Keywords for Media Studies

Edited by Laurie Ouellette and Jonathan Gray

NEW YORK UNIVERSITY PRESS New York

NEW YORK UNIVERSITY PRESS
New York
www.nyupress.org

© 2017 by New York University
All rights reserved

References to Internet websites (URLs) were accurate at the time
of writing. Neither the author nor New York University Press is
responsible for URLs that may have expired or changed since the
manuscript was prepared.

ISBN: 978-1-4798-8365-3 (hardback)
ISBN: 978-1-4798-5961-0 (paperback)

For Library of Congress Cataloging-in-Publication data, please contact
the Library of Congress.

New York University Press books are printed on acid-free paper, and
their binding materials are chosen for strength and durability. We
strive to use environmentally responsible suppliers and materials to
the greatest extent possible in publishing our books.

Manufactured in the United States of America

10 9 8 7 6 5 4 3 2 1

Also available as an ebook

Keywords for Media Studies

Contents

CONTENTS

Introduction

Laurie Ouellette and Jonathan Gray

Keywords for Media Studies introduces and advances the field of critical media studies by tracing, defining, and problematizing its established and emergent terminology. Like the authors of other books in the New York University Press Keywords series, we take our bearings from the Welsh scholar Raymond Williams. In *Keywords: A Vocabulary of Culture and Society* (1976/1983), Williams presented a "shared body of words and meanings" for understanding "general discussions of . . . the practices and institutions which we group as culture and society" (15). Less a dictionary or an encyclopedia than a holistic conceptual map organized around words, his book charted the history and usage of "key" words as a means of "recording, investigating and presenting" problems of culture and society to which they were bound (15). Williams did not set out to define a definitive canon of important terms, or to fix their significance for all time. Rather, he charted the dynamic relationship between language, knowledge, and subjects. By tracing the origins and meaning of words across changing social, economic, and political contexts, he opened up space to interrogate and disrupt commonsense assumptions about culture and society in the present. *Keywords for Media Studies* adapts this approach to the vocabulary of critical media studies. The pages that follow present sixty-five keywords, reflected upon by leading scholars tasked to show how their meanings, histories, and usage intersect with and inform problems and debates in media and society.

Curiously, "media" receives scant attention in Williams's own *Keywords*, taking up barely more than a single page. This is likely because Williams, who wrote about television, the press, and radio, understood media less as a singular entity than as an integral and multifaceted aspect of culture and society—as suggested by his two cross-references to longer entries on "communication" and "mediation." It is nonetheless worth considering what he did say about media, a Latin term he traces to the sixteenth century, when it conveyed a "sense of intervening or intermediate agency or substance," such as between a "sense or thought and its operation" (203). In the eighteenth century, the term was adapted to newspapers, to the extent that newspapers were understood (by capitalists) as "mediums" for advertising. A "conscious technical sense" of distinctions between print, sound, and vision as media began to emerge during this time as well. According to Williams, the term "media" was not widely used until the twentieth century, when the plural phrase "mass media" became common parlance for the new institutions and cultural output of broadcasting, the press, and cinema. Only with this development did the formal study of media (initially called "mass communications") emerge, operating with a "converged" understanding of these three senses of media, says Williams (203).

We can see elements, traces, and rebuttals of these early definitions of media across the entries assembled in this book. For example, while many scholars approach media primarily as "forms and sign systems" (Williams 1976/1983, 203), newer scholarship on mediated affect has revitalized an understanding of media as acting on and between the physical body and the senses (see "Affect," chapter 3). Assumptions about technological specificity—the notion that different media (print, radio, television, the web) have specific properties that "take priority over anything actually said or written or shown"—are still commonplace, even as many scholars reject technological determinism (203). As Williams points out in his entry on mediation, the "modern use of media or mass media" continues to assign various degrees of power to media institutions to distort the "real" and impose mediated relations (ideology) on social consciousness (206). The term "communication," understood as early as the seventeenth century as "to make common to many or to impart–an action" (72), was initially applied to the development of roads, canals, railways, and other physical facilities—a focus that lives on in the analysis of "space" and "infrastructure" in this volume. Only with the development of "other means of passing information and maintaining social contract," he writes, did communication come to refer predominantly to the press, broadcasting, and other mass media (72). In long-standing debates about the power of the mass media, it also is "useful to recall the unresolved range of the original noun of action, represented at its extremes by transmit, a one-way process, and share, a common or mutual process," Williams reflected, for the "intermediate senses—to make common to many, and impart, can be read in either direction, and the choice of direction is often crucial" (72–73).

We point to these discursive lineages not to minimize profound changes in media and society since Williams published his *Keywords*, but to situate the contemporary study of media within a history of ideas manifested in taken-for-granted terms that require more contextualization and unpacking than we usually grant them. Taking cues from Williams, the contributors to *Keywords for Media Studies* are keen to historicize thinking about media and society, whether that means noting a long history of "new media," or tracing how understandings of media "power" vary across time periods and knowledge formations. We have asked our authors to situate their "key" terms within the interdisciplinary discipline of media studies, so that this book—in addition to explicating influential words—chronicles a history of ideas about the objects of academic inquiry and the conceptual frameworks in which they have been examined, interrogated, analyzed, and understood. However, even more than Williams, we have urged them to go beyond description and summary, to take stock of media studies now, to intervene in debates, and to chart new arguments. This book introduces those new to the field to some key terms, research traditions, and debates, and their contexts and histories, while also offering both these readers and those who have been teaching and researching in the field for years a sense of new frontiers and questions. We've often been inspired and encouraged by reading these entries, and hope our readers will similarly use them perhaps to understand the field of play better, yes, but also to see prospects for future work.

What Is Media Studies?

Critical media studies is usually traced to the 1940s, when theorists associated with the Frankfurt School cast their gaze on the burgeoning US mass media and cultural industries. From the 1970s and 1980s, the critical study of media developed at rapid pace, influenced by literary studies, film theory, medium and technology theory, feminist criticism, television studies, and, perhaps most important, British and American cultural

INTRODUCTION   LAURIE OUELLETTE AND JONATHAN GRAY

studies. These varied (and sometimes contentious) bodies of scholarship differed from the social scientific mass communication tradition that arose in the 1920s in their engagement with qualitative analysis, social, cultural, and political theory, and power relations. In this book, we understand media studies to be focused on this critical tradition, which is (and has always been) broadly interdisciplinary.

While media studies is (and has always been) an intellectually diverse endeavor, it has developed recognizable paradigms, traditions, and perspectives that can be mapped for incoming and established scholars. Institutionalized in university departments of media studies as well as designated "areas" within compatible fields such as communication studies, visual studies, and cultural studies, critical media studies remains an especially popular academic inquiry, with introductory and specialized courses offered at the graduate and undergraduate levels. Indeed, at a time when many academic disciplines are suffering from reduced enrollments and diminished institutional support, critical media studies continues to thrive and grow, producing media workers, critical consumers, and new generations of teachers and scholars. Because the development of new media technologies, globalization, privatization, and other sociohistorical factors continues to alter the media landscape, the critical study of media has been forced to remain especially innovative, self-reflexive, and vibrant. While rooted, as Williams insisted, in a discursive past, critical media studies is also experiencing a conceptual renaissance, as scholars and theorists work to keep pace with the transition from mass media to customized, on-demand media culture, interactive relationships, and global media flows.

Keywords for Media Studies maps the enduring concepts and traditions of critical media studies, as well as emerging developments and new directions in theorizing media now. The sixty-five entries present an expansive guide to the terminology associated with critical media analysis in the broadest sense. Instead of categorizing media in narrow, medium-specific terms ("film," "TV," "radio"), we have followed Williams's emphasis on broader conceptual frameworks and modes of analysis (such as "gaze," "flow," and "sound"). In addition to covering familiar media-centric terms such as "institution," "technology," "production," "representation," and "audience," we have also chosen terms such as "hybridity," "identity," and "labor" that understand media within wider social, cultural, political, economic, and global contexts. Finally, we have included foundational terms for critical media analysis (such as "myth" and "hegemony") alongside newer analytical terms (such as "affect" and "assemblage"). As a result, the pages that follow present a comprehensive and forward-looking resource for emerging and established scholars alike.

Studying media is hard, for despite common usage that can imply "the media" is a monolithic, singular object, media are plural and varied. New media constantly join the pantheon of "old" or existing media, shifting the entire landscape at times, or slotting simply into age-old patterns at other times. Society itself changes, thereby revising the stakes or relevance of various media. Technological change and/or aesthetic innovation can repurpose a medium. Norms of production, distribution, delivery, exhibition, and use change. Thus, any study of the media occurs at a point in time, and all studies are open to revision. This book brings together some of the leading thinkers in media studies to assess where we are right now, in some cases explaining how we got here, and in some cases gesturing to possible roads ahead. It is not a dictionary, aiming to define terms that surely all our authors would regard as volatile and ever changing; nor is it an encyclopedia, aiming to give the elusive totalizing account of a word and promising an equally elusive objective rendering. Rather, we are inspired by Williams's interest in approaching a broad terrain by exploring what are the words that matter discursively. Which words' complexities need to be understood to in turn better understand how media work? We charged our authors with presenting these complexities. We also charged them with noting where the word is right now. And we invited them, should they wish, to intervene in the word's life, and to call for new or additional approaches.

Comparisons and Selection

If one compares our table of contents to those of earlier keywords collections in media and cultural studies—not only Raymond Williams's *Keywords: A Vocabulary of Culture and Society*, but also Tony Bennett, Lawrence Grossberg, and Meaghan Morris's 2005 *New Keywords: A Revised Vocabulary of Culture and Society* and John Hartley's 2011 *Communication, Cultural and Media Studies: The Key Concepts*—the addition of some words over time might gesture to their rising currency. Most obviously, as new and digital media have played increasingly dominant roles in both society and the analysis of media, a host of associated issues have risen to prominence, resulting in the additions of a cluster of words—among them "access," "convergence," "copyright," "data," "interactivity," "personalization," and "surveillance"—that did not appear in the earlier two books. Less obviously, the increasing sophistication of critical scholarship on the intersection of media, the body and identity, and the development of new approaches to studying mediated identities and subjectivities has warranted new terms not in any of the three books, such as "appropriation," "cosmopolitanism," "intersectionality," "play," and "reflexivity."

However, we'd pose that scrutinizing tables of contents to see "what's new" belies much of what is in fact new. If we hope to see a field in motion, we are more likely to witness that mobility in the evolution of definitions for similar words from 1976 to 2001 to 2005 to 2017. Thus, for instance, "ordinary" appears in Williams, yet Graeme Turner's entry on "ordinary" in this volume was written in an era of ubiquitous social media and reality television that has recalibrated our relationship (as amateur content providers and audiences) to the ordinary. "Race" (or, for Williams, "racial") appears in all four books, yet Herman Gray's entry here is situated within the current moment of ubiquitous visibility, biopolitics, and a supposedly "postracial" America. Susan Douglas's entry on "feminism" considers much of the same history as does Bennett, Grossberg, and Morris's entry, yet provides updates for the current moment. And a whole host of other terms—"audience," "author," "citizenship," "industry," and "text" among them—are by no means new additions to media studies' critical vocabulary, yet the field's understandings of them have shifted considerably in ways that our assembled authors delineate. We invite readers, if they are interested, to track definitions over time and across volumes.

By pointing out continuities and differences across various keywords collections, though, we aim not to start an odd academic game of Matching Pairs, but to underline the very point of an exploit such as the creation of a keywords collection. Words can carry layers of meaning, and they can be not only *sites* of conflict, change, or conservatism but key *actors* in the forces of conflict, change, or conservatism. They can be rallying cries that unite, weapons that assault, or salves that calm and heal. For all their visual simplicity (as with the short words "race," "class," or "labor") and even when a lazy dictionary might suggest they are fixed and unspectacular, some words matter immensely and are anything but simple. This book sketches out something of a cartography, a relief map of media studies and its own prominences by defining, discussing, critically engaging with, and in some cases redefining some of the most important words in the field.

Inevitably, some readers' favorite keywords won't appear in these pages. We aimed not to canonize, nor to suggest that only these words matter. Presented with finite pages and words, we had to make decisions about whether friendly concepts might be able to travel together under one heading, and at times about which words demanded redefinition and which may already have been handled well elsewhere. Nevertheless, we assembled a group that is simultaneously eclectic, interesting, and austere enough to cover a range of traditions and research questions within media studies. While we have offered a brief answer to the question "What is media studies?," the pages that follow present a heftier and more engaging answer in aggregate.

In closing this introduction, we offer our thanks to our authors, for being so easy and fun to work with, and for allowing us to be appreciative readers, not (just) taskmaster editors.

I

Access

Elizabeth Ellcessor

"Access" is usually understood to refer to the opportunity, ability, or right to gain entry to a space or possession of a thing. One of the most common formulations is *to have access to* a given object, action, or context. Discussions of *media access* have followed this usage, in terms of gaining access to the means of production, granting access to positive or realistic representations, enabling access to telecommunications networks and mass media content. Typically, media access is prioritized in matters related to news, politics, and economics, while it is less commonly made relevant to discussions of entertainment or social media.

"Access" has a positive and positivist bent; each of the examples above presupposes that it is beneficial for people to have access, and that access is a discrete state that can be identified and achieved. Given these tendencies, it is unsurprising that the use of "access" in media policies and within media studies has routinely conveyed some combination of media availability, affordability, or consumer choice. The limitations of such a discourse of access are evident when we consider US media policies in relation to access and then in relation to disability.

From the Communications Act of 1934, which established broadcasting as a commercial service operating in the public interest, access to mass media has referred to the ability of individuals to act as consumers, making choices from available media technologies and content. "Access" as availability and (limited) choice figured the public largely as receivers of media, rather than as producers. Access to the airwaves was limited by licensing, which ostensibly ensured the public interest and certainly reduced the diversity of producers and enabled the development of broadcast networks and later media conglomerates.

Telecommunications law, by contrast, initially established access in relation to availability and affordability through concepts of universal service and common carriage. Under these provisions, common carriers (such as telephone companies) were protected from liability for the content carried by their networks. This was justified through a mandate for universal service, whereby these carriers would extend access to and use of the network to all, making telephony a public utility managed by private interests.

Yet, availability, affordability, and consumer choice were insufficient tools with which to include people with disabilities in the mediated public sphere. For example, without specialized hardware, the availability and affordability of telecommunications were irrelevant to d/Deaf Americans. Similarly, without closed captions or audio description on television, the public interest of d/Deaf or blind viewers was not met. Routinely, laws, technologies, and studies of media have played catch-up, assuming an able-bodied media user and only later considering how people with disabilities might require different conditions in order to access media (Goggin and Newell 2003).

Disability reveals some of the limitations of dominant discourses of "access," and these limitations extend to any conception of *having access to* media technologies, affordances, and content. This understanding of "access" leaves out the infinitely variable material and experiential dimensions of access. Media access may take many forms; unorthodox means of accessing media may produce new articulations of bodies, technologies, policies, and culture. The volunteer captioning, informal distribution, and group viewing of films by d/Deaf audiences during the mid-twentieth century represented an intervention into cultures of filmgoing, the practices of Hollywood, and ultimately federal policy, as the nonprofit Captioned Films for the Deaf was brought under the aegis of the federal Department of Health, Education, and Welfare in 1958 (Schuchman 1988). Conceiving of media access as an object or state of being to be possessed hides such histories and fosters a unitary and potentially exclusionary vision of what access entails and how to promote it. For instance, although graphical user interfaces increased access to personal computing for many people, they created a barrier for blind users; then, in combating the digital divide, programs promoted access to computers that used these systems, reinforcing a singular vision of "access" and further ostracizing those for whom such access was insufficient. The legacy of such histories is that Americans with disabilities remain significantly less likely to have access to, or use, digital media.

Media studies needs to move beyond the noun form of "access" to consider it as a verb. "Accessing" should be seen as a variable moment or process by which one may enter a literal or figurative space, acquiring desired items, activities, or outcomes. If, instead of *having access to* something—possessing access—we were to think in terms of *accessing* that thing, more versions of access and subsequent media engagement can be observed, studied, and made the basis of theory. With this perspective, "watching television" ceases to be a taken-for-granted activity and becomes a variable assemblage of screens, remote controls, captions and audio descriptions, tablet computers and mobile phones, domestic and public spaces, individual and group practices. Furthermore, "accessing" must take on a subject; any statement about access must consider *who* is accessing, forcing considerations of diversity and marginalized perspectives by refusing the normativity of an unnamed subject. In doing this, analyses of media access can make increasingly meaningful interventions in the democratic roles of media content, technologies, and policies. Like formulations of access as availability, affordability, and choice, the framing of access as an object can go only so far. "Accessing" enables deeper, more nuanced, and more inclusive studies of and interventions in the ways in which people and media are brought together.

2

Aesthetics

Lev Manovich

The most common meaning of "aesthetics" today associates it with beauty. We use this term to refer to principles and techniques to make something beautiful, and to our experiences of that beauty. It comes from the ancient Greek *aisthetikos*, which meant "esthetic, sensitive, sentient, pertaining to sense perception"; that word was derived from *aisthanesthai*, meaning "I perceive, feel, sense."

Many human cultures developed explicit principles and rules to be used in order to achieve beauty. Such principles may concern proportion, symmetry, harmony, composition, use of colors, narrative organization, and so on. In between the seventeenth and nineteenth centuries in the West, many philosophers developed theories of aesthetic experience, while art academies were teaching artists the practical principles to make beautiful artworks. In the twentieth century, such prescriptive aesthetic systems became less important, but some principles remain widely used (such as Euclid's golden ratio). Modernist photographers, artists, and architects such as Le Corbusier continued to use the golden ratio as fundamental to their works.

The concept of "aesthetics" has a unique relation to media studies. I can't think of another concept that is so central to the modern culture industries and yet also to the creation of media by individuals—such as the tens of millions of people worldwide today who use digital tools to make aesthetically refined photos for posting on Instagram, or the hundreds of millions who have the means to purchase beautiful designer clothes and home décor items. The Pinterest social network, which reached a hundred million users in 2015, is dominated by images of beautiful clothes, home décor, crafts, fashion, party ideas, and so on. The photos that we see around us every day have been refined in Photoshop to achieve visual perfection, and cinematography similarly uses digital tools to control precisely the aesthetics of every shot and frame.

In fact, digital tools and software workflows that industry gradually adopted in the 1990s have led to an "aesthetic revolution." Until that time, many forms of modern media such as television, cinema, and newspapers had limited ways to control their aesthetics. These media did not always use color, or did not have technologies to control its nuances. Digital editing tools and the web as a distribution platform changed this. Now every pixel, line, frame, face, and body can be edited to achieve the desired aesthetic effect. Never before have we been surrounded by so much "engineered" beauty and perfection, especially in the visual sphere.

At the same time, the concepts of beauty and aesthetic pleasure have been almost completely neglected in theories of media. One finds little to no analysis of media aesthetics in media studies textbooks, or in the works of major media theorists after the middle of the twentieth century. Scholars in recent decades in English-speaking countries have focused on the content of media and their social and political effects, and often ignored the forms of media artifacts. Thus, for example, Jill Nelmes's (2011) *Introduction to Film Studies* (564 pages) does not even have "aesthetics" or "beauty" in the index, while a search of Campbell, Martin, and Fabos's (2011) *Media and Culture: An Introduction to Mass Communication* (616 pages) returned 5 pages where the word appeared, with no single sections or chapters devoted to it. I certainly don't want to critique these and many other excellent textbooks in media studies. Their authors represent the topics, theories, and historical and contemporary academic media analyses that are most influential today, so their omissions of references to aesthetics and beauty are only because these concepts and corresponding industry practices are not widely studied in media and communication theory and history today.

This exclusion is unfortunate. Form and the relations between form and content are what make art (including modern mass media and user-generated content) a unique type of human communication and experience. Concern with form and beauty has been fundamental in all human cultures for many thousands of years. Rhythm, composition, patterns or repetitions, expectation and variation, systematic use of color, ornament, grids, and other methodical ways of organizing elements of any cultural artifact in space and time are found in every human culture. Today, all students taking studio courses in art, media and graphic design, film, television, fashion, and other creative fields are taught how to use form effectively, and how to achieve desired aesthetics. And while prescriptive aesthetic concepts and rules of beauty are no longer enforced today as they were in the art academies of previous centuries, particular aesthetic choices and systems (such as minimalism in design or pleasing background blur in photography and cinematography) dominate professional fields.

Therefore, if we are interested in historical or contemporary media culture and media arts, we need to study not only the content of artifacts but also their form. However, if you focus too much on "form" in media studies, you may be labeled a "formalist." I assume that many people who use the label "formalist" assume that media (and the study of media) are about content (or "representations"), that progressive media artists should be creating particular representations to advance some social or moral cause, and that the job of scholars is to analyze cultural representations either to show how they excluded or misrepresented some groups in the past, or to support progressive artists today who want to use representations to make society more fair.

These are certainly legitimate ideals. However, labeling others who are interested in media aesthetics as "formalist" is very dangerous. While today media and art critics may associate formalism with a certain tradition in Western art criticism of the twentieth century (such as the works of Clement Greenberg), this label was also utilized in communist countries to imprison and kill artists who did not want to create correct representations. After Russia's 1917 October Revolution, the new Soviet state was first tolerant of some experiments in art, as long as they did not contain anything that could be taken as "counterrevolutionary." (The literature that could not be published included Dada-like movement in Russian poetry, for example.) But already in the 1920s, the term "formalism" was used in the Soviet Union to criticize in print and in public debates all those who were interested in anything other than ideologically "correct" subjects (including the representations of workers, building of socialism, etc.), and who did not use traditional (nineteenth-century) realist language.

Between 1930 and 1953, many thousands of leading Russian artists were sent to work camps or prisons or were killed based on such criticism. Often an article declaring that this or that artist was a "formalist" or had some "formalist tendencies" was published first in a major newspaper, and after that this artist was stripped of his or her positions, could not find work, and often was arrested. The term "formalism" continued to be used in a very negative sense by Soviet media and art critics until the end of 1980s. Most communist countries followed the examples of the Soviet Union and used the same practices.

But this attack on artistic form and use of the term "formalism" to destroy many artists did not mean that a communist society rejected all forms of aesthetics. On the contrary, once Stalin decided it was time to put arts, culture, and media to work helping to construct a new society—and, at the same time, to offer hardworking citizens pleasurable experience—concerns with form and aesthetics became important. In 1930, the Soviet government dissolved all independent artistic organizations that united Russian modernist artists, and started promoting "classical" and "realist" aesthetic norms in arts. Soviet architects began to build monumental buildings that used rich decorations and followed classical architectural aesthetics (such as the golden ratio). In cinema, rapid disorienting montage and usual points of view were gradually replaced by classical Hollywood film language, and by the focus on beautiful stars adored by millions. The Moscow Metro, constructed in the 1930s, offered citizens of the capital and visitors an unprecedented aesthetic experience—dozens of stations featured marble, mosaics, sculptures, and other decorative elements created by the best Russian artists of the time. Clearly, the future communist state would ideally have many places like this metro, with every building and interior designed to offer the best aesthetic experience. If communist leaders had had Photoshop, Final Cut, Flame, Autodesk, and other contemporary media software, they would have been required tools for all artists to refine the aesthetics and beauty of their creations, from paintings to films, photographs, and print.

One can only hope that the field of media studies will stop conceiving of terms like "formalism" negatively, and begin to study and teach media in ways that better reflect global media production, environments, and experiences today. If aesthetics and beauty are so central for media producers and audiences—including not only professionals but also millions of people who produce aesthetically refined content and share it online—media studies needs to pay equal attention to these dimensions.

How can we add considerations of aesthetics to media studies curriculum and textbooks? Given the centrality of aesthetics to the contemporary media industry and user experiences, this topic should be given sufficient space. Its presentation should not treat aesthetics in isolation, but instead show its roles in the history of media, structures of media industry, social relations, and other topics.

3

Affect

Carrie A. Rentschler

The concept of affect has opened up the study of media practices and technologies as carriers and mechanisms that articulate, direct, intensify, and orient feeling within context-specific social and political configurations. Affect theory provides a way into these configurations, by rethinking and privileging the *felt* aspects of everyday life, social change, and durable structures of power, in their (in some cases) nonrepresentational aspects. In studying affect, scholars aim to analyze what is not typically accounted for in media studies: how things feel, for whom, and with what potential. As Terri Senft (forthcoming) puts it, the concerns of affect theory exceed what can easily be located in the traditional study of meaning, representation, symbols, and signs.

In *The Affect Theory Reader*, Melissa Gregg and Greg Seigworth define affect as "what arises in the midst of *in-betweenness*, in the capacities to act and be acted upon." It is the term given "to those forces—visceral forces beneath, alongside, or generally *other than* conscious knowing" that "drive us toward movement . . . thought and extension," but can also overwhelm, arrest, and frustrate. Simply put, affects are "forces of encounter" and "gradients of bodily capacity" (2010, 1–2; see also Ahmed 2004). They are not necessarily *strong* in their intensity, but different qualities of intensity register the different work affect does and is doing. For Zizi Papacharissi, affect "is the active ingredient that infuses structures of feeling with different measures of intensity" (2014, 117).

Much of the emphasis in media scholarship on affect is on what affect enables and does rather than what it might mean or represent. Affect theory offers new ways of conceptualizing and studying social collectivities and their structures of affective transmission. It approaches the experiential qualities of embodiment through the capacity to feel, move, and be moved and provides a different set of perspectives on what connects collective social bodies, their modes of relating, and their affiliative, felt structures of togetherness. Affect theory recenters the body *as media* in media studies analysis (see Gregg and Seigworth 2010) in its phenomenological and dispositional relations to technologies and communication infrastructures (see Lisa Parks, "Infrastructure," chapter 32).

To study affect requires an ability to interpret the signs and traces of affect's communicability, its transmissibility (Brennan 2004). Affect tends to be studied via the processes through which it registers and becomes communicable: as ritualized, as means of transmission, and as forces for making experiences audible, visible, and felt. This requires externalized signs and markings of affect's work and structuring presence, its structures of feeling. Typical research questions ask what affect enables, what it moves or makes movable, what it intensifies, and what it links or articulates. Media practices and communication technologies are central to these movements and articulations of affect, for as Anna Gibbs notes, "media and bodies appear as vectors, and affect itself as the primary communicational medium for the circulation of ideas, attitudes and prescriptions for action among them" (2002, 339).

In film studies and media studies alike, affect theory's approach to the body as medium interprets bodily gestures, faces, and modes of bodily comportment for nonverbal markings of affective states of being, a physiognomic practice of reading the body, and particularly the face. Some studies interpret exterior surfaces of bodies and their proxies for capacities to feel together. As Beth Coleman (2011) argues in relation to her study of avatars, in "putting a face to things" through emoticons and avatars, networked communities create powerful feelings of copresence that, without facialized interfaces, are difficult to sustain. Some scholars also draw on the physiognomic ideal that one can interpret the exterior of bodies, buildings, and other surfaces in order to access other inaccessible qualities of affective and emotional states of being. Such physiognomic tools of reading are used as a means to interpret collective modes of feeling and bodily response in groups, such as in photographs that capture similar facial expressions made by on-the-scene witnesses to terrorist attacks (Sliwinski 2011). Physical movements and bodily gestures might suggest how affective states of being are occupied, carried, and lived, but there is also a risk that media makers, analysts, and viewers might essentialize the body as a machine of affective inscription, a surface of appearances that reveals the truth of shared embodied feeling states.

Affect is also studied through the lens of emotional labor and media work, in recognition that affect is both something that is worked on and something that constitutes a *kind* of work. One way scholars study how affect structures media making and communicative labor is through the structures of expression that accompany this labor and its surrounding public cultures and sites of meaning making—in training texts, public discourse, management documentation, interviews, and other research materials. These texts leave affective marks and traces, both in what they say through language, image, and sound, but also through how they move, are shared, and are used. Affective labor gives shape to activist communities and networks that take rhetorical and generic form in Twitter scripts, emoticons, tagging, avatar overlays, button clicks that message "I've got your back!"

and other modes of expressing feeling, care, anger, rage, disappointment, and other shared, and potentially collectivizing, emotions via social media (Gregg 2011; Losh 2014; Papacharissi 2014; Rentschler 2014). Affective labor has increasingly featured in studies of media production cultures, industry studies, and the un- and underpaid labor of social media content creators, participants, and commentators—work often described as "labors of love" (which they can sometimes be, but ought not be a reason for undercompensation). Increasingly, work in this area attends to the seemingly banal and unremarkable functions of emerging platforms and apps, what Morris and Elkins (2015) call "mundane software." Apps and other software tools themselves do forms of affective labor, as commodity experiences of comforting sounds, touch-based pulsating color screen responses, verbalized affirmations, and mechanisms of routine, order, and quantifiable care.

The attention to affective labor in media studies, while long a topic of study for feminist researchers, provides one of the more compelling approaches to affect as something labored on and through, and produced by laboring bodies. Media studies scholars studying activist and cultural labor in affective terms, and the role of affect in social mobilization, concretely locate the stuff and work of affect in what it does, and what people do with it. Through these means, scholars study affect as it becomes communicable—audible, visible, and otherwise palpably felt.

Finally, affect theory provides essential tools and frameworks for robustly analyzing the work that feeling and emotions do in bringing people together, and shaping and moving social collectives, in the process of popular organizing and movement mobilization. Scholars such as Lawrence Grossberg (1992) and Linda Kintz (1995) examine the cultural resonances that media practices tap into, politically—from youth culture and popular music to Christian right book series and intimacy videos—to analyze the links between politicization and the capacity to move people (see Ryan 1991). These links are made, and revealed, in concrete organizing strategies that leave documentary and other mediatic trails, in movement texts, training documents, and marketing plans for Christian publishing houses, among other kinds of materials. Jennifer Petersen refers to these materials as "the discursive side of feelings," those "under-examined parts of political communication and the role of media in politics" that are largely affective in nature (2011, 14). Networked affective publics also leave digital trails, through hashtags and other devices of aggregation and tonal expression (Mottahedeh 2015; Papacharissi 2014; Rambukkana 2015). To understand this requires that we get behind, analytically, the forms of activist and cultural labor that summon, gather, train, and direct affective experiences around collectivized political movements, often in conditions that are not expressly political. It also suggests that media connectivity is, of itself, an insufficient condition for collective action.

4

Appropriation
Beretta E. Smith-Shomade

When everyday people talk about appropriation, they use words such as "theft" and "rape"—often speaking about how their favorite artist was pirated. These same terms are used to describe the dilemma of intellectual property—downloading and hook snatching reminiscent of a time not so long ago, when those who paid homage (the Beatles) and those who didn't (Elvis Presley and Mick Jagger and the Rolling Stones) were endemic to how entertainment industries operated. Scandals such as payola in radio, voice-overs in film, black music video exclusion in cable, and reality television in general link to greed but also tie directly to the undergirding notion that if you do not have the means or foresight to copyright your work, or an audience valued by advertisers to protest, your work becomes an unintended category of fair use. Moreover, even when the work is protected, some lives, cultural producers, and cultures appear to matter less than others.

One of the central debates around appropriation is capital: Who gets recognized and remunerated for their cultural labor? Whose songs, style, and innovation become the raw materials for the next million-dollar advertisement for a major corporation like Nike or Pepsi? What dominant (read: white) rapper (Iggy Azalea), producer (Mark Ronson), or filmmaker (Quentin Tarantino) will next capitalize on the cultural work of black and brown creative output? Posing these questions should make it clear that appropriation has material consequences.

Consumers, audiences, and scholars have argued for sampling as a defense against the charge of appropriation. Sampling as an artistic function drives both the rap and the hip-hop industries. The difference, however, is twofold. First, artists typically sample from the same ethnic and cultural mix as those who produced the original track. In other words, sampling and race exist together in respect for the culture. Appropriation, on the other hand, is the distillation and recuperation of imagery, ideology, beats, style, and sometimes lyrics of not only another artist but, more often than not, of a culture different from the taker's own. For example, Justin Timberlake's dance (as Madonna's did decades prior) and Miley Cyrus's twerk borrow heavily from black and brown men and women—creative and otherwise.

Many contend that the most egregious examples of appropriation happen in the wearing of a costume. Whether the costumes are donned by college students hosting pimps and hoes parties (code: black), or folks at a Laverne Cox party (code: trans and black), or plain cowboys and Indians play (code: racist from way back), parody becomes the de facto defense of appropriating culture read as non-normative and/or foreign. The material consequences of this play are real. In other words, questions of origin and belonging such as "where are you really from" (code: Asian or Latino) are tied to the ease with which identity can be performed. Such injury as a result of appropriation leads to perceived incompetence, denied opportunity, and heightened rationales for fear.

Appropriation is to the twenty-first century what the 1980s culture wars were to the originators of hip-hop—a fight for recognition and respect and a reflection on origins. To this end, some culture war discourse still lingers in contemporary debates on appropriation, particularly the boundaries around parody and pastiche. Michael Giardina and Cameron McCarthy contend, "increasing processes of electronic mediation have now seemingly separated culture altogether from place; difference has become an abstract value that can be taken from specific groups and settings and combined and recombined in ways that allow . . . magnates . . . to appropriate elements of hip hop culture and sell these elements back into the inner city itself while . . . simultaneously marketed, with overwhelming success, to a White consumer audience" (2005, 148).

Over the past several years, a number of controversies over appropriation have raged in the popular press. The idea that the righteous anger around appropriation and oppression should be checked by the same dominant culture doing it furthers the damage appropriation does. Media studies needs to question what is at stake when media "represent" ethnic culture. What do the continuing changes and shifts in technology transnationally mean for understanding and appreciating divergent cultures? What do filmic homages to black and brown movements, histories, and people couched in white savior motifs mean for day-to-day interactions? Media studies scholars have understudied appropriation. Addressing some of the conundrums that appropriation poses may help enrich and broaden other areas of the discipline.

5

Assemblage

J. Macgregor Wise

"Assemblage" is the common English translation of the French term *agencement*, used by philosopher Gilles Deleuze and radical psychoanalyst Félix Guattari to theorize the arrangement and organization of a variety of heterogeneous elements (1975/1986, 1980/1987). The concept of assemblage has proved generative in media studies in its articulation of both the discursive and material aspects of media, and in its consideration of media as arrangements of humans and nonhumans.

It is important to note that Deleuze and Guattari's approach to philosophy is one that emphasizes immanence over transcendence, multiplicity over individuality, and becoming over being. Assemblages are not static structures but events and multiplicities; they do not reproduce or represent particular forms but rather forms are expressed and each expression is the emergence of something creative and new.

Assemblages have four dimensions. Along one axis the assemblage stratifies or articulates what Deleuze and Guattari (1980/1987) call collective assemblages of enunciation with machinic assemblages of bodies. Collective assemblages of enunciation consist of a regime of signs, of "acts and statements, of incorporeal transformations" (88). Machinic assemblages are assemblages of bodies, actions, and passions, "an intermingling of bodies reacting to one another" (88). When thinking about media from this perspective, we need to take into account a series of processes with both human and nonhuman components. We need to draw the lines between a myriad of devices and bodies, note their affects, intensities, and speeds, and consider how these material arrangements of bodies are stratified with codes, apps, conversations, tweets, and more as a collective assemblage of enunciation.

Along the second axis of the assemblage are relations of territorialization and deterritorialization, that is, on the one hand, the ways the assemblage is being organized and stabilized and, on the other hand, the ways that it is coming apart, its elements being carried away. Territory becomes especially important in understanding both the contingent and infrastructural aspects of mobile media assemblages.

The idea of assemblage has been important for the "material turn" in media studies (Packer and Wiley 2012; Parikka 2010). Rather than studying the meaning of a text (a tweet or online video), this scholarship looks at its arrangement and circulation among other messages and codes through particular contexts of production and reception as well as networks, software, and hardware, the affordances of which contribute to and shape what the message can do. Materialist media studies understands both humans and nonhumans (such as codes, routers, and mobile screens) as having agency in this assemblage. This uptake of assemblage has utility in recent work theorizing mobile media, new forms of television, media and social movements, and surveillance.

Three final points with regard to the concept of assemblage: First, it is not enough to dissect or map an assemblage's elements. We must consider its capacities: what an assemblage can do, "what its affects are, how they can or cannot enter into composition with other affects" (Deleuze and Guattari 1980/1987, 257). Second, assemblages are not accidental or just contingent but purposeful. "It is not simply a happenstance collocation of people, materials, and actions, but the deliberate realization of a distinctive plan (abstract machine)"

(Buchanan 2015, 385; see also Wise 2011). And, third, to think with the concept of assemblage it is not sufficient to simply add up or combine the elements that media studies usually considers (texts, technologies, individuals) and leave it at that. N. Katherine Hayles reminds us the concept of assemblage is a critique of the idea that a unified subjectivity preexists events: subjectivity is produced by the assemblage and not assumed in its construction (2012, 24).

6

Audience
Matt Hills

As Kate Lacey has observed, there is "an inescapable collectivity suggested by the word 'audience'" (2013, 13-14). Indeed, Raymond Williams's *Keywords*, despite not including the term, analyzes what might be meant by the audience within an entry on "masses," conveying the cultural and political ambivalences that have historically surrounded the mass audience. The "masses," we are told, can be "a term of contempt in much conservative thought, but a positive term in much socialist thought" (Williams 1976/1983, 192). Where the former has often viewed mass audiences as lacking in good taste, rationality, and expertise, the latter has instead thought of the mass as standing in for "the people" and the "popular," that is, acting as a force for democracy. Sonia Livingstone argues that "in audience research, both meanings of audience retain some purchase" (2005, 23)—sometimes audiences represent a problem to be criticized, and sometimes they are a force to be celebrated. In *New Keywords*, David Morley holds on to the importance of audience as collectivity, contrasting physically copresent audiences with "the mass audience for contemporary forms of broadcasting, which perhaps today supplies us with our primary sense of what an audience is" (2005, 8). However, Morley indicates that the mass audience can no longer be assumed to unify media consumers in space and time. Instead, "cross-border forms of broadcasting often now bring together audiences of people who may be geographically dispersed across great distances, to constitute diasporic communities of various sorts" (2005, 9).

Thinking about media audiences, then, seems to involve evaluating the cultural-political character of these groupings. At the same time, audiences have been said to fall into different categories on the basis of whether they are copresent in space and time (the physical audience), copresent in time but dispersed across different spaces (the mass audience), or scattered across different temporalities and sites (the fragmented or individualized audience). A tripartite taxonomy of audiences has thus become common (Sullivan 2013, 2), with one of the most influential versions of this to be found in Nicholas Abercrombie and Brian Longhurst's *Audiences* (1998). Abercrombie and Longhurst analyze "the simple, the mass and the diffused" audience (159). While the "simple" audience means that which is copresent at events, and the mass remains emblematic of large-scale TV audiences watching at the same time according to "linear" scheduling models, the "diffused" audience represents something more than simply fragmentation in line with "nonlinear" video-on-demand or time shifting. Rather, Abercrombie and Longhurst are interested in how being an audience member has escaped the spatiotemporal boundaries of the moments in which we consume media. We are now audiences more of the time, whether this involves reading news about TV shows or film franchises we follow via social media, tweeting and blogging about our favored media consumption and fan objects, watching trailers via YouTube, or so on. In a pervasive media culture, audience identities are not simply enacted in the spaces and times in which we encounter specific media texts—they have become performances of identity that stretch out long before and after such encounters, and hence the term "diffused" audience.

Such audiences become altered kinds of producers of meaning in addition to being consumers, and so hybrid terms such as "produsage," blending "production" and "usage," have sprung up to account for new ways of audiencing (Bruns 2008, 215), along with a focus on the "paratexts" that audiences create (Gray 2010). These can include online reviews (Frey 2015) or comments (Reagle 2015), as well as fan fiction, fan vids, or GIFs (Booth 2015). However, we need to avoid exaggerating a sense of media transformation, as if "simple" and "mass" audiences have been displaced by "diffused" audiences incessantly busy shaping user-generated content via Web 2.0. And we should avoid implying that "linear" media have been entirely supplanted by "on-demand cultures" of audience activity linked to the likes of Netflix and Amazon Prime. Some of the time we may choose to "binge watch" or "media marathon" TV shows (Glebatis Perks 2015, ix), but we may combine this with attending live events such as gigs, going out to the cinema, or collectively watching "event" TV when it is initially broadcast, such as a *Dancing with the Stars/Strictly Come Dancing* final. Rather than viewing audience types as a rigid taxonomy or a reductive narrative of media "eras," we need a far more empirical, nuanced, and theorized sense of how and when these modes interact. As Abercrombie and Longhurst caution, it is important to address the processes that connect simple, mass, and diffused audiences.

With the mainstreaming of social media/Web 2.0, we can argue that such interactions between simple, mass, and diffused audiences have become more intense. Take the UK television premiere of BBC TV's flagship drama *Sherlock* and its special episode "The Abominable Bride," which aired on New Year's Day 2016. Audiences could watch this as part of a mass audience, or they could catch up with the show via the BBC iPlayer, forming part of a diffused audience. The episode attracted ratings of over eleven million people, making it the most-watched TV program in the United Kingdom across the festive period. But fans also had the option to shift from a mass audience position and enter "simple" audiences by choosing to view "The Abominable Bride" at cinemas.

By choosing to share *Sherlock* in-person with an anticipated audience of like-minded viewers—as well as treating its cinema release as an elevation and validation of the show's brand—fans could move between "mass" and "simple" audiences, with this consumer-oriented choice effectively acting as a badge of fan distinction, and separating fans out from the mass of *Sherlock*'s viewers. But as well as shifting between "mass" and "simple" audiences as a way of performing their dedication to *Sherlock*—the cinema that I attended included a number of cosplaying fans dressed up in Victorian costumes—audiences could also migrate from a "diffused" to a "mass" audience position. This movement was possible via the sharing of online reviews and tweets within a "zone of liveness" (Crisell 2012, 45, 93) following transmission.

Such a "massification" of *Sherlock*'s fragmented audience is not strictly unified in time, however, as these viewers can watch the episode at different and individualized points after initial broadcast. Yet UK TV ratings now factor in this partial erosion of the "linear" schedule by counting viewers who watch time-shifted recordings up to a week after transmission; this results in a "consolidated" Broadcasters' Audience Research Board (BARB) rating as opposed to the initial "overnight" count of those who watched at the time of broadcast (the US Nielsen ratings system likewise includes "live plus 7" figures). These quantifications of the "mass" audience therefore stretch the concept to include those encountering a media text within seven days, assuming a weekly schedule or cutoff of TV viewing that rolls on to following episodes.

Audiences can also use social media to migrate from "simple" audience modes to those with "mass" or "diffused" currency, for example tweeting photographs taken at a red-carpet film premiere or a preview screening. In some cases, audience tweets can be picked up by the mass media and recirculated within entertainment news stories (this happened in media responses to awkward representations of feminism in "The Abominable Bride"); in other cases, tweets and videos can circulate as "spreadable media" within the "networked audience" (Jenkins, Ford, and Green 2013; Marwick 2013, 213).

But if so-called simple, mass, and diffused audiences have increasingly become modes that audience members can move across by using social media or making specific consumption decisions, then Web 2.0's diffused audience—where viewers continue to perform their audience identities over time—has also made audiences increasingly visible to one another. Media studies typically conceptualizes audiences as collectivities for particular texts, such as studying *The Lord of the Rings* audiences (Barker and Mathijs 2008) or reality TV audiences (Skeggs and Wood 2012). But there is a notable paradigm shift associated with the rise of social media and "diffused" audiences: audience communities can (and do) now encounter and confront one another far more readily.

I am no longer simply an audience for media texts; I also consume other audience members' consumption of other media, and as part of fan communities I engage with other fan communities: reading reviews, blogs, Facebook groups, and forums, for example. It is striking, then, that although media studies has deployed a concept of intertextuality for many years as part of its understanding of media culture, there has been little development of any comparable sense of interaudiences whereby audiences are analyzed as relating to other audiences. It is commonplace to consider texts in dialogue with other texts (adaptation, genre, satire), yet still seems unusual to analyze audiences not only in relation to texts but also transversally, if you like.

Scholarship has begun to focus on "anti-fandom" (Gray 2003), where diffused audiences—sometimes known as "haters"—perform their visceral dislike of particular media texts online via hate sites or commentaries. Such dislike often spills over into an othering of the audience for the disliked text, which is assumed to lack taste, knowledge, or even rationality: young women's culture from *Twilight* to One Direction has been patriarchally and problematically dismissed in this fashion. And work has also considered "inter-fandom" (Hills 2012), where fans of one media text denigrate fans of another, such as older, male *Doctor Who* fans being dismayed by the allegedly hysterical "squeeing" of younger female *Sherlock* fans. But despite such developments in audience studies, there has yet to be a systematic theorization of interaudiences and viewers' meaning-making relationships to other (imagined and mediated) audiences, across media and even across national boundaries.

Audiences should no longer be defined only in relation to the media texts they read, but should also be approached as a matter of interaudience interactions, coalitions, and otherings. This is one crucial lesson of the tripartite division into simple, mass, and diffused audiences—the more we carry particular audience identities with us through mediatized culture and via user-generated content, the more we engage with other people's audiencing alongside "official" media content. As a result of this everyday textualization of other people's views, we find ourselves watching "in common" more routinely than ever before, attending "to television's intersubjective viewing practices . . . [and] watch[ing] in conversation—direct and variously mediated—with other viewers" (Shimpach 2010, 58). Media audiences are not silos of interpretation cut apart from one another, emerging around isolated media texts. However, reading many prior audience studies, one might be forgiven for thinking that was the case. But studying interaudiences "distances us . . . from the normal media studies assumption that what audiences do . . . is already a distinctive set of media-focused practices rather than an artificially chosen 'slice' through daily life that cuts across how people actually understand the practices in which they are engaged" (Couldry 2014, 217).

At the same time, we need to be aware that many claims are made on behalf of and in relation to audiences; ratings and box office figures are presented as evidence of brand value or popularity. And some interaudience interactions can mean projecting what other viewer groups are like in order to dismiss them, for example assuming that soap audiences think the actors are the characters, or presuming that horror audiences straightforwardly enjoy representations of gore and immorality. Audiences may seem ever more visible to us within the world of social media, but this visibility masks the fact that "no representation of 'television [or other media] audience,' empirical or otherwise, gives us direct access to any actual audience. Instead, it evokes 'fictive' pictures of 'audience,' fictive not in the sense of false or untrue, but of fabricated, both made and made up" (Ang 1991, 34–35). We can never gain access—either as scholars or social media users—to the entirety of an audience. It isn't even clear what this would mean: what boundaries or parameters would we have to posit to contain this "full audience"? Instead, audiences are always a kind of fiction or construct, as Ien Ang (1991, 35) has argued.

But this does not mean that the study of audiences is futile. Quite the reverse, it means precisely that we need to analyze and challenge how representations of audiences are used by media industries, as well as how audience discourses are deployed in interaudience interactions, or by authorities and pundits. How are audiences characterized or gendered; how are their behaviors culturally valued or denigrated? Theorizing the audience thus means, among other things, critiquing forms of cultural power that can seek to naturalize constructed images of specific audiences.

7

Author

Cynthia Chris

By some measures, media studies has not had a strong tradition of foregrounding authorship, in comparison to literary and film studies' robust and even contentious traditions. At times, those traditions have influenced media scholarship. But in analyses of television, video games, social media, transmedia, and other forms, some media scholars have set aside the preoccupation with singular authors that is commonplace throughout literary and film studies. In doing so, we have regularly instead made visible the interplay of corporate imprimatur, creative and technical personnel, and active audiences. And yet other media scholars have engaged with author theories in a limited manner, adapting them to television's mode of production, and focusing on a small set of individual *auteurs*. Why is the author so categorically emphasized in regard to some media texts and products—and not others? That is, *why is an author*? Why has media studies taken approaches that differ from those of our apparent disciplinary cousin, film studies, or what has been at stake in our limited engagements with those approaches? What is gained, and what may be lost, in each approach? The answers to each of these questions are quite entangled.

In the postwar period, French film critics embraced both the resurgence of European filmmaking and an influx of Hollywood films that had been in short supply during World War II. In the magazine *Cahiers du Cinéma*, Francois Truffaut and other critics championed new generations of directors who often doubled as screenwriters, and whose works displayed persistent expressive styles and themes: among them, Max Ophuls, Jean Renoir, and Robert Bresson (Truffaut 1954/1976, 16). British film scholars including Peter Wollen (1972) allowed for oppositions and ruptures within an oeuvre, among other complications. Still, film studies—taking its cue not only from these influential scholars but from the film industry itself, which develops authorship as a kind of branding strategy—fundamentally recognizes the director as the primary authorial agent.

Interdisciplinary media and communication studies, with roots in sociology, psychology, and social theory, long privileged other approaches. A dominant tradition within communication studies has focused on media effects and the role of the audience—not the author—in making media. Striking out in another direction, Theodor Adorno identified the "culture industry" as an authorial agent—one that is profit-seeking and routinized rather than expressive, and mechanistically marked by "an eternal sameness" (1967/1975, 14). If Adorno excised, to a fault, human subjects at the site of production, he also laid groundwork influencing generations of scholars concerned with how industrial conditions shape mass culture.

Later, other influential theorists sought to decenter the biographical author, reminding us that the role is historical, ideological, and not inevitable (Barthes 1967; Foucault 1969/1984). Subsequently, media studies continued to explore diffuse and layered modes of authoring. Following a spate of corporate mergers in the 1980s and 1990s, many scholars intensified scrutiny of the exercise of corporate power in the film and media industries. For example, Jerome Christensen's notion of the "corporate studio" as a nonperson author (2012, 13) draws on Thomas Schatz's work on the Hollywood studio system, which identified studio executives—producers, such as Irving Thalberg at MGM—as authors responsible for "house style" (1988). Others explore collaborative and collective modes of authorship typical throughout media production but often obscured by the practice of designating individual authors commensurate with corporate branding strategies, copyright regimes, and institutionalized creative hierarchies. As Jonathan Gray states unequivocally, "Nothing has a single author" (2013, 93). This direction has proven enormously rich, developing as production studies (see Caldwell 2008; Mayer, Banks, and Caldwell 2009b), and accounting, often ethnographically, for the authoring roles of both above- and below-the-line labor. Yet another direction for the study of media authorship reframes the audience as an authoring partner. Stuart Hall offered a model in which, at the point of "encoding," authorial creativity is practiced within "routines of production, historically defined technical skills, professional ideologies, institutional knowledge, definitions and assumptions, assumptions about the audience and so on" (2001, 167). At the point of "decoding," the viewer (or reader, or listener) makes meaning shaped by available linguistic and cultural referents, social position, and other factors (Hall 2001, 168–69).

Following Hall, scholars have found the authoring roles of the viewer/player/user particularly conspicuous in interactive and narratively open-ended forms such as video games and those dependent on user-generated content. In the former, the player makes narrative-twisting choices within a defined universe. In the latter case of so-called social media, the user appends content to a corporate platform. Some scholars—such as Axel Bruns, who recognizes each social media user as a producer—champion "participatory culture" as democratizing (2008, 256). Others persuasively argue that digital media corporations readily exploit users' immaterial and largely unpaid labor (Andrejevic 2013a). After

AUTHOR CYNTHIA CHRIS

all, "the new Web is made of the big players, but also of new ways to make the audience work"—by occupying the role of author (Terranova 2000, 52).

Even as scholars create new models accounting for authorship in interactive and social media, others borrow directly and indirectly from *auteurism*. In television, for example, all but a few innovative producers, such as Norman Lear and Aaron Spelling, long remained largely obscure in both popular and scholarly discourses. Many have argued that television has, in recent decades, displayed tremendous aesthetic and narrative complexity (Mittell 2015), and both popular and scholarly critics laud some of its producers, now known as "showrunners." But the medium is not solely composed of the likes of Matthew Weiner's *Mad Men* and David Chase's *The Sopranos*, the products of some of the most acclaimed men working in the medium; I choose the gendered examples purposefully, given their status in a still relatively exclusionary canon.

The notion of a canon brings us back to one of the questions that motivated this inquiry: *why* is an author? Inarguably, the category of author—in the form of director, writer, showrunner, or game designer—is useful: useful to media industry marketing machines, and useful to scholars analyzing bodies of work. But it is only one of many possible approaches to studying media. If critics and scholars *over*-valorize a few individuals' bodies of work, we may reproduce hierarchies of taste and power, and underestimate the diversity and vastness of any particular medium. Alternatively applied, as Patricia White argues, the authorship framework may allow for "act[s] of historical retrieval"—even, the designation of new *auteurs*—where "women's access to the means of production has been historically restricted" (2015, 2–3). Of course, it is not only female authors but an array of marginalized creative subjects who may be excluded from critical canons. It takes other methods to recognize the social structures that shore up such restrictions. Inevitably, authors do not stand alone—and cannot be understood in isolation from the conditions of production, tactics of collaboration, and audience response that shape their work in any medium.

8

Brand

Sarah Banet-Weiser

The brand is typically understood as the cultural and emotional domain of a commercial product, or the cultural expression of a company or corporation (and increasingly of traditionally noncommercial entities, such as religious and nonprofit organizations). The brand is the recognizable, regularized, and standardized "message" of a company, the result of a complex "branding strategy" (often called marketing). The success of a brand often depends on its stability, and ability to maintain over time a coherent narrative and recognizable expression. In more economic terms, the brand is a way for a company or corporation to distinguish itself from the competition, a way of standing out in a clutter of advertising, marketing, and products. In the contemporary cultural context, branding is not limited to products, but ideologies, feelings, and the self are also branded (Banet-Weiser 2012).

While the brand is often associated with the Industrial Revolution and the emergence of mass production and mass consumption, branding was an important part of earlier forms of commerce and exchange (Moor 2007). Before the brand signified a particular signature of a company, it was seen to denote ownership of property. In the United States of the eighteenth century, branding was the process of creating and distributing a brand name that was protected by a trademark. This was signified most overtly by the branding of cattle so that ranchers could differentiate their own herds. Yet cattle were not the only species branded to signify ownership. People have also been branded as property; slaves in the United States and elsewhere were branded not only to mark ownership for slave owners, but also, and perhaps more importantly, to signify that African slaves were considered property, nonhuman objects to exchange and profit from in an economic market.

Industrialization—the emergence of mass production in the nineteenth century alongside changes in technologies (including printing and design), transportation, and labor practices—ushered in a new era of branding, when commodities began to take on cultural "value" because of the way in which they were imaged, packaged, and distributed in an increasingly competitive commercial landscape (Arvidsson 2006; Lury 2004; Moor 2007). Mass production allowed for more goods to be produced in a cost-effective way, so companies saw a need to distinguish their products as quality goods; branding was the mechanism to achieve this. Importantly, branding in the era of mass production expanded the consumer base for all kinds of products, and thus helped establish the contours of a mass market. Branding became a shorthand, a way of recognizing products and companies through a repeated and regularized logo or trademark.

The brand depends on communication and media technologies. A convergence of modern factors—such as the invention of photography and typewriters, a rising literacy rate, the rise of mass media, the increase in railways, the emergence of the telephone, and more efficient postal systems—all greatly facilitated the success of brands.

In the mid-twentieth century, companies recognized the importance of the brand as having cultural as well as economic value, and leveraged branding as a way to market to a mass culture, one that took shape in a context framed by immigration, social and cultural conflict, and world wars (Moor 2007). Brands took on a role that extended beyond mere economics; during a time of cultural and political upheaval, brands became functional in emotional as well as economic ways. Following World War II, federal housing policies that privileged white middle-class families, suburban development and the subsequent marginalization of racial and ethnic communities to urban spaces, the ideological solidification of the nuclear family, the role that white middle-class women played in the wartime workforce, and the new and increasingly normative presence of the television in the privatized American home all played significant roles in the shifting public and private terrain of consumer culture and were important in establishing the brand as a normative expression not just of consumer products, but also of emotional and cultural identity (Coontz 1992; Lipsitz 1998; Weems 1998). Market-driven networks of communication, such as mass magazines, broadcast television, Hollywood films, and advertising, facilitated relationships between political and social identities and consumption behavior, a practice that only increased as new markets—for women, African Americans, and families—were created and then capitalized upon (Cohen 2003; Cross 2002; de Grazia and Furlough 1996). During this time, major companies like Procter & Gamble, General Foods, and Unilever developed more sophisticated brand strategies and management, as the competition among similar products intensified.

In the later twentieth and early twenty-first centuries, branding began to fulfill an even greater role in the United States (and Europe), in part because the election of conservative governments in the Britain and the United States ushered in an era of privatization and deregulation. This shift meant, among other things, that corporations were considered in a similar way as individuals in a "free market," so there were fewer regulatory constraints on how corporations could brand and advertise to consumers. As Naomi Klein (2000) has argued, during this time, corporations and businesses began to concentrate less on manufacturing and more on the marketing of goods, labor began to be outsourced from the United States in significant numbers, and branding began to take on a heightened economic significance and cultural value. The cultural economy of advanced capitalism, ever more rapid innovations in technologies and user interactivity, and more sophisticated marketing provides an environment that among other things enables brand strategies in its production of goods, services, and resources. These cultural dynamics create a context in which not only are commodities branded, but identities, difference, and diversity are managed, contained, and even designed as brands. Brand cultures facilitate "relationships" between consumers and branders, and encourage an affective connection based on "authenticity" and sincerity. That is, rather than being targeted as buyers in a purely economic sense, consumers within brand culture are urged to establish a relationship and experience with brands that is personal and intimate, an essential element of their everyday lives.

In the late twentieth and twenty-first centuries, it became clear that advertising and brand managers were developing new strategies to capture the attention of ever more savvy consumers by appealing to affect, emotion, and social responsibility. In fact, the definition of the contemporary "consumer" points not simply to what kinds of purchases one might make; more than that, the "consumer" is a political category or kind of citizenship (Banet-Weiser 2007; Cohen 2003). And, consumption itself is part of what one *is*, part of the complex framework that constitutes identity. In the contemporary terrain of global, national, and narrow-scale marketing, brands have begun to assume increasingly complex sets of political and activist functions

(Arvidsson 2006; Lury 2004). Within the multidimensional contexts of branding, marketers are increasingly turning to campaigns that encourage consumers toward highly cathected, deeply emotional, and personal relationships to brands, so that products bear what is called in market speak "love marks" (Roberts 2005).

Brands are not merely part of economic strategies, but cultural spaces that are often difficult to predict and characterize precisely. Brands, as "love marks," mean to invoke the experience associated with a company or product, a story they tell to the consumer, and perhaps even a kind of love for oneself. But the story surpasses any tangible product, and becomes one that is familiar, intimate, personal: a story with a unique history. Brands become the setting around which individuals weave their own stories, where individuals position themselves as the central character in the narrative of the brand: "I'm an iPhone," or "I drink Coke." While brands are materially visible and often audible through symbols, logos, jingles, sound, smell, and design, the definition of a brand exceeds its materiality. In many ways, commodities have always been bound up in social life. But the contemporary brand is different. The brand is also a cultural outlook, a way of understanding and shaping the world that surrounds us.

A brand is the perception, the series of images, themes, morals, values, feelings, the essence of what will be experienced, a promise. Together, these characteristics consolidate to project a version of authenticity. Because a brand's value extends beyond a tangible product, the process of branding is different from commodification. The process of branding impacts the way we understand who we are, how we organize ourselves in the world, what stories we tell ourselves about ourselves—and importantly, it is increasingly through our relationship with brands that we feel authentic and "real," such as when Dove soap tells women to "empower themselves" or Special K cereal implores women to "own it."

The brand is different from a commodity. While ever more sophisticated in advanced capitalism, commodification remains a relatively static process (though its results may be dynamic). To commodify something means to turn it into, or treat it as, a commodity; it means to make commercial something that wasn't previously thought of as a product, such as music or racial identity. Commodification is a marketing strategy, a monetization of spheres of life, a transformation of social and cultural life into exchange value. The process of branding, however, is more complex and dynamic than commodification. Branding is clearly inextricable from commodification, but it is also not merely its extension, and is more expansive than turning something into a commodity.

As Viviana Zelizer (2011) reminds us, economic exchange is organized in and by cultural meanings. But contemporary brand culture also comes at this dynamic from the opposite direction: *cultural meanings are organized by economic exchange*. The process of branding is created and validated in these interrelated dynamics: developing a brand entails the making and selling of immaterial things—feelings and affects, personalities and values—rather than actual goods. It engages the labor of consumers, so that there is not a clear demarcation between marketer and consumer, between seller and buyer. It is the extension of marketing to arenas of life thought to be outside, and sometimes even oppositional to, the market (such as branded social activism). Significant to media studies, the process of branding also involves the mediation of human action through technology, where within digital spaces boundaries of power are blurred, potentially engendering new relationships that take shape within branding logic and language. In a contemporary moment dominated by social media and micro celebrity, branding is intimately connected to media spaces. These entangled discourses are all part of the process of branding.

Celia Lury notes that one of the key stages in late twentieth-century branding practices "is linked to a changed view of the producer-consumer relationship: no longer viewed in terms of stimulus-response, the relation was increasingly conceived of as an exchange" (2004, 24). This changed relationship requires labor on the part of both consumers and marketers, and cannot be explained as commodification, or as the incorporation of cultural spheres of life by advanced capitalism. As Tiziana Terranova (2000) has pointed out, explaining the labor of consumers as commodification or corporate appropriation usually presumes the co-optation of an "authentic" element of a consumer's life by a marketer: the use of songs of revolution to sell cars on television commercials, for instance, or manufacturing T-shirts emblazoned with "This is What a Feminist Looks Like," which are then sold at chain retail stores. The brand here also functions as part of one's political identity, expanding its reach beyond consumption of products.

Understanding the brand in twenty-first-century Western culture requires a complex frame of analysis, where incorporation is, in Lury's words, "not about capital descending on authentic culture but a more immanent process of channeling collective labor (even as cultural labor) into monetary flows and its structuration within capitalist business practices" (2004, 38–39). This channeling of labor into capitalist business practices is precisely what mobilizes the building of brand cultures by individual consumers.

Alongside the increasing emotional components of the brand, twenty-first-century consumer culture focuses on the individual entrepreneur, "free" to be an activist, a consumer, or both. The brand is increasingly important to this newly imagined subject, defined not in the traditional sense of being a business owner or investor, but as an entrepreneur of the *self*, a category that has exclusive hints to it but also gains traction as something that ostensibly can apply to anyone (Rose 1999). At the same time, digital technologies and other media have also facilitated the emergence of "networked publics," where networks between individuals help form collective communities, such as those revolving around feminist, gay, or environmental issues, to name but a few (boyd 2008).

The collapse between business brand strategy and personal identity construction has logic in an economic context where the individual is privileged as a commodity, and where cultural and social life is increasingly organized and experienced through the terms and conditions of business models. Within this context, we witness the development of an increasingly normative brand of the self, or self-branding. As the brand becomes seemingly more diffuse, permeable, and therefore wider-reaching, there is also a continuing blurring of distinctions between and within "products" and "services" so that the dynamic of commercial exchange is increasingly understood within a framework of affective relationships, engagement, and sociality.

This is evidenced in a common marketing slippage between people and brands, where brand managers insist that "brands are like people" and "people are like brands." This dynamic emerges in force within the variegated practices and policies of neoliberal capitalism. The marketization of social life and the individual indicates that economic practices have been retooled in efforts to reach individuals in ways previously levied by the state or culture, involving key strategies of emotional engagement, authenticity, and creativity.

9

Celebrity

Suzanne Leonard and Diane Negra

By the time Caitlyn Jenner's reality program, *I Am Cait*, premiered in the summer of 2015 featuring the athlete-cum-reality show star, she had already helped to instigate a national conversation about transgender lives. The celebrity phenomenon surrounding Jenner, which arguably mainstreamed the issue of transgender rights in ways that had not been done before, testifies to the cataclysmic reach of the celebrity platform, the increasingly convergent nature of media celebrity, and the imperative to grapple with how a proliferation of "no-holds-barred" access to stars has transformed the notion of twenty-first-century celebrity from earlier models.

The study of stardom and celebrity maintains a distinct but not fully integrated position in media studies, despite the centrality of fame to the production, distribution, and consumption of all media forms. Though scholarly accounts of stardom emerged almost as early as the discipline of film studies, the first scholarly journal devoted to the subject (*Celebrity Studies*) did not appear until about twenty-five years later, in 2010. The foundational work on stardom adheres closely to mid-twentieth-century developmental paradigms in which film studios carefully groomed and trained stars as properties over long periods of time. Twenty-first-century celebrity, by contrast, often appears more disposable, less dignified, and rooted in flimsier and more superficial modes of identity (Collins 2008). The Internet and the proliferation of reality television have provided impetus

for celebrity discourse as well as the financialization of public knowledge about celebrities and new relations between celebrity, neoliberal subjectivity, and entrepreneurial self-branding.

Many of the modes and mechanisms of contemporary celebrity originate in the prehistory of film, television, and digital media. Celebrity, Brenda Weber points out, is "commonly theorized as the by-product of a twentieth- and twenty-first-century media culture that inundates us with indiscriminate images of stars, thus allowing for consumer fetishization through fanzines, web sites, entertainment programming, celebrity talk shows, inside editions, etc." Yet, she contends that "in the centuries before our own celebrity was experienced with no lesser intensity" (2012, 15). In fact, the advent of print cultures, vaudeville theater, and human interest journalism, which burgeoned in the nineteenth and early twentieth centuries, centralized and democratized the concept of celebrity. Whereas prior to this period fame was anchored by the perception that celebrities were special, different, and distinguished by achievement or birthright, according to historian Charles Ponce de Leon (2002), a twentieth-century turn rendered fame widely available to anyone in the public eye, and highlighted personality as a structuring principle.

As this history suggests, the consistently shifting boundary between "exceptionalism" and "ordinariness" constitutes a central tenet of the field. Stars' commonplace qualities counterbalance their ability to serve as aspirational figures, and their position with respect to this dichotomy often indexes their commercial value. Silent film star Mary Pickford, for instance, offered up a "girl-next-door" image in her life and in films like *Poor Little Rich Girl* (1917), a presentation deftly anchored by her wholesome femininity and whiteness, according to Sean Redmond (2007). What this representation belied, however, was "Little Mary's" (as she was often termed) position as a savvy businesswoman who well understood her commodity value to Paramount Studios, and who ultimately helped to found United Artists, an independent studio that challenged the distribution dominance of her former employer.

Scholars of stardom and celebrity have grappled to determine the extent to which stars' images are produced by their works, their lives, or, crucially, the overlaps and interactions between them. Typically, stars' personae worked in conjunction with their casting, though there is reason to believe that lives tend to trump specific acting roles. According to Richard deCordova (2001, 99) "with the star, the actor became the character in a narrative quite separable from his or her work in any film." Stars remain at once inside and outside their mediatized roles as "characters," and Richard Dyer's landmark contribution to the field has been to emphasize the paratextual aspects that make the "star-as-person" indistinguishable from the "star-as-performer" (1998). Dyer coined the term "star image" to explain this concept, and pointed out the need to study ancillary texts associated with stars, which include "everything that is publicly available" about them, such as "the promotion of those films and of the star through pin-ups, public appearances, studio hand-outs and so on, as well as interviews, biographies and coverage in the press of the star's doings and 'private' life" (2004, 2). A central insight arising from the early "wave" of intellectual inquiry into the cultural functions of stardom is that star personae are "always intertextual and syncretic" (in deCordova's phrasing) sustaining a "coherent continuousness" over and above individual roles and appearances (2001).

Stars' meanings within the larger cultural milieu are also anchored by their privileged status and ability to serve as aspirational figures. Speaking about the early twentieth century, Sumiko Higashi (2010, 265) observes that "consumption, as signified by stars, became the most visible mark of success for the striving 'new' middle class and involved not only acquiring goods but transforming selves." Stars ground ancillary consumption of material goods, stage lifestyling scenarios, and generally foster regimes of capitalist desire. In an early and influential account, Charles Eckert (1991, 39) goes so far as to suggest that early Hollywood, "drawing upon the resources of literature, art and music, did as much or more than any other force in capitalist culture to smooth the operation of the production-consumption cycle by fetishising products and putting the libido in libidinally invested advertising." Examples of the ways that stars exerted such influence can be found in Charlotte Herzog and Jane Gaines's (1991) investigation into the craze for knock-off dresses of the kind worn by Joan Crawford in *Letty Lynton* (1932); Simon Dixon's (2003, 96) contention that star homes be read as "ambiguous ecologies" customarily conceptualized and presented in magazine layouts as showcases for the preferred meanings of the star; and, finally, Rebecca L. Epstein's (2000) argument for a repositioning of the star as a fallible consumer whose fashion choices are to be raked over by a public whose fundamentally critical role displaces the more adulatory relations of the past. It is evident that the contemporary social field is characterized by strengthening links between a range of lifestyle concerns and celebrity authority.

In assessing the trajectory of this discipline, it bears mention that most early theories of celebrity were developed in relation to film stardom, with television typically placed in a subordinate cultural position. "The dominant tendency in star studies has been to denigrate the stature of television stardom, to argue that television does not actually produce stars of the complexity, depth, and cultural value that film does, largely because of the medium's lesser cultural status and its essential familiarity and intimacy," maintains Christine Becker (2005, 9). Yet, during the medium's earliest eras, a television star's ordinariness was in fact a calculated strategy: positioning stars as natural and authentic helped to court viewers and to ensure that star pitches for various products were seen as genuine (Murray 2005). The notion that celebrity is not only tied to but ameliorated by familiarity and ordinariness has, if anything, gotten only more pronounced in the current era, readily evident in the conceptualization and caption phraseology of entertainment magazine *Us Weekly*'s "Stars: They're Just Like Us." Those stars designated as "ordinary" hence typically enjoy a greater sense of connection with their publics, an effect film critic Richard Schickel (2000) calls "the illusion of intimacy."

Ground zero for such developments is, of course, reality television, thanks to its emphasis on transparency and accessibility: as Joshua Gamson has argued, "For reality TV, ordinariness becomes a credential for stardom, not its antithesis" (2011, 1065). Indeed, the advent of reality television, and particularly its valorization of self-commodification and self-branding, is crucial for understanding the functioning of stardom and celebrity in the twenty-first century. In such realms, selling oneself replaces being "discovered," talent is no longer conceptually fixed, and qualities such as scrappiness and determination inexorably come to the fore. Such shifts have implicitly gendered subtexts, particularly given the intensified appetite for female celebrity misfortune and scandal and the gendering of "overexposure" in a fame environment that regularly contrasts the low status of reality celebrity with the artistry and craft attributed to the stars of "quality TV" (Holmes and Negra 2011). Reality regimes witness how infotainment and celebrity gossip edge out conventional news, and serve the synergistic promotional needs of major entertainment organizations. They exemplify new norms of unapologetic and incessant self-promotion and evidence the fact that a public persona increasingly serves as a multiply leveraged commercial asset in a fame economy in which promotional zeal outweighs talent.

In addition to the necessity of appearing ordinary, current stars must negotiate the requirements of new media, which not only allow but often demand stars' own self reporting (via Twitter, for example), and signal a heightened responsibility to responsiveness. Elizabeth Ellcessor notes that "Internet celebrity is founded even more firmly on illusions of intimacy, expressed not so much in terms of television's regularity as through perceived access to private, backstage behavior" (2012, 51). Similarly, Alice Marwick has explored how "the mindset and practices of micro-celebrity are made possible by social media technologies, which enable average people to gain the audiences of traditional celebrities" (2013, 115). A recurring element across recent celebrity incarnations has thus been a commitment to transparency in the context of lifestyling discourses that celebrate myriad forms of self-knowledge, and the requirement that stars self-disclose in this way has become de rigueur.

Recently, celebrity use of social media may be seen to up the (techno-consumerist) ante on fantasies of affiliation, engagement, and communication between celebrities and their publics as social media forms facilitate the creation of what Ellcessor (2012) deems "star texts of connection." As Rachel Hall suggests, new expectations/imperatives for celebrity disclosure should be contextualized within a field of social discourse that denotes transparency as an important credential of security state citizenship (2015, 109–10). We contend that the contemporary convergent environment largely intensifies the predispositions of earlier cycles of celebrity production. Whereas access to film stars was desired by publics but often denied by studios that exerted tight control, acts of self-disclosure and self-branding are now a cornerstone of star labor. We note, then, a transition to a "post-talent" fame ethos where a celebrity's promotional work is his or her most important (or only) work, and where even the most banal forms of celebrity are zealously multi-platformed to maximize their commercial value.

Despite this emphasis on ordinariness, a gap arguably exists in theorizing the multiple modes of celebrity in play in the highly stratified contemporary field. Fame remains facilitated and arbitrated—a contemporary set of gatekeepers including Simon Cowell, Perez Hilton, Ryan Seacrest, and Kris Jenner are inheritors to some extent of the roles once played by Hollywood gossip columnists and agents. Other developments include the lowered social value of privacy, the widely shared view that fame-seeking celebrities invite constant scrutiny, and the value of disclosure in a tabloid culture (often around the makeover as a device for "authentic" self-disclosure).

While customarily disregarded as trivial and ephemeral, celebrity discourse in the early twenty-first century continues to powerfully model and adjudicate changing social norms, as the example of Olympic athlete Bruce Jenner's transformation into Caitlyn attests. In recent scholarly work Rachel E. Dubrofsky and Megan M. Wood sound a cautionary note in regard to the assumption that Twitter offers a route to authentic celebrity discourse in ways that challenge or even undo long-standing entertainment industry objectification of women. They find that "tabloid stories about women celebrities use Twitter activity to verify and authenticate them as willing sexual objects, while in stories about male celebrities, Twitter serves as no more than a professional tool" (2015, 106). As such accounts suggest, gendered double standards persist in the realm of celebrity discourse, even as delivery methods have been transfigured. Micro celebrity, self-branding, and the promotional terrain of forms such as Facebook, LinkedIn, YouTube, and Twitter facilitate fantasies of proximity and affinity with entertainment celebrities, yet testify to the corporatization of sociality. As it stands the premiere function of the focus on minutiae of celebrity activity may be as a substitute and compensatory form of public sphere activity; it fills the space that should be taken up by the deliberations of democratic citizenship and the functions of a watchdog press. Celebrity watchfulness, that is, serves a politics of distraction—while we're looking one way, powerful and increasingly inaccessible and unaccountable figures in political and economic life are going another.

10

Censorship

Terry Flew

For as long as humans and societies have communicated using media technologies, there have been measures to regulate media content. At their strongest, such controls have constituted censorship, defined as the restriction, suppression, or prohibition of forms of speech and media content deemed to be contrary to the common good. The word comes from the Latin *censor*, which referred to the officials in the Roman Empire who took the public census, and whose role was also to supervise public behavior and morals. While governments are not the only institutions that can engage in censorship, it has generally been connected to the government of social conduct and the security and protection of the state (M. Dean 2010).

The development of the printing press in the fifteenth century enabled the dissemination of printed works on a large scale. As this challenged the monopoly of the Roman Catholic Church over the production and circulation of religious texts, what followed was a struggle, over more than three centuries, for the right to publish. The long struggle for freedom of the press in seventeenth- and eighteenth-century Europe was connected to the ideas of the Enlightenment and political liberalism. Liberal philosophers proposed that society was founded upon the inalienable rights of sovereign individuals, who should freely and collectively determine how they are governed. This required that the powers of the state should be codified in law through some form of constitution, as well as separation of powers between the executive, legislature, and the judiciary. In order to enable a functioning liberal democracy, there needed to be freedom of the press (the "Fourth Estate") in order to ensure that individuals could freely access all relevant information and opinion relevant to their conduct as citizens in public life. A free press was an integral part of what Habermas (1974) would refer to as a public sphere.

In the spirit of these Enlightenment ideals, the First Amendment to the US Constitution, passed in 1791, proclaims, "Congress shall make no law respecting an establishment of religion, or prohibiting the free exercise thereof; or abridging the freedom of speech, or of the press; or the right of the people peaceably to assemble, and to petition the Government for a redress of grievances." In the wake of the French Revolution of 1789, Article 11 of the Declaration of the Rights of Man and of the Citizen also stated, "The free communication of thoughts and of opinions is one of the most precious rights of man: any citizen thus may speak, write, print freely, except to respond to the abuse of this liberty, in the cases determined by the law." Article 19 of the Universal Declaration of Human Rights, proclaimed in 1948, states, "Everyone has the right to freedom of opinion and expression; this right includes freedom to hold opinions without interference and to seek, receive and impart information and ideas through any media and regardless of frontiers." An influential philosophical statement of opposition to censorship was that of John Stuart Mill, in his 1859 essay *On Liberty* (Mill 1859/2011). Mill proposed that "the only purpose for which power can be rightfully exercised over any member of a civilized community, against his will, is to prevent harm to others" (Mill 1859/2011, 68). In practice, however, there have long been restrictions on the freedom to communicate in both liberal democratic and authoritarian societies. The freedom to communicate has always been subject to general civil and criminal laws, including defamation (communication of a false statement of fact that harms the reputation of another party), breach of copyright, contempt of court, *sub judice*, vilification, obscenity, blasphemy, and sedition. In addition, there are laws, policies, and regulations that have been specific to the media, including program standards that relate to depictions of sex, nudity, or violence, restrictions on some forms of commercial advertising, and requirements relating to "fairness" and "balance" in news programs.

There have also been "emergency" measures that have been put in place during times of war, but have remained in peacetime. In the United States, the Espionage Act of 1917 was passed shortly after the country's entry into World War I, and was intended to prohibit interference with military operations or recruitment, to prevent insubordination in the military, and to prevent the support of US enemies during wartime. It has since been extensively used against political dissidents and whistle-blowers, including Daniel Ellsberg when he released the Pentagon Papers in 1971. More recently, the Espionage Act was used to convict Private Chelsea (formerly Bradley) Manning for transmitting classified military documents to WikiLeaks, and to charge Edward Snowden for releasing documents exposing the National Security Agency's PRISM mass surveillance program.

Among the more contentious areas have been pornography, or the depiction of sexually explicit acts through the media, and depictions of violence in the media. Prior to the 1960s, the definition of a particular work as being likely to "deprave or corrupt" was made largely at the discretion of censors themselves. In the landmark case surrounding the publication of the D. H. Lawrence novel *Lady Chatterley's Lover* in Britain in 1960, the courts found that such decisions would need to account for the context in which any individual act is placed within an overall work, the artistic or other forms of merit of the work in question, and the question of whether such material would give offence to a "reasonable person" in light of contemporary "community standards."

From the 1960s onward, censorship increasingly gave way to classification, and to distinctions being made as to whether a work was deemed to have artistic merit or not, where the work was made available (in a film festival or at an art gallery, for example), whether it was to be made accessible to children or only to adults, and what community attitudes in general were to such material. The introduction of film ratings by the Motion Picture Association of America in 1966, with classifications such as "R" (restricted) and "NC-17" (no one under the age of seventeen admitted), as well as "X" for clearly pornographic films, enabled a much wider range of films to be produced than was the case under the previous Motion Picture Production Code (the so-called Hays Code), whereby film censors could directly intervene in creative production processes.

The Internet has radically transformed debates surrounding the classification of media content. Whereas media content has traditionally relied upon various distribution gatekeepers (publishing editors, broadcast networks, film distributors, etc.), and has been predominantly nationally based, Internet content is potentially global in its reach, platforms are open to huge volumes of user-created media content, the distinctions between public and private media consumption are far less clear, and age-based access restrictions are inherently difficult to apply. An early attempt in the United States to restrict access to "indecent" content on the Internet, the Communications Decency Act of 1996, was struck down by the US courts as unconstitutional in the *Reno v. ACLU* case. In his judgment, Judge Stewart Dalzell concluded that "the Internet has achieved, and continues to achieve, the most participatory marketplace of mass speech that this country—and indeed the world—has seen" (Godwin 1998).

But debates about censorship on the Internet remain ongoing. The OpenNet Initiative found that, in 2013, forty-three of the seventy-five countries it surveyed engaged in some form of Internet filtering, for political, social, religious, or cultural reasons (OpenNet Initiative 2014). The nation with the world's largest Internet-using population, the People's Republic of China, is known for extensive blocking of Internet sites and state monitoring of online content. Even among countries that do not engage in such practices, government agencies often restrict content or issue takedown notices where material is illegal or contravenes social norms: child sexual abuse material, "extreme" pornography, and material that advocates violence against others or terrorism is blocked in multiple jurisdictions (Edwards 2009).

The sheer volume of content on the Internet, and the impossibility of state agencies being able to monitor it, has meant that Internet-based companies themselves increasingly undertake such filtering tasks on their websites. Online platform providers have terms of service associated with user access that provide them with considerable discretion in their ability to take down content they deem to be objectionable. The role played by social media platform/service provides such as Google/YouTube, Facebook, Instagram, and others in routinely taking down content on the basis of criteria that may range from obscenity to vilification to breach of copyright has opened up issues about the forms of accountability and transparency that accompany such de facto censorship. The issues raised range from the lack of external scrutiny that can be applied to such decisions to the application of different rules in different jurisdictions (e.g., geo-blocking content that may offend religious or political sensitivities in some countries), the relationship this has to wider questions of algorithmic governance, or the growing importance of technological algorithms as a means of regulation in the digital realm (Gillespie 2014).

II

Citizenship
Laurie Ouellette

The relationship between media and citizenship is contradictory and evolving. Since the rise of mass media, social scientists and critics have worried about its deleterious impact on democracy. Such concerns typically hinge on the assumption that commercial media trade on trivial pleasures, emotions, and consumer values that inhibit public participation in political affairs. However, mass media have also been understood as "citizen machines" (McCarthy 2010) that can be harnessed to guide and shape the citizenry (or segments of it) for democracy and public life—an agenda that gave rise to twentieth-century national public broadcasting systems (Ouellette 2002). The proliferation, fragmentation, and globalization of media culture in recent decades, and the development of new conceptual frameworks (such as cultural studies) to analyze it, have required a critical reevaluation of citizenship. While the marginalized and degraded state of "serious" news and public information remains a pressing concern for many, a growing body of critical scholarship recognizes the role of popular entertainment in constituting citizenship as a social identity and everyday practice that is not limited to the formal political sphere.

Citizenship has traditionally referred to the status of belonging to a political body and having rights and duties as a member or subject. The term stems from the Latin word *civitas*, or people of a city, the locus of organized government in ancient times (Bellamy 2008).

With the rise of nation-states, Benedict Anderson (1991) famously argues, citizenship became bound to "imagined communities" that transcended local connections. The commercial printing press was crucial to this process: books, newspapers, calendars, and other printed materials standardized language and discourse, encouraging dispersed citizen-subjects to recognize commonalities and making it possible to govern within a national framework. For Anderson, this emergent "print capitalism" was pivotal in the shift from monarchy to democracy.

Founded on liberal ideals of self-government, early modern democracies like the United States continued to experiment with direct, face-to-face participation in political rule, as exemplified by the agrarian town hall. However, exercising citizenship on a national scale ultimately involved layers of mediation: the selection of representatives to "stand in" for the people, the distribution of symbolic resources (such as universal education and information) to steer public participation, and the construction of national identity itself. The speed and scale of industrial capitalism, waves of immigration and urbanization, and the solidification of consumer culture secured the mediated nature of modern citizenship. While mass media (penny newspapers, magazines, cinema, radio) were crucial to the development of mass democracy in the West, these mass communication technologies threatened the viability of democratic processes in the eyes of alarmed intellectuals and early media researchers. With each new mass medium, complaints about the distracting, "dumbed down" influence of entertainment on the populace surfaced, and by the 1920s, social critics like Walter Lippmann were questioning whether popular participation in democracy was desirable or even possible given the banalities and distortions attributed to media and modern life. Lippmann's treatise *Public Opinion* (1922) called for a

class of educated experts to "restore reason to politics" and relieve the masses from the burden of having an "informed" opinion (Ouellette 2002, 111).

Mass communication research codified this recommendation in the theory of the "two-step flow," which identified a subset of "opinion leaders" who read newspapers and sought out public affairs broadcasts modeled after print journalism as the natural leaders of democracy. This rationalization soothed anxieties about the masses of consumers who preferred the cheap distractions churned out by commercial radio and the new medium of television. The equation of democracy with the printed word partly evidenced nostalgia for the era of print capitalism, but it also cast the socially legitimated tastes, habits, and dispositions of educated white men as prerequisites for "enlightened" participation in the political process.

This tendency was not unique to social science. The ideal of the rational and informed citizen has long been a trope in critical media analysis as well. This work often evokes the public sphere, theorized by Jürgen Habermas (1989) as public spaces separate from the market and the state, where people can act as citizens by deliberating issues, advocating positions, and forming "publics" with collective interests. Habermas cites the coffee houses of the eighteenth century, where learned men would gather to discuss and deliberate upon public affairs as prototypes; today such public spaces are often mediated and virtual. While public sphere theory points to the urgent need for independent media not beholden to market pressures, proponents have glossed over the bourgeoisie origins and dictates of the public sphere in practice. Rules of decorum and the emphasis on rational discourse over emotionally and bodily invested forms of participation (such as union meetings or protests) have historically excluded women, the working classes, and people of color from exercising agency in the "public" spaces described by Habermas, a problem abundantly noted by many feminist critics, Marxist theorists, and critical race scholars (see Fraser 1990).

Despite these critiques, the model of citizenship associated with the bourgeois public sphere continues to resonate well beyond the university. The notion of a rational public committed to debating differences and advancing common interests within predominantly national contexts retains currency, even as developments in late capitalism (including the intensification of market values, transnational cultural flows, and the proliferation of ever more specialized consumer niches) undermine this ideal. Since the 1990s, media scholars trained in cultural studies and political theory have questioned this definition of political citizenship, and tracked the shifting shape that citizenship takes in contemporary times. Some of this work situates the perceived failures of democracy within the broader tensions of liberal capitalist democracies. For example, Toby Miller (1993) has persuasively shown how the competing demands of the consumer economy (which encourages selfishness, pleasure, and hedonism) and the political order (which requires rationality, discipline, and responsibility) generate a perpetual sense of inadequacy. Because citizens are perceived to be perpetually "at risk" of failing to fulfill their duties and obligations, initiatives from public broadcasting to Univision's Citizenship Month have operated as corrective cultural technologies or forms of citizenship training.

Other scholars have questioned the assumption that popular media impede rather than enrich the political process. Jeffrey Jones (2006), for example, rejects the hierarchy that values the democratic function of news over entertainment. Jones contends that the consumption of popular media can also foster political engagement and that satirical fake news programs like *The Daily Show* may encourage a more critical understanding of the "reality" of politics and the state than traditional news or public affairs media (380). Jones's "cultural approach" to mediated citizenship offers an optimistic alternative to purists who lament the decline of newspapers and associate the ritualized consumption of television with antidemocratic attributes such as passivity, hedonism, and "distraction." Along similar lines, Liesbet Van Zoonen (2004) contends that the convergence of politics and entertainment in recent decades—from the election of Hollywood icons for political office to the appearance of television dramas built around government officials like *The West Wing* and *House of Cards*—signals the "rejuvenation" of democratic citizenship, not its end point. While these perspectives reclaim an affirmative role for popular media in political culture, they themselves risk upholding the equation of democracy and citizenship with the official events, institutions, and figures of the political sphere.

Feminist and queer scholars have called for a more radical revision of what counts as "political" and where and how citizenship takes place. The robust scholarship on the daytime talk shows of the 1990s explored how these heavily stage-managed and ratings-driven television programs brought ordinary people and the intimacies of everyday life into the public sphere. While talk shows turned private experiences and problems into spectacles, they also presented a mediated forum for discussing social issues such as rape, poverty, mental illness, and discrimination from the ground up. The personal was (at least potentially) deeply political, and the rules of decorum and social exclusions of the white, masculine, bourgeois public sphere did not apply. For scholars like Joshua Gamson (1999), talk shows expanded the boundaries of political life and offered a rare opportunity for marginalized groups to "represent" themselves within the constraints of commercial television. As the political climate of the 1990s shifted, these shows gave way to authoritarian forms of citizenship training, epitomized by *Judge Judy* (discussed below).

Another intervention challenges the nationalist framework in which mediated citizenship has traditionally been conceived. Globalization, migration, and the transnational flow of media culture have encouraged "disjunctures" in national identity (Appadurai 1990) that require scholars to theorize citizenship in new terms. In his research on media use among diasporic communities, Stuart Cunningham (1991) argues that the national public sphere has given way to ethno-specific "sphericules," or social fragments that provide a site for public communication and hybrid forms of belonging (often through commercially traded video-cassettes, music videos, and other popular media forms) beyond boundaries of the nation-state. Lynn Spigel (2007) takes this further, arguing that nationalism "as a cultural dominant" is also losing currency in Western democracies like the United States, because it no longer fits with the economic and cultural practices of late capitalist media and society. As narrowcasting, niche marketing, and an appeal to subcultures have become "central to global capitalism," media content has assumed a "culture that is deeply divided by taste, not one that is unified through national narratives" (640). The fragmentation of media culture in the age of five hundred channels also changes the contours of mediated citizenship, as evidenced by the rise of niche-oriented political brands like Fox News.

While the nation remains the basis of legal citizenship, the practice of citizenship has—for better or worse—become more consumer-oriented. Today, our sense of belonging is often rooted in our consumption practices and brand communities as much as in formal political bodies. Drawing from the cultural theorist Néstor García-Canclini (2001), Sarah Banet-Weiser contends that if the nation-state retains currency as a basis for membership and belonging, its definition has come to hinge on interpretative communities of consumers. Within the current context of proliferating media channels, narrowcasting, globalization, and transnational cultural flows, she contends, the "shared identity of consumers is increasingly one of the most meaningful national connections among members of a community" (2007, 10). Banet-Weiser sees the shift toward what she calls consumer citizenship as a reconciliation of the competing demands of the consumer economy and the political order theorized by Miller. Increasingly, brands (including media brands like Fox, MTV, and Bravo) encourage us to actualize our rights, duties, and sense of belonging as citizens *within* the sphere of consumption. The children's cable network Nickelodeon, the focus of Banet-Weiser's study, claims to "empower" its viewers to exercise their right to make consumer choices and simultaneously escape adult rules through membership in the Nickelodeon Nation. The network fuses the promise of political and cultural power—and cleverly connects both to participation in and identification with the niche-oriented Nickelodeon brand.

The rising currency of corporate social responsibility, which has largely replaced state regulation of the public interest in media culture, stitches political citizenship into consumer culture and brand communities in more explicitly political ways. Most media conglomerates, including Disney and Time Warner, now pursue robust "socially responsible" agendas as part of their corporate brand strategies. From encouraging volunteerism and charitable giving to inserting prosocial messages into television content, media corporations pursue citizenship training to bolster their corporate image, which can translate into profit. My own work on media ventures like *Oprah's Big Give* and the ABC TV network's Better Community Campaign (Ouellette 2012) shows how corporate social responsibility stitches the demands of the political order into the symbolic boundaries of media brands, which then become venues for traditional forms of civic belonging as well as newer forms of consumer membership. Within this context, the pursuit of "good citizenship" does not contradict the aims of the consumer economy, but is folded into them.

In recent years, a burgeoning strand of media scholarship has tracked the offloading of duties and services historically performed by the state onto corporations and individual consumers. The shift from the regulation of the public interest, which assumes public oversight, to corporate social responsibility is one example; the surge of media devoted to transforming individuals into more enterprising, responsible, self-reliant, and marketable versions of themselves is another. Reality TV has received particular attention as a "technology of neoliberal citizenship" that translates shifting ideas about democracy and government into regimes for everyday living. Reality TV gained visibility and currency in the early 2000s, in the wake of attempts to privatize public institutions and downsize the postwar welfare state. Neoliberal policies and discourses that apply market logic to every dimension of society were gaining hold in political discourse and the policy sector, and reality programming in the United States was one of the clearest cultural expressions of this political shift. Scholars have noted how reality TV competitions, makeovers, docusoaps, and interventions equate "good citizenship" with personal responsibility (see Ouellette and Hay 2008), while also offering market-oriented social identities, behavioral norms, advice, and templates for self-maximization and personal entrepreneurship. Scholars around the world, especially in Europe, have observed similar neoliberal tendencies in reality TV, as market logic has intensified and programs of privatization and welfare reform have taken hold on a global scale.

The growth of the Internet, social media, and interactive mobile devices (including phones) in the past decade has intensified the long-standing debate over media and citizenship—with no clear resolution. Some scholars are pessimistic about new media's capacity to undo problems of commercialism and political passivity. We may be able to "vote" for our favorite TV idols, share political information and opinions (as well as GIFs, memes and the contents of our lunch) at the touch of a button, or even participate in new forms of "clicktivism" and hashtag activism, but doing so—they argue—is merely a new form of distraction that prevents substantive participation in democracy and stymies political change (see J. Dean 2010). Other scholars, however, are cautiously optimistic about the extent to which social media, mobile devices, and other new media technologies afford opportunities to redefine the public sphere, formulate mediated publics around diverse issues and identities, and develop new forms of political engagement. Such possibilities are not automatic or inherent to new technologies, but they can manifest under particular social and political conditions. One thing is clear: just as earlier activists understood the pivotal role of mass media in their efforts to transform political life, as suggested by the infamous slogan "The Whole World Is Watching," today's social and political movements recognize the centrality of interactive digital media platforms. From WeChat's role in political activism in China to the use of Twitter by the Black Lives Matter movement in the United States, new media technologies are equally integral to contemporary demands being made on the nation, the public, and the state.

12

Class
Laura Grindstaff

Media scholars who study class lament the relative lack of attention it gets in both the academy and the culture at large, citing the diverse meanings of class (socioeconomic, cultural, behavioral, etc.) and, in relation, the fact that class is not marked on the body's surface as consistently or visibly as gender or race. Nevertheless, media studies research on class exists, exploring class both "on-screen" (in media texts) and "off-screen" (in spaces of production and consumption, broadly conceived).

Studies of class "on-screen" typically analyze individual texts in context. Whether the focus is *Amos 'n' Andy* on radio, *Norma Rae* on film, *Keeping Up with the Kardashians* on television, or Fred the "trailer-trash" kid on YouTube, close readings identify class-coded meanings expressed through character, action, and narrative development. At its best, this work helps us see class dynamics and their relationship to broader social formations outside the text. A good example is Julie Bettie's (1995) analysis of *Roseanne*, an American sitcom about a white, working-class family starring Roseanne Barr. Drawing on Bourdieu (1984), Bettie foregrounds the ways in which class is cultural and performative, expressed by and through body, as well as an outcome of particular labor practices and consumption patterns. She also links the TV program to the changing demographics of class disadvantage in the United States, arguing that as economic restructuring funnels increasing numbers of women and people of color into low-wage service work, Roseanne (who waits tables at a diner) is an important corrective to the conflation of "the working class" with white, blue-collar masculinity embodied over the years by the likes of Ralph Kramden, Archie Bunker, and Homer Simpson.

Historical studies of class representation often foreground social context even more explicitly. Focusing on Hollywood film from 1930 to 1980, John Bodnar (2003) compares the portrayal of working-class characters on-screen with rhetoric about the efficacy of liberal democracy espoused by politicians at the time, while Ross (1998) documents the rise of a working-class film movement during Hollywood's silent era, noting its repeated clashes with censors, industry leaders, and federal agencies over the kinds of images audiences would be allowed to see. By making the social context a key "player" in the analysis, historical studies show that media portrayals of class are not merely representations *of* class but interventions *in* class-based political struggle on a broad scale. In a different but related vein, longitudinal research on media representations of class is able to identify themes and patterns over time. One important theme is the relative invisibility of the working classes. In his analysis of six decades of family sitcoms on US television, Richard Butsch (2015) concludes that working-class life is grossly underrepresented compared to affluence; moreover, when working-class households *are* portrayed, husbands/fathers are stereotypically cast as dumb, irresponsible buffoons, in contrast to working-class wives and middle-class parents, who appear wise and sensible. Butsch ties the persistence of this pattern to production pressures at the network level along with the white, middle-class male profile of writers and producers. Another persistent theme is the portrayal of class as an individual rather than structural phenomenon. Diana Kendall (2011) draws on *New York Times* coverage over many decades as well as television entertainment programming, including reality TV, to argue that affluence is presented as normal and desirable in US media, while class inequality is legitimated through stories that express class as a matter of money and individual lifestyle rather than a social location shaped by differential structures of opportunity.

Studies of media reception adopt an "off-screen" focus on real people consuming media in their everyday lives. Cultural histories of reception chart the rise of popular commercial entertainment in the United States and its appeal to working-class audiences alongside efforts by cultural elites to gentrify those audiences (Butsch 2000; Nasaw 1993), whereas cultural studies approaches—largely inspired by the work of Stuart Hall, David Morley, and Dorothy Hobson of the Centre for Contemporary Cultural Studies at the University of Birmingham—examine why and how people of different class backgrounds use media and/or interpret specific media texts (e.g., Bird 1992; Press 1991; Skeggs and Wood 2012). Research on media reception offers an important counterpoint to representational analysis, in that it forces a consideration of the differences between consumers' understandings of media texts and those of scholars, as well as differences in interpretation among consumers, and between consumers and producers. This work shifts analytic focus to the experiential spaces outside the text created by the production-consumption chain. In their research on reality programming, for example, Skeggs and Wood (2012) focus less on how programs are interpreted as text or representation and instead explore how the encounter between viewers and genre constitutes what they call "a mediated social relation" in which viewers negotiate the class-coded moral boundaries between "self" and "other"—a complex exercise given the genre's explicit mandate to blur the line between spectator and performer.

A different way of looking at the operation of class in "off-screen" media contexts is to examine the politics of media ownership and control. Political-economic approaches as pioneered by Herbert Schiller, Noam Chomsky, and Robert McChesney, among others, are quite obviously about class but face criticism within media studies because of their presumed economic determinism. This work analyzes the ways that established corporate interests influence the production and distribution of media content within and across national borders to shape public consensus in their favor. Commercial media essentially function as propaganda for an international "power elite"—and thereby diminish democracy and increase inequality—because of the way media firms interface with, depend upon, and take up the perspective of powerful social institutions. Political-economy research is rooted in foundational sociological theories of class (including the work of Karl Marx on class conflict, Louis Althusser on ideology, and C. Wright Mills on power) and exists in productive tension with more grounded, meaning-centered scholarship adhering largely to a Gramscian tradition. The tension between top-down versus bottom-up paradigms is particularly salient in global studies of media, where the interplay of local and global forces may itself be a key focus of analysis. As those studying specific manifestations of "glocalization" note, one needn't deny the unprecedented control exercised by Western transnational corporations over the dissemination of media on a global scale in order to appreciate that indigenization is not a special moment of resistance to, or an unintended by-product of, Western media hegemony, but rather is fundamentally constitutive of it (Tomlinson 1999). This, too, is a class struggle of sorts.

A third thread of "off-screen" scholarship falls under the rubric of production studies, often focused on media industries and workplaces. An excellent example is Vicki Mayer's (2011) book on labor in the globalized television industry in which she challenges the industry's mythical account of itself as a creative economy populated by auteurs and elites rather than contingent, precarious workers whose contributions are often marginalized or rendered invisible. Earlier studies of media production coming primarily out of sociology in the 1970s and 1980s dealt with class more obliquely, in the course of exploring everyday decision making among high-status professionals in Hollywood or among journalists whose standard reportorial practice prioritizes the perspectives of institutional authorities over those of ordinary people. This early work—along with scholarship on emotional labor, cultural capital, and the politics of civility—inspired my own ethnographic research on daytime talk shows, which employed extensive participant observation behind the scenes to unpack the class implications of the production and performance of "ordinariness" on television, with "ordinary" more often than not serving as producers' euphemism of choice for "lower class" (Grindstaff 2002).

In this work, I sought to understand how and why real people with real problems and conflicts in their lives, many of who were indeed poor or working class, willingly delivered "trashy" performances on television via a grammar of heightened emotional and physical expressiveness. To say that talk show guests were seeking fifteen minutes of fame is to describe rather than explain the phenomenon. Like most people, guests wanted to leave a mark on the world by participating in public discourse in a locally meaningful way. For them, "public discourse" meant mainstream television, and they accepted the unflattering terms of entry because, given their systematic exclusion from media participation, they saw few other options for fulfilling this desire. This speaks volumes about the refraction of class through television at the cusp of the reality TV boom:

the out-of-control body was a relay for the "lower" classes not because it came naturally to talk show guests necessarily (if it did, producers would have spent less time preparing guests for their roles) but because it was consistent with deeply held cultural assumptions about class and was the most legible terrain for producers and guests to mine. Consequently, despite the common comparison between talk shows and freak shows, I argued that talk shows were like modern-day minstrelsy, with guests performing in "poor face." The slippage between "class" and terms like "white trash" and "trailer trash" as applied to talk show guests afforded producers a convenient alibi, enabling them to cultivate "trashy" performances on the basis of behavioral and cultural criteria without naming race or class per se.

Daytime talk shows constitute but one genre in a broader constellation of genres generally known as "tabloid media" (others would include supermarket tabloids, celebrity gossip magazines, and certain news and current affairs programs). Tabloid media underscore the implicit correspondence between the cultural and socioeconomic dimensions of class, invoking class meanings in allegorical as well as literal ways. Tabloid media are "lowbrow," marked by sensationalism, personalization, and emotional excess; with roots in nineteenth-century melodrama, they blend oral traditions of gossip with the human interest story to serve "popular" as opposed to elite tastes, and in contrast to the "serious" or "legitimate" press (Bird 1992; Glynn 2000). Class difference is implicated in the presumed opposition of dominant and subordinate interests—what John Fiske (1989) characterizes as "the power bloc" versus "the people"—translated into culture form. The same could be said for the study of fans and fandoms, which, at first blush, might not appear to be "about class" at all. Because media fans favor popular over elite culture, and because their ways of engaging media texts are often direct, expressive, and participatory rather than distanced or restrained, fans embody a class aesthetic stereotypically associated with the "lower" classes regardless of the actual socioeconomic status of individual fans (Jenkins 1992). Consequently, fan studies could be said to invoke and obscure class simultaneously. More recently, with the ascendance of the Internet and Web 2.0, the participatory ethos once confined to fan culture has become a more pervasive media phenomenon and blurred the (already blurry) distinctions between production and consumption. This in turn has prompted considerable debate about whether such developments signal opportunity for and/or exploitation of media consumers, along with concerns about class-based digital divides based on unequal opportunities and resources for media participation (Jenkins, Ford, and Green 2013).

And finally there is reality TV, which has radically transformed television culture over the past two decades in ways that bring on- and off-screen dynamics together. The class implications of reality TV are profound, not only because of the class meanings and dynamics unfolding on particular shows or subgenres (e.g., makeover television, in which ordinary people are perpetually in need of expert intervention) but also because of the economic and cultural formations wrought by the growth of the genre as a whole. As many scholars have observed, reality programming is a thoroughly neoliberal enterprise, rising hand in fist with economic policies that have deregulated and privatized media industries while weakening labor unions. At the same time, it passes itself off as a democratizing force by extending the possibility of media participation (and potential celebrity) "downward" to ordinary people. With its legions of ordinary-people participants, reality programming simultaneously "democratizes" media access and upholds a business model predicated upon a radical restructuring of labor, not the least of which is the elimination of actors and screenwriters. Consequently, "ordinariness" in the context of reality TV is both a category of participation driven by a neoliberal programming strategy *and* a mandate of performance tied to the display of emotion and affect. The performance of ordinariness on reality TV and the potential celebrity it confers are "classed" to the degree that it is precisely in a context of increasing economic precarity that "performing the self" becomes an ever important resource for value extraction (in reality TV and elsewhere), to the degree that heightened emotion and affect continue to signal class difference despite the growing cultural imperative toward performativity across the class spectrum, and to the degree that "ordinary celebrity" is considered inferior to traditional celebrity because reality TV itself is subordinate to scripted dramatic television. Ironically, reality TV occupies the low side of the high/low cultural divide while lining the pockets of the industry's one percent and underwriting the risk of producing "quality" dramatic programming for more "desirable" audiences.

If nothing else, the study of reality TV stages a challenge to the lament that class is largely invisible in media studies. Even setting reality TV aside, class has been explored in a multiplicity of ways by different traditions of scholarship, both on- and off-screen. Although the meanings of class are mobile and wide-ranging, this is precisely what makes class interesting—and imperative—to explore and understand, using all the theoretical and methodological tools at hand.

13

Commodification
Alison Hearn

The term "commodification" names the process whereby things, services, ideas, and people are transformed into objects for sale in a capitalist economic system. It can also refer to the ways in which human practices normally considered to be outside the market, such as art, religion, or medicine, are being integrated into the capitalist marketplace. Taken more broadly, "commodification" signals the expansion of capitalist processes of accumulation across the globe and into every corner of our lives. Under these conditions, in the words of Karl Marx and Frederick Engels, there remains "no other nexus between man and man than naked self-interest, than callus 'cash payment'" (Marx and Engels 1998, 20).

While scholars have long been concerned with the impact of commodification on human creativity, communication, culture, politics, and freedom, their work all follows from that of Karl Marx and his foundational analysis of capitalism. For Marx the commodity is key to understanding the capitalist system in general. Although markets and commodities predate the rise of capitalism, Marx argues that capitalist societies are unique insofar as they position the exchange of commodities as "the central driving force of growth and profit" (Murdock 2011, 18).

The commodity has a twofold character. It has a specific individual use value, but once it enters the market, all that matters is its value in exchange for another commodity. In order to facilitate that exchange, goods must be made equivalent or comparable to each other; this process of making goods equivalent requires the introduction of an exchange value. According to Marx, exchange value has nothing to do with the inherent qualities of the two goods being exchanged, but rather expresses "in equal quantities something common to both" (2011, 43)—the amount of "socially necessary" labor time required to produce each good. Eventually one primary commodity emerges through which the exchange value of all commodities can be expressed. This "general equivalent" is money. Under capitalism, the amount of socially necessary labor time expressed in a commodity via its money price on the market *is* value, displacing all other forms of value, such as a good's moral or environmental impact, aesthetic appeal, or contribution to the public good.

Crucial to the process of commodification is the fact that it obscures or "mystifies" how and under what conditions value is really produced in society. It masks "a definite social relation between men" (our productive social relations as workers) with a "fantastic form of a relation between things" (commodity exchange) (Marx 2011, 83). For Marx, commodities are "fetish" objects because they propagate an illusion that value is inherent in the goods themselves, when value is really constituted by the labor of human beings under definite social conditions of production; the "relations of commodities as exchange-values" in the market "are really relations of people to the productive activities of one another" (Marx and Engels, cited in Prodnik 2012, 277). The capitalist marketplace, then, becomes the ultimate social mediator, disguising the social relations and fundamental antagonisms of production (between worker and capitalists) as shiny, magical goods and services that appear to come out of nowhere. As a result, our relationships to the processes of production, to each other, to our own humanity, and to society are alienated; they are mediated in and through commodities and are no longer under our own control. So while commodities seem autonomous and independent of humans, they are really agents of our oppression. The fetishism of commodities is a kind of mystification, or form of ideology, that arises out of the material, economic functioning of capitalist society (Prodnik 2012, 283).

In order to ensure its reproduction and avoid crisis, capitalism must continually expand. This necessarily involves the creation of new commodities. This can occur either by invention or by the generation of new demands and commodities to meet those demands—work that is the special purview of media, specifically advertising and marketing. New areas of commodification are also created by colonizing or "enclosing" areas of human life or the natural world that have previously existed outside of market logics.

In 1847, Marx predicted that there would come "a time when the things which until then had been communicated, but never exchanged, given, but never sold, acquired, but never bought—virtue, love, conscience—all at last enter into commerce—the time where everything moral or physical having become a saleable commodity is conveyed to the market" (Marx 2008, 86–87). For Marx, capitalism is more than a simple economic system; it reshapes our morality in its own image, resulting in growing alienation, inequality and greed, and environmental degradation and the concentration of wealth and deepening of poverty.

Within the field of media studies, concerns about capitalism and the dehumanizing processes of commodification have generally followed two distinct tracks. One focuses on the commodification of cultural production, examining the ways the market logics of equivalence and sameness, exchange and profit have infiltrated artistic expression and practices of meaning making more generally. The other examines the corporate and industrial arrangements of the media and creative industries themselves, focusing on the ways they produce and sell audiences to advertisers. Both perspectives, however, argue that media texts, industries, and technologies mediate and shape our work, desires, identities, and social relations, and play a central role in capitalist domination and expansion.

Mid-twentieth-century Marxist critics influenced by the work of Sigmund Freud focused specifically on the ways in which capitalism and commodification impacted the human psyche, human relationships, and all forms of cultural expression. This group of German scholars, commonly referred to as the Frankfurt School, examined both the ideological and economic role of mass-produced popular culture (TV, movies, radio, popular music). Their central argument is that industrialized, mass-produced culture is now imposed on us from above, drowning out organic, grassroots forms of cultural expression. Mass-produced cultural forms are subject to the same homogenizing logics of equivalence, accumulation, and fetishism as all other commodities. So, while there might appear to be infinite choice and significant differences in the cultural marketplace, the actual products themselves are all very similar; they are standardized, formulaic, and generic, composed of interchangeable parts. As a result of its commodification, they write, "culture now impresses the same stamp on everything" (Horkheimer and Adorno 1944/2002, 120).

The formulaic and standardized products of the culture industry in turn produce a passive kind of engagement on the part of consumers, reinforcing social conformity. They stimulate consumers just enough to help them relax after a hard day's work, but not enough to elicit any kind of critical thinking or dissent. The culture industry's job is to equate "the Good and goods," to "both stimulate consumption and deflect critical thought" (Agger 1992, 64–65). Like other commodities, media and cultural products are fetish objects, positioned as the source and very definition of our happiness. By perpetually manufacturing and reinforcing false needs and creating and managing demand for goods through advertising, the culture industry also works to legitimate and expand commodity capitalism. It forecloses our ability to engage in meaning making in an autonomous and authentic way, ensures social control, and seriously constrains our political freedom. Members of the Frankfurt School showed how the commodification of cultural expression and popular media effectively results in the commodification of our consciousness—a view that has continued to be influential in media studies.

The second major way in which commodification has been analyzed in media studies is through what is commonly referred to as the "critical political economy of communication." This area of media studies focuses on the industrial arrangements of the media industries, examining the ways in which the material processes of media production influence the actual content of the texts, films, and music we consume. These critics also examine the effects of concentrated media ownership, governmental policies, and regulatory structures, and the differences between commercial and public broadcasting systems.

Arguably the most direct way in which these thinkers engage the concept of commodification is through the "audience commodity thesis," an argument first introduced by Canadian scholar Dallas Smythe. In his seminal essay "Communications: Blindspot of Western Marxism" (1977), Smythe takes issue with forms of analysis that focus solely on media's role as a "consciousness industry" propagating capitalist ideology. Instead, he insists that we focus on the specific economic role media industries play and the real commodities they produce. Smythe contends that the media industries make

a profit by selling audience attention to advertisers; they produce the "audience commodity." The audience commodity is generated by what Smythe calls the "free lunch inducement"—television programming, magazines, or pop songs that whet "the prospective audience members' appetites and thus (1) attract and keep them attending to the programme, newspaper or magazine, and (2) cultivate a mood conducive to favourable reaction to the explicit and implicit advertisers' messages" (5). At the same time as our attention is sold to advertisers, Smythe argues, we are socialized to accept capitalist processes and values. In both our work time and our leisure time, then, we are exploited as laborers by the capitalist system. Smythe's work points to the fact that our commercial media systems play a central role in the commodification of all aspects of our lives.

Like the work of the Frankfurt School, Smythe's audience commodity thesis set the stage for future analysis about the material ways in which processes of commodification impact our media and communication systems and "play a key role in determining the forms of consciousness and mode of expression and action which are made available to people" (Murdock and Golding, 1973, 205). Along with the scholarship of Graham Murdock and Peter Golding (1973) and Herbert Schiller (1973, 1989), Smythe's work is considered foundational to the study of the political economy of communication, influencing the work of many media scholars.

Over the past few decades, processes of commodification have both intensified and become more diffuse, largely as a result of new communication networks and media technologies. As capitalist modes of value production have become more immaterial, flexible, and global (Harvey 1989), we see traditional boundaries between work and leisure, producer and consumer, mass-produced and organic culture, and private and public life break down. Nowadays, we live in a "social factory" in which we are all "socialized workers" producing value through our communicative capacities and social relationships (Hardt and Negri 2000; Lazzarato 1996).

Corporate technology and social media giants such as Google, Apple, Facebook, and Amazon dominate the media and communication industries, driving the creation of new commodities and new forms of labor. Companies such as Netflix have gone "over the top" of traditional broadcast models by producing their own content to be shown over the Internet, and websites like YouTube are fueled by content that is entirely user-generated. E-commerce and ubiquitous connectivity enable us to buy and sell anything, anytime, anywhere, transforming the market from a material place into an electronic field of perpetual transactional opportunities (Manzerolle and Kjosen 2014). Online surveillance via the use of cookies and other technologies tracks us across the web, designing personalized advertisements that show up wherever we go, configuring each one of us as a tiny micro-market. New forms of "crowdsourced" "micro-work" offer to pay workers pennies to complete "human intelligence tasks" that computers cannot do, and legions of young people labor unseen to scrub social media sites clean of violent or offensive material. In an increasingly precarious and unstable work environment, individuals work to self-promote and brand themselves online with the hope of possibly cashing in down the line (Banet-Weiser 2012; Hearn 2008). Internet companies engage in "opinion mining" and "social media intelligence," offering to manage the digital reputation of corporations or individuals for a fee (Andrejevic 2013b). And, as "smart" technologies take over, every time we engage with social media or use our mobile phones or bank cards, we are generating metadata that can be mined, packaged, and sold to the highest bidder in real time by companies such as BlueKai (Turow 2012), or used to generate predictive analytics, which will work

to manage and control our movements and interactions into the future. As we tweet, post, like, and share online, then, these privatized media affordances and their data analytics turn us into atomized bits of metadata to be traded and speculated upon in the capitalist marketplace.

All of these developments illustrate new modes of value extraction and accumulation; our identities, social relationships, personal tastes, and opinions are now subject to the homogenizing logics of exchange value, becoming directly productive for capital. Under these conditions, we are simultaneously worker, natural resource, and consumer, but have very little control over the way we are circulated or represented and no access to the profits that are derived. Clearly, the processes of capitalist commodification first described by Marx and developed by media studies scholars throughout the twentieth century are still very much at work. In the digital media age, the magical, shiny promises of perpetual consumption and social connection, increased democratization, and easy access to fame and recognition obscure the real social conditions and relations of production, alienating us from meaningful control over our work, our social relationships, our sense of identity, and our humanity.

14

Convergence
Jean Burgess

Convergence is a dynamic of change. In the most neutral and general sense, it describes the tendency for separate streams or pathways (whether of matter, of technologies, or of biological life) to come together. Its complement is *divergence*—the tendency for these same paths and streams to branch, fork, and drift apart.

In the context of media and communication, convergence is the tendency of separate media technologies, cultural forms, and/or social practices to come together to perform similar functions and make new hybrid media systems. In this sense, it is a key driver of economic, technological, and cultural change in the media environment. Convergence, then, is one of the constitutive dynamics of new media (Hartley, Burgess, and Bruns 2013). To be able to describe and understand the different forms convergence takes is to begin to unravel one of the deepest and most long-standing issues in the history of media studies: the nature of the relationship between technological and sociocultural change.

From the late 1990s through the mid-2000s, the concept of media convergence was especially prominent. It featured in media scholarship, in popular reporting about the Internet and digital media, and in media policy circles. There is even a well-respected academic journal that took its title from the concept and the dynamics of media change it represents: the title *Convergence: The International Journal of Research into New Media Technologies* implicitly suggests that "convergence" is the primary dynamic of new media.

During this peak in the 2000s, the concept was strongly associated with a certain optimistic vision of participatory culture—springing especially from the fact that audiences and fans were now talking about, evaluating, curating, and remixing media content via the same digital networks that media producers were using to distribute and market it. Henry Jenkins is most famously associated with this model of media convergence, and he elaborated the concept in his influential and much-debated book *Convergence Culture: Where Old and New Media Collide* (2006).

Tracing the origin of the concept of media convergence to Ithiel de Sola Pool (1983), Jenkins begins with the most orthodox technological definition, which has two parts: on the one hand a single physical medium might perform a number of functions that were previously handled separately (in today's terms, think of smartphones especially); while at the same time a single cultural function or service can be carried by several different technologies (think of "television" content, which we can now access in a dizzying variety of ways, including via "smart" television sets that run mobile operating systems and connect to app stores). *Convergence Culture* explores the changing relationships among cultural producers and consumers under these conditions, which are driven both by "top-down" and "bottom-up" logics (Jenkins 2006, 18), focusing particularly on the potential for these new relationships to lead to a more participatory culture—hence, the optimism. Jenkins does acknowledge the dangers of convergence, including concentrated media ownership, despite the lower barriers to cultural production afforded by new media technologies. He warns that the "cultural shifts, the legal battles, and the economic consolidations that are fueling media convergence are preceding shifts in the technological infrastructure," and that "how those various transitions unfold will determine the balance of power in the next media era" (17).

However, other scholars have raised concerns about Jenkins's approach to convergence—so much so that an entire special issue of the journal *Cultural Studies* was given over to scholarly critiques of the "overuse" and conceptual limitations of the term, some of which are directed at Jenkins specifically but also at "participatory culture" approaches more generally (see Hay and Couldry 2011 for an overview). Across the twelve contributions to the collection, the recurring themes concern a perceived lack of attention both to history and power, and to the socially and environmentally destructive impacts of technological and economic convergence.

Given the acuteness and intensity of this debate in the mid- to late 2000s and its focus on Jenkins's work, the concept of convergence might seem specific to the digital era. But media and communications have always been shaped by convergence, and new media scholars have long been attentive to both the creative possibilities and the social dangers associated with it. On the industrial side, James Carey was concerned about the centralization of power associated with the "electronic revolution" that was connecting and reconfiguring public, commercial, and personal communication in the mid-twentieth century (Carey and Quirk 1970). On the consumer side, technological inventions have generated surprising new combinations—convergences—of practical uses not intended by their inventors. The telephone is an excellent example—intended for broadcast and business but taken over for intimate, personal communication—thereby transforming both the telecommunications infrastructure and the practices of everyday, domestic life (Marvin 1988).

Convergence is more significant and challenging than ever, in both economic and critical terms. Since the mid-2000s, social media like Facebook, Twitter, Instagram, and YouTube have—in their own distinctive ways—created new forms of *cultural* convergence among the modes of communication and self-expression formerly characterized as personal media (self-portraiture, daily journaling) or public communication (journalism, news distribution). Zizi Papacharissi and Emily Easton (2013, 171–82) have discussed how technologies of social convergence like Facebook and Twitter produce a new *habitus*—a new way of living in and through media that emphasizes authorship, "accelerated reflexivity," and the blurring of boundaries between cultural production and the practice of everyday life, and that have normalized the very idea of living in a state of constant newness. The boundaries between public and private have always been both constructed and dynamic—think of the quasi-public sharing of holiday photographs via the humble slide projector and the vernacular form of the slideshow, on the one hand, and the public exposure of private information through "gotcha" tabloid journalism on the other—both of which predate digital media by many decades. But social media combine public communication with interpersonal communication and self-expression in specific ways, not only across platforms but also within single platforms like Facebook, leading scholars to talk about new concepts like a "private sphere" (Papacharissi 2010) for the circulation of public communication via personal stories, or "context collapse" for the convergence of our public and private personae (Marwick and boyd 2011), for example.

The logics of *industrial* convergence are having profound and concerning effects in the social media moment too; and the "platform paradigm" is a crucial and distinctively contemporary form of this (Burgess 2015). Mega-platforms like Facebook and Google are seeking to provide more and more of the services that used to take place in other platforms. Google has risen from a scrappy start-up to search giant to global connectivity and digital services company, and a single Google sign-on can connect your workplace (through Google Drive and Gmail) to your personal entertainment system (through Android TVs, tablets, and mobile devices), and your most intimate relationships (through geolocative dating apps, for example). As part of its Internet.org infrastructure project, Facebook, transforming from being a place for college kids to meet up and hang out, is planning to beam its own version of the Internet from the sky to developing countries—indeed, Facebook arguably wants to supplant the open web in favor of its own operating system. For Uber and other "sharing" economy businesses, the convergence of personal transport coordination and workforce management within a mobile app is only the beginning of a historically significant disruption of our employment and civic infrastructures and how they are managed and governed.

Convergence, then, is a dynamic of new media that operates technologically, socially, and industrially. It is neither a revolutionary event that can be located in the mid-2000s, nor a state that can be permanently achieved—it's a persistent tendency, but never a fact. As Papacharissi and Easton note, the dynamics of new media are "founded upon the premise and the promise of constant change and permanent evolution" (2013, 171). In the restless logics of the digital economy, there needs to be enough apparent stability to enable us to integrate new media into our everyday lives and for cultural entrepreneurs and Silicon Valley start-ups to build new cultural forms and viable business models around them, but there also needs to be enough change and disruption (which can come from media consumers as much as from tech companies) to enable *new* new media to emerge.

15

Copyright
Kembrew McLeod

Copyright law emerged from the technological, economic, and legal-philosophical transformations produced by the invention of the printing press, the rise of capitalism, and the ideological construction of the author as owner. The term "copyright" is self-defining, for it means, quite literally, the *right* to *copy*. Copyright protects all types of original expression—including art, literature, music, songs, maps, software, film, and choreography, among other things. In order to be copyrightable, a work merely needs to rise to the most minimal level of originality. But not everything does. For example, the US Supreme Court ruled that telephone books and other such databases are not copyrightable, because an alphabetical list of names and numbers is simply not original or creative enough to be protected by copyright law (*Feist v. Rural Telephone* 1991).

In 1710 Britain passed the Statute of Anne, which is often recognized as a predecessor to modern copyright law. Then, in 1790, Congress passed the first copyright law in the United States—a country that also was the first to acknowledge copyright and patent rights in its Constitution (something that several other nations have emulated). Thomas Jefferson, Benjamin Franklin, and their peers were wary of perpetual patents and copyrights, viewing them as state-sanctioned monopolies that deterred the progress of learning, creativity, and innovation. The Framers of the US Constitution developed a utilitarian theory of copyright that rewarded creativity and encouraged new works to circulate. In short, they did not want to give creators complete control over their work in ways that would inhibit the "progress of science and useful arts," as is stated in the Patent and Copyright Clause of the US Constitution (Boyle 2010).

This "progress" is encouraged "by securing for limited times to authors and inventors the exclusive right to their respective writings and discoveries." In exchange for these temporary rights, inventions and creative works must enter the public domain after a limited amount of time (copyright terms originally totaled twenty-eight years, but have been lengthened several times over the past two centuries, though patent term lengths have remained twenty years). Another limitation on copyright protections is the concept of "fair use," which evolved through common law and was eventually codified into US federal law in 1976. The fair use statute allows people to quote or repurpose elements of copyrighted works without asking permission, as long as it is for educational, critical, journalistic, or other transformative purposes.

Today, fair use functions as a kind of free speech safety valve within copyright law, which has sometimes been used as a tool of censorship. Fair use grew even more important after the passage of the 1998 Sonny Bono Copyright Term Extension Act, which lengthened copyright terms by another twenty years. Copyright terms now last for the author's entire lifetime, plus seventy years, and corporate authors are protected for ninety-five years. The Bono Act had the effect of shrinking the public domain and, as a result, the number of cultural goods that could be freely repurposed or commented on. When the copyright term ended after twenty-eight years, for instance, one could freely use a creative work without censorship being an issue, but fair use is now increasingly being used to make sure copyright law does

not trump the First Amendment (McLeod and DiCola 2011, 234–41).

For much of the twentieth century, these were relatively obscure policy issues; in fact, the phrase "intellectual property" did not achieve wide circulation until the 1980s and 1990s. Often understood as a synonym for copyright, "intellectual property" is a deceptive descriptor, because copyrighted, patented, and trademarked works do not resemble *property* in the traditional sense. They are merely government-granted rights that contain several exceptions and limitations, such as restrictions on the length of copyright terms (Vaidhyanathan 2001, 11–12). "Intellectual property" is a problematic term because it naturalizes the notion that copyrighted works are akin to physical property. This encourages many false analogies, such as the oft-repeated argument that downloading a copyrighted song without permission is like breaking into someone's car and driving it away. This is a flawed analogy. When physical property is stolen, it is no longer accessible to the owner, unlike what happens when a copyrighted work is appropriated. Physical property—such as a car or land—is what economists refer to as a rivalrous good. Copyrighted works, on the other hand, are nonrivalrous, because one consumer's unauthorized use does not preclude simultaneous consumption by another.

Copyright law has regularly evolved in response to new technologies, such as the invention of photography in the mid-nineteenth century or the phonograph at the end of that century. The US Copyright Act of 1831 protected musical works for the first time, giving the sheet music industry a considerable amount of legal and economic power. But aside from suing pirate sheet music presses, the first major lawsuits filed by song publishers targeted the emerging recording industry in the early twentieth century. Ironically, the same record companies that sued twenty-first-century file-sharing networks out of existence were considered the original music industry scofflaws, because they distributed recordings of copyrighted songs without securing permission.

Much to the song publishers' chagrin, the courts sided with "pirate" record labels because the existing copyright law did not specify that it was an infringement to record the performances of compositions (or "cover songs"). In response, the 1909 Copyright Act was passed to protect music publishers from uncompensated performances of the songs that they controlled, while at the same time allowing for covering other songwriters' songs. This practice was enabled by what is commonly referred to as a compulsory license, wherein publishers are compelled to allow record labels to release versions of songs as long as they pay a fee (set by Congress) for each record sold.

Because the music industry did not have the same lobbying power that current content industries enjoy today, the 1909 act was able to respond to the phonograph in a reasonable and balanced way. This is certainly not true of the current digital moment. The controversy provoked by hip-hop artists who digitally sampled copyrighted recordings in the 1980s was the first to provoke a heated conversation about copyright, after years of obscurity in the policy trenches. The musical and technological innovations developed by artists who sampled produced a ripple effect that dramatically changed the way popular music is created. They forced artists and audiences to rethink conventional notions of creativity, authorship, and ownership. Unfortunately, copyright law has largely ceased to evolve in a way that ensures a balance between compensating creators and encouraging creativity that is enabled by new technologies (McLeod and DiCola 2011, 1–18).

"The primary objective of copyright is not to reward the labor of authors, but '[t]o promote the Progress of science and useful Arts,'" Supreme Court Justice Sandra Day O'Connor stated in the 1991 ruling *Feist v. Rural Telephone*. "To this end, copyright assures authors the right to their original expression, but encourages others to build freely upon the ideas and information conveyed by a work. This result is neither unfair nor unfortunate. It is the means by which copyright advances the progress of science and art."

Many content industry advocates contend that only strong and inflexible intellectual property law protections can create incentives to innovate, but this is an oversimplification. The Internet owes its very existence to the fact that most of its foundational protocols, codes, applications, and architecture were *not* heavily protected or locked up; this gave the programming community enough freedom to improve upon what already existed in the commons of ideas, creating the foundation for today's Internet. That is a lesson we should hold on to in this hypercommercialized, free-market age—in which everything (from education to human genes) has fallen prey to the logic of privatization.

16

Cosmopolitanism
Lilie Chouliaraki

What is cosmopolitanism, and why does it matter? How can the communication of cosmopolitanism function as both a framework for the critique of power and a catalyst for imagining alternative orders? In addressing these questions, my aim is to recuperate cosmopolitanism as a normative project that challenges its Western conditions of possibility and recognizes vulnerable others as those with their own claims to humanity and justice.

Our everyday life is saturated by images and stories of distant sufferers, whether refugees crossing the Mediterranean, war victims in Syria, or hurricane homeless in the Philippines. Mundane as these stories may appear to be in our everyday media flows, they are not insignificant. They are fundamental. This is not simply because they are there to inform us of world sufferings or campaigns for charity. They are fundamental because they maintain the self-definition of Western liberal democracies both as political regimes of national welfare and, crucially, as ethico-political projects of transnational solidarity in the name of "common humanity" (Linklater 2007).

The heart of Western democracies lies not primarily in the political institutions of the nation, but rather in our capacity to feel, think, and act for distant others. And while some would reserve our capacity to care only for the suffering members of our nation, insofar as Western democracies place the well-being of the "human" at the center of their political legitimacy, their communities of solidarity extend beyond the nation and encompass the world (Chouliaraki 2006).

Cosmopolitan solidarity, defined as the moral imperative to act on human suffering without asking back, arises precisely out of this double imperative of Western politics: to govern within the nation, but to extend the nation's scope of care to faraway others. Evidence of the tensions inherent in this imperative is the European response to the migration crisis in 2015–16, the greatest moment of human mobility and mass suffering after the Second World War. Motivated by the cosmopolitan commitment to offer hospitality to the vulnerable, Europe's dominant narrative was primarily about rescue and humanitarian assistance, yet its practice was fraught with internal conflicts and inconsistencies. Open borders turned to closed, as, after twenty-one years of free interstate mobility, the Schengen Agreement was reinstated in March 2016 so as to block refugees' advancement from Greece to Northern Europe; hospitality claims swiftly became excuses for exclusion, on economic or demographic grounds; and guilty grief for children drowning in the Mediterranean morphed into suspicion for potential terrorists, especially after the 2015 Paris terror attack that recast refugees as a security risk rather than a humanitarian priority. While this example clearly shows the precarious basis of cosmopolitan politics, it also strongly reminds us that cosmopolitanism acquires its most compelling normative significance when it is communicated within the problematic of Western liberalism and its dual relationship to democratic practice: not only as national but also as transnational commitment to human suffering. Unless this commitment remains alive, there is little hope for those who live outside Western safety and prosperity.

There are, undoubtedly, various other normative values that inform competing visions of cosmopolitanism. As a cultural project of actually existing fusions of tastes, choices, and lifestyles, cosmopolitanism aspires to establish a moral imagination of multicultural conviviality (Beck 2006). As a political project driven by global institutions of international law and human rights, it aspires to work toward a peaceful and fair international order (Held 2010). And as a methodological project of comparative research that rejects nation-bound knowledge production, cosmopolitanism encourages scientific interpretations of the world as communities of fate linked by shared risk (Beck and Szneider 2006).

While these social, institutional, and epistemological approaches are valuable, the most meaningful vision of cosmopolitanism relies on communicative acts that recognize the humanity of vulnerable others and engage with their vulnerability without demanding reciprocation. It is in this recognition that cosmopolitanism becomes both empirically relevant to the realities of our world, as the refugees example demonstrates, and politically useful, as a much-needed catalyst for critique and social change. Indeed, unless cosmopolitanism is communicated as an ongoing project of *both* critical reflection upon its own conditions of possibility *and* moral imagination about the nature of humanity itself, it runs an important risk: becoming reduced to a Western vision of global togetherness that, instead of foregrounding social inequality, is co-opted in new projects of power.

Skeptical accounts of the cosmopolitan project rest precisely on this diagnosis that, for all its promising rhetoric, cosmopolitanism reproduces an ethically dubious and politically harmful disjunction: it may claim to rest on the respect of global plurality but is, in fact, a universalist form of (Western) hegemony. Cultural cosmopolitanism, to begin with, has been accused of celebrating difference yet ultimately misrecognizing a free-market world as the realization of borderless paradise (Calhoun 2003). Political cosmopolitanism is under attack for, despite its celebration of human rights, it privileges a neocolonial geopolitics in North-South global relationships (Hardt and Negri 2005). As for the methodological project, it has been met with suspicion on the grounds that it may acknowledge transnational connectivities, yet promotes Western research agendas and interpretations (Pries and Seeliger 2012).

While different in many respects, these critiques of cosmopolitanism converge on one assumption: insofar as the concept is born out of the liberal imagination itself, it is condemned to reproduce liberalism's own impasses—namely its entanglement with its colonial past and its embrace of the market. In contrast to this determinist diagnosis, cosmopolitanism's complicity with Western democratic politics granted, there is no a priori verdict dictating how its moral vision is articulated, at different historical moments. Insofar as cosmopolitan morality is communicated through specific stories and images of human suffering, the possibility is always there both for a rethinking of what the human is and for reformulating what the global order is and which interests it should serve.

Notwithstanding its legacies with history and power, cosmopolitanism as a communicative project has the potential to act as a critical tool, problematizing and reimagining the very political order that enabled it to emerge in the first place. And one key precondition for this potentiality lies in the capacity of media and communication studies to produce sensitive accounts of two properties of cosmopolitanism: its historicity and its performativity.

The *historicity* of cosmopolitanism raises questions about its enfoldment in the technological, political, and economic contexts that give rise to it, in particular moments in time. Is the cosmopolitanism of the early twentieth century the same as that of the Cold War era, and does the latter resemble today's multilateral order?

How are they different, and in which ways are these differences associated with the distinct possibilities and constraints afforded to the cosmopolitan moment by the technologies, political ideologies, and economic relations of its time? A comparison between various media platforms and communicative genres of solidarity, such as appeals, celebrities, concerts, and disaster news in the past fifty years, identifies a paradigmatic shift in the cosmopolitan sensibilities of the West. While the period between decolonization and the mid-1980s was largely marked by an "other-oriented" morality in the name of salvation and revolution (the grand narratives of saving lives or changing the world), today we are witnessing a "self-oriented" morality, which still invites care for distant others but increasingly relies on minor self-gratifications and transient pleasures as our motivation for action on their suffering (Chouliaraki 2013).

The *performativity* of cosmopolitanism refers to its enfoldment in practices of meaning making, such as language, image, or the body, which regulate the communication of the sufferer as human and invite particular forms of action upon her or him as legitimate, at the moment that they claim to simply "report" on them. What are the aesthetic properties of communicating suffering, and in which ways do differences between them produce different claims to cosmopolitan care? Why and how does this matter? These questions have motivated intense debates among professionals, humanitarians, journalisists, and scholars alike. While some argue that the political economy of the media, far from making a difference, ends up commodifying spectacles of distant suffering, others blame the colonial legacy for the continuing dehumanization of the sufferer, in contemporary humanitarian campaigns or the news. Although these questions may ultimately be unresolvable, given these fields' complicity with enduring histories of dehumanization and othering (Said 1978),

they also sustain important conversations about how aesthetic form and narrative content may contribute to encouraging affective dispositions of humanity and care.

In conclusion, while the need for cosmopolitanism values remains urgent, the project of cosmopolitanism is undermined by its histories, conceptualizations, and applications. Given the problems of war and suffering, poverty and injustice, forced mobility and dehumanization that the world faces today, the challenge for cosmopolitanism is to move away from benign visions of global togetherness and to communicate its normative value as a systematic critique of global power and an imagination of a safe and fairer global order for every human being.

I7

Data

Melissa Gregg and Dawn Nafus

Data play a major role in orchestrating contemporary power relations through the collecting capacities of knowledge-generating machines. For media studies, "data" is an increasingly important term as information gathered and shared through personal and public communication channels becomes subject to new kinds of tracking, quantification, and analysis. Media technologies like the smartphone combine multiple functions of broadcast, storage, transmission, and capture, turning everyday experiences into information that can be measured, sold, or used for political claim making. But discussion of "data" didn't start in media studies. The terminology is drawn from traditions of information science, sociology, and the natural sciences. In these disciplines, recorded observations combine to create frameworks for understanding social phenomena and the behavior of populations, whether birds, humans, or microbes. The systematization of data in these disciplines previously required a human agent to conduct the analysis. Today computational machines are just as likely to provide the source of empirical revelation, as software packages and backroom analytical engines perform commands that allow for large-scale composition and representation of data. This automated assessment of data, the large-scale amassing of insights that is sometimes referred to as "big data," can have the effect of stripping important contextual cues and details from the activities being measured. For example, geospatial data are time-stamped, but the meaning being measured is often transported over time through space—a route, say—which likely involves sociocultural rhythms and meanings merely evoked by the data themselves, or perhaps erased entirely. Or consider graph/network data, which pretend they are time-free but are actually a snapshot of a specific moment in history. Simple attribute data that seemingly tell an eternal truth (fingerprints, blood type, or light from a star) are sampled once in time but are presumed to refer to an incontrovertible essence. Data have different types and functions depending on context; their meaning rarely remains fixed.

For most people, data tend to connote an individual record of activity. Using new types of media technologies, recording our activities can provide a source for reflection, self-enlightenment, and motivation. Looking beyond the individual, however, data can act as a shared record of human endeavor. The following is a list of further qualities we ascribe to data in this sense.

Data are collected insights. They begin with an individual fact—a *datum*, the Latin singular—and attract further instances to lay the foundation for an argument. Historically, the word has conveyed different meanings, but it has always referred to the tension between truth and persuasion.

Data always have a date. Date and data share the same etymological root. Data are recorded in time, and provide a trace, even when the recordings of time itself are erased through subsequent calculation. Patterns in time—cadences, steady declines, recurrences, and spikes—point to phenomena not otherwise recorded in conjunction with the data values themselves. At a technical level, the time stamp is a critical key that allows heterogeneous data sets to be brought together in the same calculation or visualization.

Data gain significance through association. "Data" is a word used in the singular and plural for good reason.

A datum does not stand on its own, but requires other datums to mean. They come together to say something. But to do so, first they must be assembled. This work of crafting association is necessarily rhetorical, since it is never possible to capture all information adequately. For data to mean something, the network of associations at some point must be cut.

Data's potential is to facilitate narrative. But whether they ultimately do so is a secondary question. An isolated activity that produces no evidence does not become data. It remains solitary, rogue, discountable, exceptional. It is a tree falling in the woods. The work involved in articulating data to elaborate new stories takes years, sometimes centuries. Data incite narrative bundles: culturally scripted accounts explaining what a sign indexes. Data have the capacity to destabilize the categories that underpin narratives, reinscribe them, or do both at the same time.

Data may or may not point toward culturally stable referents. Data point to a possible whole phenomenon, which in turn might not be a coherent assemblage. Take the example of an electricity monitor. It partially indicates energy consumption, but it might make only more evident the mysteries of what is actually involved in "energy consumption" beyond electricity. The impulse that data should be "actionable" is grounded in the assumption that data already have a social and cultural coherence—a routine of acting and knowing we are already trained to perform, and which data prompt us to do. Often they do not.

Data are neither qualitative nor quantitative. Data can appear as lines of text, or images, or categorical information, "qualitative" information that can potentially be counted, and rendered quantitative. Numbers, conversely, contain both symbolic and aesthetic qualities. When visualized, data "prepare the senses" in Michael Pryke's (2010) phrase—their shapes contain qualities that people respond to in ways beyond the merely intellectual. In Pryke's study of financial data in stock market trading, visualizations worked as a kind of sensory prosthetic, bundled into the embodied gestures of anticipation in the practice of market trading.

Media technologies capture data. They provide the recording vehicles for activity, and means of communicating the stories told with data. In media studies, these stories tend to take three forms. The first contains *self-assembled information about individuals where data* capture is self-nominated and people have some say in crafting the narrative. In the Quantified Self subculture, for example, people choose to adopt tracking technologies such as wearable fitness monitors to record physical activity, heart rate, and sleeping patterns. Productivity software works similarly to record the screen activity of technology users so that an archive of practices can be generated for subsequent reflection. In both of these cases, data visualization and statistical measures are outputs that operate as points of reflection. This is their rhetorical power: data prepare us for an exploration about the body, the mind, or the senses that works in between our observation. Data allow us to alter aspects of a hidden lifeworld not always available to the conscious mind or witnessing eye. Compelling data prompt reform, improvement, reflection, or an aesthetic impulse.

Second, media also capture information about individuals, assembled by others. These are data that are captured and aggregated en masse by third parties for particular purposes, with or without an individual's consent. When National Security Agency analyst Edward Snowden acted as a whistle-blower to reveal the extent of data surveillance conducted by the US government, individuals responded by claiming new rights to privacy to oppose such widespread monitoring of intimate life. Payment transactions, traffic routes, energy consumption, and phone conversations are some of the most well-known data sets amassed by external bodies and institutions. This emerging context for popular governance is complicated by the fact that citizens are not always told about or actually understand the ways their data are collected. The most common justifications for the capture of nonidentifying behavior are the convenience of predictive services (e.g., Google Maps) or matters of civic patriotism, safety, and self-care (e.g., against terrorism or in response to natural disasters). Following Hurricane Sandy in 2012, Occupy Sandy activists collected on-the-ground information about the location and troubles affecting victims of the storm so that civic services could be mobilized. Without these door-to-door surveys, existing relief agencies would not have known who or how to help (Superstorm Research Lab 2013). The politics of data thus reflect broader tensions and inadequacies in the equitable provisioning of services in public life.

A third category of data collection and deployment is *community-oriented and purposive in nature*. Ventures in citizen science involve collecting and harvesting data to represent issues that may be difficult to learn about otherwise. Data activism allows minority groups a vehicle for telling urgent stories that are not in commercial interests to tell, from the impact of refinery pollution to the damage wreaked by fracking sites. Participatory geographic information systems aim to represent ownership or other types of claims for marginalized peoples. For motivated parties, data can be the evidence needed to secure more just and accountable social ends for the conduct of industry and government.

Beyond these three categories of data collection, the expansion of ambient means of gathering information, especially in contexts of professional work and management, harbors a range of in-between states of measure that are not fully voluntary or involuntary. In workplace programs of activity tracking, whether through wearable tracking devices for fitness and health care benefits or email- or screen-based monitoring for enterprise security, employees are subject to varying levels of coercion and persuasion. This reflects a broader trend toward normalizing oversight of behavior by a technically mediated managerial gaze that captures both labor and lifestyle activities. It is unclear how much choice consumers or workers will have in this passive experience of surveillance as more of our everyday infrastructure becomes capable of monitoring activity through intelligent, embedded sensors.

In all of these instances, *data are collected with the intention to produce actionable insights—knowledge that prompts a response, even if that response is further reflection.* The difference between the forms of data collection lies in our awareness of or involvement in the process. When data are self-assembled, we may experience a feeling of control. But this feeling is haunted by an awareness that while data offer the capacity to tell stories about activities, we will never fully grasp the meanings of the data assembled. The notion of freedom frequently celebrated in the design of recording technologies is one that privileges individual will as the best kind of agency. Circumstances that force us to collect our own data—diabetes, allergies, sleep disturbances of mysterious cause—might involve a more begrudging obligation than freedom, but there remains scope for autonomy over when, and how, and, to some extent, what recording is performed. Conversely, when data are collected without assent, we become subjects of others' discourse. Our activities are recorded in the terms set by others, for the purview and measure of an external entity or authority. As Mark Andrejevic (2014) notes, a "big data divide" is emerging, where individuals have little chance to influence the terms upon which their information is gathered and used. This power asymmetry is one of the main points of concern for contemporary media studies.

The idea of an asymmetrical data economy in media studies (see also Nissenbaum 2009) reflects an inheritance from the early work of Michel Foucault (1978) and the notion of *pouvoir-savoir*, or power/knowledge. Over a series of studies, Foucault explained how modern institutions rendered activities visible and knowable by capturing them in discourse—by witnessing or describing behaviors in such a way that they could be named and categorized. Using media technologies today, this principle applies to the extent that accumulating data demonstrates new activities befitting new kinds of categories and narratives, and to the extent that these activities prompt external authorities to abstract the significance of individual narratives to generate new modes of regulation and order. But what has changed with the growing processing power of billions of connected data-capturing devices is that there is no human agent capable of adequately assessing the amount of identifying information people create in aggregate. Media studies needs new frameworks to understand a global marketplace and an international territory for governance that is distributed in complex ways, yet determined by large digital data sets.

Our research develops different metaphors and frameworks to answer this challenge. To explain the often unspectacular experiences of data exchange in everyday life, we are attracted to organic concepts, for example, the notion of *data sweat* (Gregg 2015a). Sweat is a natural phenomenon that happens to all of us. It describes an emission of meaningful information depending on context—weather, anxiety level, proximity to others, social engagement. It is also a form of information flow that toys with our ideas of control and agency, since sweat responds to different social and cultural cues. What media studies can sometimes miss, partly because of its focus on text and format, content and audience, is the difference that place makes in perception. More recent theorists (e.g., Bachmann and Beyes 2013; Sloterdijk 2011) are beginning to identify the significance of environments in our engagements with media.

The current fascination with data metrics and analytics can be read optimistically as an interest in technology's role as facilitator for new kinds of stories. This is the last gasp of what has been called "participatory media." When communication technologies and people are equally mobile, we are no longer observing discrete bodies interacting with static media entities of transmission and aggregation so much as we are elaborating a hybrid relationship of occasional collaboration. The media studies to come will need to explain our involvement with data and their capturing devices as an accommodation, a cohabitation, a shared breath, a mutual dwelling.

18

Discourse
Nico Carpentier

No academic concept offers the luxury of being completely stable and uncontested, but the interdisciplinary nature of discourse studies (with strong influences of linguistics, political studies, and philosophy) has resulted in a particular diversity of meanings and uses. At the same time, exactly this diversity is its strength, offering many different entry points for the study of media, and encouraging us not somehow to choose the "best" approach, but rather to look at the menu that discourse studies has to offer, and then wisely select what fits the appetite best.

In order to unpack the diversity of meanings attributed to the concept of discourse, we can first distinguish between micro- and macro-textual approaches (Carpentier and De Cleen 2007; see also Gee 1990). In the micro-textual approaches of discourse, the concept's close affiliation with language is emphasized, an approach we can also label, following Philips and Jørgensen (2002, 62), discourse-as-language. Van Dijk's (1997, 3) definition provides us with a helpful illustration: "Although many discourse analysts specifically focus on spoken language or talk, it is . . . useful to include also written texts in the concept of discourse." Macro-textual approaches use a broader definition of text, much in congruence with Barthes (1975), seeing texts as materializations of meaning and/or ideology. In this macro-textual approach, where discourse becomes discourse-as-representation, or discourse-as-ideology, the focus is placed on the meanings, representations, or ideologies

embedded *in* the text, communicated *through* language, and not so much on the language itself.

A second distinction that allows us to map the different meanings of discourse is the distinction between micro- and macro-contextual approaches. Micro-contextual approaches confine the context to specific social settings (such as a speech act or a conversation). We can take conversation analysis as an example, where—according to Heritage's (1984, 242, emphasis added) interpretation—context is defined at a micro level: "A speaker's action is context-shaped in that its contribution to an on-going sequence of actions cannot adequately be understood except by reference to the context—including, *especially, the immediately preceding configuration of actions*—in which it participates."

But it would be unfair to claim that micro-contextual approaches remain exclusively focused on the micro context, even if that is where they are rooted. Socio-linguistics, with its emphasis on social groupings, class positions, social relations, and sociocultural and situational rules (Dittmar 1976, 12), is a case in point. Nevertheless, the role of context in macro-contextual is structurally different, as these approaches look at how discourses circulate within the social, paying much less attention to more localized settings (or micro contexts). This leads to much broader analyses, for instance how democratic discourse (Laclau and Mouffe 1985) or gender identity (Butler 1990) is articulated within the social.

The diversity of approaches in discourse studies makes it difficult to combine an all-encompassing overview with at least some in-depth analysis. For this reason, I focus on the macro-textual and macro-contextual approach of poststructuralist discourse theory, to show how discourse is used in media and communication studies. This is not the only macro-textual and -contextual approach in discourse studies, though. Also critical discourse analysis (CDA) can be located within this (sub)field. CDA does have its own joint research program (see Fairclough and Wodak 1997), but also different approaches, such as Wodak's historical-discursive approach (2001), to name but one. But also within the (sub)field of poststructuralist discourse theory, there is quite some diversity. For this reason, the choice is made to use Laclau and Mouffe's strand of poststructuralist discourse theory as an example, as first fully developed in *Hegemony and Socialist Strategy* (*HSS*, 1985), and not so much the Foucauldian strand of discourse theory, as for instance can be found in *The Archaeology of Knowledge* (1972), or any other strand for that matter.

Laclau and Mouffe's *HSS* is a highly valuable but complex and hermetic work, which—as has been argued elsewhere (Carpentier and Spinoy 2008)—can be read on three interrelated levels. The first level, which we can call discourse theory in the strict sense, refers to Laclau and Mouffe's social ontology (Howarth 2000, 17) and to the importance they attribute to contingency. At this level, we can find the vocabulary and the mechanics of discourse theory, explaining the building block of a discourse. A second—and strongly related—level is what Smith (1999, 87) has called Laclau and Mouffe's political identity theory, which is tributary to conflict theory. Key concepts at this level are antagonism and hegemony. Here, (more) attention is given to how discourses, identities, and their nodal points are constructed and obtain fixity through political processes. Laclau and Mouffe's post-Marxist approach becomes even more evident at the third level, where their plea for a radical democratic politics places them in the field of democratic theory.

Because of its clear focus on political theory, Laclau and Mouffe's discourse theory has often remained confined to the study of politics and the political. Despite the rather limited attention from discourse theorists for the realm of the media, Laclau and Mouffe's discourse theory has been used for analyzing media, and we can even see a modest increase in popularity. An early example is James Curran's (1997) attempt to articulate a radical democratic (normative) theory of the media, which he distinguishes from the more traditional liberal, Marxist, and communist theories. Although Curran does not explicitly refer to Laclau and Mouffe's work, a clear link with their radical democratic theory is present. Examples from the early 2000s are my own analyses of community media identities, audience identities, and media professional's identities (Carpentier 2005). During the 2010s, in particular in Belgium, several authors continued to use discourse theory to analyze media settings (De Cleen 2015; Van Brussel 2014; Xu 2014), but also more theoretical (or nonempirical research-based) reflections on media appeared elsewhere (Dahlberg and Phelan 2013).

A preliminary version of a discourse theory and media studies research agenda can be found in Torfing's (1999, 210–24) chapter on discourse theory and the media. He distinguishes three domains where discourse theory (and, in a broader sense, discourse studies) can be put to work: (1) studying discourses *about* the media and their place and function in society; (2) focusing on discourses *of* media, that is, on the form and content of the discourses produced by the media; (3) defining media *as* discourse, which is a more contextualized version of (2). This early version continues to be relevant, for discourse studies as a broad field of study, and for discourse theory as one of its subfields. Media can be defined as finding places, or reservoirs, for discourses to be analyzed, which opens up the door for a limitless list of research foci. But there is an equally notable production of discourses on media (whether analogue or digital), media actors, media technologies that can also provide the focus of discourse studies' inspired research.

From a discourse-theoretical viewpoint, it remains important to stress that media are seen not just as passively expressing or reflecting social phenomena, but as specific machineries that produce, reproduce, and transform social phenomena. The media field is not just one of the societal sites where discourses circulate, but they are machineries that can be considered—using Foucault's (1972, 37) concept—"systems of dispersion" for discourses, with their proper and specific rules of formation, themselves also embedded in discursive frameworks that impact their affordances. This core idea is something that all discourse study approaches—albeit in different degrees—take into account, but which is particularly present in the macro-textual and macro-contextual approaches.

To discuss the relevance of discourse theory for media studies, we can return to Laclau and Mouffe's first level, discourse theory in the strict sense. Their theoretical starting point is that all social phenomena and objects obtain their meaning(s) through discourse, which is defined as "a structure in which meaning is constantly negotiated and constructed" (Laclau 1988, 254). Discourse thus becomes a very necessary part of our social reality, as it provides us with the frameworks of intelligibility: "The concept of discourse in Laclau and Mouffe's theory captures the idea that all objects and actions are meaningful, and that their meaning is conferred by particular [discursive] systems" (Howarth 2000, 101). This does not mean that our material worlds do not exist, and that there is nothing outside discourse, but simply that discourses are necessary to give meaning to our material worlds (Butler 1993, 6; Hall 1997b, 44). One implication of this line of thinking is that the discursive becomes seen as a dimension of our social world that spans it, in its entirety, and not as a delimited part of it. Laclau and Mouffe "reject the idea that ideological practices simply constitute one area or 'region' of social relations"

(Howarth and Stavrakakis 2000, 4). In other words, discourse-as-ideology or discourse-as-representation enters the media field, in a variety of ways. Not only the many different ways that media organizations attribute meaning to particular social phenomena and processes show the workings of the discursive, but also how they construct themselves, for instance, as the center of our societies (Couldry 2003). What it means to be a journalist, an audience member, a media owner or manager receives meanings through discourses.

Another starting point of Laclau and Mouffe's discourse theory that makes it particular and useful for media studies is that discourses are seen as contingent and obtain their meanings through political struggles. This means that discourses are not necessarily fixed and their meaning is to be taken for granted. On the contrary, it means that particular groups in society engage in struggles, attempting to render "their" discourses dominant, also by eliminating competing meanings and discourses. In Laclau and Mouffe's work, discursive constructions become defined as contingent processes that are always open to change, and not as unchangeable essences fixated for eternity. Of course, in some cases there is a discursive victory that results in a discursive fixation and stabilization, even in sedimentation. This situation of a particular discourse becoming dominant, being turned into a horizon that defines and delimits our thinking, is what Laclau and Mouffe call hegemony, following in Gramsci's (1999) footsteps. This discursive fixation can be very stable, but at the same time, contingency continues to play its role, allowing for other discourses to come up and undermine a hegemonic discourse. As Mouffe (2005, 18) formulated it, "Every hegemonic order is susceptible of being challenged by counter-hegemonic practices, i.e. practices which will attempt to disarticulate the existing order so as to install other forms of hegemony."

Here, by way of example, we can return to the identity of European broadcasters. Broadcasting was first hegemonically defined as a public service—necessarily and exclusively focused on the provision of the public good through large-scale and professionally organized media organizations, financed by national states. In the 1970s and 1980s, we saw the development of new discourses on the identities of broadcasters, with community media constructing an identity based on state independence, small-scale and horizontal organizational structures, and nonprofessionalism, and with commercial broadcasters, who in their turn to the market and profit, contested not so much the organizational media model, but the affiliation with the state and the public broadcasters' objectives. These media organizational identity discourses structurally weakened the public service discourse, and replaced the public service hegemony by coexistence of the three discourses (with the market discourse in a leading role). What remained hegemonic for decades to come was the idea that these communicational processes should be handled by *organizations*. Only in the 2000s did we see discursive contestations coming out of Internet activities, where alternative organizational models grounded in the notions of community and network were developed to counter the dominance of the media organizational model, opening up a new area of discursive struggle. What this example shows is the role of the discursive in providing meaning to media activities, and the workings of contingency, where Laclau and Mouffe's discourse theory provides us with ample theoretical support.

19

Domesticity
Mary Beth Haralovich

In media, domesticity is everywhere. Media present a vision of being happy and settled in the home, but also dysfunctional families and estrangement from the home. Domestic life has been part of media history from the very beginning. One of the first films ever made was an actuality of the Lumière family, parents feeding the baby (1895), perhaps the first filmed record of domestic life. Throughout media history, domesticity has been a site for examining and challenging identities. Much of media's wrestling with identity politics—gender, sexuality, class, race, and ethnicity—often takes place in the realm of domesticity.

Domesticity is also an industrial force, an economic pillar of the media industries connecting audiences to programming and markets. Radios and television sets, the means of delivery, have often been tied to domesticity through design and placement in the home—from the bulky corner radio with a single speaker to the television console integrated into living room furniture, handheld radios and portable televisions, and the home theater with surround sound, big screens, and comfy chairs. Consumer product designers consider the placement and function of media in the home and seek to integrate receivers into a family's leisure life.

As a textual element of storytelling, domesticity is present throughout the range of television formats: talk, reality, advice, drama, comedy, music video, and so on. Content is imbued with assumptions about domestic roles. To follow the strand of domesticity in media history is to observe how media perceive and respond to the changing context of their living audience. The history of domesticity reveals preferred discourses but also challenges to notions of gender, economic class, race, ethnicity, and sexuality.

Gender role challenges, particularly for women, have been closely linked to domesticity from early cinema. Putting on makeup was a sign of impending insanity for a young woman in *The Painted Lady* (1912). Silent film created drama by contrasting the morality of women: the sultry sexual vampire competing with the wife and mother for the affections of the husband (city woman vs. country woman in *Sunrise* [1927], which received the first Academy Award for best picture). Virtue was tied to the cohesive family, which the desiring woman sought to disrupt. The emotional trajectory of melodrama would lead to the satisfaction of a happy ending in which domesticity was restored and secured. This dramatic strategy continues throughout media history.

The Hollywood studio film was a haven for the white family and the "women's weepie" was a staple of the studio years. In the weepie, domesticity is emotionally fraught. Mothers demonstrate a noble willingness to sacrifice their own happiness for the economic and/ or emotional security of their children—even to the point of giving up their maternal rights (the lower-class mother weeps with happiness as her daughter marries into the upper class in *Stella Dallas* [1937]; in *Imitation of Life* [1934], Bea gives up her boyfriend when her daughter develops a crush on him while Delilah gives up her daughter so that the daughter can pass for white).

"Desiring women," the femme fatales of film noir and crime drama, do not savor domestic space and are not tied to family. Children would complicate the lives of noir women. Romantic attraction is tinged with sexuality and violence. For these women, domesticity is twisted, elusive, or not available. Phyllis Dietrichson, the infamous spider woman of *Double Indemnity* (1944), introduced the cold, calculating femme fatale and film noir to the screen.

Genre conforms domesticity to its needs, creating a rich hybrid story. Domesticity is embedded in every film, it seems—even those genres wherein the family stays at home (perhaps in peril) while the man goes off on a mission (contemporary *Interstellar* [2014] or period drama *The Right Stuff* [1983]) or an adventure (nearly any superhero film). The promise of domesticity gives the hero a reason to succeed. His return to domestic space (Iron Man saves Pepper Potts) also signifies that the nation or world is also secure. Even television crime drama antiheroes (meth fabricator Walter White in *Breaking Bad*) and antiheroines (crime family matriarch Mags Bennett in *Justified*) are motivated by domestic life. Their criminal activities are intended to protect the family and its interests.

Romance is perhaps the most pervasive domesticity genre, lending itself to hybrid texts. The romantic comedy puts gender roles on display as characters interact in the search for a suitable companion. Romance may beckon but domesticity is elusive. By the end of the story, the heterosexual companionate partners, delayed by quirky, funny, and/or eccentric dating rituals, will be united in domestic life—a satisfactory ending to savor as the credits roll. This tension around the formation of the couple is a staple of series television, whether sitcom (Sheldon's search for a girlfriend in *The Big Bang Theory*) or episodic drama (the politician's need for a marriage partner in *The Good Wife*).

In drama, a family's domestic stability can be threatened by the actions of a family member: an extramarital affair in the psychological thriller *Fatal Attraction* (1987); the psychopath wife in *Gone Girl* (2014); economic struggles (cancer treatment in *Breaking Bad*). In disaster, horror, and sci-fi, otherworldly creatures (such as Jurassic dinosaurs) threaten the family. In television crime drama, romantic partners solve crimes in the romance/procedural hybrid. The lab in *Bones*, for instance, employs several couples. Across genres, stories depend on threats to companionate couples seeking happy domesticity for thrills and tension.

This mediated domestic family has embraced and put forth idealized notions of romance, romantic eligibility, attractiveness, and companionate marriage. But it is not only on-screen that domesticity matters in media. Assumptions about the domestic lives of audiences off-screen inform marketing strategies, production, and programming. Across media industry history, one can see the attributes of domesticity change. In radio in the 1920s, the male voice replaced the female voice, granting an assumed masculine authority to the young medium and to news reporting for decades to come. The economic value of the idealized middle-class woman—for cinema and for television—occurred during the formative periods of both entertainment forms. In the 1910s, film theaters and film stories attracted white middle-class women, thus broadening the social position of film.

Half a century later, as television saturation grew across the United States, the television screen replaced ethnic and working-class domestic comedies (Swedish immigrant family in *Mama*, a Jewish family in *Molly*) with white middle-class families who were living the post–World War II promise of consumer goods and the single-family home located in a suburban neighborhood and maintained by the wife-mother (the Cleavers on *Leave It to Beaver*). The white middle-class family dominated television while film told "adult theme" stories with topics that television's Standards and Practices would not permit on the small screen at home. Released from Production Code censorship barriers, film was populated with dysfunctional families

presented in widescreen and/or color—"You're tearing me apart!" Jim Stark cries in agony at his comfortable middle-class parents in *Rebel Without a Cause* (1955). To experience emotional and complex challenges to television's discourse of domesticity, one had to go to the movie theater.

The domestic family endures on television today. For most of media history, the white heteronormative family dominated. With multichannel, "post-network" television, cable networks, premiere channels, and web series reach out to explore niche, "quality," and cult programming. Domesticity is reconstituted as not only biological nuclear families (such as *The Simpsons*), but also extended families (*Downton Abbey* and *The Walking Dead*), workplace families (the TV station in *The Mary Tyler Moore Show*, the bar in *It's Always Sunny in Philadelphia*, or the workplace in every hospital drama), and modern families (1970s single moms *Kate & Allie*, today's hip-hop family on *Empire*, transgender domesticity in *Transparent*).

In the 2000s, television and film sometimes challenge earlier media versions of domesticity, whether through parody (*South Park*, *Bridesmaids*) or Oscar-nominated dramas like *Carol* (2015) that explore how miserable it could be to be a white heteronormative woman in the 1950s. Romantic couples have complex personalities, such as bipolar disorder in *Silver Linings Playbook* (2012). *Juno* (2007) and *Precious* (2009) examine teen pregnancy in two very different socioeconomic contexts for domesticity. The drama *Mad Men* positioned its characters on the cusp of civil rights and second-wave feminism, generating self-examination as characters made choices about domestic life.

Every aspect of media is imbued with domesticity. Production design creates an environment in which characters are situated in domestic space. Screenplays explore how characters confront problems and respond to each other. Relationships are established and taken apart; they can grow and they can die. Identities about gender, sexuality, race, ethnicity, and class are examined through the pathways of domesticity. Characters do not have to be biological families to function as domestic characters. "We're family"—words spoken in a workplace setting, on earth or in outer space—motivate protective action, offer reassurance, and demonstrate commitment to others. Throughout media history, domesticity has offered expectations that characters embrace, struggle against, and challenge. Domesticity is a foundation for the richness of media.

20

Fan
Henry Jenkins

"Fan" is an abbreviated form of the word, "fanatic," which has its roots in the Latin word *fanaticus*. In its most literal sense, *fanaticus* meant simply "of or belonging to the temple, a temple servant, a devotee," but it quickly assumed more negative connotations, "of persons inspired by orgiastic rites and enthusiastic frenzy" (*Oxford Latin Dictionary*). As it evolved, the term "fanatic" moved from a reference to excessive forms of religious worship to any "excessive and mistaken enthusiasm," often evoked in criticism to opposing political beliefs, and then, more generally, to madness, "such as might result from possession by a deity or demon" (*Oxford English Dictionary*). Its abbreviated form, "fan," first appeared in the late nineteenth century in journalistic accounts describing fans of professional sports and popular theater, and in both cases these fans were seen as having an inappropriate attachment, displaying the wrong beliefs or emotional attitudes toward activities that others saw as not worth those investments (Jenkins, 1992, 12).

Many of these earlier associations persist, shaping what even sympathetic scholars write about fans, resulting in connotations of the excessive, the obsessive, the delusional, or the religiously devoted. Yet, at the same time, popular usage of the term has become more widespread. Today, the culture industries use "fan" to describe anyone who clicks a like button on social media, as they seek to intensify fan engagement as a mechanism for insuring loyal attention within a cluttered media environment (Jenkins, Ford, and Green 2013). Where "fan" once carried some social stigma, more and more people self-identify as fans, describing a broad range of different relationships with popular media content, ranging from casual attachments and mild preferences to identification and involvement within a subcultural community (or fandom). Industry discourse typically depicts fans as having singular attachments to particular franchises (Trekkies, Potterheads) rather than as nomadic members of one or more subcultural communities displaying a set of shared values and practices that get applied to a broader range of different texts. A fan, in that sense, is a fan *of* something, rather than a participant *within* fandom, distinctions that have to do with the relative power ascribed to texts, industries, and audiences.

Many of the earliest academic accounts described fan as a scandalous category that challenged assumptions shaping traditional academic reading practices (especially with regard to notions of rationality and distance) and disrupted the operations of the media industries (especially with regard to notions of intellectual property ownership). Today, fandom is a much more mundane category, more and more accommodated (or contained) within industrial logics. At the same time, the fan subculture has often provided a base by which consumers could challenge Web 2.0 practices that transform their creative expression and social interactions into forms that can generate revenues for media companies. And the shared practices and languages of fandom offer models for new forms of political activism and civic engagement (Jenkins et al., 2016).

Fandom studies is an outgrowth of cultural studies as practiced by the Birmingham School (Storey 2009), especially as those ideas got transplanted and adapted to the particulars of American culture. Early cultural studies had challenged hierarchies that shaped traditional

humanistic analysis of culture, insisting that grassroots creativity and transformative consumption were "ordinary" aspects of how cultures grew and seeing culture itself in dynamic terms, the outgrowth of an ongoing struggle between competing groups to assert their voices. As with other media audiences, fandom is a site of media consumption, with early fan research drawing on existing models of how audience members negotiate with or actively resist textually preferred meanings (Hall 1973/1980). Fandom took shape as cultural studies was starting to blur the distinction between consumption and production, with fans valued precisely because they used the contents of mass media as raw materials for their own forms of cultural production. Like subcultures (Gilder 2005), creative expression in fandom occurs through appropriation and resignification, with fan culture emerging through acts of poaching (de Certeau 1984) or hijacking signs or semiotic guerrilla warfare (Eco 1986; Fiske 1989), all concepts running through early work on fandom. Fandom also constituted a kind of reading formation with its own reception norms that shaped what kinds of interpretations were seen as meaningful or valuable. Like publics, fandom constitutes a space where significant debates take place as different groups seek to shape the cultural and political agenda. More recently still, fandom has been discussed in terms of performativity, as participants act out or embody particular identities, display particular emotions, or demonstrate their mastery over shared fictions (Hellekson and Busse 2006). As fandom studies has emerged, the emphasis shifted from fan identities (i.e., who fans are) to fan activities (what fans are doing) to fan communities (where fans belonged), with fandom often understood as a mechanism for cultural diversification.

Fans at the same time were also read in relation to notions of taste and discrimination (Fiske 1992) and affect (what set fans apart from more distanced academic observers.) A more recent strand of research has defined fans in opposition to nonfans (people who are indifferent to popular texts) and antifans (people who define their identities in opposition to those texts), suggesting that we might locate a broader range of different affective relationships to popular media (Gray, Sandvoss, and Harrington 2007). Such work has expanded the vocabulary of fandom studies, but also risks reducing fandom to "the adoring audience" (Lewis 1992)—that is, the opposite of antifans—rather than dealing with fans as negotiating readers, shaped by both fascination and frustration with the texts from which they appropriate raw materials for constructing their own culture.

The emergence of fandom studies can be understood as part of a larger shift taking place as cultural studies came to the United States: fandom studies linked a strand of American feminist writings which had discussed fan fiction as a form of women's writing (Hellekson and Busse 2014) with feminist critiques of Birmingham work on subcultures, which argued that it stressed masculine "street culture" over the more intimate subcultural practices associated with domestic lives of young women (McRobbie 1980). Coming from these roots, American fandom studies stressed the collective and expressive dimensions of fandom (what tied it to subcultures or publics), though there has since emerged a body of literature (Hills 2002; Sandvoss 2005) that considers fans from a more individualized perspective.

Many of the blind spots in contemporary fandom studies reflect the field's starting points. So, there is a tendency to be more invested in recovering female fan expression while ignoring more masculine forms (assumed to be more hegemonic); to focus on fans who are resistant or transgressive rather than negotiating or accommodating; to celebrate fans who transform the original over fans who are more affirmational or, more generally, fans who produce rather than consume or collect cultural materials. There is a tendency to make strong distinctions between fans of science fiction or cult television and fans of sports teams, soap operas, and rock performers (the first seen as more subcultural, the second as more mainstream) (Duffett 2013) and to focus on Westernized fan culture while only belatedly exploring different models found in other parts of the world. Perhaps, most damningly, fandom studies has tended to be racially segregated, writing, often without explicit acknowledgment, about the activities of white fans while ignoring or marginalizing fans of color and, along the way, cutting itself off from important strands of cultural theory having to do with race and ethnicity that should have been part of a larger conversation about cultural participation (Wanzo 2015). All of this points to the need for a much more expansive understanding of the fan, one that will inspire and inform yet another wave of scholarship, critique, and advocacy, and one that will keep alive the contradictions as we move deeper into the twenty-first century.

21

Feminism
Susan J. Douglas

On September 7, 1968, Robin Morgan, a former child television star, along with other feminists, organized several busloads of women to stage a demonstration against the Miss America pageant. There, on the Atlantic City boardwalk, they crowned a sheep "Miss America," set up a "Freedom Trash Can" into which various trappings of femininity like curlers and bras were hurled, and held up signs that read "Welcome to the Miss America Cattle Auction" (Douglas 1994, 13). It is hardly surprising that the first major feminist demonstration of the late 1960s targeted one of the highest rated programs on television; second-wave feminists, starting with Betty Friedan in *The Feminine Mystique* (1963), had singled out the mass media as a central culprit in promoting sexist representations of women. By 1970, when feminists staged a sit-in at *Ladies' Home Journal* to protest its retrograde depiction of women, women at *Newsweek* and *Time* sued the magazines for sex discrimination, and the Women's Strike for Equality in August featured guerrilla theater ridiculing the widespread objectification of women, it was clear that media criticism had become a foundational tenet of feminism.

Feminist scholars embraced this agenda, and feminist media studies was born. It was driven by the conviction that sexism and discrimination against girls and women in employment, education, relationships—indeed all aspects of everyday life—were driven and legitimated by dismissive stereotypes of women in the media. And its analytical framework was simple yet intellectually transformative: that society was structured, institutionally and ideologically, through patriarchy—the domination of men over women.

In its early stages, feminist media studies sought to corroborate activists' charges that women in magazines and advertising, on television, and in films were primarily young, white, slim, shown almost exclusively in passive or helpmate roles or, worse, used simply as sex objects, and conformed to very narrow, corporately defined standards of beauty. In addition, with very few exceptions, there were no female television reporters or news anchors, and in entertainment programming women rarely had careers. Much feminist media scholarship in the early 1970s, labeled as analyzing "sex role stereotypes," relied on content analysis to quantify what kinds of roles women had in TV shows or how often female voiceovers (as opposed to male) were used to sell a host of products like laundry detergent or cosmetics (answer: only 6 percent) (Busby 1975). One study found that 75 percent of all ads using females were for products found in the kitchen or bathroom (Dominick and Rauch 1972). The communications researcher George Gerbner coined a term for this, "symbolic annihilation": the systematic underrepresentation of a particular group or groups and/or media representations that favor stereotypes and omit realistic portrayals (Gerbner and Gross 1976). Other scholars developed a "consciousness scale" to rank the depictions of women, from level 1, women as quintessential dumb blondes, victims, or sex objects, to level 4, the rare depictions of men and women as equal, to level 5, more rare, where women were shown as individuals or even in roles typically reserved for men (Butler and Paisley 1980; Pingree et al. 1976).

Meanwhile, feminist analyses of film, like Molly Haskell's *From Reverence to Rape* (1974) and Marjorie Rosen's *Popcorn Venus* (1973), documented how women had been represented in the movies and the increased sexualization of women and rising violence against them in films. Thus, initial analysis of women in the media employed both social science and humanities methodologies.

In Britain, a very different turn took place that revolutionized feminist analyses of the media. First, in 1972, art critic and novelist John Berger's *Ways of Seeing* launched a full-bore critique of how women were represented in oil paintings and later in advertising. Berger argued that female nudes were painted for the pleasure of male viewers, that women were constantly under surveillance, and that such depictions persisted right up to the present. As a result, women had learned to constantly watch themselves being watched. They were "split into two," seeing themselves as "surveyed" (being looked at), and surveying themselves through male eyes, essentially turning themselves into objects (1972, 46–47). The book had an enormous impact on feminist media studies because it demystified the portrayal of women in art and advertising, and urged readers to see these images as part of an ongoing system of patriarchal representation that structured (while obfuscating) the very way we take in gendered images without much thought.

Then, in 1975, the British feminist film theorist Laura Mulvey published "Visual Pleasure and Narrative Cinema" in the journal *Screen*, a scant thirteen-page article that broke entirely new ground in how scholars analyzed female imagery. Mulvey was not concerned with the various roles women played in films or whatever stereotypes inhered in them. Rather, she took on the filmic apparatus of how viewers, in a darkened movie theater, saw women on the screen, through what she identified as the three "gazes"—that of the male director and cameraman and then the male costars, which positioned the audience's gaze as that of a heterosexual man.

Hollywood cinema turned women into sexual objects, "to-be-looked-at," sexual spectacles, and nothing else. Men were the active agents advancing the narrative of the film, "making things happen," while women interrupted or worked against the advancement of the story line (Mulvey 1975, 11–12). Thus, like Berger, Mulvey insisted that beyond analyzing stereotypes, the very ways in which our viewing of imagery is structured and maps onto our psyches were crucially important to feminist media studies.

Mulvey's work electrified feminist media scholars. Some took up her call to apply psychoanalytical theory to film analysis, some began to rethink how female spectators related to media texts, while others challenged what they saw as her overarching position about how all film spectators were positioned as heterosexual men. And feminist scholars began to apply theoretical frameworks from neo-Marxism and poststructuralism, especially Michel Foucault's notion of "discourses" or discursive regimes, ways of constituting knowledge and power relations that gain an aura of truth and produce particular forms of subjectivity. The concept of fragmented subjectivity—that women, especially, are socialized to inhabit multiple subject positions, some of them in conflict with each other, and learn to identify with contradiction itself (Williams 1984)—also gained considerable influence in conceptualizing how women engaged with media texts. And Antonio Gramsci's (1971) concept of ideological hegemony—the process by which beliefs and values that benefit elites become a kind of "common sense" that nonelites consent to and adopt—also influenced feminists' analysis of how the media affirmed, but also at times undermined, patriarchy.

Two threads began to emerge then in feminist media studies in the late 1970s and early 1980s. One continued to explore how various media forms, especially those geared to women, like romance novels, soap operas, or melodramas, promulgated patriarchal values that reaffirmed sexism and helped keep women in their place. What was important here was that feminized media texts previously considered beneath contempt became objects of study. The British scholar Angela McRobbie, in her reading of *Jackie* (1978), a magazine for teenage girls, laid out how dismissing such a publication as "silly, harmless nonsense" ignores the powerful ideological work it does in socializing girls into restrictive codes of femininity. Another line of work, however, began to ask why women might take pleasure in media texts created for them even if such texts were denigrated as examples of "trashy" mass culture. McRobbie's colleague Charlotte Brunsdon (1997) focused on the "despised" British soap opera *Crossroads* and argued that such shows both engage with genuine, everyday challenges women face and, more to the point, assume and cultivate particular viewing repertoires that are complex and add to women's pleasures in the text.

A pioneering work here was Janice Radway's *Reading the Romance* (1984), in which she interviewed dedicated readers of romance novels. Taking on scholars who saw women's engagement with the highly popular Harlequin novels as evidence of a kind of false consciousness, and a willing subjugation to patriarchal ideology, Radway found that despite narratives that affirmed women's subordination to men, the novels also provided satisfying fantasies of women humanizing the male heroes, making them more nurturing and caring. Radway's work pointed out that while it was important for feminist scholars to deconstruct media texts, it was also crucial to pay attention to the female audience, to understand how they read media texts both with and against the grain.

Several scholars took up the charge of studying female media consumers to report what meanings they—and not academic analysts alone—got from media texts. One of the most important of these studies was Jacqueline Bobo's *Black Women as Cultural Readers* (1995) because the overwhelming majority of feminist media studies in the 1970s and 1980s was written by and about white women. In 1988, the filmmaker Alile Sharon Larkin (1988) wrote one of the first analyses of the recurring stereotypes of African American women in film—as mammies, maids, and "tragic Mulattos"—the interconnections between racism and sexism that informed them, and how black women filmmakers were seeking to reclaim their own image making. Bobo's book was the first in-depth study of black women as cultural consumers, and she interviewed them about their responses to novels and films featuring African American women. Like Radway, she framed them as an interpretive community every bit as legitimate as academic scholars, whose cultural domination and social activism powerfully informed their textual interpretations, often in empowering ways.

Andrea Press took up the charge of attending to the audience as well. In *Women Watching Television* (1991), Press interviewed forty women of different ages and socioeconomic status, and found that social class powerfully shaped the extent to which women identified with TV characters and found TV to be "realistic." And Press was one of the early scholars to identify the rise of "postfeminist era television" characterized by a superficial acceptance of feminism coupled with a "trend for women to be shown back in the home" with their family role emphasized and a deemphasis on female friendship and solidarity (38).

As a historian interested in media texts, I wanted to explore how the representations of women had evolved over time, particularly with the rise of the women's movement. And I was especially influenced by feminists' emphasis on women's contradictory relationship to and readings of popular culture, and by feminist film and video makers like Joan Braderman, whose *Joan Does Dynasty* (1986) simultaneously luxuriated in the pleasures of the show and offered a thorough deconstruction of its ideological work. My book *Where the Girls Are* (1994) sought to review both the sexist and progressive images of women in the media post–World War II up to the early 1990s, and to argue that in their efforts to address and contain women's aspirations in the 1960s, the media inadvertently helped launch the women's movement.

As the field branched out, scholars like Mary Celeste Kearney (2006), Sharon Mazzarella and Norma Pecora (1999), and Joan Jacobs Brumberg (1998) focused on girls and the media and other scholars began to study television shows like *Buffy the Vampire Slayer* and, later, *Twilight*, and their appeal to female audiences. Suzanna Walters (2003), Larry Gross (2002), and Katherine Sender (2005), among others, corrected the neglect of LGBT representations and audiences, and chronicled the rise of gay visibility in the media. All of this further expanded the field's objects of study and its modes of analysis.

One of the most significant challenges for feminist scholars at the turn of the twenty-first century was, indeed, confronting what had come to be labeled "post-feminism," a discursive framework that assumes full equality for women has been achieved, that feminism is therefore unnecessary and outdated, and that women can and should, as Yvonne Tasker and Diane Negra put it, "enthusiastically perform patriarchal stereotypes of sexual servility in the name of empowerment" (2007, 3). Feminist scholars also had to incorporate in their work analyses of neoliberalism—the notion that the market, not the government is the best arbiter of the distribution of goods and services—to account for the media's insistence that the most important product women now create is themselves, so they can compete effectively in that market. Rosalind Gill in *Gender and the Media* (2007a) analyzed the renewed and intensified sexualization of girls and women in the media at the very same time that feminist ideas are also taken for granted. Angela McRobbie's *The Aftermath of Feminism* (2009) powerfully documented "a new kind of anti-feminist sentiment" (1) in the media in which feminism is indeed "taken into account" in media texts primarily so that it can be dismissed as no longer necessary, "a spent force." This work was crucial to my own analysis (Douglas 2010) of the rise in the twenty-first century of "enlightened sexism," a new, sneaky, subtle form of sexism that seems to accept female achievements on the surface, but is really about repudiating feminism and keeping women in their place. Enlightened sexism insists that women have made plenty of progress because of feminism—indeed, full equality has allegedly been achieved—so now it's okay, even amusing, to resurrect sexist stereotypes of girls and women.

The impact of feminist analysis in media studies has been profound and far-reaching. It has transformed how scholars analyze not just entertainment media, but the news, media effects and reception, industry structures and employment practices, programming decisions, and the small number of women, still, who get front-page bylines and op-eds in newspapers and serve as sources and experts in the news media. It has launched analyses of how various masculinities are represented in the media, as well as work on sexuality and on the intersections between race, class, and gender on multiple media screens. And now a new generation of scholars is turning its attention to the possibilities and perils for women in the world of the Internet and social media, where facelessness and anonymity are both giving feminists a new platform and enabling the expression of virulent misogyny. The fragmentation of the audience, the proliferation of user-generated content, the multiple platforms through which media texts are consumed, and the ongoing war between feminism and antifeminism are presenting new challenges and opportunities for further elaboration of feminist media analysis to the ongoing, explosive changes in our digital environment and how it too is now profoundly shaping gender identity, performance, relationships, and the still elusive hope for gender equality.

22

Flow
Derek Kompare

When first formulated in his seminal 1974 book *Television: Technology and Cultural Form*, Raymond Williams's concept of flow was a compelling metaphor of the ideological power of television. Focusing on the output of five television channels (from Britain and the United States) over several hours, Williams deconstructs programming into discrete segments, and then explains how these segments, as delivered in a succession of sounds and images, become more than the sum of their parts. In doing so, he expands the scope and vocabulary of textual analysis by showing how the overall flow of the broadcast schedule, with its constant breakup and reassembly constitutes "perhaps the defining characteristic of broadcasting" (86).

Over the past forty years, the concept of flow has been used in media studies as a conceptually influential, but ultimately limited model for the textual analysis of television content, or more broadly as a metaphor for postmodern culture, of which television is the ultimate exemplar. The former usage shows up in close analyses of television content in the immediate wake of the publication of Williams's work. Scholars trained in literary and/or film theory incorporated Williams's concept into their studies of television as an ongoing semiotic system that reinforces dominant ideologies while inoculating audiences with glimpses of "resistant" perspectives (see Altman 1986; Browne 1984; Feuer 1983; Modleski 1983). Tania Modleski, for example, critiqued Williams's construction of the (ostensibly male) prime-time viewer in her analysis of how the frequent interruptions of daytime television's flow (particularly commercial breaks) bolstered the "decentered" experience of women's housework. By the 1980s and 1990s, this usage had evolved into the more general use of flow to describe the depthless circulation of disconnected images and sounds that exemplify the postmodern condition. In this interpretation, flow is less a machinery for ideological reinforcement and more of a description of formless content, fleetingly visible, and devoid of deeper meaning. As John Corner (1999, 60) noted, flow had become unmoored from its origins and was too often used by scholars as a broader synecdoche for TV's semiotic excess, in second- or thirdhand ways that could not "sustain the weight of theory which has often been placed upon it." Media studies had rendered flow into a general description rather than a critical tool; according to the editors of the *Flow TV* anthology, based on the conference and blog inspired by Williams's concept developed at the University of Texas at Austin in the mid-2000s, "though it has acquired the patina of a well-worn theory, flow remains more of a critical provocation than a coherent analytical method" (Kackman et al. 2011, 2).

Given the expansion and fragmentation of television, and the rise of digital media (both offline and online), since the 1970s, it is more than appropriate to revisit and reengage with the concept of flow. While the ten pages in which Williams explains flow have always garnered the most attention, he actually spent most of the book meticulously tracing a broader history of the relationships between communications technologies and their surrounding societies as "a social complex of a new and central kind" (1974, 31). His description of twentieth-century citizenship as increasingly ensconced in the consumerist machinery of "mobile privatization"—best exemplified by television—has proven particularly

cogent (26–27). Through this prism, he even foresaw significant aspects of twenty-first-century media systems, such as subscription and on-demand media. Williams's flow is thus best engaged with today not only as a historic semiotic by-product of the television schedule, but as a productive way to consider the more complex relationships of information, infrastructure, and capital coursing through globalized digital networks.

Williams's claim that "an increasing variability and miscellaneity of public communications is evidently part of a whole social experience" is more apt today than ever (1974, 88). The televisual flow that Williams analyzed in the 1970s was experienced through a citizenship engaged by viewing and listening to mediated local and national spaces. However, the hegemonic flows of the early twenty-first century (in the most technologically advanced societies) converge upon the relatively more instrumentalized "user," a node in seemingly endless online networks. Entry into the mediated citizenship of Williams's 1970s was gained through the private achievement of material class markers (private home, TV set, leisure time, etc.). But an individual functions as a node in twenty-first-century information networks virtually from birth, as key data (name, government ID number, financial information, etc.) are entered and circulated online. The 1970s TV viewer was a relatively anonymous part of a one-way ideological system functioning largely at a macro level, but the 2010s social media user is constantly registered, addressed, and compelled to participate as a series of discrete and distributed data points.

Accordingly, flow today incorporates the very systems that propel global capitalism and determine our positions within it. The consumption of mediated textual sequences is important, but only one small aspect of this grand flow, which incorporates flows of energy, raw materials, labor, finance, and information across the globe. The very devices we use to access "television" are designed, manufactured, distributed, and consumed by intricate global networks of information and capital. Our individual connections to these networks—registered in IP addresses, user accounts, and time stamps—in turn generate the flows of email inboxes, social network feeds, streaming media queues, and ever demanding notifications. In addition to the temporal flow of the television schedule, we must "scroll through" the temporal and spatial flows of mail, messages, images, videos, and other information. As Douglas Rushkoff observes, keeping up with these flows is the source of "digiphrenia": the anxiety about being out of synch with our online identities and information flows (2013, 69–129). Extending Williams's claim about how television's flow was "the central television experience" (1974, 95) that kept us viewing for hours, regardless of particular content, the many flows of the Internet today draw us in around the clock.

While much of these flows consist of the same sorts of social abstractions that Williams found on television, these information flows have a different and more intimate relationship to our lives: they are addressed directly to us, and often require our response. Moreover, given that it is increasingly difficult, though not yet impossible, to function in advanced societies without access to the Internet, the data we generate fuel flows of capital *from* users *back out into* the global information flow. Without this user-generated flow, culturally and financially powerful media platforms like Facebook, Twitter, Google, and YouTube would be empty software shells.

Television's place amid these interactive flows is both more nuanced and less central. The volume and diversity of channels and (now) platforms are much greater than the handful of choices available in most advanced societies when Williams wrote, and their role in the media ecosystem must be put in relation to the rapid rise of the Internet more broadly. Accordingly, in a landscape of old and new television brands strewn about broadcast, cable, satellite, home video, and online platforms, where programming is still accessed on fixed schedules, but increasingly on demand at any time, the deconstruction of textuality that Williams performed has become an effectively pointless task. In the era of audience fragmentation and time shifting, when much (if not most) viewing will take place in the hours, days, weeks, or even years after an initial broadcast, and when program segments are regularly extracted from their original flow and recirculated into others as video clips, what textual sequence could possibly constitute "planned flow" in any broad sense? While there have certainly been some important social and formal analyses of television textuality in recent years (particularly in work focusing, respectively, on reality TV and serial drama), in terms of the wider view that Williams took of "watching television" as part of a larger media system, the parameters and qualities of *particular* forms and discourses matter much less than the extent and functioning of the system itself. That is, *what* flows is secondary to the continuous movement of flow itself. As the *Flow TV* editors argued, and at the risk of metaphorically crossing from physics to biology, while there are genuinely fascinating "trees" out there on television, it's the "forest," as an entire ecosystem, that matters most (Kackman et al. 2011, 2).

In this regard—flow as "the impulse to go on watching"—Williams's concept is neither a fascinating but outmoded critical tool, nor a broad brush to apply to any cultural incongruities, but still a compelling model with which we can analyze how communications systems structure societies (and vice versa).

23

Gaze
Michele White

Classical Hollywood cinema and contemporary media forms often depict women as objects and make them available for the pleasurable and controlling look, or gaze, of spectators, who are coded as white heterosexual men. Critical scholarship on the gaze is concerned with how gendered, raced, eroticized, and controlled bodies become visible within media and other texts, and how individuals look at, identify with, and are constructed by visual representations. The conceptions of desire, identity, and identification articulated in this work are sometimes critiqued for being inattentive to racial differences and the varied ways people view representations. However, reconfigured theories of the gaze can address gender, race, sexuality, and other identities and reveal how new media intermesh gazing, touching, and accessing (White 2006, 2015).

Truth's "Left Swipe Dat" thirty-second antismoking video, which is screened on TV and online, facilitates an expanded conception of gazing. The video informs viewers that they will get twice as many dating matches if not smoking in profile pictures. The message is that being visually assessed is desirable. Truth's antismoking texts are supposed to empower "everyone" with "tools to make change" but "Left Swipe Dat" limits the ways women's agency and appearance are understood. The video depicts Harley Morenstein, who produces YouTube's *Epic Meal Time*, alone in a restaurant booth with stacks of food. Morenstein displays a dating application on his phone and he and viewers evaluate the depicted "hottie" with a "pretty face, tight waist, and nice body." However, he "couldn't overlook one small fact, she smokes like an old man at the race track." Morenstein speaks for empowered heterosexual male viewers by assessing and then dismissing the woman with a left swipe of his finger. The technology and video enhance this position and gaze by indicating that Morenstein can personally summon her through the interface, touch her through contact with the screen, and dismiss her with the same hand gesture that he uses to flick a breast-like pancake and strawberry off a stack of flapjacks. While the video is about smoking cessation, it establishes heterosexual men, even men whom it renders as asocial and gluttonous, as privileged Internet viewers who can access and reject women. In contrast, women are objectified as they admire and politely reject men. With these representations and technologies, the gaze of white heterosexual men is amplified by the ability to touch and control new media and women's bodies. Truth, like many new media companies and representations, promises to, but does not empower, everyone.

Media and other scholars continue to use Laura Mulvey's "Visual Pleasure and Narrative Cinema" (1975) to consider the gaze and dyadic constructions of power, despite its limitations. Mulvey's psychoanalytic reading attributes the production of sexual difference, or the articulation of inscribed male and female positions, to the structures of pleasure and identification in classical Hollywood cinema. She indicates that the subject of the gaze is male, and the camera and projector support his empowered position, while its object is female, and she exists in order to be viewed and functions as to-be-looked-at-ness. Mulvey and other feminists have reconceptualized psychoanalytic theories, including Jacques Lacan's formulation (1981) and propose more subjective conceptions of the gaze.

Mulvey indicates how the text and apparatus work to produce white heterosexual identifications and desires. However, she does not specifically label this as an operation of racial privilege or heterosexuality. Terrell Carver (2009) uses the term "heterosexual male gaze" because of the desires and identity usually linked to viewing. Many forms of looking relationships occur in contemporary society, but the normative white heterosexual male gaze is a key process of heterosexuality and racial exclusion. It establishes such things as movement, egress, spatial relationships between bodies, the right to view, and the qualities and accessibility of women. This right to view is articulated by Truth's video and heterosexual male Internet viewers who demand that women provide depictions but harshly judge their cleavage shots, angled pictures where they hold cameras overhead, and other self-representations as too sexual and as falsifications.

Film, photography, and other representational technologies enable the gaze and social control. Michel Foucault (1979) discusses how gazing and architectural structures, including Jeremy Bentham's panoptic prison, facilitate social regulation. Individuals situated within these structures know they are being watched but not when observation or punishment might happen and therefore learn to adjust their behavior. For instance, Truth deploys surveillant aspects of Internet dating to trigger self-regulation. Women's personal information is posted online without consent as a means of textually constructing the gaze and informing women that they are being surveilled, can be harmed, and should self-regulate. Programmer and author Kathy Sierra stopped publicly appearing when images of her being smothered and her home address were posted online. Some feminist bloggers have reduced their prominence because of threats.

John Walker and Sarah Chaplin indicate how being "gazed upon can be pleasurable or painful" in their visual culture research (1997, 97). Their useful ways of itemizing the look include the look of producers and cameras toward the view being rendered, the looks traded between characters, the look of spectators at representations, and the depicted looks between characters and spectators. I propose that their list be used to conceptualize the gaze, including the gaze of producers and cameras toward property that can be bought, entered, or commodified; the looks exchanged between white male and female characters, people of color, or other disenfranchised characters; the gaze of spectators at otherwise inaccessible lands, unavailable bodies, or hidden views; and the looks that seem to be exchanged between differently empowered characters and spectators. The gaze can be textually constructed and convey such things as approval, disgust, and dismissal.

Critics can be complicit in these configurations. Some feminist film scholars, according to E. Ann Kaplan (1983), are fascinated with Hollywood films and the male gaze, even as they assess these structures. In *Black Looks*, bell hooks (1992) foregrounds the racial aspects of acquiescent views, their history in slavery, and the ways black children have been trained not to look. She proposes that people of color use oppositional gazes to look back at mainstream texts and read against the grain and dominant narratives. Chris Straayer (1996) encourages resistant readings and scholars to question if the gaze is heterosexual and if people need to comply with such heterosexual positions. In a related manner, Diana Fuss (1992) theorizes the ways fashion magazines invite white women to consume products by gazing at, overidentifying with, and desiring other women. According to Reina Lewis and Katrina Rolley (1996), fashion magazines educate readers into a form of lesbian response and gaze. My research (White 2015) suggests how lesbian and queer responses are produced in Internet settings when women, who self-identify as heterosexual, are encouraged to declare their love of sites, products, and other women. This includes the proliferation of heart emojis in posts, heart-shaped favorite buttons, and passionate declarations from women about the beauty and sexual desirability of women on wedding sites.

Gazing and being surveilled produce affective as well as identificatory experiences. For Laura U. Marks (1998), haptic media viewing includes graininess, camera positions close to the body, and other depictions that evoke the senses. The horror genre underscores how viewing is incorporated into the body, felt, and conceptualized as distant gazing. Horror characters and spectators, as suggested by Isabel Cristina Pinedo (1997), do not completely see, recoil from painful sights, enjoy fluid spectacles of gore, and fully view and comprehend. Bodily movements in theaters can be related to Internet participants' gazes, swipes, and other actions. Internet viewers jerk back from upsetting material, swipe away representations, and move along with game characters. In a different conjunction of viewing and swiping, Tinder provides representations of a white heterosexual woman who is supposed to be available through its swipe-based dating application and develops female to-be-looked-at-ness by placing play and cancel buttons over her. Women nail polish bloggers reorder presumptions that women will make images of their faces, breasts, and buttocks accessible by depicting their working hands, but mainstream society still links them to frivolous aesthetics. Such practices, sites, and technologies connect gazing, hand movements, touch, and access as a means of physically intensifying experiences and too often perpetuate male power. Analysis of such text and gazes also foregrounds overstated claims that individuals are equally empowered by digital media.

24

Gender
Rosalind Gill

Looking back from the vantage point of the twenty-first century, early analysis of gender and media is notable for the extraordinary *confidence* of the analyses produced. Reviewing a decade of studies in the late 1970s, Gaye Tuchman (1978b) unequivocally titled her article "The Symbolic Annihilation of Women by the Mass Media" and wrote of how women were being destroyed by a combination of "absence," "trivialization," and "condemnation." Such clear evaluations were not unique and were often accompanied by similarly robust calls to action—whether voiced as demands for more women in the industry, campaigns for "positive images," or "guerrilla interventions" into billboard advertisements. Writing about this period of research on gender and the media, Angela McRobbie (1999) characterized it as one of "angry repudiation."

By the late 1980s, this angry certainty had largely given way to something more equivocal and complex. As Myra Macdonald (1995) noted, one reason was that media content changed dramatically. The notion that the media offered a relatively stable template of femininity to which to aspire gave way as media offered a more plural and fragmented set a of signifiers of gender. There was a new playfulness in media representations, a borrowing of codes between different genres, and a growing awareness and interest in processes of image construction. Media content was shaped by producers and consumers who were increasingly "media savvy" and familiar with the terms of cultural critique, including feminism (Goldman 1992). Feminist critiques made their way into media content, exemplified by Nike advertising that critiqued media for offering unrealistic images of women, and L'Oréal advertising that addressed female anger about constantly being addressed in terms of unattainable images of female beauty (Gill 2007a). Another striking feature of advertising of the 1990s and early 2000s was its use of strategies highlighting female empowerment, agency, and choice—taking a cue from feminist ideas but emptying them of their political force and offering them back to women in terms of products that may make them feel powerful (but won't actually change anything) (Gill 2008).

The early twenty-first century has seen further important shifts, including a proliferation of different theoretical languages for discussing media representations of gender. What Liesbet Van Zoonen (1994) has characterized as the "transmission model" of media was replaced by more constructionist, poststructuralist-influenced accounts. These tend to see meaning as fluid, unstable, and contradictory, and to emphasize the media's role in constructing subjectivity and identity.

Scholarship has also been influenced by queer theory, which has produced "gender trouble" (Butler 1990), interrogating traditional understandings of a gender binary, based on cisgendered males and females, and highlighting performative rather than essentialist readings of gender. This has brought to the fore questions about trans and genderqueer, opening up space for thinking about both gender and sexuality in more open terms, which might include, for example, "female masculinities" (Halberstam 1998). Queer theory has also been influential in offering alternative readings of cultural products, and in "queering" contemporary media.

Another shift is growing interest in representations of men and masculinity. This has been particularly evident in film studies and research on the proliferation of men's magazines or "lad mags" such as *FHM*, *Loaded*, *Zoo*, and *Nuts*. Some research has examined the way the media are implicated in dominant representations of masculinity such as the figures of "new man," "new lad," "metrosexual," "hipster," or "lumbersexual"—which come to be powerful popular means of reading and understanding masculine identities, endlessly recycled in marketing, PR, academic, and journalistic texts until they come to seem like reflections of reality rather than particular constructions. Another focus is on changing representations of the male body in sites such as advertising or fashion magazines—including the mainstreaming of eroticized or idealized images of the male body that represent a challenge to earlier understandings that "men look and women appear" (Berger 1972; Mulvey 1975). Iconic figures such as David Beckham and David Gandy have been central to this shift, which has led to discussions about whether "sexual objectification" is now a routine practice for depicting men as well as women, and raising questions about masculinity "in crisis."

A concern with "intersectionality" (Crenshaw 1989) has also animated contemporary interests in gender and media. It seeks to understand the connections between multiple axes of oppression and exclusion, on the understanding that these are not simply "additive" but constitute distinct experiences and subjectivities. In media studies, the notion has challenged singular definitions of "woman," and—with postcolonial and mestizaje interventions—has argued for a far greater specificity in accounts of how gender is mediated, thereby helping to create space for a multiplicity of foci on—for example—constructions of Latina/Chicana, African American, or Asian American women in the media, and pushing beyond the whiteness of dominant theorizing.

This is linked in turn—though is not reducible to—a marked interest in questions about global media among gender scholars. At its most straightforward, this has translated into a greater international focus and more cross-national comparisons, such as the Global Media Monitoring Project, which, in a series of reports since 1995, has indicated the woeful representation of women in news genres across the world—showing up disproportionately as victims rather than as journalists or experts. An interest in globalization has also produced a focus on how representations "travel" (Machin and Thornborrow 2003) or, alternatively, how they are designed to have appeal across multiple contexts. Michelle Lazar (2006) has produced fascinating research about globalized advertising in Asia, pointing to the construction of an almost "identikit" image of desirable youthful femininity: the ideal model should look a little bit Indian, a little bit Thai, and a little bit Malaysian and is carefully designed to exemplify a "pan-Asian blend" of "consumer sisterhood." More recently, Ofra Koffman, Shani Orgad, and Rosalind Gill (2015) have examined how ideas about "girl power" materialize in different national and transnational contexts, constructing an idealized neoliberal feminine subject.

Another major development has been the "turn to production" in media studies, which for gender analysts has focused attention on persistent inequalities in the media labor force. This is horizontally segregated and vertically segregated, meaning that women are both concentrated in particular areas—for example within filmmaking they are disproportionately found in "makeup" or "wardrobe" functions—and are also concentrated lower in the hierarchy of desirable roles. Martha Lauzen's important research on Hollywood highlights the long-term lack of women in key creative roles such as cinematographer or director, with only one female Academy Award winner for best director—Kathryn Bigelow—in its history (2015).

Some research has been concerned with whether the lack of women in key creative roles impacts the kinds of media that get produced. Television seems to be doing better than film both in the diversity of its workforce and in the range of shows that get made, with *Girls*, *The Good Wife*, *Orange Is the New Black*, and *Damages*, for example, featuring "strong" women on both sides of the camera. Other research has examined the reasons for continued inequalities in media worlds that pride themselves on being "cool, creative, and egalitarian," but seem in reality to be anything but. Deborah Jones and Judith Pringle (2015) have pointed to the dominance of small-scale, project-based employment in the media and creative industries, arguing that it gives rise to "unmanageable inequalities"—through processes of finding work, hiring, and evaluation that are largely informal and lie outside legislative apparatuses designed to protect equal rights. In turn, others have called attention to the meritocratic and neoliberal dominance of media and cultural fields, which instill an idea that sexism (and racism) are "over" (Ahmed 2012) and cultivate a climate of "gender fatigue" (Kelan 2009) in which inequalities become "unspeakable" (Gill 2014)—problems that are connected to a postfeminist sensibility (see below). Feminist research on media labor has also generated new topics of interest such as aesthetic labor and affective or emotional labor—highlighting the extent to which an ever increasing range of "soft" skills and qualities are put to work in a moment of passionate capitalism (see Elias, Gill, and Scharff 2016).

Meanwhile, the boundaries of media production have been called into question by reality TV programs featuring "ordinary people" rather than professionals. New media are also said to have collapsed distinctions between producers and consumers, rendering many of us—simultaneously—as both. Early feminist research on the Internet looked at gendered practices in online sites such as chat rooms and multiuser dungeons. Approaches tended to be polarized between, on the one hand, techno-utopians who believed the World Wide Web would offer unparalleled opportunities to transcend the body and to explore futures devoid of social divisions such as gender, and, on the other, the cyber-pessimists who argued that the technology could never escape its origins in the military-industrial complex and who pointed to new forms of oppression that were practiced in online communities, for example, flaming, trolling, and cyberbullying. In the past few years, the excesses of both positions have given way to more measured and cautious research, exploring (for example) the impact of dating sites on the way in which people conduct their intimate relationships, or the emerging forms of sociality on network sites such as Facebook and Snapchat. Self-representation has become a key topic of interest (for example, selfies, sexting), as has the proliferation of different forms of surveillance—from the "top-down" surveillance of media companies such as Google and Facebook to the peer surveillance (Ringrose et al. 2013) and the "girlfriend gaze" (Winch 2014) of social media or the self-monitoring of mobile phone apps that track exercise, calorie intake, weight, and beauty regimes (Elias and Gill forthcoming).

A crucial concept in contemporary studies of gender and media is "postfeminism." The term is used to highlight the "entanglement" of feminist and antifeminist ideas, and a sense in which, as Angela McRobbie (2009) has argued, feminism is both "taken for granted" in contemporary culture yet also "repudiated," as women are offered opportunities for individual success and advancement, on condition that they disavow collective projects for social change. Postfeminism does not simply denote a complicated and contradictory relationship to feminism, but also is constituted through the pervasiveness of neoliberalism in which the enterprise form

is extended to all forms of conduct and "normatively constructs and interpellates individuals as entrepreneurial actors in every sphere of life" (Brown 2005, 42). It appears that women to a greater extent than men are constituted as active, autonomous, and self-reinventing subjects, called on to "make over" their selves again and again.

Indeed, makeover is a central theme of postfeminism—seen not just in the hostile scrutiny of women's bodies on shows such as *10 Years Younger* or *The Swan*, but more broadly regarded as a central part of a neoliberal disciplinary apparatus (Heller 2007; Ouellette and Hay 2008; Ringrose and Walkerdine 2008). It has been argued that this makeover paradigm increasingly moves beyond homes, gardens, bodies, and intimate relations, but now calls forth a transformation of subjectivity itself, a central element of what elsewhere I have called the psychic life of postfeminism. One clear example of this is in the contemporary incitements to confidence (Banet-Weiser 2015; Gill and Orgad 2015) in which women are exhorted to "lean in" and become more confident and involved at work (Sandberg 2013), to "love your body" (by brands like Dove, Gap, and Weight Watchers), and to believe that "confidence is the new sexy" (Bobbi Brown). *Elle* magazine had a Confidence Issue in 2015, and even the Girl Guiding Association now offers a badge in "body confidence"—one indication of the force and reach of this postfeminist imperative.

Postfeminism has proved a valuable and productive lens for exploring contemporary mediations of gender. The term is contested—referring to historical, epistemological, and backlash versions. One productive and much-used formulation regards it as a cultural sensibility that should be the object of critical interest—rather than a position or a perspective. Elements of this sensibility seen across media culture include the notion of gender as grounded in the body, and with an intensified focus on women's appearance; the shift from objectification to subjectification as a mode of representing women; an increased emphasis upon self-surveillance, -monitoring, and -discipline; a focus upon individualism, choice, and empowerment as the "watchwords" of postfeminism; a resurgence in ideas of natural sexual difference; and an emphasis upon consumerism and the commodification of difference (Gill 2007b). These elements coexist with and are structured by stark and continuing inequalities and exclusions that relate to "race" and ethnicity, class, age, sexuality, and disability. The contemporary foci on postfeminism, neoliberalism, and subjectivity offer challenging and exciting directions for new work on gender and media.

25

Genre
Jason Mittell

"Genre" is a keyword used broadly outside academia, a concept that seems so widespread and self-evident as to not require detailed analysis. We all know what we mean when we talk about sitcoms or musicals, Westerns or cartoons, right? But what most people probably imagine when they think about genre—the particular programs, films, books, or more generically "texts" referenced by a genre label—is not actually what makes up a genre. Instead, genres are produced by the very process of categorization itself, making the topic more interesting and sophisticated than it might seem.

What might it mean to think of genres as categories, rather than collections of texts? In the first instance, we should consider a genre as a product of cultural practices, rather than a stable, self-evident term. Genre categories do not simply emerge from the texts that they categorize, but rather are created, debated, refashioned, and dismissed in various cultural sites. While most genre criticism uses textual analysis to closely examine the formal features and interpretive meanings in any given genre's texts, another way of studying genre looks at genre categories themselves as key cultural practices (Altman 1999; Mittell 2004).

It is easiest to understand such an approach to genre categories by exploring a specific case study. Take soap operas, a well-known television genre category—thinking of the term "soap opera" probably generates some examples in your mind. Perhaps it's specific daytime dramas that ran for decades on US television, such as *General Hospital* or *The Young and the Restless*. Or maybe you think of prime-time soaps such as *Dallas* in the 1980s or *Empire* today—quite popular programs at a given moment but that rarely run beyond a decade. Or perhaps your context lies outside of the United States, with exemplary soap operas such as the long-running British drama *Coronation Street* or the Columbian telenovela *Yo Soy Betty, La Fea*. Regardless of the series, a genre typically evokes specific textual reference points as stand-ins for the category as a whole.

However, a genre is not just an empty placeholder for the texts it categorizes, as the category itself bears a cluster of assumptions and meanings impacting how we use the term and think about the programs it refers to. The term "soap opera" is quite an odd genre name, as it refers to nothing within the programs themselves—no prominent soap opera features operatic singing or is about detergents! Most genre names reference typical plots (mystery, romance), settings (Western, fantasy), or viewer reactions (horror, comedy) that their component texts presumably feature. "Soap opera" as a term originates from dismissive press coverage of 1930s daytime radio serial dramas in the United States, with male commentators coining a term juxtaposing their highly melodramatic "operatic" plots with the mundane domestic realm of female listeners and the detergent companies sponsoring the series (Allen 1985). Genre labels rarely stick when designed to dismiss and malign the texts they refer to, but "soap opera" became widespread and eventually reclaimed by fans. Thus the term itself already conveys a negative evaluative attitude toward both the programs categorized by the genre, and their presumed female listeners. All genres bear such cultural assumptions about their value, legitimacy, and their consumers' identity—for instance, calling *The Simpsons* a satirical sitcom makes it appear more culturally legitimate than labeling it a cartoon, even though the series belongs to both genres.

If the term "soap opera" doesn't point to any defining elements of its texts, what defines the genre? The (often contested) process of definition is a key factor in any genre's cultural operation. One undisputed formal element of soap operas is seriality, featuring stories that continue across episodes, but their specific serial parameters are debated—some critics claim that soap operas are open-ended by definition, referring to US daytime dramas that are designed to run forever, while others include series with definitive endings, like telenovelas and prime-time serials. The scheduling of seriality also varies, as daytime soaps broadcast new episodes each weekday without breaks, while American prime-time serials typically air weekly with seasonal breaks—thus the daytime series *Days of Our Lives* features more than 250 new episodes annually, while a prime-time series airs only 10 to 24 episodes each year, a radically different formal structure. Seriality is also not exclusive to soap operas, as many series across genres have embraced ongoing storytelling in recent decades; thus there is no consistent formal criterion for soap opera's serialized structure.

Another core element of soaps is melodrama, featuring highly emotional storytelling often marked by excesses in performance style and dramatic cues such as music or camera work. But melodrama is also a disputed term, with scholars like Linda Williams (2012) claiming that the mode need not be excessive; she labels the highly realist cop drama *The Wire* a serial melodrama, but not a soap opera. Even *Mad Men*, which is certainly both serialized and melodramatic, is not regularly called a soap opera—in fact, calling such a critically acclaimed and highbrow series "soapy" would be regarded by most as a dismissive condemnation. This defensive stance against being labeled a soap opera points to how genre categories function not by clear formal definitions, but by cultural assumptions of value, identity, and hierarchy. Tied to such assumptions are ideological meanings reaffirming dominant social values, such as the centrality of heterosexual romance within soap operas and most melodramas, making genres an important site to analyze how media reinforce power relations (Ryan and Kellner 1988).

Central to most genre categories are assumptions about audience and how they consume a genre's texts. The soap opera audience has always been presumed to be female, with a stereotype of less educated "homemakers" who can be easily manipulated both by melodramatic narratives and advertisers' commercial appeals. Throughout the genre's history, calling a program "soapy" denigrates the viewers who enjoy the series, perpetuating assumptions of a lowbrow unsophisticated female viewership. The actual demographics of daytime soap operas are much more diverse, often with one-third male viewers, and spanning class, race, education, and age categories—the audience became even more varied as video recorders grew commonplace in the 1980s, with viewers time shifting series to avoid schedule conflicts (Allen 1985). Regardless of demographics, actual soap audience behaviors and practices have always been more varied and complex than presumed passive manipulation—vibrant intergenerational viewing communities were a staple of the genre, using various communications media from printed zines to online social networks to collectively discuss, critique, and analyze storylines spanning the lifetimes of characters and viewers alike.

The industry that produces, distributes, and markets media texts actively uses genre categories. For commercial television broadcasters, genres help attract viewers and sell their attention to advertisers, using scheduling, channel branding, and cross-promotion to reinforce and reshape genre categories. For most of television history, soap operas were a highly profitable way to attract an audience that advertisers wanted to reach, so networks filled their daytime schedules to appeal primarily to women viewers—throughout the 1970s and 1980s, more than a dozen soap operas ran each afternoon. As soaps declined in popularity in the twenty-first century, the industry tried new ways to reach viewers, such as launching the cable channel Soapnet to air soap operas in time slots outside of daytime, or creating online extensions or streaming versions of soaps; however, the genre has dwindled to only four daytime soaps left on network television. Arguably, soap operas endure via the prevalence of serial melodramas in American prime-time schedules and the hugely popular global circulation of telenovelas and other international serials. However, it is debatable whether such series fit into the category of soap opera, especially given their drastically different airing patterns and broad refusal to be labeled soaps in reaction to the genre's negative connotations (Ford, De Kosnik, and Harrington 2012).

Hopefully this brief case study shows that genres are not as simple as they might appear. Every genre category gathers a cluster of assumptions and practices that connect to its presumed cultural significance, viewership, aesthetic value, and industrial strategies. Genres are fully embedded in their contexts, shifting across historical moments, national origins, and subcultural groups. The ways that a category is used are what makes it important and relevant to understanding media culture. We should continue to use genre categories even if they are not straightforward and self-evident, but be attentive to the very practices of categorization, definition, interpretation, and evaluation that make genre into such an important keyword.

26

Globalization

Aswin Punathambekar

In December 2015, one of my hometowns in south India (Chennai, formerly Madras) was experiencing one of the worst natural disasters in its modern history. Incessant rains had left the city and its suburbs flooded and the city's infrastructure wrecked. With the state government struggling to respond adequately, people across the city, the nation, and the world took charge. Even as people in Chennai threw open their homes to neighbors and virtually anyone who needed a safe and clean space, others across the country and in the diaspora began using a range of mobile and digital platforms to share ideas and resources. Using Twitter, various messaging services, Facebook pages, Google Docs, and crowdsourced maps, a tech-savvy group of people mobilized to produce an infrastructure of care that the government simply could not. It also became clear that not everyone was treated equally. A number of news reports revealed that lower-caste and Dalit neighborhoods and communities in Chennai and in towns and villages across the state of Tamilnadu were denied access to basic relief supplies, clean drinking water, and medical care.

While this crisis unfolded in south India, heads of over a hundred nations met in Paris in what was widely being described as *the* most important climate summit. Not surprisingly, India's role in shaping negotiations made front-page news with a number of activists and politicians pointing out that the disaster in Chennai was a direct consequence of global warming and climate change. #Chennairains quickly became linked to #cop21 in Paris.

These events were yet another reminder that we are connected across time and space on a daily and routine basis by global media and communication technologies and networks, and that we apprehend and make sense of the world in and through the media. Regardless of the event, perspective, or vantage point we choose to begin thinking about globalization, we can say this about life in the early twenty-first century: we are all concerned about the world, and perhaps more importantly, we are aware that our lives, social relations, and activities—however local they may seem—are shaped by forces and connections that span the globe. This profound shift in consciousness has been the consequence of over four decades of economic and cultural globalization, processes in which the media have played a central and defining role.

I am not concerned with asking here whether the globalization of media is a "good" or "bad" thing for communities and nations that lack financial resources or geopolitical clout, whether a handful of media conglomerates are in control of the production and circulation of media, or whether cultural identities are slowly but surely being transformed under the influence of English-language Western media. To be sure, we should continue asking questions about Western media dominance despite the emergence of other centers of global media production, the very real constraints on audiences and users in a predominantly capitalist world media system, and regulations and policies that shore up unequal flows of capital, talent, and content. However, I want to develop a broader perspective here to consider the impact of media globalization on three interrelated aspects of human life—*place, time,* and *imagination.* The globalization of media has transformed links between place, culture, and identity; the globalization of media has transformed our experience of daily life by reconstructing our experience of lived time; and the globalization of media has helped cultivate a global imaginary, an awareness that we live in a shareable, common world.

For well over three decades now, academics, journalists, artists, and media producers have reflected on the many interconnected economic, political, and sociocultural dimensions of globalization. While approaches and vocabulary differ, there is a general consensus that that term "globalization" is indicative of a world in which human life and activity are less constrained by geography. Increased mobility of people across regional and national borders, accompanied by new technological developments that ensure the flow of information and images across borders, has transformed social relations and challenged any easy assumptions about the relationship between culture and place. As Clifford Geertz put it, we live in a world where "difference is encountered in the adjoining neighborhood and the familiar turns up at the ends of the earth" (1988, 14). There is nothing local, in other words, about any locality in the world.

Beyond a measure of doubt, easier and cheaper access to television and a range of mobile and digital media technologies have played a central role in making us aware of distant events and happenings. Shot through with images and ideas from across the globe, not to mention online social interactions that crisscross local, regional, and national boundaries, our daily lives are global not just in the sense of knowing what's happening "out there" in public domains, but more crucially in the private spheres of our homes. It is worth noting, moreover, that media globalization is by no means solely a "Western" phenomenon. Beginning in the 1980s, the media landscape across Asia, Africa, Latin America, and the Middle East has been altered dramatically as transnational and regional television networks displaced and, in some cases, reinvigorated centralized, public, and often state-regulated media systems. This process has only intensified in recent years as digital distribution and online video networks (both legal and extralegal) have expanded their footprints, creating new circuits for the flow of media content that crisscrosses national, linguistic, and other political and cultural borders.

Furthermore, since the early 1990s, a number of cities and regional hubs across the non-Western world—Hong Kong, Chengdu, Mumbai, Bangalore, Accra, Lagos, and so on—have emerged as important nodes in a transnational network of media and ICT (information and communication technology) design, production, and circulation. In rich accounts of media industries (Curtin 2003; Govil 2015) and digital cultures (Chan 2014), scholars have shown how media and tech capitals emerge through a complex interaction of local, regional, global, as well as national forces and factors including state policy, technological advances, the built environment, talent migration, and the desires and ambitions of media moguls and venture capitalists. Far from leading to a homogenized world system in which Anglo-American media, culture, and values overwhelm local culture(s) everywhere, the globalization of media has given rise to new and highly hybrid scales and forms of cultural production and cultural identity.

To be sure, these transformations in the media sector were part of broader transitions involving the adoption of neoliberal economic policies and the deregulation and privatization of different sectors of the economy. And in many nations, the turn to market-oriented reforms and the embrace of cultural and consumerist forms of citizenship went hand in hand with new forms of religious nationalism and other reactionary movements (Abu-Lughod 2005; Fernandes 2006). But on the whole, we can see now that in remaking the link between place and culture, media globalization has led to proliferation rather than a destruction of identities (Tomlinson 1999).

Indeed, the idea that cultural identities are tied to a particular place in the world becomes even harder to sustain when we consider the issue of migration. The movement, resettlement, and rebuilding of life and identity, often under harrowing circumstances, speak to the challenges as well as possibilities of forging and sustaining social relations that link together multiple places. For migrants, media are not mere artifacts evocative of a home left behind. Films, music, television, and interactions via digital networks reconfigure memory, nostalgia, and long-distance ties in profound ways, in addition to facilitating the rebuilding of communities in new lands. Given the ability we now have to connect with people via cell phones, at an interpersonal level or with tens of thousands, it should come as no surprise that for millions of refugees making perilous journeys across land and water, access to cell phone networks and charging stations has become a matter of life and death. As one news report put it, new media technologies make up a "digital passage" that is just as vital as other infrastructures (Latonero 2015).

Of course, there is great unevenness in the way people encounter and deal with this emergent global space of media, technology, and culture. Experiences of mobility and displacement differ widely, and the resources for moving, settling, and rebuilding lives and social networks are distributed in highly unequal ways. The critical geographer Doreen Massey is right to point to a "power-geometry" of globalization in which "some people are more in charge of it than others; some initiate flows and movement, others don't; some are more on the receiving end of it than others; some are effectively imprisoned by it" (1994, 149). This spatial approach also helps us discern entrenched hierarchies in media

production and circulation despite the emergence of centers of media production and technological innovation that rival Hollywood and Silicon Valley. From visual effects labor to offshore outsourcing for software development to crowdsourced work platforms like Amazon's MTurk, media globalization rests on highly precarious forms of labor.

Taking a moment to think about work and labor alerts us to another aspect of human life that has been transformed by globalization—*time*, how we experience it, and how it structures our lives. There is a tendency to think about globalization as having radically disrupted the pace of life and to discuss this in terms of speed, immediacy, and instantaneity. To be sure, 24/7 television and the relentless stream of emails, messages, tweets, and Facebook updates leave many of us feeling that our experience of time has accelerated. But such a view ignores not only the complexity of lived time but also the fact that different media technologies, platforms, and genres have very particular modes of structuring and communicating time.

For instance, Paddy Scannell's (1996) account of broadcasting in England reveals that "dailiness" was the organizing principle at work, particularly as listeners oriented the rhythms of daily life—school and office routines, teatime, dinner and bedtime habits, and so on—to radio program schedules. Scannell's take on the temporality of broadcasting applies well beyond the British context. In India, for example, the launch of national broadcast television services during the early 1980s had the effect of synchronizing the time of everyday life to the time of television. Across urban India, the beginning of daily television services at four in the afternoon, a popular sitcom at eight thirty on Friday evenings, the broadcast of a Hindi-language film on Saturday evenings, and, famously, the Sunday morning broadcast of Hindu mythologicals all became crucial temporal markers for organizing daily and routine activities.

We also have to take into account what Emily Keightley calls "textual time," the ways in which "time is organized, represented, and communicated in media content" (2012, 4). The real-time claims of 24/7 television news, the planetary time of natural history documentaries, the fear of missing out on the latest that lures us to digital platforms, and so on are all reminders of the diverse and entangled "media times" that make up our personal and social lives.

Furthermore, the question of how different media construct our experience of lived time depends very much on who we are, where in the world we are, and what kinds of media we have access to. Even within a single space—a software company in a global IT city like Bangalore, for instance—time operates differently for the software engineers than for other laborers (janitors, canteen cooks, shuttle drivers, etc.) who have less freedom to calibrate their own time. When lived time is differentiated in such a manner, media access and use also vary widely. The idea that the globalization of media has accelerated life everywhere makes little sense; it is far more interesting and important to attend to the interplay of media with different temporal frameworks that shape human life and activity—waiting, traveling, talking, remembering, expecting, and so on—in varied social contexts.

Finally, as the media become ever more vital resources for us, shaping our personal and social lives, we have to ask what kind of world(s) we are able to imagine. As Silverstone puts it, the world we live in is "shareable but not necessarily shared" (2007, 27). The stories we hear and tell, the representations of people and communities we encounter and make sense of, and the incidents and events we pay attention to all depend on a rich, yet deeply flawed global media environment.

Consider again the account of #chennairains that I began with. What became evident during the #chennairains event was not just that deeply held caste and class prejudices determined rescue and relief operations. To be sure, news reports that shed light on such moments of exclusion are important and valuable. But millions of Indians only ever read or listen to a story or two about the lives of lower caste and Dalit communities in relation to natural disasters, moments of political violence, or protest movements. It is, as Chimamanda Ngozi Adichie (2009) would put it, a "single story." Accustomed to largely negative stories in mainstream media, the vast majority of Indian citizens are simply unable to imagine and recognize other dimensions of lower-caste life and experience. And of course, substituting "race" for "caste" in the American context or exploring "race" and "migration" in Western Europe will reveal a similar lack of imagination and profound misunderstandings. Alternative media and digital activism (#Dalitlivesmatter, #Blacklivesmatter, etc.) are vital counterbalances to mainstream media narratives, but they are not enough.

If we agree that we share a responsibility to understand each other and our place in the world—at times across vast distances and at times in our most immediate surroundings—then we have to imagine and work toward a more open and hospitable media environment.

27

Hegemony
Justin Lewis

Hegemony is a way to describe people or ideas that become—and seek to remain—dominant in society. The development of the term "hegemony" in media studies follows the work of Antonio Gramsci (1971) and Stuart Hall (1973/1980, 1982, 1996), and generally refers to "soft" rather than "hard" power. Gramsci and Hall were concerned with the way in which certain groups and ideologies maintain their power in democratic societies. They were interested in dominance achieved by consent rather than by force, maintained by ideology rather than repression. In this context, hegemony's tools are words, images, rituals, and practices rather than weapons, courts, and prisons. Indeed, Hall's interest in the media stems from his view that, in modern democracies, media and cultural forms are central to the maintenance—or disruption—of hegemony.

Hegemony is not merely a description but a process, one that makes the dominance of certain groups or ideas in society seem normal, natural, or inexorable—even to those in subordinate positions. Hegemony often involves masking or solidifying various forms of inequality so that they seem part of everyday life, making customs and contrivances that favor some people over others *appear to be* common sense. Indeed, hegemony is often at its most effective when it is least visible, when ideological work goes on without our noticing it.

We see this in many forms of media representation. Take, for example, a fairly routine advertisement. An attractive women in her late thirties—perhaps she has a stressful job—is worrying about finding the time to prepare a meal for her family. Salvation comes in the form of a highly processed ready meal, which, in the rapid denouement of the thirty-second TV commercial, we see served to an appreciative husband and children in a contented domestic setting.

There is nothing especially remarkable or unusual about this story. Most people would watch it without dwelling upon the assumptions it promotes. Change the script slightly and it could be for an appliance or a cleaning product. But imagine, for a moment, that we change the gender of the central character: we see, instead, a man worrying about what to cook his family for dinner. There is nothing strange or unnatural about a father cooking for his wife and children, and yet in the highly gendered world of TV commercials it looks odd. We might expect to see a comic reference to the man's ineptitude in the kitchen, or some other acknowledgment that gender stereotypes have been upset. But to simply replay the script portraying male rather than female domesticity disrupts our expectations. This reveals hegemony in action: advertising tends to reinforce expectations that domestic duties are performed by women rather than men.

In much the same way, we may accept most TV drama or factual programming, in which a majority of those on-screen are male, as "normal" representations of the world. So while we may know that there are roughly equal proportions of men and women in society, we do not necessarily notice it when men dominate time on screen (which, surveys show, they do across most genres). If programs occasionally reverse the gender bias we are more likely to notice the gender imbalance. The overrepresentation of men on television thereby reinforces assumptions that male dominance is the norm.

These assumptions are enshrined within a set of patriarchal attitudes that tend to favor men. The fact that gender bias in media portrayals may wash over us almost without our noticing is, in part, because of a long history of gender stereotyping. The processed dinner advertisement attaches itself to this history, thereby reinforcing an ideological notion that favors one group over another.

Like most forms of hegemony, the assumptions behind these stereotypes have long been contested. Feminists have, for some time, campaigned for media representations that present equal choices for men and women. And yet the persistence of gender stereotypes in advertising (and in many other media domains) represents a victory for patriarchy over a counterhegemonic, feminist critique of gender inequality.

If we look a little closer, we can see that the advertisement also takes a hegemonic position in relation to the politics of food. It reflects—and normalizes—the dominance of a particular system of food production and consumption. This system tends to favor the manufacture of processed food, which has more potential for "adding value" to cheap ingredients and is often more profitable than, say, selling fruit or vegetables. It may be healthier to avoid eating too many processed ready meals, but in the world of advertising we are far more likely to see a pitch for precooked lasagne than for lettuce, leeks, or lentils. With no sense of irony, advertising has thereby naturalized the buying and selling of processed, less natural food.

This form of hegemony is more difficult to identify, because it favors a system rather than a particular class, race, or gender. It favors profits over palates and fast-food outlets over healthier alternatives. The "slow food" movement, which developed in response to the increasing dominance of processed food chains, is in this sense counterhegemonic. An advertisement for slow food—showing us someone buying a set of ingredients and cooking them—is unlikely to appear unless it involves shopping at a supermarket chain large enough to fund a TV ad campaign.

In a more general sense, the advertisement is also part of the hegemony of consumer culture (Lewis 2013). It is part of an ad world where good things—whether happiness, respect, popularity, friendship, love, security, or fulfillment—always come with a price tag. In advertisements, a scene of family harmony is always linked to a specific product. Hence, in our ad, the consumption of a brand of processed food is linked to happy family life. The fact that this link could be (and is) made to market almost *any* product—from a car to a breakfast cereal—tells us that these associations are fairly arbitrary. Indeed, the way in which advertisers can link their products with positive social values (connecting, for example, Coca-Cola with happiness) without it seeming bizarre or preposterous is part of a hegemonic process in which we accept such connections as routine.

Ads will never propose the more plausible idea that happy family life comes from a set of social relationships (rather than which car you drive or what kind of prepared food you eat). Consumerism thereby presents a narrow view of the world, one that always connects the good things in life to the purchase of goods. This idea is hegemonic is most capitalist societies. It sustains a whole set of economic and cultural priorities, where governments focus on trying to deliver more consumer choice through economic growth rather than organizing societies in ways that more directly create human fulfillment and well-being.

The advertisement—like most commercials—is also hegemonic in focusing not only on the pleasure of consumption but on the *moment* of consumption. Production is usually invisible—on the few occasions when we do see working conditions, they are invariably romanticized. This is, in part, because many of the things we buy may be made in ways that involve poorly paid groups of workers, or manufactured using an array of toxic chemicals and greenhouse gases. And, in the case of our processed dinner, a set of unwholesome ingredients and industrial processes. The fact that the low cost of consumer goods often depends upon forms of inequality and exploitation (only a tiny percentage of purchases are certified as fair trade) is hidden in the world of advertising, something to be skipped over or ignored as we carry on consuming.

The mountains of waste produced by all this consumption are also invisible. There will be no camera shots lingering over the discarded fast-food or soft-drink containers that pollute our urban and rural environments, or pictures of people in the third world rifling through exported toxic piles of waste, or any inkling of the increasing *public* cost of waste disposal. Waste, in the ad world, is somebody else's problem, something that is generally *not* built in to the cost of the product, leaving the taxpayer to pick up the tab. This is another aspect of the hegemony of consumerism, in which environmental problems are seen as subordinate while the needs of a consumer culture are dominant.

In all these cases, the processed dinner advertisement is typical of the way in which hegemony works in media representations. It forms part of a system that repeats certain kinds of images, roles, and ideas while neglecting others. And, in so doing, it makes certain dominant views of the world seem natural or simply part of ordinary life.

28

Hybridity
Marwan M. Kraidy

A notion that emerged in biology, thrived in postcolonial theory, then entered media studies as it metastasized throughout the humanities and social sciences, hybridity is emblematic of our era. Used to describe mixtures of cultures, races, languages, systems, even paradigms, hybridity emerged in the 1990s as a master trope, a necessary heuristic device to understand a world in flux. As of this writing, the heyday of hybridity—when it animated entire subfields and spawned heated arguments between celebrants and critics—is behind us. Now largely absent from book titles, conference themes, and intellectual polemics, hybridity has taken residence in interdisciplinary venues like media studies, as a once-dominant concept now content with latent taken-for-granted-ness and banal usage. We now assume, rather than argue over, hybridity.

The notion of hybridity developed in the study of genetic variability. The word entered the English language in the late 1830s, and half a century later it had made the leap from biology to culture, when the *Oxford English Dictionary* in 1890 used hybridity to compare linguistic to racial mixture. Synonyms of hybridity were in circulation much earlier. Both *métissage* (French) and *mestizaje* (Spanish) harken back to the Latin *miscere*, "to mix." In the twelfth century, Old Provençal included the word *mestif*, and in 1615 the feminine *métice* was in use. The Spanish term *mestizo* appeared in 1600, and the French *métis* in 1690. *Mestizaje* emerged as the official ideology of newly independent Latin American nations, as a discourse integrating local identities and cultures in a politico-economic system dominated by the creole elite, born in the colonies from Spanish parentage. Various historical contexts have spawned assorted notions: *mestizaje*, *métissage*, transculturation, creolization, syncretism (see Kraidy 2005).

A heated, wide-ranging debate has revolved around hybridity and power. Notions of fusion lend themselves to rival interpretations, one focused on celebrating hybridity's progressive potential, one emphasizing that hybridity reflects relations of dominance, since it is often colonized, occupied, and subordinate cultures that get hybridized, on the terms of the dominant party. Overlapping with ancient scuffles and contemporary skirmishes about culture and influence, the question of power has remained important to uses of hybridity in media studies. This is manifest in global media studies and in research on migrant and diasporic media.

Hybridity arose in global media studies after decades during which dependency theory and media imperialism enjoyed primacy, and elicited concerns that scholars were jettisoning the study of inequality and power in global communication favored by those approaches in favor of glib celebrations of cultural mixture (Boyd-Barrett 1998; Mattelart 1994). Indeed, some studies of media texts through the prism of hybridity tended not to focus on issues of power (Lee 1991; Olson 1999), but critics of hybridity often elevated caricatures of hybridity theorists before savaging them (for example, Ahmad's attack on Bhabha, in Ahmad 1995). Nonetheless, the impassioned debate made the vexed relation between hybridity and power salient. In critically minded global media studies, this concern translated into efforts to understand hybridity as the very condition of culture, and to comprehend how constantly shifting material and discursive structures shaped various manifestations of hybridity (Kraidy 2005).

Hybridities, then, are better understood in the plural, and by being particularly attuned to this, Latin American scholars decisively influenced the deployment of hybridity in media studies. This is shaped by the peculiar history of Latin America, the ways global movements of people and resources under violent imperial dominion have shaped nations characterized by cultural and racial mixture. Ever since the Cuban writer Fernando Ortiz (1940/1983, 1995) conceived of the vibrant mixtures characteristic of Cuban culture through the notion of transculturation, hybridity has been pervasive in Latin American cultural theory. But most influential in media studies during the past quarter century have been contemporary scholars like the Spanish-Columbian Jesús Martín-Barbero and the Argentinean-Mexican Néstor García-Canclini (for a survey of Latin American cultural and media theory, see Rodriguez and Murphy 1997).

A key contribution of the rise of hybridity has been to expose media centrism and promote alternative conceptions of the role of media in culture. Martín-Barbero's seminal work (1987, 1993) made the ostensibly basic but actually momentous argument that focusing research directly and solely on the media was insufficient, even misleading, in the quest to understand how communication operates in cultural terrains. Central to his intervention was the notion of *mestizaje*, which to Martín-Barbero captures not only cultural fusion, but also continuities and ruptures between social, economic, and cultural dynamics. These processes, defined as mediations, underscore a vision of hybridity that is historically deep and geographically wide, and one that articulates communication to culture and politics. The contemporary *telenovela* (serialized television drama) connects to older folk/popular cultural forms like Mexican *corridos* and Colombian *vallenatos*, while containing traces of Latin American magical realism. Hybridity is at once the process by which cultural hegemony is achieved and its outcome. It is permeated by power and inequality, and to understand it we must develop complex approaches that jettison dualistic perspectives—modernity versus tradition, rural against urban, local contra global—on media and culture (Martín-Barbero 1987). Hybridity augurs an exit from cultural dualism and binary analysis in media studies.

Another key contribution of scholarship on hybridity has been the reintroduction of a cosmopolitan aesthetic sensibility to media studies, one nonetheless grounded in politics. Rejecting magical realism and dependency theory, two dominant conceptual apparatuses for understanding Latin America, García-Canclini (1989, 1995) instead proposed hybridity as a tool capable of grasping the complexities of the "multitemporal heterogeneity" and mixed political systems of Latin America. Seeing in hybridity a map of the fraught and multiple interrelations between traditional culture and modern forces, García-Canclini coined the notion of "impure genres." The hybrid aesthetics of genres like graffiti and comics illustrate contradictions between various political, economic, technological, and social forces shaping contemporary culture, but also enable an understanding of the complex interplay between these forces. This notion of hybridity is political because it accounts for strategic practices of inclusion and exclusion with which modern societies filter traditional culture. Hybridity for García-Canclini is a theory of "oblique power," focusing on the interweaving of power and culture between and within social classes, ethnic groups, and national communities.

Grounded in hybridity and in assorted notions (creolization, transculturation, etc.) that demonstrate the bankruptcy of narratives of cultural purity and national distinctiveness, the imperative to eschew dualistic approaches and to consider power as indirect, ambivalent, and diffuse affected studies of media and culture in different parts of the world—popular culture in Hong Kong

(Lee 1991), globalization and nationalism in Indian television (Kumar 2006), citizenship and Latino identity in the United States (Amaya 2013), global blockbuster movies (Wang and Yeh 2005), Japanese popular culture in Asia (Iwabuchi 2002), the complex tripartite hybridity of French, Japanese, and US cultural production (Darling-Wolf 2015), and the Arab culture wars triggered by reality television (Kraidy 2010). The imprint of hybridity theory was more or less direct, but always manifest, in these and other studies.

By offering a compelling alternative to media centrism, grounding cultural fusion in political power, exposing the tenuousness of discourses of purity and homogeneity, and emphasizing the importance of aesthetics, the rise of hybridity compelled work that tackled at once the three traditional realms of media studies—production, text, and reception—helping usher a field more attuned to cultural complexity, less provincially Anglo-American, and more at ease with the nested ambivalences of cultural forms.

This could already be seen in diasporic and migrant media studies that emerged in the 1990s. Immigrants like Punjabis in the United Kingdom, it turned out, watch television in ways that subvert the culture of the host country (Gillespie 1995). But more importantly, these studies documented practices of cultural production for migrant communities that create hybrid texts that at once attract people with hybrid identities and foster further cultural hybridization. The Iranian community in Los Angeles, for example, had an intricate network of production and broadcasting facilities and resources. The community used these to enact hybridity through practices of mimicry, consisting of pictorial superimposition, ambivalent characters, and incoherent plots and narratives on Iranian television in Los Angeles (Naficy 1993). But with the increased affordability and availability of media production equipment, immigrants, like Croatians in Australia, started producing videotapes about their lives and sending them to their home country (Kolar-Panov 1997). Thus migrant media studies underscored that communities with mixed cultural identities produce hybrid media texts, in a transnational circuit in which production occurs in the host country while the home country provides creative energy.

This foreshadowed the rise of do-it-yourself (DIY) digital culture, which can be understood as one end of a spectrum that articulates hybridity with human agency and intentionality. On one end, we have media audiences attracted to hybrid texts (created mostly by professional media workers) that resonate with the hybrid identities of viewers. This is, to a large extent, a reactive hybridity. On the other end, we have producers of digital culture, often amateur, actively creating intentionally hybrid texts meant for wider circulation. The Russian formalist critic Mikhail Bakhtin distinguished between intentional and organic hybridity, the former spawned by auteur-agents mixing cultural genres, the second emerging from long-term patterns of cultural fusion (Bakhtin 1981). The advent of digital culture, with its formal simplicity and DIY aesthetic (Goriunova 2013), has accelerated and amplified intentional hybridities.

In an age of attention scarcity, aesthetic hybridity is increasingly important in mobilizing publics, and in so doing it becomes an important component of political power and resistance. Forms of artful dissidence that emerged in the Arab uprisings since 2010 are quintessential cases of intentionally hybrid texts strategically designed for maximum impact on the largest possible audience. Consider *Top Goon: Diary of a Little Dictator*, a Syrian finger puppetry show that skewered Bashar al-Assad and went viral in 2011. It is hybrid in multiple ways. It blends the age-old art of finger puppetry with the genre of video and with the digital circulation afforded by the Internet. It summons familiar global tropes (the Tom Cruise blockbuster *Top Gun*) and the global reality television hit *Who Wants to Be a Millionaire?* and uses these as a platform on which it grafts local political struggles. As a result, it displays the cultural equivalent of what geneticists call "hybrid vigor"—it is vibrant, funny, punchy—which enabled it to cut through the deafening chatter of thousands of revolutionary videos coming out of Syria and achieve global, mainstream, visibility. By combining the global and the local, the old and the new, the miniature and the monumental, *Top Goon* is an exemplary case of "creative insurgency" (Kraidy 2016).

Hybridity no longer being an ostensible and provocative theoretical standard-bearer does not signal the conceptual demise of hybridity. Rather, it underlines the success of the concept in becoming a latent instrument in media studies' analytical toolkit. The turbulent world we live in, for better or worse, militates for the enduring necessity of hybridity, the analytical vocabulary in anchors, and the types of analysis it enables. A perfect storm of global developments—the contentious decade that has seen the Arab uprisings, the Occupy movement in the United States, *Podemos* in Spain and a motley crew of social movements, the rise of xenophobic, anti-immigrant, anti-minority rhetoric in the European Union and the United States, and the exploding movement of people fleeing war, hunger, and misery, particularly but not exclusively via the Mediterranean, not to mention the ongoing globalization of media industries—underscores the salience of hybridity as theory and method, not to mention its necessity as a moral discourse opposed to the specter of racial purity and political exclusion. Hybridity, in whatever guise it is invoked, remains a necessary antidote to stereotypes of identity and fantasies of homogeneity. As such, it is more salient than ever to media studies.

29

Identity

Myria Georgiou

Identity is an intriguing concept with a plurality of applications and meanings that make it attractive but also contested. Associated with questions such as "Who am I?" all the way to "Would I sacrifice for my community?" identity reflects multiple associations and dissociations, including, while not limited to, ethnicity, nationality, social class, gender, sexuality, and religion. One of the most influential concepts across social sciences and the humanities, identity has particular resonance to media and communications, especially as it raises important questions about media power: Is identity reflected or shaped in the media? What are the implications of media representations for different groups and their identities? Do media enhance understanding or hatred toward others? These questions have enduring relevance, but answering them has become increasingly complex, especially as media diversify, exposure to proximate and distant others expands, and digital connections—asymmetrically but effectively—manage spaces of belonging within and across physical boundaries.

A concept that is malleable, identity is used in academia, as much as it is used in everyday and political contexts. In everyday life, it primarily relates to the presentation of the self to others: identity is no less than an ordinary performance, Erving Goffman argues (1969). The ways people dress in public or present themselves in social media are about performing identity and finding ways to locate the self(-identity) in the world (social identity) through acts that are socially recognized as carrying certain meanings. Thus identity is as much about self-making as it about the position individuals take in social systems. As Paul Gilroy puts it, there is a constant "interplay between our subjective experience of the world and the cultural and historical settings in which that fragile subjectivity is formed" (1997, 301). This dialectic becomes most evident when identity is mobilized to support political claims, or even to justify violence. Propaganda radio broadcasts in Nazi Germany and during the Rwandan genocide projected the "purity" of German and Hutu identities respectively against "impure" and "inferior" identities of the Other (Appadurai 2006). Either in responding to or in shaping powerful narratives of identity, propaganda radio did in the twentieth century what extremist websites do at present: symbolically mark identity and difference through powerful mediated discourses and imagery.

As these examples reveal, the relationship between identity construction and media and communications is long-standing and prominent. Many argue that this relationship's significance has grown in time, not least as opportunities for identification with communities (e.g., fans), places (e.g., cities), and cultures (e.g., celebrities) have multiplied due to the digital expansion of media technological affordances and representations. This claim gains more validity especially if we examine it in relation to three key macro-processes associated with the organization of contemporary social and cultural life: globalization, migration, and mediation. Each of these macro-processes has implications for identity, some of which are captured by three concepts that have gained eminence in analyses of identity and in relation to these macro-processes: reflexivity, hybridity, and performativity. Not unlike the concept of identity itself, these concepts—which can also be considered as conditions of identity formation—have wider and global relevance, though their particular meanings are always contextual and particular. As Stuart Hall puts it, identities "are subject to the continuous 'play' of history, culture and power" (1990, 223). Thus, questions of identity are best understood at the juncture of macro-processes that make history and society and the distinct and particular micro-processes of everyday life—what in social sciences is vividly captured through the debate of structure (given norms and limits) versus agency (individual capacity to make choices).

Debates on the relation between structure and agency raise critical questions: How much control do individuals have over their own identities? How reflexive and aware are they of their choices? Anthony Giddens (1991) responds to the binary opposition of "structure versus agency" by proposing their dialectic interdependence. Identity matters and involves a process of *reflexivity*: individuals make decisions based on their awareness of norms and boundaries and while mobilizing their capacity to negotiate and even resist such structural boundaries and norms (Giddens 1991). Audience research has supported such arguments. David Morley's now classic study of *The Nationwide Audience* (1980) demonstrates that class identities were central to interpretation of television programming, while more recent research emphasizes the role of gender, ethnic, and national identities in negotiating media norms and values (Georgiou 2006; Nightingale 2014). These discussions also recognize that individuals' and groups' reflexive engagement with the media has grown in complexity at global times.

Globalization has challenged traditional societies, not least through the faster and wider circulation of information on different cultures, subcultures, and value systems. The more information becomes available to people about the particularity of their own identity vis-à-vis the range of other identities and experiences in the world, the more identity turns into a reflexive but also fragile project. Media constantly show their users that very little can be taken for granted as universal truths or as globally accepted norms—family life, work cultures, and lifestyles vary, and all this diversity is regularly visible to them. Identity of one's own and of others is constantly under scrutiny, even under threat, especially as media remind their audiences of risks, such as terrorism, close by and at a distance, and of others' constant presence on screens (Silverstone 2007) and on the street, especially as a result of migration.

Yet, access to information and communication remains uneven—not everyone sees themselves and others in the media to the same extent. Unequal access to media and communications and uneven representations of different groups, especially on the basis of race, gender, sexuality, class, and location, can privilege certain groups against others. Returning to the questions of whether individuals have control over their own identities and if identities represent a global reflexive project, one might need to consider whether media power and control are directly involved in producing identity hierarchies. This question becomes even more important if we approach identities as symbolically constructed. Mead (1934) argued that different symbols allow individuals to imagine how others see them and act self-consciously in response to that. Such symbols can be a passport or a language that represent nationality, but they can expand across a range of identifiable or subtle representations, such as media representations. Does it matter that ethnic minorities are underrepresented on national television in most countries of the Global North? Does it matter that stereotypical images of femininity are reproduced across different media? And does it matter that Internet access between continents varies enormously with both technological and content control overconcentrated in the Global North? Feminist and postcolonial scholars (see Gill 2007a; Hegde 2016) have emphasized the role of the media in constructing, not just representing, identities; Teresa de Lauretis (1989) powerfully argued that cinema is a technology of gender, that media representations *are* the constructions of gender, class, race, not just their reflection. While media and communication scholars widely recognize these challenges, their responses vary. Some emphasize the significance of fairer and regulated representations of diversity in mainstream media as a necessity for different groups gaining recognition and respect for their cultural identities and difference (Downing and Husband 2005). Others argue that digital media have changed the game altogether by diversifying identity representations; increasingly media users become producers of their own desired representations of the self and of their communities (Bruns 2007).

Discussions on participatory and reflexive engagement with the media have gone hand in hand with debates on the fragmentation, multiplicity, and *hybridity* of identities. Digital technologies have boosted mediated mobility between spaces, but migration has enhanced physical mobility and identification with a range of collectivities and communities for much longer. A core element of global change, intensified and diversified migration has presented a range of challenges to the concept of identity, not least as this has historically been associated with the nation and bounded communities. Influentially, Benedict Anderson's (1991) theorization of imagined communities established the close relation between the nation and the media throughout modernity. Sharing the same news and the same media within the boundaries of the nation has reproduced shared imagination of collective identities among people willing to commit and even die for the nation, he argues. Currently one in thirty-three people is an international migrant (United Nations Population Fund 2015), while more than half of the world's population lives in cities, largely as a result of mass migration. Do national media still have the power to widely and effectively circulate symbols of a community? Or do current formulations of media and culture destabilize identities that used to be dominant, like national identities, but even social class, gender, and religion?

A range of approaches respond critically to these questions, especially by problematizing the limits, relevance, and biases of the concept of identity. Kevin Robins (2001) talks against identity altogether, arguing that as a concept it has become irrelevant to the experience and imagination of people who live between different physical and mediated environments. Ien Ang (2003) recognizes the value of identity, especially in recognition of its mobilization for political projects of emancipation, as seen in the case of indigenous and ethnic minority movements. At the same time, she highlights the dangerous territory of identity, as it is sometimes mobilized within national and transnational communities to promote hostility to difference and to diversity. In response, she turns to hybridity as a concept helpful to understanding "a world where we no longer have the secure capacity to draw a line between us and them, the different and the same, here and there, and indeed between 'Asian' and 'Western'" (2003, 141). Hybridity has become an attractive concept, especially in critical approaches to identity, as it opens up a space for understanding and promoting togetherness-in-difference rather than being preoccupied with identity's separateness (Ang 2003). Is the binary of togetherness/separation the inevitable result of a politics of identity, or is there space for a politics that recognizes both difference and commonality? W. E. B. Du Bois's concept of "double consciousness" speaks of a "two-ness," of feeling "an American, a Negro" (1903/1986, 364), a line of thought followed by Gilroy's (1997) conceptualization of the "changing same" in regard to diasporic identities' multiplicity and ambivalent perspectives. Continuity comes with change and identifications with new places and people. Urban music often reflects such hybrid, complex, and ambivalent systems of identification (Georgiou 2013): R&B and hip-hop lyrics and musical themes sometimes capture experiences and histories of migration and diaspora, while at the same time identifying struggles firmly grounded in urban, marginalized locales.

Music, graffiti, advertising, as well as social media currently constitute elements of mediated communication, as much as the press, television, and radio. Thus, information and symbols of identity—from world news to "likes"—are circulated widely through a range of networks including those controlled by media conglomerates, but also by communities, such as music fans, diasporas, and extremist groups. As a result and inevitably, debates on the inclusion and exclusion of different groups from media production and representation have now expanded far beyond mass media. Who speaks and on behalf of whom and with what consequences for identity is a question requiring more complex responses than in the past. Arguably, media power has grown, not least as all different elements of communication—interpersonal, community, professional, local, and transnational—are increasingly mediated. Roger Silverstone (2007) argues that mediation comes with significant changes in social and cultural environments and regulates relations between individuals, groups, and institutions. The diversification but also the ever presence of media in everyday life open up prospects for more democratic and diverse recognition of identities and difference, argue some; yet others emphasize the danger for further regulation and containment of identity—theories of *performativity* have been influential to both claims.

For Judith Butler (1990), identity is more about what you *do* rather than about what you *are*. Identity is a regulatory fiction, she argues, reinforcing limits and control upon individuals. Following Michel Foucault, Butler argues that gender, like all identities, is the result of repeated performances "that congeal over time to produce the appearance of substance, of a natural sort of being" (1990, 33). Inscriptions of identity are reproduced through the repetition of certain symbols, not least through media representations. If media's influence in culture and society is growing, as mediation scholars claim, then important questions are raised in regard to the mediated reproduction of identity hierarchies—such as heterosexuality versus homosexuality, whiteness versus blackness, West versus East. Scholars who criticize the growing commercialization of the Internet (Mejias 2013) express concerns about digital media reinforcing the status quo and current political and cultural hierarchies. Yet, others turn to performativity to emphasize the possibility for resistance to such hierarchies in digital media (Cammaerts 2012). If identity is not natural, as claimed by Butler but also by most contemporary identity theorists, there is always a possibility for resistance to its inscribed substance—this is for example seen in the case of transgender identities that destabilize the binary man/woman and reveal that all identities are performed. When it comes to the media in particular, performative complexity becomes most visible in social media: for example, in cross-gender screen identities or, more importantly, in digital projects of self-making that challenge limits of identity. Onscreen performances and confessional narratives that appear on YouTube and blogs are powerful reflections of experimental articulations of the self and provide evidence of the continuous appeal of communities, though and importantly, not only of communities of origin but also of choice. Digital environments can be seen as providing the evidence of shifting spaces of identity. Yet they can be more than that: they can both reflect and construct identity in its performative and imagined dimensions. Most importantly, digital media, like all media, reveal the relevance of identity as a concept used to understand but also to express claims to recognition, as a category of emotional but also political significance that captures and reveals the always incomplete struggles of individuals and groups for a place in the world.

30
Ideology
Jo Littler

Today, "ideology" is usually taken to mean a system of beliefs or a set of ideas that both constitute a general worldview and uphold particular power dynamics. Media are particularly significant in this context, as the stories they tell and the belief systems they promote can be powerful amplifiers of particular ideologies. For instance, magazine articles that repeatedly address or call to and "interpellate" us first and foremost as consumers—as buying subjects—are on some level promoting an ideology of *consumerism*. The promotion of such an ideology might be understood as variously helping to marginalize those who cannot afford to buy; to shape the subjectivities of those who can, by encouraging them to desire more and more consumer goods; to prioritize our identities as individual consumers above and beyond that of producers or citizens (by, for example, encouraging us to monitor our health via vitamin intake but not to campaign together for reduced working hours or against the wider problems of privatized healthcare provision); and, on a broader level, to contribute toward the atomization and "individualization" of our social relations and our ways of being in the world.

The disagreements over the extent to which ideology is a useful term and the different meanings ascribed to it can in part be understood as a product of its contorted history, in which it vacillates between a tool that can be applied to any position and a term of slander for those holding worldviews considered fanatical or erroneous.

Ideology was first used in English in 1796, translated from a French word, *idéologie*, used by Desutt de Tracey to distinguish "the science of ideas" from ancient metaphysics (Williams 1983, 153–54). Here we can see the early outlines of its use as an analytical tool for social science. Later, ideology was used and popularized by Napoleon Bonaparte as a term of abuse for what he thought was happening in the French Revolution, which for him involved the self-conscious "doctrine of the ideologues" warping the "rightful" (i.e., conservative) laws of nature (Althusser 2014, 171; Williams 1983, 154). This pejorative use of ideology was adopted and adapted by Marx and Engels, who similarly used it as a critical term, only from the opposite end of the political spectrum: in order to identify how social relationships under capitalism spawned ideas which in turn worked to legitimate capitalism. The inability to recognize how such ideas actually connected to relationships of production and exploitation within capitalism was understood by Marx and Engels as a system of "false consciousness" which offered an upside-down version of reality (Marx and Engels 1987, 47). While ideology as illusory false consciousness is uppermost in Marx and Engels's writing, in various parts of Marx's work it has a more capacious, less pejorative meaning: where ideology is still an expression of economic interests, but is not "mere illusion"; rather ideology involves terms and values that people can be conscious of, and fight over (Williams 1983, 156).

It was this strand of meaning that was to be foregrounded by the writings of Italian communist Antonio Gramsci, for whom struggles over ideology were part of an active struggle for power and hegemony. Gramsci's more capacious understanding of ideology was to become influential in media and cultural studies when his work was translated into English in the 1970s and became used by practitioners in this new field, notably the Centre for Contemporary Cultural Studies (CCCS) at Birmingham in the United Kingdom (Gramsci 1971; Hall 1996; Larrain 1996). During this decade the French Marxist Louis Althusser also published his work on ideological state apparatuses (ISAs), which drew on Gramscian theory alongside psychoanalysis to propose an understanding of how social formations and relations are reproduced, normalized, and internalized via state-sanctioned institutions such as schools, churches, and media (Althusser 2014). ISAs are relatively diverse and plural yet function to reproduce the ruling or dominant class through the ideology they project and the rituals they involve. For example, newspapers are varied in the United Kingdom and United States, yet coverage does not reflect anywhere near the extent of left-wing thought in the population at large, focusing, for example, on consumer "inconvenience" during strikes, or ignoring them, rather than extensively covering the reasons why workers feel forced into that position. A reading drawing on theories of ISAs would consider that this is because they are beholden to reproducing the vested interests of the dominant capitalist class through, for example, their structural dependence on advertising revenue and the vested corporate and establishment interests of their owners. Similarly journalists are participating in what Althusser outlined as the *ritual and material* function of ideology when they feel unable to cover strikes because such coverage doesn't fit with accepted institutional "news values."

Critical media and cultural studies from the 1970s onward enthusiastically embraced ideological analysis, drawing on Althusser and Gramsci alongside a wider range of analytical tools and techniques. For instance, in her 1978 CCCS stenciled paper "Jackie: An Ideology of Adolescent Femininity," British cultural studies scholar Angela McRobbie considered how the values presented by this girls' magazine offered a map through which "teenage girls are subjected to an explicit attempt to win consent to the dominant order—in terms of femininity, leisure and consumption" (1978, 35). In this reading, ideology is therefore understood as the expression of "a set of particular values" that promote a particular understanding of what it means to be a teenager. Here, ideological values relate to both the material interests of the company (the union-busting DC Thomson) and wider and interrelated cultural norms of gender and consumption. McRobbie, for instance, notes the magazine positions work as "a necessary evil," feting consumption as part of the "freedom" of leisure time, through "a lightness of tone, fun and romance"; and that its "focus on the *individual* girl and *her own* problems comes to signify the narrowness of the woman's role in general and to prefigure her own later isolation in the home" (1978, 35). This reading of *Jackie*'s "immensely powerful" "ideological discourse" (1978, 50) was therefore considering how dominant material relations extend beyond the immediacy of waged labor and through to the wider context of social reproduction, in which particular roles for working-class men and women (breadwinner, housewife) were still very much in evidence.

It is notable that "Jackie: An Ideology of Adolescent Femininity" used the phrase "ideological discourse," and this is because the wider cultural implications of ideology as part of conceptualizing the struggle for hegemony were at this moment being purposefully explored. The use of the term "discourse," in the cultural rather than the purely linguistic sense, was to expand in the 1980s in critical media and cultural studies, either in conjunction with or as a preferable term to "ideology," a trend fermenting under the influence of French philosopher Michel Foucault (1979, 1981). For Foucault, "discourse" was a far more capacious and politically neutral term than ideology and thus analytically preferable.

But while it handily bypassed the undeniable problems inherent in the idea of "false consciousness,"

discourse was also only too amenable a term to dispose with any attention to class relationships whatsoever. In some more apolitical academic quarters from the 1980s onward, during the zenith of postmodern media analysis, "discourse" came completely to supplant the use of ideology as a term, its neutral value-free resonance fashionably chiming with the new postmodern (neo) liberalism of the era.

More critically engaged media scholars, however, who engaged with the theoretical challenges of post-Marxism, tended to use both terms. For Stuart Hall, it was a mistake to attempt to treat Marx's writings as an exact "social science," the letter of the law; rather, it was crucial to put them into dialogue with other theories—including those of Gramsci, Althusser, Valentin Volosinov, and Ernesto Laclau—in order to try to grapple with "the *problem* of ideology: to give an account, within a materialist theory, of how social ideas arise" (Hall 1996, 26; Laclau 1977; Volosinov 1973). The problem of ideology, in these terms, "concerns the ways in which ideas of different kinds grip the minds of the masses, and thereby become 'a material force'" (Hall 1996, 26). To understand how this happens we need to use our critical imagination and look all around us. By ideology, Hall wrote, "I mean the mental frameworks—the languages, the concepts, categories, imagery of thought, and the systems of representation—which different classes and social groups deploy in order to make sense of, define, figure out and render intelligible the way society works" (1996, 26).

Opening up consideration of how particular ideas come to dominate social thinking, "so as to inform the struggle to change society and open the road toward a socialist transformation of society," was, in these terms, the only reason why studying ideology was important. For such an approach to understanding the shifting power dynamics and contours of the present, openness to methodological experimentation was more important than doctrinal insistence on terminology. Consequently, Hall argued, "I don't much care if you call it ideology or not. What matters is not the terminology but the conceptualization. The question of the relative power and distribution of different regimes of truth in the social formation at any one time—which have certain effects for the maintenance of power in the social order—that is what I call 'the ideological effect'" (Grossberg and Hall 1996).

This open approach to considering ideological complexity, and its effects, was and remains influential in critical media studies; and notably, Hall's work had already highlighted how the interest in ideology in the 1970s was to no small degree encouraged by "the massive growth of the cultural industries" (Hall 1996, 26). Such an open stance, which marked the work of scholars at CCCS and beyond, welcomed hybrid theoretical approaches in order to make sense of the cultural, social, and economic power dynamics of the context at hand and the potential alternatives. McRobbie's analysis of *Jackie* magazine therefore emphasized that while its ideological discourse was "immensely powerful," her reading "does not mean that its readers necessarily swallow its axioms unquestioningly" (1978, 50), and suggested alternative ideologies that magazines could feature, including frank discussion of sexualities, masturbation, and abortion, or teenage girls becoming active musical performers rather than mooning over pop stars (1978, 51).

Trying to understand complexity is therefore a necessary part of ideological analysis. As David Croteau and William Hoynes put it, "The most sophisticated ideological analysis examines the stories the media tell as well as the potential contradictions within media texts, that is, the places where alternative perspectives might reside or where ideological conflict is built into the text."

In these terms, the ideological influence of media can be seen "in the absences and exclusions just as much as in the content of the messages" (2014, 162). Such nuanced approaches have been used to analyze how contemporary capitalism operates in and through the media. For example, in the 1980s the Glasgow Media Group analyzed television news in the United Kingdom, proving that it was biased toward the powerful and omitted voices of the poor (Eldridge 1995); and more recently, excavations of the workings of neoliberal ideology have discussed how corporate media messages increasingly promote ideals of competitiveness and individualism and marginalize ideals of cooperation and sharing (Grossberg 2008; Hall, Massey, and Rustin 2014; Harvey 2007).

We can also consider the ideological uses to which the term ideology *itself* is put in popular culture. For example, in the United Kingdom in the 1990s Prime Minister Tony Blair declared himself "beyond ideology," thus identifying his political project with the neutral "center" ground of "common sense." This was part of a wider neoliberal context whereby any identifiable left position was clearly marked as "an ideology" and thus rejected as unnatural and unreasonable, while the acceptable center ground shifted further to the right. Identifying a political position as "ideological" in political discourse has long been a tactic used to demarcate one's enemies as unnatural or the product of firebrand fanatics. Such a popular invocation of "ideology" draws on the lineage of the pejorative meaning of the term, which runs all the way back through the work of Marx and Engels to its conservative use by Napoleon Bonaparte.

The recent embrace of "socialism" by political candidates Bernie Sanders in the United States and Jeremy Corbyn in the United Kingdom provides one example of how the ideological terrain of what is "normal" and "possible" is shifting. For example, Britain's left-liberal newspaper the *Guardian* has been notoriously reluctant to present any positive coverage of Corbyn, and the extent to which it is thought to reflect the ideological interests of an existing political establishment has itself become a subject of online debate. But through the complexities, and the gaps, of the newspaper coverage (for instance, through coverage of Corbyn critiques backfiring and working to generating support, and through the alternative ideological messages presented on social media) different ideological stances have gained increased traction. Whether dealing with politicians or handbags, transsexuality or gun control, the shifting presentations of media—through what they say, through the way they say it, and through what they do *not* say—plays a powerful role in presenting us with ways to understand, and to challenge, the ideological power dynamics of the present and the boundaries of the possible.

31

Industry
Amanda D. Lotz

"Industry" within media studies describes the broad field of conditions and practices that play a role in the creation of media. Industry includes the immediate environment of production, but also mechanisms of distribution, the organizations that enable production (studios, labels, publishers, etc., as well as their conglomerate owners), their workers, the policy makers and regulatory environment in which these entities operate, the mandate of media—typically either commercial or public service ends—and the technologies that are used in making media (Havens and Lotz 2016).

Industry traces its roots to Adorno and Horkheimer's treatise on "The Culture Industry" (1944/1972). Their decision to use the terminology of industry was clearly meant as an exclamation point to a screed on the impossibility for art and creativity to exist within activities driven by commercial goals. As Hesmondhalgh (2013) explains, culture and industry were perceived as opposites when they wrote the chapter in the middle of the twentieth century. Moreover, their use of the singular form of industry to reference a wide range of entertainment, leisure, and information industries effectively conjured an all-powerful monolith. Marxist critiques subsequently viewed any commercial media as likely to perpetuate the dominant ideology.

Hesmondhalgh traces the terminology of "culture industries" to the work of French sociologists beginning in the 1960s and 1970s who sought more complex understandings of these industrial operations and identified their contradictions and variations instead of posing them as a unified field as had Adorno and Horkheimer (see Miège 1987, 1989). A robust exchange of ideas debating definitions of cultural industries and theorizing models and logics to explain them exists among Francophone media scholars, but a small amount of their work has been translated, preventing wider influence on non-French-speaking scholars. Industry also appears as an entry in Williams's (1976/1983) *Keywords*, where he traces the full breadth of the term, though, as Hesmondhalgh (2011) explains, the most relevant component of his use is of industry as "an institution or set of institutions for production or trade" (Williams 1976/1983, 165).

Despite this long lineage within theory, until recently the term "industry" has been used less than "production," although the words are frequently used interchangeably. In Hall's (1973/1980) explanation of the encoding/decoding model, the phase of encoding was seen as "production," although industry might have better acknowledged the multifaceted components of making media. Likewise, production was the term identified as the cultural process related to the making of media in the "circuit of cultural production" put forward by Johnson (1986–87), then enhanced by du Gay et al. (1997), and most recently refined by D'Acci (2004). In these uses, however, production stands in for more than the tasks and activities of the making of a particular text—though this was the level of focus of most early studies. Although these models use the term "production," they include the broader forces constraining and enabling production understood as part of industry as well. "Production" may be the term present in these key theoretical models, but "industry" emerged as the term at the definitional core of media studies as an approach that addresses or considers the triumvirate of "text, industry, and audience."

There is little to be gained in quibbling between the propriety of industry versus production. In many ways, production more accurately captures the scale of many studies that indeed focus upon case studies of particular productions. As studies of the creation of media surged in the 2000s, "production studies" became a term more associated with the making of particular "productions" that were informed by observation or ethnography and tended to emphasize analysis of media labor. Industry studies exists as a broader category of inquiry that includes production studies as well as investigations of media distribution and the ecosystem within which production takes place.

This transition between production and industry likely owes in part to varied intellectual traditions and contexts in which media have been studied. The work most important to media studies emerged first in Britain and explored media with a public service mandate that might not readily be considered as an industry in the same manner as their commercially motivated US counterparts. Considerable variation exists among and within various sociological, cultural studies, and political economy traditions of studying media industries, the subtleties of which are detailed by Hesmondhalgh (2011).

Outside academia, industry is a simple categorization, as Williams notes: the set of institutions that produce particular media. No singular or coherent media industry exists; the variation among media industries nearly always requires identification of a particular industry to make meaningful claims. Even when focusing on the "television industry," for example, further specification is required. Is it a commercial television industry, broadcast television industry, cable television industry, or subscription-supported cable industry that is of interest? Many scholars emphasize the plurality by discussing media industries rather than the singular form of the word when speaking of the media sector more generally.

Because of the breadth and scope of media industries, studies consequently investigate a wide array of sites and can employ a similarly broad range of theories and approaches (Lotz and Newcomb 2011). At the most macro level, industry studies explore how matters of national and international political economy and policy produce implications for the operation of media companies and the products they make. Schiller (1989), for example, examines the expanding corporate control of various cultural entities such as museums, theaters, and performing arts centers. Holt (2011) explores the shifting regulatory environment in the United States from 1980 through 1996 and its role in encouraging conglomeration among what had been distinct film, television, and cable media industries.

Studies of specific industrial contexts and practices provide a bit more focused examination. These studies explore questions about the operation of particular media industries, often narrowed to particular periods of time. For example, Gitlin (1984) examines a variety of practices characteristic of the US television industry in the early 1980s, and Havens (2008) investigates the norms of the practice of international television distribution in the early 2000s.

Yet more narrow focus can be found in industry studies that examine particular organizations such as studios, production companies, and networks. The questions asked in studies of this level may engage with broader industrial conditions—such as how the practices of a particular studio adapted to the increased reliance on computer-generated images in filmmaking, or such studies may provide a more general case investigation of the norms and practices at a particular moment in time. For example, Perren (2013a) explores the evolution of the Miramax film studio in the early 1990s from an independent producer-distributor into a studio subsidiary and the implications for the films it made. In another case, Born (2005) studied the decision-making behavior of the British Broadcasting Corporation in order to develop more comprehensive understanding of the day-to-day practices of a public service media organization.

The most focused level of industry study examines individual productions and, as already noted, is often characterized as production studies. The value of studies at this level is the depth of understanding that can be developed and the ability to link industrial conditions with particular outcomes in creative goods. Such case studies are most valuable when the specific context can be connected to broader phenomena. For example, D'Acci (1994) explored the production of the television series *Cagney & Lacey*. At the time, it was most unusual to include analysis of industrial conditions of a television show, and D'Acci's book remains canonical in the field because of its integration of analysis of the production of the series with the text and audience response.

An alternative site for narrowly focused industry studies is on individual agents. Most studies at this level have focused on film directors; however, television writers and producers have also become identifiable creative voices for investigation (Newcomb and Alley 1983). In a few cases, media executives have also provided a site of analysis. These works tend to be more biographical and autobiographical in nature, though they can be read with an eye toward scholarly insight (Bedell 1981; Tartikoff 1992).

Though it no longer defines the area of industry studies, it is important to acknowledge the legacy of once considerable hostility between political economy and cultural studies approaches. Intellectual disagreements in the early 1990s retarded the development of studies of industries drawing from a cultural studies tradition, as did the close identification of cultural studies with first textual analysis and then audience studies.

Before the 1990s, studies of US media industries typically drew from the North American version of the tradition of political economy (Mosco 2009). Such studies often focused at the most macro level of industry operation and focused on who owned media companies as the most important consideration in industrial analysis. This approach matched conditions within US media well, as considerable consolidation of media companies in all sectors took place in the 1970s through the 1990s. The research in this tradition identified how large national media companies increasingly took over what were once local media and how both consolidation within particular media and conglomeration among companies with different media holdings drastically reduced the number of media companies and hence the number of voices in the mediated public sphere.

The tradition of political economy that emerged in the United Kingdom has always been somewhat distinct from its US counterpart (see Hesmondhalgh 2006), likely because it developed in an environment of ample public service media that demanded different foci of analysis than the near uniformly commercial media of the United States. Studies of media industries in the 1970s in both the United States and the United Kingdom focused on news production, employed sociological methods such as interviews and observation, and reflected concern about "everyday culture" emerging from early cultural studies (Gans 1979; Schlesinger 1978; Tuchman 1978a). Studies relying on sociological approaches revealed different information about how ownership and an organization's mandate affected newsroom operations, journalistic decisions, and the content of the news than accounts that cataloged who owned media organizations.

Although political economy or cultural studies approaches might be used in studies at any of the levels of analysis, cultural studies approaches are more commonly found at the more focused sites. This is because cultural studies approaches often employ methodologies such as interviews and observation to make sense of norms, routines, and practices involved in making media that are identifiable only at more specific levels of analysis. Cultural studies approaches also integrate evidence and analysis of industrial conditions with specific textual outcomes in a manner uncommon within political economy approaches and characteristic of a midlevel approach (Havens, Lotz, and Tinic 2009). The centrality within cultural studies of understanding media within a circuit of historical and contextual conditions articulated within a matrix of production, reception, and textual considerations necessitates such integration (D'Acci 2004; du Gay et al. 1997).

Both political economy and cultural studies assessments of industry explore questions related to the operation of power within industry, although the theoretical bases vary. Much political economy research, particularly the North American variation, derives its approach to power through Marxist theory. Cultural studies' thinking is related, but draws more from neo-Marxists who identified power relations other than those rooted in class such as Gramsci (1971) and Althusser (1971), and also Foucault (1979). Where Marxists primarily conceive of power operating through the media's ideological extension of capitalist power, cultural-studies-based research also explores power in discourse "that privileges specific ways of understanding the media and their place in people's lives" and in the operation of power within media organizations (Havens, Lotz, and Tinic 2009, 237).

32

Infrastructure

Lisa Parks

The word "infrastructure" surfaced in the early twentieth century as "a collective term for the subordinate parts of an undertaking; substructure, foundation," and first became associated with permanent military installations (*Oxford English Dictionary*). Since then, the term's meanings have expanded to encompass power grids and telecommunication networks, subways and freeways, sewer systems, and oil pipelines. While critical media studies scholars have investigated "networks" for decades, they have only recently begun to think of "infrastructures" as part of their research field. Work on media infrastructures has explored the material conditions in which broadcast, cable, satellite, Internet, and mobile telephony systems are arranged to distribute audiovisual content to sites around the world. While such systems have historically been referred to as "telecommunication networks," the reconceptualization of them as "media infrastructures" signals a shift toward exploring issues of scale, difference and unevenness, relationality, labor, maintenance and repair, literacy, and affect (Parks and Starosielski 2015). For this reason, research on media infrastructures requires interdisciplinary engagements across fields such as sociology, urban studies, anthropology, history, urban studies, architecture, and science and technology studies.

Studying the systems and material conditions that enable media distribution involves adopting an *infrastructural disposition*. When consuming or critiquing media it is vital to think not only about what media represent and how they relate to a history of style, genre, or meaning, but also more *elementally* about what they are made of and how they arrived (Parks 2015). For architect Keller Easterling, an *infrastructure* has a *disposition* to the extent that it is a "mode of organization" that is "actively *doing something*" (2014, 73). Astutely, she defines "disposition" as "an extra diagnostic tool for assessing undisclosed capacity or political bearing in infrastructure space" (93). Recognizing this, she explains, is to be able to "uncover accidental, covert or stubborn forms of power—political chemistries and temperaments of aggression, submission or violence—hiding in the folds of infrastructure space" (73). In the process of elaborating a philosophy of "elemental media," John Durham Peters describes what he calls "infrastructuralism" as a "fascination for the basic, the boring, the mundane, and all the mischievous work done behind the scenes . . . a doctrine of environments and small differences . . . of things not understood that stand under our worlds" (2015, 33). Then, conjoining media and infrastructure, Peters sets out to boldly expand the conceptual radius of media theory, insisting, "To understand media we need to understand fire, aqueducts, power grids, seeds, sewage systems, DNA, mathematics, sex, music, daydreams and insulation" (2015, 29).

As Peters's provocative inventory implies, the concept of infrastructure has been used to expand the kinds of objects, sites, and practices within the purview of media studies. In the spirit of this expansion, I sketch a continuum for thinking about infrastructure and affect that brings phenomenological and political autonomist approaches into dialogue, marking them as distinct yet equally important and ultimately related to one another. There is a need, on the one hand, for a broader imagining of *infrastructural affects*—experiences, sensations, structures of feeling—generated through people's material encounters with media infrastructures (not just interfaces but physical sites, installations, hardware), while, on the other hand, there is a need for further critique of the ways affect serves as part of the *base* of media infrastructural operations.

Affect is "a gradient of bodily capacity—a supple incrementalism of ever-modulating force-relations—that rises and falls not only along various rhythms and modalities of encounter but also through the troughs and sieves of sensation and sensibility" (Gregg and Seigworth 2010, 2). Infrastructures become part of such "force-relations" as people's encounters with them in everyday life generate rhythms, moods, and sensations. For many people, the default disposition to infrastructure might be indifference or apathy, but it is also possible that a broad spectrum of infrastructural affects remains unknown, simply because certain kinds of questions have not been asked.

A phenomenology of infrastructure and affect might begin by excavating the various dispositions, feelings, or sensations people experience during encounters with infrastructure sites, facilities, or processes. This critical imaginary might take shape as a continuum that recognizes, on one end, the general tendency of infrastructures to normalize behavior (such that they become relatively invisible and unnoticed), and, on the other, the potential for disruption of that normalization, which can occur during instances of inaccessibility or breakdown. By creating this continuum, it might be possible to build on Wendy Chun's crucial work on networks of control and freedom (2008) and to suggest that an array of infrastructural affects lies in the gray zone between them. The intention of this critical move, then, is not to reduce affect or turn it into a list of discernable emotions, but rather to catalyze further thinking about the ways people perceive and experience infrastructures in everyday life and how these experiences differentially orient people in the world.

Beyond this phenomenological approach, it is also important to consider the relationship between media infrastructures and *affective labor*, a concept derived from critiques of late capitalism's shift from factory labor to "invisible" or "immaterial" forms of labor involving various social skills, services, and modes of care (Hardt and Negri 2005, 108). As Brian Massumi puts it, "affect is a real condition, an intrinsic variable of the late capitalist system, as infrastructural as a factory" (2002, 45) The case already has been made that network infrastructures like the Internet rely upon the affective or *immaterial* labor of users to function and sustain themselves over time (Terranova 2004). Media infrastructures' reliance on immaterial labor is a historical and predigital process that dates back at least to the emergence of telegraphy in the mid-nineteenth century. What we have in the current conjuncture is a compounding and intensifying demand for immaterial labor as industrial societies have undergone a shift from only one telecommunication infrastructure—telegraphy—to a postindustrial order in which multiple systems—telephony, radio, television, cable, satellite, Internet, and mobile telephony—cooperate and compete for user time, attention, and energy. Landline telephony has fewer users today than it did one decade ago not because the system no longer technically functions, but because most people simply do not have enough time, attention, and money to use their landlines *and* their mobile phones. Satellite radio networks shower hundreds of niche signals into continental footprints, but listeners do not have enough time to hear them all.

Such scenarios are suggestive of the compounding affective demands that have become part of media infrastructures' current conditions of operation. The capacity to produce and distribute networked data not only creates what Mark Andrejevic describes as "infoglut"; these conditions, he suggests, turn affect into "an exploitable resource" that becomes "part of the 'infrastructure'" (2013b, 52). Andrejevic builds upon Daniel Smith's assertion that affects "are not your own, so to speak. They are . . . part of the capitalist infrastructure" (2011, 137). Within such conditions, media infrastructures once thought of as *public utilities* have been reorganized as *utility publics*—that is to say, infrastructures not only deliver utilities to publics but, in the process, reutilize publics as part of the base of their operations.

With multiple competing media infrastructures in the marketplace, it remains to be determined whether there is enough human bandwidth to sustain them all, as well as figuring out what *sustaining them* means. Human time, attention, and energy are not boundless, even if capitalism operates as if they are (Crary 2013; Sharma 2014). One incentive for mobile phone and satellite operators to tap the so-called O3B—the "other three billion" people on the planet without Internet access—is to be able to exploit a more global pool of affective labor. Plans for integrating the developing world into the Internet are also ways to expand digital capitalism's human resources. Within such conditions, formulating analyses of media infrastructures and affect seems more important than ever.

33
Interactivity
Tama Leaver

Critically understanding interactivity—the way people interact with media of various forms—has been a core concern of media studies since its inception. Long before personal computers and mobile devices arrived in family homes, media and cultural studies sought to make visible the different impact that mass media, including film and television, could have in people's lives. This undertaking is exemplified in Stuart Hall's model of encoding and decoding, which, at its most basic level, argues that media are not passively received, but rather actively decoded and interpreted by every audience member, every recipient (Hall 1973/1980). Hall's model acknowledges that media are produced and consumed within specific contexts and power structures that often promote a dominant reading, a way of interpreting a media text aligned with the producer's intended meaning. Yet it is Hall's argument that an oppositional reading is possible, that audiences may interact differently and take a different meaning from a media text, that is most important. Hall thus argues that all media viewing is an act of interpretation, and the perspective of viewers and the context in which they are viewing will have an impact on how they interact with each and every media text in their lives.

While interactivity at the level of meaning is comparatively difficult to make visible, in early studies of fan culture interactivity is particularly evident. From Henry Jenkins's canonical *Textual Poachers: Television Fans and Participatory Culture* (1992) onward, fan studies have argued that fans' deep interaction with their chosen media is both an active and creative process. As fans started using the Internet, and then the web, the scale of this creativity and participation has increased exponentially.

As digital technology developed, the centrality of interactivity in terms of tactile engagement via an interface such as a keyboard, mouse, or screen led to a range of studies attempting to offer all-encompassing definitions of the term. However, consensus came only in the broadest possible terms, with scholars agreeing only that interactivity involves communication between people and technology (Downes and McMillian 2000; Kiousis 2002). The paradigm of human-computer interaction and the fetishization of the digital and technological as new repositioned interactivity as a tactile engagement rather than a process of interpretation. Yet in *The Language of New Media*, Lev Manovich (2001) warns that trying to define digital or new media in terms of interactivity is tautological: these media forms are accessed on computers or devices that are, by definition, interactive systems. Moreover, before the ubiquity of digital screens, accessing television or even books involved some level of interaction, from turning pages to selecting channels on a dial, although this relatively minimal level of physical interaction pales in comparison to playing *Angry Birds* or other casual games on a mobile device.

As networked communication matured in the "Web 2.0" era, the participatory culture that Jenkins explored in terms of fan culture purportedly become the online norm. Blogging platforms and social networks allowed every user to become a publisher; YouTube allowed all users to "broadcast themselves"; Flickr and Instagram allowed all users to capture and share their lives in photographs; and a plethora of apps and platforms made media easy to create, easy to manipulate, and easy to share. Interactivity is inescapably in the DNA of participatory culture, a point reinforced even further with the ubiquity of mobile media devices, with tablets and camera phones able to capture, create, and consume media. However, the focus on interactivity at the level of the interface at times occludes the implicit point that users are always already negotiating the meaning of media texts as they engage with them.

Participation, however, does not take place on an even digital terrain. Critiques of participatory culture have argued that users and fans can often be exploited as free labor and advertising under the guise of participation and interaction. In a case study of television fans and online forums, Mark Andrejevic convincingly argues that in terms of fan labor, "creative activity and exploitation coexist and interpenetrate one another within the context of the emerging online economy" (2008, 25). When, for example, Joss Whedon invited fans of his self-funded online web series *Dr. Horrible* to submit their own fictional audition tapes for the Evil League of Evil, the inclusion of this often highly produced fan-created work on the commercial DVD of the series as an extra feature begs the question as to the boundary between participation and exploitation (Leaver 2013).

Interactivity is one of the defining features of video games, arguably the first indigenous digital media form. Indeed, as game studies emerged as a field of media studies in its own right, the core definitional debate was whether video games should be thought of first in terms of narrative, the stories they create, or the way interactions create an experience (Frasca 2003). While the debate basically ended with proponents on both sides agreeing that the mix of narrative and interaction was what mattered most, studying digital games can be very useful in illuminating how digital affordances make interactivity even more important to understand. As many games offer quite different experiences depending on the choices players make and how they interact with the game itself, analyzing interactivity in terms of digital games entails looking at how players make meaning during game play, how their physical interactions impact their experiences, and resulting differences of game play.

Networked games of various forms, including massively popular social and casual games, have led designers and game companies to focus on interactivity in very specific and often quite narrow ways (Leaver and Willson 2016). It is now trivial to record and analyze every mouse click, every tap or swipe of a screen, and to collate these data in an attempt to understand player responses. This has led to the era of big data and predictive analytics in which literally every interaction is a form of user labor, helping companies build insights algorithmically to create more commercially successful products. Zynga's *Farmville* is the classic example, not least of all as the company famously declared itself "an analytics company masquerading as a games company" (Willson and Leaver 2015). Yet for Zynga, as with many social media platforms and games driven by big data analytics, the underlying presumption appears to be that people are basically all the same, and that extracting enough information about user interactions will allow analytics to determine a better version of the game in which players spend more time and, importantly, more money (Andrejevic 2011). Zynga's approach, which ignored the specificities of players and their different contexts, may partly explain why *Farmville* and its various clones have fallen from popularity so dramatically. Myopically focusing on the minutiae of interactivity as it is captured in big data can occlude both contexts and thus cannot account for the specificities of individuals.

Interaction between people and media forms is a generative process. Audiences necessarily interact with media, creating meaning, albeit often within specific boundaries. In an era of mobile devices and apps, interaction can generate new forms of creative expression, participation, and engagement. Yet it can also be harnessed for the purposes of surveillance and cynical monetization. An era of big data, it turns out, leads to equally big questions about the ways interactivity is situated and understood. It is the job of critical media studies to continually map these shifting and competing contexts and make them visible.

INTERACTIVITY TAMA LEAVER

34

Intersectionality

Brenda R. Weber

"Ain't I a woman?" asked Sojourner Truth at Akron, Ohio's, Women's Convention of 1851. "That man over there says that women need to be helped into carriages, and lifted over ditches, and to have the best place everywhere. Nobody ever helps me into carriages, or over mud-puddles, or gives me any best place! And ain't I a woman? Look at me! Look at my arm! I have ploughed and planted, and gathered into barns, and no man could head me! And ain't I a woman? I could work as much and eat as much as a man—when I could get it—and bear the lash as well! And ain't I a woman? I have borne thirteen children, and seen most all sold off to slavery, and when I cried out with my mother's grief, none but Jesus heard me! And ain't I a woman?"

Truth's point, told loudly and clearly, was that universal categories like "woman" reinforce an exclusionary norm of privileged and elite whiteness, leaving a vast majority of working-class women and women of color unrepresented, even invisible. The Women's Convention at which Truth spoke was one of many geared toward expanding the rights of women in the United States. The Akron event came on the heels of other such gatherings, such as the Seneca Falls Women's Rights Convention of 1848. This conference put forward the now famous Declaration of Sentiments and Resolutions, declaring that women (just as men) had a constitutional right to pursue happiness, to develop individual self-determination, to be educated, to speak their mind, to address an audience in public, to participate fully in the public sphere, and to vote (a political act not nationally allowed by law until 1920, some seventy-two years later). Yet somehow in the mighty coalition building that started in the eighteenth and nineteenth centuries and extended into the twentieth, Sojourner Truth's declaration went unheard, in that the specificity of personhood was not fully considered.

Fast forward to 1963. Betty Friedan writes a book called *The Feminine Mystique*, which is now widely credited for starting second-wave feminism. In 1957, Friedan had been asked to conduct a survey about her former classmates at Smith College, a private liberal arts school for women in Northampton, Massachusetts, and one of the Seven Sisters, or the "female Ivies," before women were allowed to attend Ivy League schools. Friedan argued that among those she interviewed, most were unhappy with their lives as housewives despite their middle- and even upper-class living conditions. Friedan credited "the problem that has no name" for a malaise that gripped the American woman, tied to house and home, her career ambitions and artistic talents directed to child care and a husband's needs. Friedan's book was a watershed moment in US gender politics, since it revealed the "happy homemaker" as a myth few women were able to uphold and began a conversation on women's work-life balance that is still ongoing.

But in its essentialism—its positioning of white elite women as *all* women—Friedan's rendering of the feminine mystique failed to consider women of color, working women, non-US women, and non-heterosexual women as part of the feminine mystique, thus positioning them outside the category of woman altogether. Friedan's work was no doubt important as a stakeholder in a much larger debate about women's rights, and she wasn't alone in using a universal standard of woman to forward women's rights. But because *The Feminine Mystique* lumped all women into one category, it ignored the important matters of identity such as race, class, religion, national identity, and sexual orientation that constantly influence how all of us understand and negotiate our own personhood and how we are treated by others. By the 1970s, black women like Alice Walker were pushing back, arguing that woman as monolith failed to account for the particularities of race and class that infused every element of their experience of female identity. In 1981, bell hooks took Sojourner Truth's declarative question—"Ain't I a Woman?"—as the title for a book that examined the effects of both racism and sexism on black women, the civil rights movement, and feminism. In 1989, feminist sociologist Kimberlé Crenshaw coined the term "intersectionality" to give name to this increasingly important mandate. In effect, more feminist scholars began to insist that comprehensive analyses needed to engage with multiple axes of identity to better understand interlocking and overlapping systems of oppression and power. It was not enough to speak simply of sex—male and female. A comprehensive study of power had to engage in multinodal understandings of identity.

All of these matters bear important relevance to media, which often traffic in shared ideas, common templates, and recognizable archetypes, even in this post-network age of niche programming and narrowcasting that speaks to one or two million viewers at a time rather than hundreds of millions. Yet, media content has a problem with disproportionate representation and misrepresentation, in that certain people and bodies (those who are attractive, thin, white, physically and psychologically able, perceived to be heterosexual, and middle to upper class) are chosen more often than others to sell us products, tell us stories, and stand as cultural authorities and role models. When people hailing from non-normative identity locations gain recognition through representation, they have often served

as cautionary tales or as scare tactics or, in some cases, as the exceptions that prove the rules (a version of tokenism that seems to suggest that the presence of one queer person or black person, much less one queer black person, stands for all people within these categories). So intersectionality goes hand in hand with diversity, but it applies to one person's many forms of identity affiliation rather than letting one element of identity stand for the whole.

Intersectionality is critical to media studies because it requires that scholars and activists avoid short-handing identity. It is also a critical tool for media scholars because if intersectionality begins to function as a watchword of not just gender studies but also media studies, it suggests these same scholars must be attentive to the politics of identity. Let me illustrate. A few years ago, I was at a conference where scholars were discussing the classic war film *The Great Escape*. Someone in the audience asked for comment on the gender politics of the film. "Well," another scholar replied, "there are no women in the film, so there really aren't any gender politics." Yet of course a film with only male characters has statements to make about gender, just as it has statements to make about race, class, sexuality, and nationality. To the degree that all elements of media—producer, consumer, product—are occupied by people, intersectional identities are critical to how things are made, how they are understood, and what they are interpreted to mean and by whom. *The Great Escape*'s homosocial fantasy about prisoners of war who evade their captors contains rich information about power, masculinity, ethnic identity, class, and, yes, sexual orientation. Its mode of production, its almost cult-like following, its "tough guy" cast, its historical place in the culture, all tell us more when approached from an intersectional vantage point. And indeed, much important film and television scholarship—such as reception work offered in Jacqueline Bobo's *Black*

Women as Cultural Readers (1995) or Beverley Skeggs and Helen Wood's *Reacting to Reality Television* (2012) or cultural studies critiques in books such as Kara Keeling's *The Witch's Flight* (2007)—is leading the way in doing these sorts of intersectional analyses.

Yet, intersectionality itself must also be open to discussion and critique. In 2013, *Signs: Journal of Women in Culture and Society* devoted an entire issue to new modalities for thinking through and beyond intersectionality, in both US and transnational contexts. Gender scholars such as Jasbir Puar (2007) have asked scholars to consider the ways that intersectionality as a term connotes a too-delineated relation of identity, like a car enmeshed in a great interstate spaghetti bowl, where one exits the whiteness highway to merge onto the queer express. Puar and others have recommended the governing metaphor of assemblage, or the idea that radical difference and heterogeneity often mark social relations and identities. Assemblage is more diffused, overlapping, and incoherent than intersectionality, accounting for the flow of both identity and power in ways simultaneously visible and undetectable. Indeed, assemblage is to intersectionality what transmedia are to traditional forms of media, in that both seek to engage with a complex social and ideological world of pluralized meaning making, where media serve as a powerful organizing force that is itself not always coherent, linear, or stable. As one example, the emerging field of celebrity studies indicates that one cannot "get at" the diverse appeals and contradictions embedded in fame without thinking across gendered, classed, and sexed lives but also without considering multiple and often fused media platforms, such as film, television, and social media, that influence how celebrity and celebrities become intelligible and hold cultural currency.

So, does this mean that the conscientious scholar must consider all aspects of identity when engaging in the overlap of gender and media? In some ways, yes. While a world of manageable categories and knowable metrics has a certain undeniable appeal, compartmentalized analyses obliterate much of the breadth we need to engage with the complex contours of identity, where gender, race, sexuality, class, orientation, and many other vectors work together to inform the meanings of personhood and power in the present moment.

35

Irony
Amber Day

Irony is a label that we gravitate to with ease but one that most would be hard-pressed to define. Because it involves complex linguistic and conceptual contortions, it is simplest to just assume that we will recognize it when we need to. It is that know-it-when-we-see-it quality, though, that has left irony open to opportunistic usage, defined by a given speaker based on his or her purpose at hand, used alternately as a convenient scapegoat, defensive shield, or badge of hipness.

One of the most common mistaken assumptions about irony is that because of its indirectness, it signals a smug detachment or lack of commitment to any viewpoint or cause. This conception of irony makes a perfect straw man for all that is wrong with media culture, political debate, or "kids these days." It was also this conception of irony that commentators had in mind when they famously declared the mode dead in the wake of the September 11, 2001, terrorist attacks (see Beers 2001; Rosenblatt 2001). Citing touchstones of nineties culture such as *Seinfeld* and *Beavis and Butt-Head*, many equated irony with frivolity and a lack of conscience and assumed that American culture would have to collectively wise up. Looking back, it is now clear that these commentators were wrong. Since then there has, in fact, been a notable surge in ironic media, specifically a distinctly politically invested, earnest form of irony, including programs like *The Daily Show with Jon Stewart* and *The Colbert Report*, which forged an entirely new genre of American television. Irony has been used overwhelmingly to point out contradictions and hypocrisies, not cynically to withdraw from caring, but often to assert passionately that we deserve better. These forms of ironic media have also attracted many devoted fans, serving as powerful focal points for existing communities of interest.

At the same time, irony is often sloppily invoked as a blanket defense of potentially offensive humor. There are many contemporary comedians, like Amy Schumer, Keegan-Michael Key, and Jordan Peele, who skillfully unpack social hypocrisies around gender, race, and class using ironic critique. These comedians often make incisive observations about cultural assumptions, bias, and power. However, there are many more comedians and television programs that lazily gesture to the existence of stereotypes without actually countering them or revealing anything new. These programs can hide behind a hazily invoked irony, posturing that they are not just offensively repeating stereotypes, but are doing so ironically, relying on the assumption that this makes the humor acceptable, even smart.

Whether used as a shield or lobbed as a slur, the term "irony" is being used imprecisely. Most would agree that irony involves some form of layered meaning: noticeable distance between a literal statement and its implied meaning. It is too simplistic, though, to assume that an ironic statement means precisely the opposite of what is said (which implies pure negation). Rather, it constructs an alternate meaning, as well as an implied assessment. As Linda Hutcheon puts it, irony "is the making or inferring of **meaning** in addition to and different from what is stated, together with an **attitude** toward both the said and the unsaid" (1994, 11). The second part of her definition is the piece most conveniently ignored. Irony crucially involves some sort of judgment. In the case of jokes that try to appear gutsy by dipping a toe into racism or sexism, if they do not imply any coherent judgment about these things, they are likely not ironic at all. Similarly, though we can all point to particular ironic quips launched from a place of smug superiority, if there is an implied target, irony is rarely entirely detached or cynical.

The one remaining element we cannot get from even the most precise definition, though, is the pleasure of irony. In order to land, and as an indirect form of communication, any ironic statement requires a lot of pieces first to fall into place. The listener must choose to interpret it ironically, drawing on mutually understood cues and assumptions about the speaker's intentions. It is fraught with potential misfires, but when everything aligns, it instantly provides the pleasure of connection, reminding participants of the convictions they share. And precisely because of its complexity, irony welcomes depth and complication, making it the perfect tool for challenging received truths and deconstructing pieties. Particularly in a "media-savvy" age, such as our own, when nearly all communication has been given a polished, focus-grouped sheen, there is nothing like irony for slyly peeling away the layers.

36

Labor
Vicki Mayer

In its most common uses, the term "labor" refers to either an organized system of exploitation or a personal source of pleasure. "Slave labor" relies on unfree populations forced into servitude, while a "labor of love" is a gift that an individual freely gives. These two usages are frequently conjoined, conflated, or compared to simply "work." The orthodoxies that insist on using the word "labor" over "work" are less important than ways in which the word is deployed in these seemingly contradictory ways to explain centuries of media production and their producers.

On the one hand, media labor refers to a human productive capacity. The ability to communicate, while universal to all, has a special aura in relation to media industries and their specialized technologies. Beyond simply the application of skills, media labor implies a process of self-actualization for workers to construct particular kinds of identities in society (Mayer 2011). Media labor typically requires collaboration, even if remotely, and thus places individuals within social networks that are frequently further defined by gender, race, nationality, and social class. At the base of these definitions of media labor is the understanding that symbolic production as communication is both different from all other sorts of human creations, and that the laborer communicates to others without necessarily expecting money or other compensation. This definition is rooted in the biblical language of the "labor of love" (Hyde 1983), and though it can easily slide into romantic notions of media labor, it also expresses what separates communication (a song) from other material processes (pressing the record) (Hesmondhalgh and Baker 2011).

On the other hand, media labor implies the conditioning of one's unique capacities within a social structure. In Marxist terms, the power of the media worker is traded for economic benefits such as wages. In liberal democracies, the nation-state supports these laborers to negotiate fair remuneration for their time and efforts in exchange for more tax revenues. Capitalism, however, acts as a social force to reduce the value of the labor to achieve the highest profit margins. This frequently means dividing media laborers according to occupational roles within and across various codependent industries (i.e., electronics manufacturing versus information processing versus video game design), and then conquering laborers' abilities to self-organize through unions or other types of association. Under these conditions that create downward competition and stave off solidarities, it's no wonder that media labor infers exploitation as much as actualization.

Labor as actualization and exploitation was already in play during the first media revolution. As Elizabeth Eisenstein (1983) charts, the rise of the printing press from 1450 to 1600 transformed not only media labor markets, but also the social value of printing as a special kind of labor across Europe. The painstaking process of reproducing books by hand, aka manuscripts, required increasingly skilled workers to cluster nearby to more efficiently reproduce figures, charts, and a new scientific lexicon. The earliest printers contracted experienced freelance stationers, along with a wide array of binders, rubricators, and calligraphers from the scriptoria. New trades developed. A new division of labor and press technologies freed printers to focus on the contents of their books, permitting creative experimentation and new inventions, such as footnotes, tables of contents, and cross-references. Laborers came from different social worlds and traveled extensively to market both their skills and their book lists. They often made collective decisions about the product while competing against other presses.

Laborers shared the same production and reception culture in large towns across Western Europe. Print shops became cultural centers for the growth of a cosmopolitan literati and learning communities that lured university students from lectures. Predating Wikipedia, these early media laborers had a hand in creating and re-creating books through editing, translation, and even scientific experimentation to test texts' veracity. Some even developed free-labor networks of reader-correspondents to help correct errors for subsequent editions. Printers expressed their identities though their own libraries as testaments to the "by-products of their own shop work" (Eisenstein 1983, 49).

As the printers came to be known for their book lists rather than their richest readers, the master printer came to be the first celebrity of the age. Estienne made Latin Bibles. Ortelius made atlases. The famous master printer of Mainz, Peter Schoeffer, was known for developing indexes and new editions as sales techniques. He was also infamous for his testimony against Gutenberg, sending his business partner into exile. The master printer bridged social and cultural worlds, heading complex organizations by securing the financial resources to wholesale niche goods to yet-unknown markets. They were the ultimate multitaskers, taking on the roles of publisher, seller, indexer, translator, and editor, among others. They curried favor with officials and the guilds they needed for materials and resources. They mentored their own assistants and cultivated their own talent, especially authors and artists who would attract loyal buyers. In sum, they were self-promoters and entrepreneurs par excellence, becoming socially prominent as their goods were associated with their personae throughout Europe.

Meanwhile, printers erased the names of the workers who created the volumes under them. Master printers looked to new financial syndicates to provide labor and avoid the potential for strikes. They asserted the first claims over copyright and piracy to protect their profits over authors, competitors, and all other media laborers. With time, even the most creative personnel, such as illustrators, found they were replaceable to improved machinery. Printers' power concentrated with slimmer and cheaper staffs. Ironically, printers and their publishing kin would look upon their media labor as a craft, even as they continually standardized its processes and harnessed labor power. The history of printing reveals that even as some laborers achieve status or celebrity as printers, the print industry renders far more laborers as an exploitable, and ultimately disposable, commodity.

Media labor is still a commodity to be leveraged against other materials and resources needed in operating an industry. Printers' social status in the Western world declined in relation to the growth of new automated technologies. In general, new workplace technologies have exerted the most pressure on the middle range of laborers across media industries. "Deskilling" refers to the process by which media laborers' skills have been mechanized, and thus are no longer valuable in the negotiation of labor contracts (Braverman 1974). The low status of assistants as support staff, as opposed to guild mentees, for higher-ranked media laborers was one outcome of deskilling. Another outcome has been the expansion of work duties among media laborers more generally as they are expected to do more of the tasks once assigned to others. Media labor typically involves a range of technological practices associated with time and duty management, financial and social accounting, and communication with a wider range of people outside of the workplace, such as clients, consumers, and audiences.

As automation has tended to homogenize the workforce in terms of their unique capabilities, the very definition of media labor has expanded to capture the symbolic, emotional, and communicative tasks involved in being part of an increasingly postindustrial workforce. This immaterial labor extends beyond the waged time and space of the traditional notion of the workplace and into the home as a "social factory" (Scholz 2013). Media laborers cultivate themselves as particular kinds of workers. Described in the present moment as self-branding, immaterial media labor assists in the reproduction of media labor both in terms of individuals' career portfolios and in terms of the social reproduction of jobs that are highly segregated by gender, ethnicity or race, and sexuality: from the white masculine world of high-tech hackers (Coleman 2012) to the feminine heteronormative world of fashion bloggers (Duffy 2013). In their most commodified articulations, media labor markets transform people into tradable objects. High-status star or celebrity identities operate as properties that can be managed by teams of workers, while low-status ordinary citizens give their personal data freely every time they surf the Internet.

Within these general trends, it is important to understand the ways national policies and regulations structure different kinds of media labor. The public service framework for broadcasting across most of the world, with the United States as an outlier, has meant that media laborers' ethical codes include some commitment to the noble goal of serving the "public good" even if only as an ideal. At the same time, the incursion of commercial competition globally in this industry, assisted by deregulation, as well as the expansion of new digital platforms for broadcast content have forced public service workers to achieve more in a highly competitive setting. The lowering of protective barriers in international trade also spurred the offshoring of media work previously thought to be nationally based, such as copyediting in publishing or computer graphic artistry in visual effects industries. The popular notion of a "flexible" labor force most notably occurred during the government breakup of the Hollywood studio system in the 1960s. Producers learned to shed their financial risks by outsourcing virtually all of their in-house production staffs to independent contractors (Christopherson and Storper 1989). Subsequently, the film as well as virtually all other audiovisual and digital media industries convene their laborers together solely for the duration of a single project. Under contract laws, work-for-hire laborers sacrifice job stability, benefits, and all rights associated with their creations. Similarly, weakened labor laws have spurred the boom in freelance and internship markets in order to increase the flexibility of employers. Writers, photographers, designers, and a whole range of workers involved in digital techniques and applications now act as their own employers in taking responsibility for their own welfare and job safety. Although very few media laborers work solitarily to create a product or content, the national legal structuring of employment may render some media labor forces atomized both physically and politically.

Media laborers have had to cultivate strong external social networks to stave off the feast-or-famine cycles now associated with short-term, project-based, and on-call jobs. These networks have supported some labor organizing across industries and nations, such as the Freelancers Union and the International Game Developers Association, but these formations can be fragile, and even undermined by governmental interference, industry co-optation, and internal gatekeepers. More tactical approaches have prevailed to promote diversity within media production cultures or to develop ethical codes, not just to safeguard membership in the labor force, but to share resources and encourage mutual solidarity. Web designers, for example, developed collective standards for ensuring the accessibility of their sites to users with disabilities (Kennedy 2012).

Although mass media industries typically promote the visibility of those workers located at the tops of their own organizational hierarchies—the director/producer, the publisher, the mogul—the vast majority of media labor is invisible—a term with multiple connotations. In most cases, media labor is invisible to those who consume its products. Gamers, for example, sustain an illegal labor force of "gold farmers" who are forced to play online in the developing world to help players in the developed world buy virtual goods or achieve game levels. More generally, data and information jobs dominate all stages of media production today. Yet the public is still largely unaware of the scope and scale of media workers dedicated to big data capture, collection, and curation. Media labor thus frequently involves not only those workers who are not found in a media spotlight, but also the invisible "free labor" of the public writ large who contributes their data to media production processes (Terranova 2004).

Similarly, much of media labor is invisible to employers and the state because it involves tasks or skills that are never remunerated or part of a wage structure. This invisible media labor tends to coincide precisely with voluntary practices or labors of love that drive people toward their jobs in the first place. Historically, the responsibility of most immaterial labor fell to women who fell outside of formal employment markets (Fortunati 1995). This legacy has functioned to "feminize" certain media labor tasks, which then are assumed to not be as valuable as other achieved skills or credentials, and even stratify some media labor markets by the gender presumed best suited for the invisible requirements of their jobs (Mayer 2011). Invisible media labor in this sense can result in the unequal treatment and payment of workers who participate equally in media production processes, but whose labor is valued according to different cultural standards.

Finally, media labor is often invisible to fellow media laborers. The neologism "precariat" speaks to the precarious working conditions that connect the majority of media laborers with those across other sectors of the global economy. These conditions hinder the formation of a broader media labor movement, much less the formation of a working class in and for itself—"the proletariat." This notion of invisibility has political connotations for the future of media labor. The formation of syndicates, unions, guilds, and other professional associations relies on the mutual recognition of their members as media laborers. From there the solidarity of media labor may make itself not only visible, but powerful in shaping the balance between labor as a means of exploitation or actualization.

37

Mass

Jack Z. Bratich

Every time we talk about a *mass* we invoke an *amassing*. Whether via ratings measurement, political fantasy, or aesthetic judgment, an assemblage presents itself. As Raymond Williams famously put it, there are "no masses, there are only ways of seeing people as masses" (1997, 20). He took this nominalism one step further by claiming that we interpret masses "according to some convenient formula . . . it is the formula, not the mass, which it is our real business to examine" (20).

In its nineteenth-century expression, the mass emerged as an idea composed of other ideas (of bodies, spaces, identities, and affects). On one end of the idea spectrum, the physical convergence of bodies in streets and squares pose a challenge to capitalist power consolidation: the *crowd*. On the other, the regulative ideal of a democratic assembly poised to deliberate on matters of concern: the *public*. Near this pole, experts attend to the apathy of mediated subjects, persuading them to participate in a political system ostensibly for their own benefit. Closer to the first pole, the target is *hyperpathy*, or excessive action (often through media practices) that might interrupt passage to the other extremity.

Somewhere along the continuum, we encounter the *mass*: a statistical abstraction, an amorphous subject that could trend toward either pole and thus needs governance. In other words, the mass *mediated*. As idea, it enabled the administration of the emerging collective power of mediated subjects via persuasion and dissuasion. The mass *as mediation* required an array of agencies and mechanisms to make it speak and make it silent: market researchers, propagandists, media managers, moral reformers, and cultural critics. It was configured as woman (unruly, fickle, irrational) and as inhuman (statistical abstraction, average, gray)—almost always a danger. The mass (as inchoate soup of affects) was a problem that prompted a target of interventions: measurement, management, marketing, moral control. The mass also (as concept) *resulted* from those interventions, which were solutions that depended upon giving a name to their emergent target. How could these emergent mediated powers be rendered intelligible, even useful? At the same time, how could their excess, their immoderation be neutralized?

The mass described here refers to mediated subjectivities, or what is still called by zombie lovers an "audience." On another level, mass was the modifier for the technical system broadly speaking: "mass communications," "mass media." As Raymond Williams reminds us, *mass* was always a misnomer, as the one-to-many media process of twentieth-century communications was more accurately called *broadcast*. The word "mass," by appearing in the name of both structure (mass media) and subject (masses), instituted and perpetuated their distinction. In other words, the "mass" pointed to a network of associations whose specific connections and extensions were trumped in favor of a bad abstraction. It was an escape from micro-differentiations as an effort to control the proliferation of populations and their media making.

In hindsight, we see the mass as a distraction (rather than the distraction so often attributed to the masses). Mass took us away from a more descriptive sense of the media system (broadcast) as well as from the uneven, rich, and diverse media subjectivities in different nodes of the circuit. Mass short-circuited other more robust and politically viable categories. In sum, the mass was

an abyss that breathed life into so many social agents. For Baudrillard (1983), it also represented the last hope for eliminating those agents. To put it simply, never was something so average so inspirational.

For James Carey (2009), the mass (as Catholic ritual) undergirded another approach to communication: one based on the gathering of like-spirited subjects to reaffirm a communal purpose. Perhaps we currently find ourselves in a political and scholarly version of this ceremony, specifically a requiem, for the mass. But if we have left the mass behind (in favor of niche, social, interpersonal, participatory, and interactive systems), it is in name only. The will to control mediated metamorphoses persists, now enabled by finer grained captures of variation. At the same time, the 150-year-long proliferation of associations, imitations, and solidarities is no longer occulted via conceptual sleights of hand (we leave that to protected algorithms). Instead, the mass exposes the hidden problem that it was meant to solve: the growing *capacities of a collective body whose existence is mediated*. Those initial emergent conditions of expanding powers, for so long buried and stunted, now return as the matter of making media common, mutant, and multitudinous.

38

Memory
George Lipsitz

Memory is the modality in which the past is made new again and again. As Donald Lowe explains, "There is no past in itself. It is forever lost. But each present symbolizes a past on its own terms" (1982, 39). Mediated forms of communication shape the meaning of memory through both their form and their content. The technologies of telegraphy, photography, sound recording, radio, motion pictures, and television transformed experiences of time and place by connecting the "here and now" to the "there and then." The photograph, the phonograph, and the motion picture preserved images, sounds, and performances across time, exposing audiences dispersed over space to memories of a vicariously shared "past" that they had not experienced personally. Mass communication undermined the specificity of local memories and traditions by producing new experiences of temporal simultaneity across spaces (Cooley 1909; Czitrom 1982). Accelerating processes that had been produced initially by the typographic revolution of the fifteenth century, electronic mass media transformed the subjective perception of time and space by circulating cultural texts beyond the historical moments, places, communities, and traditions that imbued them with their original social meanings (Benjamin 1969). This produced a new chronology of discourse, as each item of media entered a dialogue already in progress, an intertextual conversation in which each new image or utterance answered something that came before and

invited commentary from what came after. The artifacts of commercial culture became registers of change over time as media from earlier eras bore the marks of their senescence, shaping a sense of what it meant to live in the present through the ways it differed from visual and aural representations of the past.

Mediated works of expressive culture seek audience investment and engagement by tapping into audience memories of previous forms. The bawdy humor and social inversions of medieval carnival celebrations found their way into stories written by François Rabelais, which provided a foundation for their subsequent deployment in Elizabethan theater productions, minstrel, vaudeville, and variety shows, sound recordings, motion pictures, and radio and television broadcasts (Bakhtin 1981, 1986; Lipsitz 1990). Each new form of mediated communication contains a "materials memory" of previous forms, and traditional cultural forms, figures, devices, tropes, and genres take on novel significance each time they are deployed. Thus mediated mass communication entails contradictory dynamics of both continuity and rupture that help produce the meaning of memory as a social force.

The emergence of electronic mass media in the nineteenth century created a crisis of memory by facilitating the emergence of new epistemologies and ontologies. Typography and its attendant print culture emphasized *representation in space* that promoted inquiries about similarities and differences across places. The episteme that emerged with the rise of electronic mass media, however, emphasized *development in time*, which promoted emphases on temporal frameworks such as origin, evolution, growth, decay, and decline. New ways of knowing encouraged people to perceive their own lives as segmented phases of development, to experience time as discontinuous and external, and to look to the permanence of the nation-state or accumulated wealth as an antidote to the fragile and ephemeral nature of individual lives (Lowe 1982). Evocations of loss, longing, mourning, and melancholy have been central features of Western expressive culture since antiquity. Yet economic expansion, industrialization, urbanization, empire, and capitalist modernity inflected these affects with new salience. Perpetual pursuit of growth and development entailed relentless cycles of destruction, displacement, and dispossession. As new social projects destroyed traditional physical places and social spaces, people around the globe were left with memories of lost worlds of their childhoods and of previous generations. They often longed to return to places that no longer existed.

In his analysis of the iconic 1972 Hollywood film *The Godfather*, Frederic Jameson draws on Ferdinand Tönnies's distinction between community (*gemeinschaft*) and society (*gesellschaft*) to explain that the alienations and humiliations of the social relations required by bureaucratic mass society make film viewers desire images of what seem to be the simpler and more secure senses of belonging prevalent in preindustrial societies. Yet because growth and development require leaving these little worlds behind, their interpersonal ties are depicted as the parochial property of not-yet-modern ethnic "others" such as the Italian American families in *The Godfather*. Thus viewers can both vicariously identify with the preindustrial past depicted in the film and safely distance themselves from it through caricatured exaggerations of ethnic difference and through depictions of the violence and betrayals that the ethnic community succumbs to when it confronts the modern world (Jameson 1979). Scholars identify the same dynamic of longing for, and yet disavowal of, the preindustrial past in the traditions of the minstrel show (Rogin 1996), the gangster film (Warshow 2002), and western novels, films, and television programs (Denning 1998).

Scholars of memory and media argue that remembering and forgetting are not just things that people do, but also things that are done to people. Memory is institutional as well as individual. It may be perceived personally, but it is created collectively. Social practices, processes, institutions, and structures shape the frameworks that make remembering and forgetting possible. Nation-states seek legitimacy through narratives that place the state in the time of eternity as an antidote to the fragility, ephemerality, and disposability of the lives of ordinary people. Citizens of the state are asked to always remember and never forget the sacrifices and struggles of the past. The nation-state inscribes its temporality in the polity through its supervision of education, its management of celebration and commemoration, and its appeals to past glory as a rationale for present and future sacrifice (Bodnar 1996). The corporations that control commercial culture privilege the temporalities of personal growth and development, love and romance, and property accumulation over the temporalities of shared social struggles for rights, resources, and recognition. In liberal democracies, however, these personal temporalities can be especially useful to the state because they connect state demands for citizen sacrifices not to public obligations but to efforts to preserve the personal spheres of private property and family formation (Westbrook 1990).

Yet every effort to forge a unified national memory relies on strategic forms of forgetting that hide events, actions, and ideas that might threaten that desired national unity (Renan 1990; Sturken 1997). Nostalgic renderings of the British country estate and the North American frontier rely on strategic amnesia about the enclosures and the displacement of peasants and the conquest of indigenous peoples and the importation of enslaved Africans to labor on land stolen from them. Marketers encourage consumers to remember lost worlds by imbuing new commodities with markers of tradition like "old fashioned" or "home made," while at the same time creating artificial surplus value by promoting novelty and fashion. Yet top-down practices promoting forgetting are never completely successful; the past returns again and again: in politics through evocations of past eras as moral rebukes of the power hierarchies of the present (Gutman 1973), and in popular culture through the rediscovery and redeployment of outdated products prized because of their apparent obsolescence (Lévi-Strauss 1985). The social production of memory deployed to serve the needs of capital and the state always runs the risk of opening the wounds it intends to salve, of provoking oppositional counter-memories that recuperate hidden histories occluded by dominant temporal narratives (Jameson 1979; Lipsitz 1990).

39

Myth

Jonathan Bignell

Myth in media analysis refers to how words and images are systematically used to communicate cultural and political meanings, in texts such as advertisements, magazines, films, or TV programs. Studying myth uses the methodology of semiotics (Bignell 2002), which proposes that our perception and understanding of reality is constructed by words and other signs, hence my reference to media products as "texts." Semiotics originates mainly in the writings of Ferdinand de Saussure (1915/1974) and Charles Peirce (1958), for whom linguistics was the foundation for the science of how signs mean. For example, the linguistic sign "men" denotes a group of people distinct from "women." What makes the sign "woman" meaningful is the culturally contingent distinction between "man" and "woman" that might attribute different legal or religious status, or different rules of behavior, for example, to each gender. Thought and experience, indeed our very sense of our own identity, are formed in and through the systems of signs in a society. So understanding the mythologies built in the media through the articulation of those signs is the first step toward analyzing society, and changing it. There is nothing more important, and so there has been extensive work on media myths, including those shaping gender (Macdonald 1995; McCracken 1993).

Each sign has two components. One is its physical manifestation, like the pattern of sound that makes up a spoken word, or the marks that we write on paper, or the patterns of shape and color in a photograph. This signifier is accompanied by a signified or concept that the signifier calls forth, such as the signified cat attached to the three letters *c*, *a*, and *t*. In photographic media, the signifier usually has a close resemblance to its referent, the real cat in front of the camera, which is why photographic media seem to be inherently more realist than linguistic media.

Because we use signs to refer to and interpret the world, it can seem that their function is simply to denote a preexisting reality, and this is especially so with signs in the visual media. Signs picturing a Rolls-Royce or Buckingham Palace denote a particular make of car and a building in London, for example. But because Rolls-Royce cars are expensive and luxurious, the sign would also connote signifieds of wealth and luxury. Buckingham Palace would connote royalty, tradition, and power. In advertising, for example, linguistic and visual signs trigger connotations that are assembled by the text into lifestyle myths connected to products (Cook 1992; Dyer 1982; Myers 1994; Williamson 1978).

Myth links signs together so that they construct ways of thinking about people, products, places, or ideas. A magazine advertisement for shoes with a photograph of someone getting into a Rolls-Royce outside Buckingham Palace would not only denote the car and the building, but connote luxury via these signs, and build a mythology in which the shoes embody a privileged way of life. The French theorist Roland Barthes (see Culler 1983; Lavers 1982) first used semiotic ideas to analyze contemporary media in this way.

In 1957, Barthes published *Mythologies*, containing short essays about a wide variety of cultural phenomena, from wrestling matches to the film star Greta Garbo, from Citroen's latest car to a meal of steak and fries. These essays deftly decoded each topic's underlying social significance using semiotics. Barthes "read" social life, with the same close attention and critical

force hitherto used for the study of literature or art. *Mythologies* concluded with the essay "Myth Today," which theorized the huge implications of this approach. Its methods were taken up over successive decades, for example in Blonsky's (1985), Hebdige's (1988), and Masterman's (1984) collections of essays about media, which were homages to Barthes's book.

Myth is not an innocent language. Each myth has a social and political message, which always involves the distortion or forgetting of alternative messages, so that a myth appears to be simply true, rather than one of many alternatives. Barthes's most significant example in "Myth Today" was highly controversial. He writes about being at a barber's shop, looking at the cover of the French glossy magazine *Paris-Match*. The cover is a photograph of a young black soldier, who is saluting the French flag. That is what the photograph denotes, but the picture also has a mythic meaning, which is that "France is a great empire, that all her sons, without any colour discrimination, faithfully serve under her flag, and that there is no better answer to the detractors of an alleged colonialism than the zeal shown by this Negro in serving his so-called oppressors" (Barthes 1973, 116). Signs that already have a denoted meaning ("a black soldier is giving the French salute") become the basis for another "second level" meaning ("French imperial rule is right"), which appears proved by the willingness of the young black man to wear the French uniform and salute the French flag. This was controversial when Barthes wrote the essay in the 1950s, because France was brutally upholding its disintegrating empire in the African colony of Algeria, against black Algerians fighting for independence. The mythic signification of the *Paris-Match* cover argues in favor of colonial control over Algeria, without appearing to do so. The photograph makes the reader aware of the issue of French colonialism, and asks him or her to take it for granted that black soldiers should be loyal to the French flag and that colonial rule is perfectly reasonable.

For Barthes, the function of myth is to make particular concepts seem natural, because then they will not be contested. Our job as media critics is to remove the impression of naturalness by explaining how the myth is constructed, and show that it promotes one way of thinking while seeking to eliminate all the alternatives. The analysis of myth is political, and the key concept in this analysis is "ideology," which means a way of perceiving society in which some political ideas (like colonial rule) appear self-evidently natural and right. Barthes proposes that myth in contemporary Western civilization serves the ideological interests of a particular social class, the bourgeoisie, who own or control the industrial, commercial, and political institutions of the developed world. It is in the interests of this class to maintain the stability of society, in order that their power and wealth remain unchallenged. Existing power relations might sometimes be maintained by force, but it is most effective and convenient to maintain them by eliminating alternative ways of thinking. This is done by making the current system of political beliefs, the dominant ideology, seem commonsensical, and necessary.

Ideologies can be changed. It is no longer common sense, as it once was, to think that black people are inferior to whites, that women are inferior to men, or that children can be employed to do manual labor. But media mythologies still support ideologies naturalizing consumerism and acquisitiveness, economic and gender inequality, and environmental degradation. Analyzing contemporary myth in the media can be difficult because current ideologies are made to seem commonsensical. We still need the powerful semiotic methodologies embedded in media studies for half a century (Fiske and Hartley 1978; Fowler 1991; Hartley 1982; Seiter 1992; Stam, Burgoyne, and Flitterman-Lewis 1992).

40

Nation

Melissa Aronczyk

The nation is a container for ideas about identity and culture, borders and boundaries, common descent and shared history. In its deictic form—"we" the nation—it is rhetorically powerful, alluding to a sense of collective values and goals. When hyphenated to the state, it takes on a formal connotation, bringing to mind government infrastructure and economy. Nation has a normative dimension: we all "ought" to belong to one, or at least have roots in one; and these origins are seen to define us—and to define who does not belong.

In its cognate form—nationalism—it is used by turns in a positive sense, such as in the context of claims for autonomy and self-determination; and in a negative sense, as a label for antagonistic behaviors and exclusionary practices. The distinction is sometimes a matter of standpoint: "we" are patriotic while "they" are nationalist. Regardless, the nation is still regularly used as a metaphor for home, and for this reason it occupies a powerful place in our social imaginary.

Contemporary media studies has an ambivalent relationship with the idea of nation. Many have diagnosed it as being in ill health, pointing to symptoms of its demise in an era of global media, mobility, and migration (Appadurai 1990; Couldry 2012; Morley 2000). Work in this vein attends to the ways media processes and content now circulate unbound from national frameworks. This perspective is heightened by the seeming placelessness and anonymity of the Internet and social media platforms. Such vastly expanded potential for communication and connectivity across the limits of the nation prompts visions of a cosmopolitan mind-set, according to which we are citizens of the world and not beholden to the standards or regulations of any given nation (Beck 2013).

Others look instead to the ways the nation continues to matter in a transnational media landscape. For example, Terry Flew and Silvio Waisbord (2015, 622) argue for the relevance of national media systems in a "convergent media order." Not only do media corporations tend to be less transnational than corporations in other industries, they explain, but many local audiences (including national audiences) still strongly prefer locally produced content over global formats (Straubhaar 2007). Another example is found in the ways that media coverage of global events—from financial crises to health pandemics—reflects national frameworks of reference and appeals to national audiences (Beck 2013; Rantanen 2012). It is not just that national media systems design content to appeal to national audiences; media regulation and policy are developed and enforced in national contexts. "Global media production networks continue to rely upon a range of enabling support structures provided by nation-states that range from communications infrastructure and tax incentives to labor laws and the policing of copyright" (Flew and Waisbord 2015, 628).

Too often, such debates pit the national against the global, as if one had to win out over the other. The key, rather, is to see the national and the global as mutually reinforcing concepts that overlap in everyday media practices. Take, for instance, the recent explosion of "K-pop" music and "K-drama" TV shows outside Asia. This cultural content manifests particular ideas of Korea and Koreans even as it is transformed through its global circulation (Ju and Lee 2015). K-media is promoted as part of the country's distinct national identity by the South Korean government, but it is influenced and re-created by fans outside Korea at global festivals like KCON, held annually in places like California and Abu Dhabi (Ofek, Kim, and Norris 2015).

To study a phenomenon like the nation in the context of media studies, we can look at the ways that the idea of nation functions as a *resource*: that is, as a style of talking and thinking and acting that informs how people understand the world, even—or perhaps especially—in local, transnational, or global contexts. This is what Craig Calhoun (1997) means when he refers to the nation as a "discursive formation," or what Rogers Brubaker and Frederick Cooper (2000) mean when they call the nation a "category of practice." The nation is not a thing but a set of contingent and ongoing processes that actors mobilize for diverse purposes in a range of contexts.

Some work adopts this perspective by focusing on how the nation is "performed" (Taylor 1997), "narrated" (Bhabha 1990), "visualized" (Tawil-Souri 2011), or "invented" (Hobsbawm and Ranger 1992) in different media texts, from literature to reality television to Internet domain names (Szulc 2015). Marie Sarita Gaytán (2014) explores, for example, how early twentieth-century *co-media ranchera* folk songs and the American press constructed a stereotypical version of Mexican identity that celebrates machismo and tequila drinking. Others have sought to document how devices like currency, maps, and passports (Anderson 1991); sites like museums, monuments, and architectural structures (Aronczyk and Brady 2015); and events like national commemorations, song contests, and sports competitions all work as media to produce or legitimate the nation (Baker 2008).

This does not mean, of course, that these national images are uncontested. Media texts that claim to represent the nation can be ideologically driven, tightly controlled, or even violent spectacles (e.g., Apter 1999; Taylor 1997) designed to "de-nationalize" populations that do not seem to fit into the dominant image. If such discourses are meant to stake claims about what a given nation's values and populations should look like, they can also ignite debate, resistance, or counternarratives about what a given nation "is" and how it should be represented. Counterhegemonic narratives invoking the idea of nation are also used to emphasize cultural allegiances that function independently of territory, such as black nationalism or queer nationalism (Berlant and Freeman 1994).

One of the paradoxes of globalization is that it produces the desire for cultural difference, often expressed in national terms. This is true not only for citizens but also for consumers. Consider, for example, the ways in which nations compete for global tourists and investors by developing media campaigns that promote their distinctive national culture and heritage (Aronczyk 2013), or how commodities like wine and watches are marketed to consumers all over the world via national symbols (Bandelj and Wherry 2011). Even if those products don't actually originate in the countries being invoked, national origin is a powerful package to generate symbolic and economic value.

In a highly influential definition, Benedict Anderson (1991) calls the nation an "imagined community." "It is imagined because the members of even the smallest nation will never know most of their fellow-members, meet them, or even hear of them, yet in the minds of each lives the image of their communion" (6).

Seeing the nation as an "imagined" community does not mean that it's all in our heads. More than merely about the imagined dimension of community formation, these works balance subjective or ideational understandings of nation with material factors. Scholars working in this vein observe the nation both in terms of the claims made in its name (cultural, political, economic) and in terms of the ways these claims are institutionalized and stabilized.

41

Network
Marina Levina

At its most descriptive, the network is defined as a singular and hierarchical entity, a radio or television network responsible for transmitting messages to the audience. Increasingly, however, the term "network" has become an analytical tool embedded in global culture and information technologies, and their multitudes of connections, messages, and topographies. For instance, there is "the terrorist network," a seemingly concrete entity that proves to be a hard-to-define enemy; "a social network," a mediated forum for sharing personal information and cat videos; and finally "network" as a way of life and a cultural norm, a connectivity in perpetuity (Levina and Kien 2010). This network is decidedly not hierarchical, but is not outside of relations and systems of power (Levina 2014). In fact, these relations are probably the best way to understand what it means to live in an always-mediated network environment made possible by media and information technologies. The network is best understood as a topography that organizes everyday experiences in terms of sociality and relationality.

In his influential work, Manuel Castells attributed the rise of the network society, and, with it, a new system of power relations, to the emergence of global capital and information technology in the mid- to late twentieth century. Therefore the network was not a wholly revolutionary force, created in opposition to existing power structures, but rather an inevitable consequence of the evolution of global capitalism, or informationalism (Castells 1996). Informationalism can be best understood as a new mode of capitalist development. Whereas industrialization was oriented toward maximizing output, or production of goods, informationalism is oriented toward technological development, or distribution of information. Capitalism under informationalism has been characterized by flexibility, decentralization, individualization, and diversification. Whereas maximizing the output of an assembly line required a hierarchical and rigid structure to manage the productivity of every element, technological development and the pursuit of information required a decentralized network system (Castells 1996). In terms of topographies, this is a transition from Detroit to Silicon Valley, from a car factory to Google offices, and from organized labor to flexible work. The last topography is an especially important one, as the network is a particularly antiunion force. The network economy necessitates constant input of information, and thus a flexible work environment and flexible hours. This results in the production of "free labor"—labor essential to production and distribution of information in digital economy (Terranova 2004). Because of its flexibility, this labor is highly individualized, and therefore limited in communal spaces that often promote labor organizing and economic change. If we were required to do our online activity and work in a large factory setting, we would long question the value of hours so spent.

Some contend that due to its decentralization the network is inherently democratic. This is an argument often made in Silicon Valley—the idea that social media networks will somehow liberate their users from the hierarchy. For example, during the Arab Spring, protesters in countries where traditional media are heavily policed used Twitter to organize revolutions. In the West, the press often referred to the Arab Spring as the Twitter Revolution, a problematic term in part because it

ascribes political changes to the technology, rather than to those who paid for these changes with their blood. In this equivalency, the network is treated as an immaterial entity—a technological enterprise that erases the bleeding bodies. In order to inject blood back into the network, it is essential to understand that the network is not outside of power, but rather that power is what gives the network its body.

As a nonlinear power relation that operates through decentralized relations of sociability, network power functions through regulations of standards as opposed to the enforcement of a sovereign will. This does not mean that network power is democratic—although it can definitely be used for democratic means—but rather that it is a diffuse system of control and regulation operating through a multitude of nodes (Grewal 2008). Therefore control is exercised in the network not through a linear exercise of deterministic power structures, but rather as constitutive and social processes of network power. Network power is always relational, always circumstantial, and always mutable. It encourages relations of sociability in order to facilitate expansion. In other words, the network seeks not to exclude, but rather, through openness, to incorporate other systems into the network. The power of the network lies in its continuous and constant growth and openness to divergence and difference. This does not make the exercises of power benign; indeed network power works through incorporation of dividend elements. Nothing can or should be outside of the network (Galloway and Thacker 2007; Hardt and Negri 2000; Terranova 2004). This understanding of power moves us away from a traditional approach to power as something that can be possessed, and toward an understanding of power as a relational practice that ought to be exercised in order to further the goals of the collective. For example, when we share our personal data online, we do so not because we are compelled by someone or something, but rather because by doing so we further some common goal, be it medical research, political activism, or affective circulation of cats and cuteness (J. Dean 2010; Levina 2010). This does not make the practices of sharing inherently democratic inasmuch as they are always guided by principles of global capitalism, informationalism, and free labor described above.

This argument builds on the *actor-network* theory, which contends that power is not a possession, but rather a performance. The amount of power exercised therefore varies according to how many actors enter into the network (Kien 2009; Latour 1984). To move a token—be it an idea or a piece of information—through a network requires a multitude of human and nonhuman actors, each of whom translates the token into his or her own language in order to progress it through the network. To make this concrete, think of how *patriotism* became a powerful token in the United States after 9/11. Various individual and institutional actors, including the news media, advertising, and lawmakers, used patriotism as a justification for car buying, wiretapping, or even war. We can agree or disagree with these contradictory justifications, but it is undisputed that patriotism became a powerful token not simply because one group had the power to make it so, but precisely because so many different actors translated the token to mean so many different things. Patriotism became a totalitarian idea; to criticize any of the justifications provided was to position oneself as the enemy of the very essence of the network that is the United States. Tokens, as pieces of information and ideas, grant the network materiality; it is through tracing them through the network that we can see how power acts on the bodies of its human and nonhuman actors.

This means that information flows in the network are not inconsequential; they alter topologies, relationships, and identities. An identity constituted by information is an identity in flux. It lacks a fixed meaning, and therefore it can always be changed and altered. More importantly, it can be understood only in the context of other information, and therefore, in the network, we can understand ourselves only in terms of relationships to others. To be a part of the network is to embrace a network identity, or network subjectivity, which constructs the self as a source of a constant stream of information to be shared with others. The self becomes a node in the network as it parcels through the cyberspace bits of information. In other words, in the network not only are you your information, but also your perceived value or worth is determined by how much of that information is shared with others. Measured through "likes" on Facebook, political petitions signed on Change.org, or the number of steps logged through Fitbit, bodies in the network are in the constant business of generating and sharing information. Without that information, the network would cease to exist. In this way, we are the network.

Our bodies, however, are much more than the data they generate. Any particular information-based snapshot will be inherently incomplete, and therefore contradictory. We are large; we contain multitudes. The network in its many incarnations attempts to contain the entirety of our politics, our bodies, and our selves. The fact that it fails is the only thing that stops it from becoming an absolutely totalitarian force. Therefore, neither is network a benign description, nor is it necessarily a force for good. It is a topography that parcels out bodies into bits of information easily moved, shared, and modulated. It is total; it contains everything. The most important of which are the cat videos.

42

New Media
Lisa Gitelman

The phrase "new media" is an element of elite discourse; it is used more often by professors than by anyone else. Taking the titles of books published in English as a rough way to estimate usage, it would seem that new media as such first became a concern among educators in the 1960s. So new media arrived in something of the same fashion as "new math," as a result of anxieties about American competitiveness that accompanied technological advances amid the Cold War. (The new media in question then were instructional media, like educational broadcasting, filmstrips, transparencies, and language labs.) Anxiety lingers as part of the "new media" formulation in interesting ways, but this history was eventually superseded and forgotten, as the phrase came to refer more certainly in the 1990s to computers, digital networks, and associated technologies. This new usage is evidenced by a flood of publications, which has included such classics as Jay David Bolter and Richard Grusin's *Remediation: Understanding New Media* (1999) and Lev Manovich's *The Language of New Media* (2001). Books like these seek to understand just what is so new about the new media they address. They are classics because scholars and students still learn from them, but the media that seemed so new at the turn of the new century are of course old—or at least older—by now. Newness is a matter of perspective and a moving target.

Much of the utility of the phrase "new media" inheres in its lack of specificity. To study new media today generally means to study the contemporary moment, paying particular attention to the sociotechnical conditions of networked communication. Related designations abound—like "cyberculture," "hypertext," "the network society," "emergent media"—yet have had less staying power as digital technologies and the study of digital technologies have coevolved over recent years. The perennial newness of new media seems appropriate somehow and in keeping with the temporalities of digital media, especially the frenzied pace of network growth, technological innovation, and updates. But the onrush of technological change and the forever-arriving horizon of obsolescence have also been structured partially according to anxieties about a sense of ending or of limitation, such as in terms of processing speeds and code longevity: Moore's Law (1965) predicts an exponential increase in processing speeds that many worry can't or won't continue for much longer, while the coming of the year 2000 raised concerns that computer systems would fail because of the way programmers had rendered dates. A number of observers have also noted that digital media effectively mean the end of media history, since "everything" will soon come in ones and zeros, bits and bytes, and so all media will be unified as one medium (Kittler 1999, 1–2; Lunenfeld 1999, 7).

"New media" is a tag for present-mindedness, then, but one that calls as much attention to time—to newness and oldness—as it does to today's media system and its exceptionalism. One result has been increasing attention to "when old technologies were new," as Carolyn Marvin so aptly put it (Marvin 1988). Another result has been increased attention to what Raymond Williams identified as "residual" cultural forms (Acland 2007), as well as to the ways that new media can eventually become habitual, transparent, intuitive, unexceptional, and thereby difficult to see. The studies of old media and new are thus productively mutual, overlapping, and entangled. Like sepia-filtered Instagrams, the arrow of media history points both ways.

43

Ordinary
Graeme Turner

For those working in media studies today, the word "ordinary" is not quite as ordinary as it once was. Over the past decade and a half it has become a site of a great deal of discussion, debate, and examination. This is largely in response to the manner in which television has integrated both the label and the idea of the ordinary into the designing and marketing of their formats, and the manner in which digital and social media have established themselves as technologies with the capacity to empower the ordinary media consumer.

Toward the end of the 1990s, it became widely noticed that ordinary people—that is, people not drawn from the world of the media or entertainment—had begun to be more visible in the media (Turner 2010). Where previously they may have been visible as guests or audience members for talk shows, say, or as *vox pops* in news bulletins, ordinary people had now become fundamental components of new prime-time entertainment formats on television. The UK series *Airport* (1996) started out as a documentary before morphing into a "docusoap" when a number of its continuing characters developed followings as minor celebrities. The Dutch reality TV format of *Big Brother* was launched in the Netherlands in 1997 and was widely adapted around the globe over the early 2000s. What became the widely dispersed genre of reality TV was notable for casting participants without any background in the media or entertainment industries; the format was based on the premise that television could capture, unmediated and in full, the realities of ordinary people's everyday lives. In the case of *Big Brother*, this meant closed-circuit multicamera monitoring of every moment; although this was edited down into a narrative package for its time slot on terrestrial networks, eventually the format incorporated live, twenty-four-hour online streaming from the *Big Brother* house. The everyday lives of ordinary people thus became available to viewers as entertainment, and highly desirable as raw material for television formats around the world.

As the iterations of the format proliferated, the definition of the ordinary broadened under the pressure to find participants most likely to engage and retain an audience. There is little that is ordinary about Kim Kardashian or the cast of *Jersey Shore*, of course, and so there was considerable debate about just how "ordinary" most of the participants of reality TV actually were. Critics also asked how they could be said to be living "ordinary" lives when their every move was being captured and beamed out to mass media audiences. As many noted at the time, this was still television, not everyday life—no matter how the producers tried to spin it. Furthermore, it became clear that many of the ordinary participants had pursued their opportunity in the hope of accessing a media career or a period of celebrity. Far from being definitive, and despite its instrumental role in their securing this opportunity, their ordinariness was precisely the condition they sought to escape.

The recent expansion in the reach of celebrity, and of the publicity and promotions industries that enable it, predates reality TV, although not by much. But celebrity has long been constituted in relation to the twin poles of the ordinary and the extraordinary, and so it is not at all surprising that it was implicated in the development of reality TV (Turner 2014). Once its potential was recognized, television turned reality TV into a production line that not only invented formats and produced programs, but also created its own celebrities. The ordinary people who became reality TV celebrities cost the production companies very little, they were easily commodified and harnessed to the interests of the producers, and they were easily superseded by the participants in the next series or the next popular format.

At around the same time, another media opportunity opened up for ordinary people—they could generate their own content online, and in particular, they could create their own personal digital presence or "brand" (Banet-Weiser 2012), through blogs, videos, webcam feeds, and micro-celebrity sites gathering followers through a hybrid array of connective media such as Facebook, Twitter, and Instagram. Once an online presence was established, it was relatively easy to exploit the interface between social media and the mass media to generate wider visibility. The YouTube celebrity is the classic example of this, their content so often marked as ordinary by the banality of the site of its production—the teenager's bedroom, for instance—rather than by the ordinariness of their performance or persona (many of them were far from ordinary performers!). Again, the great irony is that, while the ordinary was an attribute of the location being used, the point of the exercise for that ordinary person was to transcend the category by making full use of the affordances of the digital environment.

This was a period when participatory digital media were often described as democratizing because of their accessibility and the ease of copying and sharing, and because they could be operated outside the control of the gatekeepers of the traditional mass media (Jenkins 2006). Power, it was said, had been reclaimed from the possession of the major media corporations by "the people formerly known as the audience," ordinary people (Rosen 2006). Sadly, that optimism has not proven justified, in that much of the media's power has remained in the same hands. Furthermore, while ordinary people may have been empowered by their increased visibility and by the scale of their participation in the new media landscape, they were also sources of unpaid labor for the media industries (Andrejevic 2013b). As Sarah Banet-Weiser (2012) puts it, participatory media manage to simultaneously empower and exploit their users.

Nick Couldry (2003) has described the social role of the media through what he calls the "myth of the media center": the distinction between the media world, which is seen as the center of the social, and the mundane nonmedia world in which the rest of us live. The category of the ordinary, as it appears in media studies today, could almost be defined as the place from which the attempt to migrate across that division, and to enter into the space of the media center, originates. Consequently, the meaning of the ordinary in these contexts has begun to mutate. While it may still reference a kind of authenticity, audiences are increasingly skeptical about its ultimate validity. To watch reality TV, or to follow a particular online persona, is to witness the performance of a category of persona rather than an unmediated capturing of that person's everyday life. In many instances, the logic of the formats ensures a high level of performativity as participants compete for the attention and loyalty of an imagined audience. Indeed, as a number of writers have noted (Roscoe 2001), one of the attractions of watching *Big Brother* lies in detecting moments when that motivated performance of ordinariness cracks, to reveal insights into the everyday ordinariness the performance was designed to mask.

The commercial exploitation of the ordinary is part of a key tendency in television over this period: that is, a tendency toward diminishing the gap between television and the social. The ordinary lives of ordinary people are, as it were, the last frontier for the media to colonize. Digital media have certainly achieved that from within, not only by occupying people's habits of consumption but also by providing them with modes of expression and sociality that could be seamlessly integrated into the practices of ordinary living. As a result, even these practices, part of the stuff of our ordinary lives, have been unwittingly outsourced to media corporations. The outcomes of that transaction are varied, even contradictory: on the one hand, the contribution of commodifiable personal data and unpaid labor to the corporations and, on the other, the delivery of individualized media consumption and participation to the consumer. While the consequences of the changing provenance of the category of the ordinary across the media continue to be described by many in terms of empowerment and democratization, the actual consequences have turned out to be far more politically ambivalent than that.

44

Othering

Angharad N. Valdivia

Othering is a strategy that reinforces the mainstream by differentiating individuals and groups and relegating them to the margins according to a range of socially constructed categories. Othering occurs via a wide range of practices from language differentiation to geographical assignation, native/nonnative status (despite legal citizenship), and photographic and filmic techniques that foreground and center some characters while backgrounding and obscuring others. As a keyword, othering is articulated to concepts such as marginalization, bordering, iconization, ethnicity, ghettoization, globalization, and social difference, while symbolic annihilation, glass ceiling, spiral of silence, and in-group out-group are all findings within media studies that further document ongoing processes of othering.

Media studies scholars utilize the concept to discuss topics ranging from race and ethnic to gender and sexuality studies. While most research focuses on representation, othering also occurs in the production of media and in the construction of media audiences. One could categorize the production of ethnic media simultaneously as a site of ethnic pride as well as a form of othering, as most ethnic media are created as a response to the mainstream marginalizing or erasing ethnic populations as well as ethnic media producers whose objectivity is questioned within the mainstream. At a more basic level, the category "ethnic" is a form of differentiating in-group and out-group within any given population, and thus its very uttering performs othering. Within Latina/o studies, Chávez (2015) expands Irvine and Gal's (2009) theorization of othering populations according to language to study the eternal foreigner status of US Latina/os, who are permanently othered within popular discourse despite preceding the presence of Anglos in the national territory (Valdivia 2010). US television practitioners regularly frame Latina/os as Spanish-speaking despite statistical evidence to the contrary. This practice underserves Latina/os and undercuts profit potential for mainstream media. US-born Latina/o youth reject this form of ghettoization as they wish to be part of the mainstream. Latina/o reporters are either suspected of compromising objectivity because of their ethnicity within the mainstream press or relegated to working in the ethnic press—a classic form of othering. Similar findings apply to African Americans, Asian Americans, and, with a vengeance, Native Americans and the media. Finally, othering also occurs in relation to audiences. Audiences perceived as marginal are either ignored or underserved through less or hard-to-reach content. Furthermore, research on audiences seldom includes marginalized people in the sample.

Othering also applies to gender and sexuality studies. The second wave women's movement included the creation of *Ms.* magazine in 1972, representing a liberal feminist effort to have a presence within a mainstream that generally othered women's issues and news. Feminist media, however, has not been impervious to othering. Women of color, women of the Global South, queer women, transwomen, differently abled women, and so on are underrepresented in media jobs, in images, and as desired audiences, and also have been understudied and undertheorized within feminist media studies. Conferences, special journal issues, and edited collections seek to interrupt this process of othering. Whereas postcolonial theory has been highly influential in feminist media studies, the academy as a site of employment of postcolonial female scholars has been less receptive.

Posting social movements—as in postfeminism and postracism—is another form of othering. Neoliberal ideology replaces their political thrust in favor of individualist and market/consumer subjectivities. Postfeminism others feminism as "extreme, difficult, and unpleasant" (Tasker and Negra 2007). Similarly postracism (Mukherjee 2015) replaces the discussion of racial inequality with rational measures that foreground the interests of neoliberal capitalism and render racial equality once more to the margins—othered. In sum, othering reinforces power oppression and discrimination.

Importantly, the field of media studies is also imbricated in othering through its disciplinary organizations, categories of study, and journals of note. For example, social science approaches other humanistic ones by relegating them to the margins, and the lack of attention to "othered" areas in prestigious venues like the *Journal of Communication* has necessitated the creation of journals such as *Feminist Media Studies* to circulate marginalized research.

45

Personalization

Joseph Turow

Personalization is a term used by contemporary media practitioners to denote the emerging process by which a media organization tailors the content an individual receives based on attributes the organization believes it knows about the individual. Although the idea of personalization in performance goes far back in time, the notion of personalization as a practical activity in media industries is relatively new. Currently practiced most commonly in advertising, personalization is also showing up in other genres of media content, including music services and video games.

Interpersonal or handicraft performance often involves personalization. A storyteller's selection of a narrative and the nuances of recounting typically reflect the speaker's beliefs about the listener. An artist creating material for a patron is likely to choose the topic and perhaps even the form based on a perception of the patron's interests. The sale of products and services also has traditionally involved personalized elements. Records dating to biblical times show that merchants have adjusted the choice of merchandise, its price, and even the location for completing the sale based on an understanding of the particular shopper.

New technologies tied to steam or electrical power that evolved from the nineteenth century through much of the twentieth tilted aspects of public communication in a decidedly nonpersonalized direction. Tied to large industries, media of those decades had the capability to reach more people, and more people within shorter periods of time, than any storytelling platforms in history. The term academics used to describe these activities—mass communication—evoked huge audiences of disconnected, faceless individuals. Charles R. Wright's (1959) model of the process reflected the consensus that when "feedback" takes place in mass communication, it involves nothing like the real-time adjustments inherent in one-to-one or even group communication.

Developments during the 1970s and 1980s began to challenge the view that dominant public-communication technologies reached mainly broad audiences. The period saw the US Federal Communications Commission allocate many additional broadcast television frequencies (on the UHF band), the privatization of broadcasting in many parts of Europe and the concurrent multiplication of radio and TV outlets, the spread of cable and satellite television, and the popularity of the video cassette recorder. The 1990s and 2000s saw an even greater multiplication of platforms and channels. Much of that growth came from the diffusion of the desktop and laptop computer to the home and its connection to the Internet (especially email and the World Wide Web). The late 2000s and 2010s witnessed the spread of mobile "smartphones" and tablets in many countries. These technologies further extended people's abilities to access and interact with (and so provide immediate feedback to) an increasingly broad gamut of entertainment, news, and information landscape.

The population's interactions with new media forms upended the verities held by many media content distributors (that is, "publishers") about the best ways to reach audiences and make money from them. One change was that so much material on the web was "free"; it could be accessed with no direct cost to the audience member. An upshot was that many traditional ("legacy") media firms relying on individual purchases or subscriptions saw their audience revenues plummet. The recording, newspaper, and magazine industries were particularly hard hit. A related challenge for publishers lay with changing inclinations of advertisers. They have historically supported many media firms by buying time and space around collections of news, entertainment, and information in order to reach potential customers. Netscape's 1994 creation of the browser cookie began a profound change in advertisers' approaches. The cookie ignited a tracking industry that claimed to be able to follow individuals within and across sites—and, by 2015, even across devices—to profile them and send them messages tied to those profiles. The traditional way was to contract with a particular publisher to reach all (or sometimes part) of its audience. The new way is to pay ad networks or ad exchanges to reach the "right" individuals wherever they are, at any of thousands of publishers they visit on the web ("online") or on apps (Turow 2012). *Real-time* ad exchanges emerged by 2015 as the hot direction in media buying. A marketer can bid to reach known individuals, or individuals with known characteristics, at the very moment that they click onto a web page, begin to view a video, walk by a particular store with their phones, or engage in another activity the sponsor finds relevant (Turow forthcoming).

All these developments encourage publishers and advertisers to see profiling and the personalization based on it as crucial to their future. Publishers and marketers are approaching the activity at different speeds. At present, publishers primarily see their role as offering up highly described people to marketers interested in individuals with specific characteristics—for example, women of a certain income with preschool children. To get even more specific with the profiles, marketers often bring their own data about individual audience members to find those same people among the publisher's audience members—or to find statistical lookalikes of those people. For example, a magazine for women with children might help a diaper manufacturer to specifically reach upscale young mothers entering its site or app who have also visited the diaper firm's website or app—or who have the same characteristics of those mothers as determined by combining both the publisher's and marketer's data.

Marketers increasingly tailor their online and app messages based on the profiles of the individuals they are reaching. A common type of personalization involves sending a message to a person's phone based on her specific location and the coupons in her phone. Much of the tailored activities at this point involve creating ads for audience groupings—young female drivers in the Midwest with young children, for example, or unmarried male drivers in the Southeast. This type of work involves segmentation rather than personalization, or what some call one-to-one marketing. Janrain, a target marketing firm, argued in a 2015 report that segmentation is actually a weak form of personalization. It said the stronger form, "truly one-to-one marketing," is "perhaps the most difficult identity-driven marketing tactic to put into practice." Nevertheless, Janrain (2015, 5) noted, "a majority of marketers believed [in a 2014 survey] that personalization would become the most important capability for their teams in coming years." That would happen by combining high-octane predictive analytics (often called "big data") with mass-customization software that could turn out eloquent messages tuned to any set of characteristics.

Publisher personalization already takes place on several music streaming services (for example, Pandora and Spotify) that present different tracks to people based on the services' understanding of their musical interests; on video games, which present different adventure sequences to individuals based on their particular decisions within the stories; and on retailer sites (e.g., Amazon, Alex and Ani) that show different products based on analyses of shoppers' web movements, previous buying history, and even location in a physical store (see Turow forthcoming). Long-form television programming (for example, news and entertainment series) have so far not gotten involved in personalization. That may be largely because of the difficulty of tailoring large bodies of often-changing content in response to continually updated profiles of millions of audience members. The feat is possible. Comcast-owned Visible World is one company that has the technology to do it, but executives believe the revenue to be gained from carrying it out so far doesn't justify the high cost (Turow 2012). Declining processing costs with rising processor speeds may one day change their outlook. A likely personalization step in the meantime will be for video providers to tailor programming guides based on what the provider of multiple programming channels—or multiple video streams—knows about particular individuals and households.

Many economic and technological considerations suggest that personalization will become an increasingly important element of media presentations in the decades to come. Discourse within the trade indicates marketers and publishers have strong competitive interests in seeing the number of data points marketers gather or purchase about customers grow (Turow forthcoming). Concurrently, marketers have strong competitive interests in building technologies that can transform those data points into sophisticated and cost-effective stories tailored to attract specific types of people and even specific individuals. Inevitably, publishers will accelerate their march to personalization, as well. They will do it to attract the very individuals their sponsors want to persuade. Perhaps they will even work with those sponsors to create programming as well as commercial messages to do that.

There are few writings on what it means for a society when a dominant mode of industrialized public media is personalized communication. Addressing the subject requires exploring the history, sociology, and political economy of media industries to understand the system, chart its industrial logic, and map its possible trajectory. The investigation also requires confronting issues of surveillance, privacy, and social inequality. "Not all customers are created equal," Janrain's report on personalization in marketing asserts. The statement may well be an epigram—and rationale—for moving forward critical media research on this key topic.

46

Play

Matthew Thomas Payne

Play is doing; play is being. Play is orderly, procedural, and rule-bound; play is disruptive, anarchic, and rebellious. Rules provide a context for playful action (Sigart 2014), and yet, rules can never predict what players will do. Play is as precocious as it is precarious; it can spring into life one instant, only to be dashed to pieces in the next. Play's experiential complexity underscores the need for critical media scholars to attend to media culture as lived, meaning-making acts and not simply as discrete texts or by-products of larger industrial structures.

Play is a valuable keyword for media studies both because it underscores that making sense of popular media requires audiences to participate in meaning-making processes (i.e., they have to play media makers' sometimes proverbial, sometimes literal games), and because it emphasizes that these interpretive practices have political stakes and consequences when audiences break from producers' expectations. This might seem like a stretch. Play, after all, isn't typically associated with scholarly inquiry or with worldly ramifications. Rather, the abandonment and imagination that give rise to states of play typically connote an escape from careful reflection or issues of social import. Play remains an underrecognized force in media studies because it is an oft-ignored element of media generally.

Play's etymological derivation from the Old English *plegan* or *plegian*, meaning "to exercise" or "brisk movement or activity" (*Oxford English Dictionary*), points to its root conceptualization as an act. Game studies has been quick to emphasize play's usefulness in assessing the significance of goal-oriented actions in digital and analog games, with Alexander Galloway (2006, 2) going so far as to identify "actions" as being "word one for video game theory." But while play's insights are particularly salient to game studies, critical media scholars should likewise consider play's role in animating non-game texts, be it the parodic intertextuality that gives "satire TV" (Gray, Jones, and Thompson 2009) its political bite, or the complex canon building of the Marvel Cinematic Universe that unites characters and storylines across film, TV, and comics. Thinking seriously about play highlights how interacting with media demands audiences engage in boundary exploration and rule testing, and how acts of media play can lead to personal transformation.

Because play is the freedom of movement within boundaries, play theorists have long attempted to define its relationship to and differentiation against non-play spaces and practices. Johan Huizinga, one of the first scholars to make a case for the civilizing effects of organized play on Western culture, noted how play unfolds in specific spaces with specific rules. One of the "play-grounds" he enumerates—alongside the tennis court, card table, stage, and screen—is that of the "magic circle," a social membrane that envelopes those engaged in a playful activity (1955, 10). Although others have since refined Huizinga's original conceptualization, the magic circle remains a bedrock concept because it captures both spatially if not experientially the ineffable sensation of playing between realms and how social groups utilize play to advance their agendas. The cultural politics of play suffuse everyday media: the display of military might of a Blue Angels flyover before a televised football game; the techno-utopian positivism of Walt Disney's Tomorrowland exhibit

(Telotte 2004); the hypermasculinity of arcade games (Kocurek 2015).

Building on Huizinga's work, Roger Caillois (2001) sought to better define play's variability by creating a typology of game modes, and by proposing a play spectrum that ranges from highly regulated interactions such as chess (ludus) to open-ended activities that might include children playing with blocks or spinning around until they fall down (paidia). While such labels are useful for categorization, play is unrelentingly fuzzy. To wit, media firms' utilization of alternative reality games—activities that integrate imaginary worlds and characters into real-world spaces—strategically exploit play's porous boundaries for promotional purposes. Moreover, because play unfolds in real-world spaces, magic circles are ready-made targets for cheaters and spoilsports (Consalvo 2007). Indeed, children regularly reify hegemonic social norms (e.g., class, gender, sexuality) through "innocent" games of "cowboys and Indians" or "playing house," and players challenge the magic circle's mystical aura by altering its seemingly sacrosanct rules of play.

The magic circle's vulnerability to ne'er-do-wells illustrates that play is not simply about borders, but is likewise about communities of play. Anthropologist Victor Turner's (1982) emphasis on the liminality of rituals, where participants are caught in identity spaces "betwixt and between" and where those from different backgrounds can access a common experience, stresses the communal value of media rituals. The spectrum of playful engagement that makes media sites of celebration and derision—from affirming cosplay to social media trolling—begs additional questions about the rules that govern how media should be played.

Despite play's definitional challenges, we can say with certainty that there is no media culture without play. Mediated play is predicated on interacting with rules—be they explicit or implicit in nature. Game studies is again instructive for its attention to understanding how the cultural industries' offerings contain mechanics and rule-based prompts that solicit a range of intertextual play practices.

Reframing media practice as media play (and not simply as a discrete, empirical happening) injects additional agency into the analyst's interpretive frame while simultaneously highlighting how the media object has been engineered with active audiences in mind. Indeed, contemporary media increasingly function as magic circle generators that are crafted with the playful user in mind at textual and extratextual levels. Consider, for example, the narrative puzzles featured in TV dramas like *Lost* that invite crowdsourced solutions (Mittell 2015), how transmedia storytelling leaps platforms in *The Matrix* (Jenkins 2006), or how the aural intimacy of an investigative podcast like *Serial* can turn legions of listeners onto new forms of radio "soundwork" (Hilmes 2013). Play is a central part of media's extratextual design strategies, too, be it as a programming block's televisual flow, or the paratextual elements of an advertising campaign (Gray 2010).

Play is potentially transformative boundary exploration that allows players to examine issues that might, in another context, seem immutably fixed. In play, media users get to try things on: they change avatars in games; toy with narrative strategies and representational tropes in fan fiction; and time shift viewing experiences with DVRs. But to engender personal change, play requires a leap of faith; it demands that players adopt what philosopher Bernard Suits (2005) calls a "lusory attitude." The value of the lusory attitude for critical analysis is that we can learn about ourselves and our media when we open ourselves up to the vulnerability of play; by risking failure in games or rejection by peers in a fan forum, we stand to learn and grow through playful experimentation.

Brian Sutton-Smith (1997), the leading play scholar of the twentieth century, argues against any universal definition due to play's varying manifestations and how disciplines have grappled with its resolute ambiguity. Sutton-Smith reminds us that any attempt to linguistically fix a ludic experience is not the same thing as that experience. Play is thus not only a highly individuated phenomenon; it is also—in some real way—beyond language. Textuality's rigid and permeable definitional boundaries, the fixed and shifting rules of play, and the varying investments of community and of self in media culture are useful reminders that human play is a historically specific and contextual event. And because play is in a perpetual state of emerging and vanishing, it is a generative term for thinking about media's critical potentiality as something that reflects existing mores and values, and as something that holds out promise for possible futures that might yet be imagined.

47

Policy

Jennifer Holt

Media policy is about power—the power to establish boundaries, norms, and standards for mass-mediated visual culture; the power to decide which perspectives will be informing social discourses, debates, news, and entertainment; and the power to police the expression, ownership, and distribution of that content. In other words, policy is in many ways about the structural power to determine "who can say what, in what form, to whom" (Garnham 2000, 4). Policy is political and is often guided by dominant ideologies regarding technology, culture, and national identity. It is what dictates the legal parameters for the structure, content, and dissemination of television, radio, and increasingly streaming digital media.

In the United States, the origins of contemporary media policy can be traced back to the Progressive Era, when administrative agencies and trust-busting were on the rise, and "the world of 'policy' came to be defined by a search for a kind of government-by-expertise that rested on neutral, objective, and in some sense scientific principles" (Streeter 2013, 490). Antitrust policy was formally instituted by the late nineteenth/early twentieth century after the Sherman Act was passed in 1890. This allowed for a form of regulation and control over industry structure, and a legal remedy (albeit underutilized) for undue concentration and anticompetitive behavior. While there is a deep historical investment in policy and the policy-making process as "neutral," policy is undeniably politicized at every stage (see Freedman

2008) despite a veneer of "objectivity" and reliance on "expertise." Steve Classen (2004) argues that the traditional valorization of legal authority and "precise, official knowledges" as the guarantors of truth in policy making has served to deny and disaggregate fundamental contexts, voices, and concerns. And as Sandra Braman (2004, 154) has explained, even the way a policy issue is identified and categorized is political "because it determines who participates in decision-making, the rhetorical frames and operational definitions applied, the analytical techniques and modes of argument used, and the resources—and goals—considered pertinent."

Policy has been described in the US context as "the set of practices by which government intervention on behalf of private corporations is reconciled with the liberal legal principles of the separation of public and private" (Streeter 1996, 16). The ensuing stakes of this struggle for reconciliation are nothing less than the preservation of free expression and maintaining the possibility that media can be (at least theoretically, if not often practically) grounded in ideals transcending marketplace economics. Policy forms regulatory actions, is subject to (and also at times created by) law, and is often driven by a conflicting and contradictory set of processes and considerations, including technological development and standards, political ideologies, economic frameworks, legal procedures, and industrial legacy structures. These dynamics are moving at different paces, and often clash when it is time to address policy for a quickly changing media landscape, as seen in debates over spectrum allocation, retransmission consent, and net neutrality.

The world of formal media policy is the province of the state. All three branches of the federal government—as well as state and local authorities—are involved in determining various boundaries for the media. The agencies and institutions active in creating media policy in the United States include the Federal Communications Commission, the National Telecommunications and Information Administration (of the US Department of Commerce), the Federal Trade Commission, the US Congress, as well as the Department of Justice, the courts, state legislatures, and even local municipalities, which control cable franchising and rights-of-way for media infrastructure, among other things. While policy is different from statutory and common/case law in origin and determination, there are significant points of overlap. For example, policy is often enshrined in law (such as the Telecommunications Act of 1996) in addition to being overseen by the courts, regulatory agencies, and/or congressional committees.

There are various tools used to implement and enforce media policy. These range from constraints (such as ownership and speech limits) to requirements (for obtaining/renewing a license), and from formal law to "terms of service" agreements required by many digital media platforms. Even industrial "self-regulation" in the form of ratings and informal regulation that is crowdsourced and decentralized (as with various components of the digital media economy—see Lobato and Thomas 2015) have become part of the media policy apparatus. Government interventions and policy formulations run the gamut from financial subsidies and tax breaks to trade negotiations, quotas, spectrum management, content mandates and restrictions, and antitrust oversight. The state also has the all-important powers to grant, withhold, renew, or revoke broadcast licenses and/or mete out fines if such rules are not followed.

In addition to the state's role in policy, there are other players and stakeholders such as corporations and industry lobbyists, NGOs, consumer protection agencies, as well as other interest groups, reformers, and activists that also have an influential role in this arena. They typically work to advocate for their constituents and influence policy decisions. The campaigns in the fights over media concentration and net neutrality are prime examples of the impact interest groups can have on media policy (Crawford 2013; Klinenberg 2007; McChesney 2007), and how ultimately neoliberal the orientation of most government regulation has been, particularly since the 1980s, despite the vaunted place of "the public interest" in policy rhetoric (see Horwitz 1989; Miller et al. 2005).

The policies of a media system are contextually specific. In the United States, media policy has been designed for a commercial system. Industry standards such as market concentration, competition, diversity (of ownership and content), and the need to serve the public interest are subject to regulatory protocols that are not fixed throughout time, but often determined by a combination of lawyers, economists, and current political appointees. In Western Europe and other liberal democracies where media systems and policies were built on a public service tradition with a history of state funding and control, policy makers have been more focused on the elements of public accountability and contributions to citizenship, diversity and educational and cultural qualities of content, and universal service than their counterparts in the United States (Hesmondhalgh 2013, 137–38). The history of core-value conflicts and struggles in the media policy arena between market-based or economic versus cultural imperatives, or between the public interest and the private interests of media corporations, has been more pronounced in the United States than in countries with a public service tradition for their media; however, that is changing with the increasing commercialization of systems such as the BBC, and the trends of deregulation and marketization in the cultural sphere that have been slowly spreading throughout countries with a history of strong public service in recent decades.

There is a new imperative to leave behind the "technologically particularistic approach" (Napoli 2001) that has characterized much of media policy history, and develop new models for convergent technologies that respond to the expanding connections between traditional screen media and digital media infrastructure. As a result of new distribution models and devices, media policy is increasingly bound up with the laws and regulations that govern the wires, networks, broadband pipelines, data, and carriers of the telecommunications services. These new relationships complicate media policy and require an extension of focus to also include telecommunications policy, Internet governance, and even social media platforms' terms of service when navigating and regulating power in the current era of media use and dissemination. This also brings in new dynamics that must rise in prominence for policy makers, including the politics and practicalities of access, digital rights, privacy, data security, and other conflicts between technological innovation and the enduring desire on the part of the regulatory community for control over new technologies and their cultural and commercial impact. Ithiel de Sola Pool presciently pointed to these current concerns when he first noted in 1983, "The onus is on us to determine whether free societies in the twenty-first century will conduct electronic communication under the conditions of freedom established for the domain of print through centuries of struggle, or whether that great achievement will become lost in a confusion about new technologies" (10).

The study of policy renders such cultural politics manifest, and makes possible forms of activism, democratic participation, and citizenship that might otherwise go unexplored. There are indeed limiting factors in the efficacy of policy and the policy-making process, including the diminished coffers of reformers and activists in relation to those of industrial political action committees and lobbyists, the well-documented problem of industry capture, the dearth of in-depth analysis in the press about media policy issues and their stakes, and the resulting lack of public access and involvement in the issues that dictate who and what controls our media culture. "Even the regulators themselves," writes Susan Crawford, "are outmaneuvered, under-resourced, constantly under threat of attack, and short of information" in comparison to the corporations that control the wires and media pipelines (2013, 16). As such, it is incumbent upon scholars, journalists, and government officials to create greater visibility for these issues, and an elevated level of public participation, debate, and engagement in the policy arena. The future of media culture depends on it.

48

Popular
John Clarke

The popular is always enmeshed in shifting meanings, evoking both positive and negative connotations. Its basic sense of something that belongs to, is enjoyed by, or is of, the people indicates why this might be so, since "the people" have long been an object of fascination, fear, and fantasy. The popular is often explicitly or implicitly contrasted with other types of culture. So, popular cultures are set against elite or high cultures, marked by distinctions of "taste" (Bourdieu 1984). Elite forms of culture are seen as set apart by the cultural skills and knowledge needed to engage in them, or appreciate them. By comparison, popular products and practices are presumed to be accessible or available to large numbers of people.

These distinctions have positive and negative evaluations attached to them. In one version, elite culture is seen as distinguished, refined, and sophisticated (indeed, as "cultured"), while popular culture is viewed as trivial, peripheral, and empty of value ("trash"). In reverse, elite culture has been attacked as elitist, exclusive, and lacking vitality, while popular products and practices are celebrated as energetic, vibrant, and pleasurable. Such contrasts intensified with the emergence of mass forms of communication that created new conditions for the proliferation of the popular. Mass publishing enabled the circulation of popular journalism and popular literary genres such as romance and detective fictions; new broadcasting technologies underpinned new popular forms of entertainment—alongside moral and political anxieties about their corrupting influences (involving sex, violence, drugs and more).

Distinctions between elite and popular forms have a long history of being articulated with class relations, connections that explain something of the intensity and persistence of the debates around the popular. But popular cultural products and practices have also had a long, if less visible, set of articulations with gender formations. Popular genres of fiction, art, and music are often associated with female audiences or consumers—from melodrama to pop (e.g., Burch and Sellier 2009, on cinema in France; Kaklamanidou 2013, on romantic comedies; and Gill 2007a, on media forms). This gendering of cultural forms underpinned a disparaging view of popular cultural forms as "only entertainment" (Dyer 2002).

Critical approaches to popular culture have explored the ways in which such forms and practices are implicated in the constitution of social divisions and differences and their accompanying patterns of domination and subordination. For example, popular "entertainments" articulate formations including dynamics of gender, class, race/ethnicity, and sexuality. Such critical work also argues that the field of popular culture is *contested* by different conceptions of social order: some conservative, colonial, and patriarchal; others subversive or destabilizing. Much work in media and cultural studies has explored these contestations of the popular (Hall 1981).

Nevertheless, such approaches—sometimes described as "cultural populism" (McGuigan 1992)—have been criticized for romanticizing or overstating the subversive, transgressive, or resistant qualities of popular cultural forms. For cultural pessimists, in contrast, popular cultural forms are commodified objects that are locked into the political economy of capitalism. As such, they both are reproductive of capitalist social relations and have distracting, pacifying, or demobilizing ideological effects. This applies to "domestic" popular cultures and to processes of "cultural imperialism"—especially the global export of US-centric popular culture (see the classic argument by Dorfman 1983).

The alternative is to view the forms and practices of popular culture as sites of contestation, located in, but not necessarily determined by, the social relations of capitalism (and other systems of subordination). This does not necessarily mean that all popular forms are resistant, transgressive, or counterhegemonic, but it does assume that the meanings within popular culture have to be struggled over—whether to maintain forms of subordination or refuse them. The popular remains a site of considerable disagreement.

POPULAR JOHN CLARKE

49

Power
Nick Couldry

Whatever "media power" means, almost everyone thinks it is important. "It all," wrote Roger Silverstone, "is about power in the end" (1999, 143). Great historians take the power of the media for granted, even as they worry about it: "as the 20th century ended, it became evident that the media were a more important component of the political process than parties and electoral systems . . . however . . . they were in no sense a means of democratic government," writes Eric Hobsbawm (1995, 581–82). Media—understood to include all technologically based means of communication, means of organizing communication, information, and data—matter.

So why do textbooks on power often say nothing about media? Jonathan Hearn's respected textbook *Theorizing Power* states that "power is the central thing that social scientists study," and "at the core of who and what we are" (2012, 3–4), yet media and communication are absent from the book's index, and feature only in a passing reference to popular culture and taste (100). If power is so important, how can a theory of power ignore one of the most important dimensions of power today: media? And yet this is what theories of power have done for a century or more, and we need to correct that. What are the obstacles to thinking about *media* power? How might we move beyond them?

We must start with a basic distinction. The word "power," in English, is ambiguous: it can mean "power to" (my *capacity* to run, speak, write an essay); and it can mean "power over" (the *domination* over you that I exercise by running faster than you, speaking better than you). Power to and power over, although sometimes opposed in sociological theory, are "inextricably bound together" (Hearn 2012, 7): my power to own and hold a gun is directly related to the power *over* you that I exercise when I point the gun at your head. Or as Des Freedman puts, with media, "'the power *to* mislead' is combined with an assumed 'power *over* audiences' to generate what we might call the 'power *of*' the media to secure . . . compliance to existing social relations" (2014, 5). Media power has multiple elements.

Critical media studies has, however, mainly been interested in media's "power over" society, politics, the economy, and so on. We have sided with leading social theorist Steven Lukes who, against 1950s and 1960s social theorist Talcott Parsons's emphasis on the "power to" of the social system, insisted that "power over" is the most important feature of power to understand. For Lukes, "power over" in its basic form means "A affects B in a significant manner" (Lukes 2005, 30). Lukes expanded the understanding of power and domination taken for granted in much sociology and political science before the 1970s by distinguishing between three dimensions of power.

The first dimension of power is concerned only with *positive* effects: "A gets B *to do* X which otherwise B would not have done"; for example, A bribes B to vote for a law that B otherwise would have opposed (Lukes 2005, 19). This first dimension misses completely a second dimension of power that includes *negative* effects: "A gets B to do (*or not do*) X which B otherwise would not have done/*would have* done"; for example, a government issues threats on television to discourage citizens from voting (Lukes 2005, 24–25). But both the first and second dimensions assume that domination is possible only when there is explicit conflict, a struggle over whether B will, or will not, *do X*. Power can be exercised, surely, in other circumstances: for example, where parents influence a child to become the sort of person who *voluntarily* takes this or that type of job. Lukes wants to focus on such cases, where A "exercises power over [B] by influencing, shaping or determining his very wants" (2005, 27). This is the third dimension of power, but how do we know that A shaped what B wants to do, when B says to us "I really did want to become a lawyer"? Lukes's answer goes back to Karl Marx: we know that A shaped B's wants when B does X, and X is *against B's real interests*. This leads to Lukes's final definition of power as "A exercises power over B when A affects B in a manner contrary to B's interests" (2005, 37).

Since there are few cases where a media message identifiably causes B to act, or not act, in a specific way (to buy/not buy a car), how can we build a bridge from Lukes's general account of power to a specific understanding of *media* power today?

First, we must take seriously a form of power that media undoubtedly have, yet much sociology has neglected: *symbolic power*. John Thompson (1995, 17) offers a very helpful distinction between economic, political, coercive, and symbolic power. These terms are relatively self-explanatory, except for symbolic power, which works through our "means of information and communication." Symbolic power is the "capacity to intervene in the course of events, to influence the actions of others and indeed to create events, by means of the production and transmission of symbolic forms" (1995, 17). Since media institutions do things through the production and transmission of symbolic forms—they make programs, ads, websites—they have symbolic power. Thompson lays here the foundations for thinking about media power, by linking back to the early twentieth-century founders of sociology (Weber, Durkheim). Media are in fact just one of many types of institutions that accumulate resources for the exercise of symbolic power: think of religious institutions, schools, universities, the makers of digital platforms and phone apps.

But Thompson's account of symbolic power does not, arguably, go far enough. We must address the consequences of symbolic resources being accumulated in very large amounts in particular institutions over time. To grasp this, we can turn to a French sociologist, Pierre Bourdieu, who offers a definition of symbolic power that is much stronger than Thompson's: "symbolic power is a power of *constructing reality*" (1991, 166). What greater power is there than this? Bourdieu means here *social reality*—what is real for us as actors in the social world that is close to and meaningful for us—not the natural physical world. By the process of "constructing reality," Bourdieu means a number of activities: constructing consensus, which Bourdieu sees as a "political function"; and the shaping of knowledge through a shared way of categorizing and ordering the world. Bourdieu is interested too in legitimacy: how do particular institutions become seen as legitimate producers of knowledge and information? Concretely, Bourdieu asks, where do we turn for the stories about our world that we treat as legitimate, more likely to be true, more likely to fit with how we believe that world to be? Through this very strong definition of symbolic power, Bourdieu, without mentioning media, grasps what we now assume is one of the *most distinctive features* of media power: the ability to influence the basic reference points of social life.

Note that institutions or individuals can only have symbolic power in Bourdieu's strong sense—the power of constructing reality—through *accumulating* symbolic power in Thompson's weaker sense—the ability to influence things via symbols. The BBC, which in Britain has the power to construct reality that Bourdieu talks about, did not suddenly acquire it: it was only through the long-term accumulation of specific forms of symbolic power (broadcasting this type of event, becoming the lead source for this type of information, producing this type of entertainment) that the BBC gradually acquired its broader symbolic power to "represent" the nation. Some might regard Bourdieu's definition of symbolic power as *too strong* to explain the multiple *competing* forces in today's media environment. But at least it gives a deep account of how media power *might* work: not just through symbols, or systems of symbols, but "through the very structure of the field in which belief is produced and reproduced" (1991, 170): through the basic relations between actors that shape knowledge production. Imagine if Bourdieu (who wrote his essay originally in 1977) were alive today and thinking about microblogging platforms such as Twitter or Weibo. He would be interested not just in analyzing particular posts or tweets, but in the whole "field" of action that Twitter and Weibo constitute, the relations and hierarchies between average users, who have a small number of followers but follow a lot of people, and celebrity users, followed by millions but following no one (Justin Bieber or the economist Paul Krugman). Bourdieu would be interested too in how the structure of this field derives from how Twitter or Weibo as platforms count and re-present data (for developments of Bourdieu's approach, see Couldry 2000, 2003; Meikle 2009).

Clearly this is just the beginning of grasping the complexities, indeed the "contradictions," of media power (Freedman 2014). To go further, we must turn to writers who specifically consider the power of contemporary media, such as Manuel Castells (2009). Castells, unlike earlier social theorists, takes it as basic that *communication* is an important dimension of power within societies. But most distinctive about Castells is his attempt to think about the *complexity* of how power today works. What is new, for Castells, and what enables contemporary power relations to be hugely complex, are *networks*:

networks of links that connect up large numbers of actors, with connections passing through a number of key "nodes," and across which the passing of communication or resource happens—transport networks, commercial networks, communication networks, social networks. Through the differences they create between who is connected into the network and who isn't, networks have huge consequences for power. For Castells, power is not simple, and we simply must think about the relations between the power in multiple networks: the power of the US state, the US military, *and* Google; or between the powers of the Chinese state, Chinese commercial corporations, *and* Weibo. Castells also usefully distinguishes between power over the building and programming of how the network operates ("programming power"), power over which other networks a network links into ("switching power"). For Castells, like Foucault, Elias, and Bourdieu, all power, including media power, is not a thing located here and not there (like a bar of gold), but a process distributed across many locations. But a difficulty remains: how to think together the power associated with networks themselves and the power of the discourses circulated through such networks.

The challenge is to grasp the sheer *complexity* of media power. Think of the different types of processes that come together in what we call "media power": the power to make symbols (images, content, websites, films, platforms), but also the *economic* power needed to invest in the design, production, and maintaining of symbolic forms; the *social* power to focus people's attention, so that they watch this particular symbolic content rather than another; the *political* power to block or directly censor symbolic content; and, most difficult to grasp of all, the power whereby types of particular symbolic content come to make a difference in our lives. Media power encompasses all of this. It makes no sense to think that all this works in one direction and to one ultimate effect: rather, we need "an approach to media power that emphasizes structure *and* agency, contradiction *and* action, consensus *and* conflict" (Freedman 2014, 29). And media power must be examined on many scales: the power of a reality TV show to influence people's beliefs or habits, but also the struggles over its production process and the struggles of actors far outside the media industries to use influence over media to achieve *their own* ends (perhaps gain economic or political power).

There is no easy answer to the conundrum of defining (or mapping) media power in all its interrelated aspects. But we need nonetheless to ask: how do we understand the "power" of today's social media platforms, such as Facebook, Weibo, WeChat, Twitter, Instagram, and so on? Older debates about the power of television offer some insights. The main debate in early media studies concerned the degree to which the organization of media messages through mainstream media, particularly television, influenced people to have beliefs, in ways contrary to their interests (Morley 1980). The dominant approach in the 1980s was to examine the organization of meaning in media texts, but that approach is particularly difficult to apply in a media world as saturated as the one we now inhabit. We might revive then a less common 1980s approach to television's power that emphasized television's role *as an institution in people's everyday lives*: what Conrad Lodziak (1987) called television's "colonization of leisure," that is, of our times and spaces for relaxation outside work. Today, as we spend ever more time on online social platforms, scholars are asking whether this amounts to the "colonization" of our social imagination (Mejias 2013, 14).

Given the complexity of how media power works in society—with the social-media-saturated environment being a good example—we would expect a wide range of views on whether media power has good consequences or bad. More optimistic approaches contrast with more pessimistic approaches. But, as our uses of media increasingly depend on the sustaining of commercially owned platforms for social *existence*, few would dispute Joseph Turow's claim that "the centrality of corporate power is a direct reality at the very heart of the digital age" (2012, 17). If so, the challenge of how to grasp media power in all its breadth and intimacy shows no sign of losing its importance in media research and public debate.

50

Production

Derek Johnson

While production is most often associated (and seen as almost synonymous) with industry and the specific study of media industries, more careful reflection on the scope of the word reveals a significantly more dynamic concept. Despite its utility in delimiting specific industrial sectors, identifying discrete labor practices and communities, as well as articulating scholarly methodologies, the notion of production holds greatest value for its potential to support intellectual inquiry across different cultural, industrial, and academic boundaries. Although we often limit study of production to specific industrial sites of cultural creation and circulation, it more usefully theorizes media industry in direct relationship to media engagement, use, and participation in less formal, everyday settings. In media studies, production can be understood as the link between industry studies and audience studies that recognizes the meaning, communities, identities, and above all the power involved in making culture.

Context is key to understanding what production means. For professionals working in film or television production, claiming to work in "production" could imply most generally that their work involves the creation and/or craft of making media content. At the same time, such a statement could draw more specific distinctions between the work of staging, lighting, and shooting content on set, compared to the work of scripting and production designing them in "preproduction" or the labor of editing and adding effects in "postproduction." Meanwhile, professionals working in other culture industries might use other language to describe their creative labor, talking about the creation of web and video game content, for example, in terms of "development" or "design" more often than with the language of production.

The polysemy that surrounds production extends beyond professional work worlds to media studies, where production is both all-encompassing and a matter of distinct cultural economic activity. In the past decade, "production studies" has emerged as a dominant paradigm for examining and theorizing media industries as well as the structures, power relationships, identities, communities, and meanings that constitute them. Framing their *Production Studies* anthology with the subtitle *Cultural Studies of Media Industries*, Vicki Mayer, Miranda Banks, and John Caldwell eagerly consider all activities conducted under the aegis of media institutions as aspects of production. "Production studies," they write, "interrogate the term 'producer' as one that identifies a specific category of media practitioners, while also marginalizing other practitioners in the production process" (2009a, 7). Nowhere is this idea clearer than in Mayer's *Below the Line* (2011), which challenges readers to think about a wide variety of workers from Brazilian television set manufacturers to community cable regulators as producers and thereby participants in the circuit of cultural creativity implied by the idea of production. In modeling production studies for those who would later take up the call, the prototype research projects in the *Production Studies* anthology folded case studies of many different kinds of labor across different industry sectors under the rubric of production. Understanding how the media industries produce culture took precedent over defining (and policing) production as a distinct field.

This theorization of production as boundary crossing pushes up against everyday use of the term as well as structuralist media industry scholarship that understands it in far more bounded ways. Early film scholars working from political economic perspectives identified production as only one part of the even more complex industrial system through which corporations exerted monopoly power over culture. While such models remain useful, they present persistent obstacles to the more dynamic theory envisioned by production studies. In her seminal essay on the Hollywood studio system, for example, Mae Huettig (1985) identifies "production" as a discrete industry sector distinguishable from either distribution or exhibition. While the vertically integrated Hollywood studios of the 1930s and 1940s enjoyed controlling interests in the markets for producing, distributing, and exhibiting films alike, Huettig sees tensions and conflicts among those different industry sectors. The status of theatrical exhibition as a source of income, for example, gave it control over the "purse strings," conditions that "give decisive policy-making power regarding the kind of films made to the groups farthest removed from production itself, i.e., the men in distribution and theater management" (291). To maximize those profits and keep exhibitors happy, studio managers determined how much content to produce, at what budget, and on what release schedule. While this suggests the interconnectedness of production, distribution, and exhibition, it also draws a firm boundary around production (the kind of boundary that newer work in production studies wants to interrogate). That boundary extends beyond the industry to consideration of audiences as well, where "by virtue of division of labor within the business, film distributors and exhibitors are much more closely in touch with the moviegoing public than are the producers" (288). While analytically and critically useful, the hierarchies and distinctions invoked by production are exactly the boundaries a production study might seek to interrogate.

Of course, the contemporary Hollywood industry looks much different today than in the studio era, and we should not expect to see the same divisions as did Huettig and others. Nevertheless, this notion of production as a discrete, bounded industry sector persists. Media scholars like Alisa Perren (2013b) and Josh Braun (2015) invoke the need for a "distribution studies" to complement the more limited focus on production sectors that seems to be suggested in the rise of production studies (again, despite hopes to the contrary by Mayer, Banks, and Caldwell). In this light, production studies is perhaps poorly named as a research agenda in that it courts reification rather than deconstruction of industry divisions and hierarchies. Understood in this bounded way, every industry sector now needs its own dedicated subfield of study just like production.

Rather than trying to impose a new unifying name on an intellectual endeavor well under way by this point, it may be better to simply embrace the theoretical potential of production study to explain how each link in the industrial chain participates in a production process more broadly and radically conceived. To fully understand production, we need to embrace production studies' interrogation of these distinctions between different types of media work and categories of media practitioners and push it even further to its logical conclusion. We need to recognize the potential that an emphasis on production offers for seeing the intersections between industry and other cultural fields. In "Encoding, Decoding," Stuart Hall reminds us that the process of communication is "produced and sustained through the articulation of linked but distinct moments—production, circulation, distribution, consumption, and reproduction" (1973/1980, 128).

Moments and institutions of production and distribution can be distinguished, for example, but both remain sites of semiotic production insofar as distributors reproduce culture while also producing new meanings and inflections. A theory of media production enables us to understand not just distinct media institutions and industry sectors, but also how those forces figure into larger processes of communication, culture, and meaning creation.

The problem with production studies, then, is not that it conflates or ignores labor in the realms of distribution or exhibition (or development, or design, etc.) in favor of focus on narrowly conceived production sectors. While such a critique does highlight the value of a parallel distribution studies, we might alternatively consider the value of production study outside of industry sectors altogether. In that sense, the blind spot of production studies may lie in the subtitle of Mayer, Banks, and Caldwell's initial call: "cultural studies of media industries." Of course, production study continues to have significant potential for media industry analysis. In making their own field-defining call for a "critical media industry studies" that shifts concern for the "micropolitics" of meaning making from "the resistive readings of individual audience members" to "institutional operation and production practice" (2009, 238), Timothy Havens, Amanda Lotz, and Serra Tinic see an ally in production studies. Noting in particular John Caldwell's focus on interviews, ethnography, and close readings of industry discourse, they see cultural studies of media production as "entirely consistent with our proposed research framework" (2009, 245). There should be no doubt that the study of production provides a powerful means of undertaking critical and cultural study of media industries. However, what might powerfully distinguish production studies is its potential to put the micropolitics of cultural production and

reproduction within media industries in greater relationship with audiences and other forces outside of it, rather than moving away from those forces purely in favor of industry. The advantage of production study, in other words, is that it need not be defined by industry or its boundaries.

From this perspective, I synthesize three global recommendations for theorizing production and organizing the study of it. First, production studies should not be limited to any one specific industry sector, set of labor categories, or professional identities. Instead, following Mayer and others, we might challenge and interrogate the way that production is limited and policed in discourse and practice to think about a broader set of productive relations through which meaning, identity, and culture are generated. We should recognize how all actors and agents working within media institutions participate in the complex processes and practices of production, regardless of their position within various divisions of labor and corporate structures. Production studies should thus continue to match concern for writers, directors, and other above-the-line creative talent with attention to the creativity of below-the-line laborers as well as the managerial work of marketers, sales distributors, agents, accountants, and more.

Second, in that more radical conception, we need not limit our understanding of production to industry alone. While Henry Jenkins's (2006) claims about convergence culture have been both well tread and frequently criticized, his central theorization of convergence as a moment in which production and consumption become blurred remains an instructive way of reconceiving the boundaries of production study. When the production of culture increasingly occurs outside the formal aegis of industries and professionalism (and as Jenkins would remind us, has always existed outside of industry in folk cultures), the study of production must necessarily turn its attention to informal settings and networks of cultural creation and distribution. Convergence may only raise the stakes and make more pressing our need for production studies that can recognize these continuities of cultural work. Mark Deuze (2007, 23–24) invokes Zygmunt Bauman's (2005) notion of "liquid life," for example, to encourage us to think about how the modern notions of production/work and consumption/leisure have dissolved into one another in flexible and precarious ways in the context of convergence. Axel Bruns's (2008, 19–20) theory of "produsage" captures this potential for a more ambitious, unbounded theorization of production too, imagining how cultural content might be continually produced and reproduced through the process of its ongoing use—much differently from the fixed products offered by the hierarchical divisions of labor and ownership logics of industry. We might critique Bruns for positing a utopian, fully separable alternative to industrial production, but he nevertheless offers a production study that can account for the hybridity of production and the impossibility of understanding it in purely industrial terms. Bruns's emphasis on the links between "production" and "use" is echoed by Elizabeth Ellcessor (2016), whose recent work revises Stuart Hall's preferred reading positions to theorize "preferred user positions" in which digital media users are positioned not just as consumers but also as active participants in the production of culture. Here, the scope and disposition of those preferred user positions shape understanding of who can participate in what ways.

This growing interest in use should not render the theorization of production obsolete, in my view, but will instead recognize how production unfolds as a process and series of moments including not wholly contained within the scope of industry and professionalism. Production studies should expand to consider the productivity of fan and amateur hobbyist cultures, to be sure, but also the everyday participation with which we use—and contribute to—Facebook and other media interfaces.

What this means, finally, is that production studies can offer a window onto how media content is made, circulated, and engaged throughout a series of moments and a process of articulations. Put another way, we might figure production studies as simultaneously a *reproduction* studies. Culture is reproduced through use. And in this sense, we might turn our attention back to industry as well and think about reproduction and use within the hierarchies and divisions of labor with which production is more traditionally associated. In my own work on media franchising (Johnson 2013), for example, concern for production is a concern for reproduction as multiple media industries manage the production of culture from shared intellectual properties across distinct markets and economies, different creative communities, and changing cultural and historical contexts. Major media brands are reproduced in response to industrial challenges and tensions encountered in crossing these different boundaries. That industrial process of production and reproduction is one centrally comprehensible through "use," moreover, as professional content creators function as temporary, for-hire labor for only moments in the decades-long management of properties over which only corporate claims of ownership can be made. Franchise producers, in this sense, are users of what corporate employers provide them and what later producers will surely use once more. In the context of franchising, media industries produce culture through the circulation of resources across multiple moments, uses, and contexts of reproduction. While other forms of industrial practice from casting to marketing may not formalize ongoing reproduction to the same obviously intensified degree as franchising, they too might be usefully figured as an opportunity to understand how production emerges through reproduction and use.

Production, therefore, is not one side in a binary with consumption, nor is it solely one moment/sector in an industrial structure. Instead, production is the process by which culture is created and re-created, within the industry and without.

51
Public
Jennifer Petersen

In modern usage, public is both an adjective (public interest, public opinion) and a noun (the public). As a noun, it suggests the judging and debating social collective. As an adjective, it marks its object as a matter of common concern and judgment of this collectivity. Both meanings derive from practices of citizen sovereignty or self-rule that arose in the eighteenth century. In the medieval and classical periods, the public did not refer to commonality but rather was associated with leaders (elites, lords) and displays of assembly (the agora) or power (feudal lords) (Habermas 1989). The notion of a public realm of social life, or the *public sphere*, in which average citizens might debate and critique political matters and state decisions, and also social matters, was part of a shift from absolutism to democratic governance (Koselleck 1988). Jürgen Habermas's narrative of the evolution of the public sphere is useful here, as a distillation of liberal theory and institutional invocations of publicity and the public sphere. He argues that a political norm of publicity as something like a citizen's right to know arose in the eighteenth century. People came to expect information about policy and other state decisions to be made accessible as a public matter, and began to critique such decisions. This engagement of citizens in discussions and critiques of decisions that pertained to all, rather than more immediate, private matters of individual or small-group concern, was the initial incarnation of the public sphere. Experiencing themselves not only as private people, but also as representatives of the polis, citizens—or more precisely, bourgeois citizens—began to make demands on the state in the name of the public, or common, good. Thus, the public sphere became the site for claims of representativeness. Ultimately, the public sphere became the reference point for the legitimacy of democratic governments, the manifestation of citizen sovereignty.

Given this history, to name something as public is powerful. It marks what is within the boundaries of the polis. The interests, demands, and opinions of some groups have historically been excluded from being public, understood in the minds of elites at least as eruptions of mere private or personal interests. Such has been the fate of women, people of color, the working classes (especially under the aegis of "the crowd"). In the nineteenth century, for example, crowd demands or riots appeared in the eyes of elites as eruptions of private interests and personal passion, bodies and sentiments out of place rather than as public actions (e.g., Butsch 2007; Landes 1998). Sex and domestic labor similarly have not been considered public matters until recently.

In order to understand the complexities of the term, its relation to gender, race, and class, and the current moment in which "the personal is political" and formerly private matters are labeled and understood as public, we need to look back to the history of the technologies of publicity. Changes in who and what can be considered public, subject to political representation, are in a significant sense artifacts of technologies of representation. Much of the meaning that the term has accrued is inherited from the means of making things public—media technologies—and the meanings humans attribute to them. New technologies do more than expand or contract the public sphere. Our very conceptions of what it means to be public have a media history in that they are produced in significant part by the material and cultural means of making public.

The modern conceptions of public described above were predicated on a particular means of publication. Printing was the means by which state decisions were made available to citizens, and the means by which citizens became aware of each other's thoughts and arguments. It was a way in which people were able to engage in debates dealing with matters beyond their neighborhoods or private networks and could experience themselves as members of a broader, more diffuse social formation held together by talk rather than intimate ties: *the public*. The circulation of print materials through the market enabled people to address this broad and anonymous group as well as to experience themselves as the subject of such an address: a member of the public, or in Michael Warner's (2005) terms, a mass subject. Of course, as many historians have pointed out, the printed word was not the only way of doing politics in this era. The theater, the street, and image-based posters were all key venues for politics in eighteenth- and nineteenth-century England, France, and the United States (Landes 1998). The centrality of print to the historiography and theory of publicity is as much metaphorical as historical.

Metaphorically, the experiences of print publication and the meanings attributed to it capture much of what is at stake in how we talk about the public. The political ideals of the public sphere draw on the textuality and modes of circulation associated with print publication (Warner 1990). Publication is, of course, to make public. It is the presentation of something new, the movement of something hidden into view. By the beginning of the eighteenth century, publishing had taken on its contemporary link with printed material, suggesting presentation to a geographically dispersed, anonymous, and indeterminate audience. Unlike pronouncements and newsletters, print publishing relied on an impersonal "to whom it may concern" form of address.

The "to whom it may concern" mode of address says much about the characteristics that have governed publicity for much of its modern life. The impersonality of the address presents itself as a form of openness (Peters 2005). For eighteenth-century thinkers, it also suggested egalitarianism. Unlike its predecessor the newsletter, the newspaper is under pressure to cover the events of the day presumed to be of interest to all. In this agnostic other-orientation, print seemed to offer a model for disinterested public discourse that allowed a pure exchange of ideas, bracketing status, and body.

The notion that print publication was an exercise in impartiality was a fiction maintained in important part by the materiality of printing. The printed word, in books and newspapers, seemed to present words without bodies, in which words took on a life and authority of their own, abstracted from the bodies and passions of speakers (Ong 1982). The ability to seem to speak from no place, to voice concerns not dedicated on personal needs or particular experience, is at the heart of the exclusions central to the public sphere. It is why some peoples, opinions, and interests have at times not been considered public. The concept of publics and public opinion was mobilized in the early twentieth century to distinguish orderly opinion formation, based in reading, from such labile passions, likely to be aroused in theater, cinema, or on the streets (e.g., Lippmann 1922; Tarde 1901/1969). Crowds, mobs, and the riots or protests they might engage in appeared to elites as eruptions of not only irrationality, but also private interests (Butsch 2007). Into the twentieth century, women, people of color, and gay men were not able to claim to speak in such a disembodied manner, or represent the common good (Ouellette 1999; Van Zoonen 2004).

Of course, in the late nineteenth century and early twentieth, the means of publication were shifting. New mass media enabled presentation of the people through sound and moving image. If the public was the people embodied in print (Warner 1990), then what was the people embodied in film, radio, or television? For many cultural commentators, the fact that cinema and then broadcast spoke to and about the working class, women, the uneducated was an intrusion of private interests—whether the tastes of suspect audiences or the financial interests of the culture industries—into the public sphere (Habermas 1989).

Arguably, these reactions were to changes in the terms of publication and publicity brought on by (then) new media. Film and broadcast media presented ideas to an indefinite audience via embodied and intimate forms of address. Both the visual image and the sound of the voice are traces of the body. They trade in an odd intimacy, utilizing a mode of address that is at once impersonal, in that they address an indiscriminate audience, and personal, in that they highlight the particularity of the speaker and often go to great lengths to craft the sense of a bond between the speaker and audience (Scannell 1996)—a rhetoric of embodiment to contrast to the "rhetoric of disembodiment" of the print public sphere (Warner 2005). In this and other ways, television flouts the rational-critical of the public of print. The intimacy of the address may be part of the reason that the audiences of radio, film, and television have so often been distinguished from publics (Livingstone 2005). The distinction marks the audiences of film, TV, and radio as private, outside politics.

The addition of these highly centralized new media has had its costs, namely, the ability of the powerful to capture and capitalize on the infrastructure of exchange. But it has also opened new possibilities. When the means of publication change, so do practices of publicity, on a large scale. Film, radio, and television presented criticism and debate in oral, visual, affective, and embodied form to a mass, or indefinite, audience for much of the twentieth century. Embodied politics are nothing new, but their legibility as representative, or public, is. Within the liberal, print-based discourse of publicity, passions and bodies could lead only to division; impersonal, abstract reasoning could pull us out of purely personal, private feelings, commitments, and interests into consideration of the public, common good. But mass media of the twentieth century spoke in such terms to all. The very massness of mass media, their ubiquity and address to as large an audience as possible for much of the twentieth century pushed liberal discussions of publicity toward a recognition of the ability of intimate address to make political claims and, more importantly, to forge commonality and consensus and thus actually be a form of public opinion in its robust meaning. In US law, actions and embodied expression, from flag waving to black armbands, to the use of the body as a tool of dissent in acts of silent protest, are increasingly recognized as public speech. Likewise, the law has recognized departures from the rational-critical norm, including the importance of the emotional force and aesthetic impact of political statements, and the public relevance of (some) rude discourse. Justices, like the rest of us, draw on the contemporaneous means of publication in determining what counts as speech and public discourse (Petersen 2014). New media of communication have thus helped expand legal conceptions of public, political discourse. While the ideal of impartiality and its cousin rationality still color lay and legal understandings of what is public, they increasingly have competition.

From sex to sentiment to emotions, there are currently a number of competing models for talking about the terms of representation, who and what can "speak" for the people. Individuals enter into discussion and turn toward the indefinite audience of others known as the public for reasons that include desire and connection (Young 1998). Emotions and attachments, understood as social processes rather than private psychology or particularity, define the contours and limits of relationships among people in public as well as private (Ahmed 2004; Lunt and Stenner 2005). Like distanced deliberation, such passions can move people from private interests toward collective ones. For instance, the affective responses to the murders of Matthew Shepard and James Byrd Jr., shared via media texts, were instrumental in the political mobilization that ensued. People were inspired and energized to form publics through sentiment, and made political demands in a language that mixed public feelings and social justice. The affective arguments publicized in media texts were ultimately successful in articulating the murders as public tragedies rather than private ones, and in advocating for the passage of first local and then federal hate crime provisions (Petersen 2011).

Currently, some of the more difficult questions about publicity arise in the context of Internet communication and social media. It is hard to determine audience orientation, what collectivity is represented or addressed in online utterances. The scale and type of audience(s) we address vary with platform settings and hidden algorithms and the "collapse" of the social contexts we usually rely on to understand public and private (Marwick and boyd 2014). Intimate bonding with close, and closed, circles of others takes place alongside more open-ended appeals, invective, and deliberation. Given the history of media technologies and publicity, the biggest questions regarding the Internet and the public sphere are not about political economy and access, as important as they are. Rather, they are about how these new conditions of publication will shift the feel and sensibility of publicity, and thus change the foundation of the public (n.), and the public sphere.

52

Queer

Karen Tongson

Queer media is an emergent category acknowledging that media forms, from film and television to an ever expanding digital sphere, are no longer just "playing to Peoria" (and the many Peorias since established) as the standard of demographic normalcy and desirability. The early 2000s saw the emergence of LGBTQ-focused programming on cable networks like Logo, and gave rise to Bravo as the unofficial home for queer programming ever since it turned queer eyes to straight guys. More recently, queer methods for storytelling have come to prominence on streaming platforms like Amazon and Netflix (which launched queer shows like *Transparent*), and social media sites like YouTube and Instagram, which provide platforms for queer and transgender people to auto-document their lives, struggles, and transitions. In short, queer niches have sprouted up across the media landscape since the beginning of the new millennium, even as LGBTQ characters have become more prevalent on prime-time network programming—ABC's sitcom *Modern Family* the most frequently cited among them.

Queer media also function as a historical index: as a phrase that encompasses, in shorthand, the medial transformations and shifts that afford such proximity with the "queer," and the cultural and conceptual changes queer life, culture, and theory have inaugurated in the United States and beyond (Villarejo 2014). In other words, we have become more attentive to the ways in which media themselves have been transformed at various historical moments by the advances of, and irruptions caused by, LGBTQ civil rights movements and calls for political and cultural representation. Scripted television "after *Ellen*," DeGeneres's herstorical coming out in "The Puppy Episode" in 1997, and the proliferation of queer participation on reality television, with its roots in PBS's 1973 series *An American Family*, are owed in many respects to the historical agitations and transformations that precipitated these moments of visibility (Villarejo 2014, 92).

"Queer media" also names a set of practices and methods for interpreting media that may or may *not* make themselves available to queer interpretation, queer worlds, and queer people—as innovators in the field of feminist, LGBTQ media studies have explored for over two decades (Doty 1993; Joyrich 1996; Modleski 2007; Rich 2013; White 1999). With a contemporary media landscape relatively rich in queer representation—from *Orange Is the New Black* to *I Am Cait* to "Same Love," the rapper Macklemore's top-forty hit advocating for gay marriage, to mainstream movies depicting lesbian marriage between All-American sweethearts (*Jenny's Wedding*, 2015)—it would seem that queer viewers are no longer bereft of the opportunity to see ourselves on screens and devices large, small, fixed, and portable.

How and why, then, do arguments about queer visibility still run the table? For example, why are we obsessed with the lack of butch lesbians in film and TV (one of Jack Halberstam's recurrent concerns on his collaborative scholarly blog, *Bully Bloggers*), at the same time we capitulate to the latest BuzzFeed hype about the openly queer, masculine of center celesbian DJ, supermodel, and actress Ruby Rose, not to mention the many would-be Ruby Roses clamoring to reboot "lesbian chic" on social media platforms like Instagram? Why amid such apparent abundance, are we still left feeling so empty? Furthermore, why in this economy of plentitude are we still struggling to describe what is queer about media, and how media themselves might be queer? These definitional problems arise in part because the category of "queer" and what exactly it indexes have always been up for debate in the academy and beyond. At times "queer" has come to mean a particular set of sexual practices, positions, and proclivities. In the past fifteen years or so, scholars have vigorously debated whether or not queer constitutes *any* form of antinormativity. Meanwhile, some of the field's fundamental questions continue to abide: Is queer an identity? An orientation? A method? A practice of reading, seeing, or hearing?

Aren't-we-GLAAD approaches to quantifying queer visibility—that is, measuring with exactness how many gay characters, shows, and actors are on TV or in films, and whether or not these portrayals are positive or negative—have created their own set of limitations around our encounters with *all* forms of media, not just explicitly queer representations with identifiable queer bodies, characters and "acts." Like the Dickensian Mr. Gradgrind, the headmaster in *Hard Times* obsessed with numbers and their Malthusian applicability to a profit-driven "greater good," queer media observers are inevitably derailed by counting how many LGBTQ shows are watched by larger audiences, and measuring their "impact" in ways that equate profit and advertiser approval with political progress. As an alternative to these metrics of quantification, and in the effort to bring back some of the vicissitudes the murky designation of "queerness" affords, we might rediscover queer media, past and present, as sites of fantasy, play, and projection.

In other words, we are so fixated on how *many*, how *often*, and how *affirmative* portrayals are that we have begun to lose sight and sound of the textures, sensations, and idiosyncrasies that fuel the pleasure of queer spectatorship and participation (Belcher 2014; Moore 2013; Rhee and Phillips 2015). To invoke Kara Keeling's more expansive medial perspective, we are in a moment during which we have the potential to craft the architecture for a "Queer OS" (operating system). As Keeling writes, "Queer OS names a way of thinking and acting with, about, through, among, and at times even in spite of new media technologies and other phenomena of mediation. It insists upon forging and facilitating uncommon, irrational, imaginative, and/or unpredictable relationships between and among what currently are perceptible as living beings and the environment in the interest of creating value(s) that facilitate just relations" (2014, 154). I'm interested in Keeling's insistence on the "thinking and acting *with*." Queer media, in other words, is as much about a queer engagement, and sometimes *resistance* to certain processes of representation and mediation in the effort to forge an otherwise, and a "not yet" (to echo the language of José Esteban Muñoz's *Cruising Utopia*): a striving for alternate and just relationality or "different paths to queerness" (2009, 15).

Furthermore, queer is anchored never simply to a set of bodies or practices, but more crucially to a set of methods and *desires*—both political and intellectual—derived from activist genealogies (e.g., the legacy of Queer Nation), the academy (since the institutionalization of queer studies starting in the 1990s), and media forms themselves. As I argued elsewhere, "Though we may have loved, fucked, eaten, sang, sewn, played softball, honked the tuba, ballet danced, taken ecstasy, and flashed jazz hands, queerly in our lifetimes before our respective sojourns in higher education, we talk, write, read, watch publish essays and books, waste our time making GIFs about, and sit in harshly lit MLA ballrooms to mull over the queer we learned in school" (Tongson 2014, 118). Extending my claims about the affinities, and the formal, as well as everyday pedagogies constituting "queerness," to media engagement, I would also like to imagine that queer spectatorship—particularly televisuality and the proliferating forms of "home-viewing" in which we participate—is also born of another kind of sensibility: a "latchkey" sensibility that we often equate with the voracious overconsumption of media that forges our queer sensibilities. I would argue, for example, that the figure we have come to know as the "latchkey kid" is the linchpin to illuminating queer media and queer relationships to media: she is the figure left to her own devices who forges improper identifications, and—to invoke Muñoz's work once more—dangerous disidentifications (1999) with media content, appropriate or inappropriate. Through the historical, metaphorical figure of the latchkey kid, we can trace a particular kind of queer relationship to media born of excess and dereliction, one in which the queer spectators project themselves into worlds beyond the ones that have chosen to ignore them.

Historically, the "latchkey kid" is among the first prototypical consumers (some would say over-consumers) of media, who cannot be imagined as a producer of any kind. Unsupervised, left alone, and either fearful or bored, the youth of suburbia have been called latchkey kids since World War II, when the label was invented to describe children transiently orphaned by work as well as war. In 1944, Henry L. Zucker, secretary of the Emergency Child Care Committee of Cleveland, and an advisory committee member of the Child Welfare League of America, lamented the term's induction into the "social work literature" of the era: "The nomenclature of social work literature has been enriched during the war by such terms as 'latchkey' or 'doorkey' children and 'eight hour orphans.' . . . The house key tied around the neck is the symbol of cold meals, of a child neglected and shorn of the security of a mother's love and affection. These new terms foretell a war-bred generation of problem adolescents-to-be in the 1950s, and of maladjusted parents-to-be in the 1960s" (Zucker 1944, 43).

Even before the concept of a nuclear family cohered in the atomic age after World War II—an age that bore witness to America's storied baby boom, its rapid suburbanization, and the rise of television—social workers were concerned with the dissolution of the family unit, because of the shifting gender roles wrought by war. With more women in the workforce, as men fought overseas in the European and Pacific theaters, children were increasingly left to seek refuge with neighbors or "aged grandparents," or worse, according to social observers, to fend for themselves. Quoting extensively from a female elementary school principal's report on her school's "war casualties," Zucker argued that the excessive consumption of media had a deleterious effect upon a child's unsupervised time:

> Edward, a bright child but extremely nervous, could not sit still or remain in his seat long enough to do his work. Both parents were working, both were extremely tired and nervous. . . . One Monday, things became so extremely bad in the classroom that the teacher asked Edward what he had done. Well, the mother had given him $2.00 to do what he wanted. He left home at ten o'clock, went to a movie at the Hippodrome, then one at the Palace, one at the Mall, then one at the neighborhood theater, arriving home at ten o'clock [PM], tired but feeling that he had had a most successful day. (Zucker 1944, 47)

Even before broadcast television became a staple of every middle-class home, and binge watching and #showholes (a recent ad campaign encouraging binge viewing through the Amazon Fire platform) entered popular parlance in the streaming era, Edward, the insatiable consumer of entertainment, proved how delinquency, truancy, and disrespect for institutions and authority are fostered by "the wrong" relationship to media.

Thus the queer viewer has always, already been something of a latchkey viewer. Our entry points to media are often askew, and require a certain overindulgence and excessiveness. The latchkey queer is the one who, like Jonathan Caouette in his homemade, indie feature *Tarnation* (2003), or performance artist Kalup Linzy in his sumptuous, if low-tech, fannish soap opera performance videos (2002–6), transposes isolate, sometimes lonely queer viewing practices of mainstream programming, from prime-time drama to daytime fare like *Guiding Light*, into the texture of another life, another story, another medium. Caouette turned his latchkey overconsumption of prime-time soaps, documented auto-ethnographically on video throughout his adolescence, into the content and texture for a feature film later he made as an adult using iMovie. Linzy does similar work with his performance videos, albeit through dramatic reenactments of his and other queers of color's reception of soapy daytime fare. Like latchkey kids who had to fend for themselves and fight for their sustenance, these queer artists reheated what was processed and packaged and turned it into something nourishing. Latchkey queers are the dykes who, like the members of the 1990s punk band Team Dresch, accidentally happened upon Mariel Hemingway and Patrice Donnelly achieving their *Personal Best* (1982) on an endless cycle of regular cable repeats of the sporty film in the afternoon, opening pathways to becoming fantastical new beings à la "Fagetarian and Dyke" on their 1995 album *Personal Best*—an oblique musical homage to the film.

The objects may continue to change. Instead of glistening lady track stars perspiring in slow motion after their athletic exertions, we may now turn to butch lesbian-identified Top Chefs sporting all iterations of the faux hawk while thrusting their "hands up, and utensils down" upon Padma Lakshmi's command. Instead of Harry Hamlin "making love" with both Michael Ontkean *and* Kate Jackson as he did as a confused bisexual man in the film *Making Love* from 1982, we may take a prurient queer pleasure in the overcooked heterodisaster-kink of a cable series like *The Affair* (2015–), or the slow-burning normporn of a show like NBC's *Parenthood* (2010–15), or the adoptive parental homonormporn of *The Fosters* (2013–) (Tongson 2015). Queer media have meant, and continue to mean to me, the sort of titillated, interpellated, yet ultimately ambivalent viewing practices, that re-enliven the reparative, and disidentificatory practices of queer fantasy—the kind of imagining that carries the potential for queer world making. To watch and listen queerly also mean to explore the ambivalent pleasures, and the attraction-repulsion queer viewers experience when watching even the most mainstream, ready-for-prime-time network programming designed for families, modern or not. These moments of queer encounter with and *within* media, with or without actual queer bodies, created the conditions of possibility for—continue to create the possibility for—righteous and radiant queer operating systems, platforms, fantasies, or what we still dare to call "worlds," from yesterday to today; for tomorrow, forever, or perhaps even never, IRL—in real life.

53

Race

Herman Gray

Race is a legal, social, and cultural invention rather than given in nature, and the knowledge of race and its deployment are *exercises of power* expressed in the encounter among groups for control over resources. The social construction of race trains our focus on the practices of race, including the terms of its creation, deployment, and enforcement as a mode of group subordination and regulation. Race as a technique of power identifies arbitrary differences such as skin color, hair texture, nose and eye shapes, and thinness of lips as sites of knowledge (classification, hierarchy, and value) about variations in human intelligence, capacity, creativity, development, indeed what it means to be human (Goldberg 2009; Wynter 2003). Constructionism provides an indispensable critical beginning (rather than endpoint) for thinking about the nature of racial knowledge taking shape today.

Nineteenth- and twentieth-century racial projects depended on social and cultural inventions as well as moral rationalizations that made racial difference the basis of classification, value, knowledge, and political practices that enforced racial distinctions by intimidation, violence, and terror. Nineteenth- and twentieth-century decolonial wars, movements for national liberation, and global struggles for civil and legal recognition by people of color around the world *ended* some of the most brutal, exploitative, and violent racial projects designed to exploit land and labor in order to shore up racial capitalism. By the mid- to late twentieth century,

these critical movements produced new subjects of history and knowledge about those subjects produced by those subjects.

Twenty-first-century racial knowledge has taken refuge in the science of the human genome, in the proliferation of cultural diversity and digital technology, and in legal disputes over race-based public policies. Ascendant twenty-first-century truths of race align with different technologies of power, modes of authority, and cultural logics. Knowledge of race ranges across several fronts simultaneously. For example, in the media the truth of race works through the proliferation and hypervisibility of racial difference as multiculturalism while genomic science uses powerful statistical procedures to identify and group populations who share genetic information. Based on statistically identified genetic variations among different populations, genomic scientists of race draw conclusions about racial classification, geographic concentration, and shared ancestry. The changing nature of racial knowledge also includes the recognition of cultural diversity and the incorporation of ethnic studies, queer studies, and feminist studies into university curricula that have become essential components of twenty-first-century knowledge of race (Ferguson 2012). These shifts in racial knowledge invite media, race, and cultural studies scholars to develop new critical analytics to identify, document, and assess the workings of race in the academy, science, law, and media.

I offer aspects of my research on racial projects as a modest illustration. This research traces the mutually constitutive role of media, racial science, and academic knowledge in the assembly of race in the twenty-first-century Global North. Arranged through various racializing practices like racial slavery, colonialism, Jim Crow segregation, and racial neoliberalism, the approach emphasizes the mutual role of representation, meaning, identity, and subjection in such projects. This mutuality stresses differential access by race to resources, forms of state-sanctioned domination (including violence and more benign forms of social terror), and attendant cultural forms and psychological stress for different populations. Racial projects are dynamic exercises of power that produce, organize, and distribute racial and ethnic groupings of populations according to socially valued attributes arranged hierarchically. One might say that race is an outcome, a production of a set of relations and material conditions that take charge of resources necessary for living. Racial projects produce, authorize, circulate, and enforce racial knowledge based on distinction, classification, value, and hierarchy that constitute the discursive truth of race within a given set of living arrangements.

In different historical periods and regions of the globe, racial knowledge designated and denigrated certain populations, targeting them for displacement, land seizure, and captivity for labor exploitation based on purportedly inferior racial attributes. The cultural assignment of value and significance and the social use of classification based on arbitrary racial differences together with scientific explanation and judicial legitimation make such arrangements into racial projects.

Racial projects arrange racial meaning discursively and social practices materially and work by circulating such meanings throughout our commonsense understandings and experiences of everyday life (Perry 2011). Racial projects operate through feelings, emotions, and the body, where we live and feel the truth of race at the most quotidian and commonplace levels. These affective practices focus attention not just on the representational but on the truth of race as intuition and sensation. Meanings and feelings are the locus of legible representation, authoritative knowledge, commonsense understandings, and affective investments in the truth of race.

Indeed, with Dorothy Roberts (2011), we might say that race is the expression of the mutually constitutive effects of media, science, the state, and economic markets. The media—the press, commercial broadcast systems, digital platforms, and digital social networks—are scenes where social relations, representations, understandings, and feelings about racial differences among us circulate.

The social relations and the knowledge of race on which they depend vary widely across geographies, histories, and populations in different parts of the world (Goldberg 2009). For instance, South Africa and Brazil, England and the United States culturally recognize racial and ethnic distinction, but differ by state formations, colonial histories, and population removal and displacement; the exploitation and exposure to vulnerability of different segments of the population depend on the assignment by states, elites, and scholars of human capacity based on race. On the basis of such purported capacities, different populations are confined to low-skill, low-wage work, targeted as high credit risks, naturalized as criminal, rendered unemployable, and disproportionately imprisoned.

To claim that we are on the terrain of digital genomic multicultural racial projects is to suggest that because of transformations in digital media, pubic policy, and diversity discourse as well as genomics, race and media have undergone conceptual and practical shifts that make this terrain somewhat distinct from its twentieth-century precursors. With the knowledge of new racial science and digital media capacities, access to gaining cultural representation, visibility, and meaning, in some social arenas, is less open to dispute in the politics of representation today than in the twentieth century, when access relied on the primacy of skin color, hair texture, or nose width as a site of knowledge and truth. Culturally, racial differences are actually celebrated in certain countries in the Global North while in others racial (and ethnic) groups are the targets of intense contestation, regulation, violence, and abjection. In the United States, to take one example, cultural practices in public and private institutions celebrate multiculturalism, while court rulings outlaw race as a basis for allocation of resources or claims to grievance in public life. In this new condition of race making, racial projects produce visibility *and* regulation, celebration *and* exploitation.

The post–civil rights conjuncture in the United States that produced the first black American president is not one where there is a paucity of images of racial difference or the cultural grammar to decipher the significance of race. In the Internet age, social media, streaming media services, broadcast, and cable are robust sites of racial engagement, representation, and belonging for all forms of racial and ethnic identifications, thanks in part to the digital technologies that make new media ecologies possible, the political struggles that make the conception of multiculturalism and diversity available, and the genomics research that makes the new science of race possible. Ironically, with the discourse of color blindness and multiculturalism, the United States may be described as one of racial excess (Fleetwood 2011).

As the truth of race moves to the level of the genomic, our cultural celebrations and social suspicions based on race are as visible as ever. In its deployment, circulation, and effect, race organizes, sorts, and informs social life even as claims in science, media, politics, and popular culture insist on the flagging salience of race. So racial projects produce racial knowledge and racial subjects within a condition of abundance and excess where, for example, in the search for one's racial and ethnic ancestry, the production of race and search for evidence of its scientific truth have gone digital and genomic, where genomic accounts of population variations based on

race (among other factors) confirm the importance of racial differences in the authentication of indigenous origins. The market logic of difference based on race (gender, age, and disposable income) arranges popular knowledge as the footing for identification and belonging and consumption on the basis of race as a lifestyle choice.

Over its resilient history in the United States, various iterations of racial science including eugenics, craniology, IQ testing, and genomics helped to install and authorize the intellectual, cultural, and social firmament necessary to produce race as a *purported* social fact. With appeals variously to religion, science, philology, and the state, racial science endeavored to show that like the world of nature, the social world of history and culture could be described and apprehended by classifying, ordering, assigning value, and searching for variation (Robinson 2007).

Considering the relationship among race, science, and media as dynamic and a technique of power (each part or component of the alignment moving independent and with different temporalities and logic) is a productive way to think about the connection among genomic racial science, digital media, and postracial discourses of diversity, multiculturalism, and color blindness. While similar relationships organized accounts of race from the nineteenth and twentieth centuries, the emphasis on the constitutive elements of new racial projects permits researchers to track race and the projects that produce them into new zones of knowledge, authority, and expression such as genomics, ancestry, new media technologies, and admixtures of racial diversity.

In the United States, the cultural visibility of race and the legal rejection of race-based policies by twenty-first-century practices of science, media, and postracial diversity provide powerful alibis to disavow race (certainly of the nineteenth- and twentieth-century sense) in the organization, distribution, and access to safety and security, and to recognize, even celebrate, multicultural identities and histories. Similarly, in the case of media platforms that include social media networks, gaming, entertainment, and streaming content, race is avowed in the form of multicultural lifestyle markets and disavowed based on consumer sovereignty and market neutrality, the cornerstone of which is economic capacity and resources, market variation, and consumer needs. Marketable distinctions, and most especially those organized around racial and ethnic differences (but marketed as cultural distinctions), drive access and representation in media. In the case of social media platforms, participation by racial groups is not precluded on racial grounds but operates on the basis of revised twentieth-century racial models of separate but equal media content, platforms, and representation (e.g., black social media networks or ethnic language media).

In genomic racial science, racial difference operates in the search for scientifically neutral and statistically significant genomic variation and genealogical clustering by populations. In other words, scientists attempt to identify and rigorously measure human variations according to (socially generated) group classification on the basis of statistical estimates of gene frequencies that differ among geographic populations. This form of racial knowledge allows for the proliferation of population variation and geographical distribution, the search for original and authentic bloodlines, and genealogical recuperation underwritten by scientific authority staked in rigorous quantitative techniques and complex computational methods and by a liberal humanism that recognizes and in some cases collaborates with members of diverse population groups. Despite this concern with rigor, scientific neutrality, and recognition of difference,

racial science of genomics operates through the social and cultural optic of racial distinction. In the commitment to social diversity in social and economic affairs and recognition of multiculturalism, both of which disavow the salience of race, ironically race is produced on the basis of racial knowledge and social meaning tempered by science, media, and culture.

Making race by disavowing racial difference, I read as a bid to parse the truth of race as still a fundamental feature of the social order and not just seeing race as a matter of targeting a specific group, identity, or location. In this sense we could say that, with intensification of race making in genomics and digital technologies, race is an effect of projects that produce racial understandings and racial truths that are no less pernicious in their social, cultural, and political effects than their nineteenth- and twentieth-century predecessors.

Two main challenges therefore confront the next generation of media studies of race. The first challenge is to track down and connect the new racial projects, the social basis of knowledge and truth of race they produce and their role in organizing the social order they help to secure. In other words, what exactly is the "truth of race" that is being claimed and secured by genomic science and deployed in the new media ecology of difference that organizes access to vulnerability, risk, and insecurity based on the truth of race proffered by racial science? Moreover, where (and exactly how) are forms of race making produced?

The second challenge is to raise critical questions and search for alternate imaginations with which to build different accounts of human variation and their role in social worlds. These might include decolonialized (including indigenous) epistemologies as well as residual possibilities that lie dormant and the creative inventions that come with living in the ruins of capitalism

(Weheylie 2014; Wynter 2003). Examples include social initiatives by people of color displaced by the 2008 housing and financial crisis in places like Detroit seeking to reinhabit and sustainably develop urban living space long abandoned by capitalist elites, and the emerging global alliances and identification among black and Palestinian youth subjected to surveillance, violence, and containment by state authorities like the police and occupying armies. Of course, as they have in social movements like the Arab Spring, Black Lives Matter, and Occupy, new media and related social networking platforms like Facebook, Twitter, Snapchat, and Instagram play roles in social projects challenging and building different conceptions of belonging and practices of sociality.

In the end, the story that I have been telling is about the changing nature of race, the truth of which is a product of the alliance of racial science, mediated technologies, cultural recognition of multiculturalism, and political disavowal of racial differences. The deployment of race takes on different forms, mobilizes different discursive and material resources, and produces different effects across time and space. Race continues to work through multiple and dispersed forms of subjection to the effects of its truth as freedom from and subjection to regulation, vulnerability, risk, and security.

With every new instantiation of this very old story, we have yet another opportunity to make race and the social worlds that it aims to build matter less to manage, regulate, and exploit populations. While we may elect to make race matter more or less in other ways, we need not proceed on this terrain uncritically and without the critical insights learned from fictions of nineteenth-, twentieth-, and now twenty-first-century racial knowledge that claim for themselves racial truth. We are once again in the position to decide how to make race matter less in shaping human history, what the truth of race is, and how it is deployed in the service of human sociality. That is to say, with the questions we ask and the truths we seek from our science and our politics, we are once again in the position to decide what difference race makes for our understanding of human potential and social relations.

54

Realism

Greg M. Smith

The most obvious way to think about realism is also the least productive. Our initial instinct might be to compare reality with its portrayal in media, but when we do so, we always arrive at the same conclusion: the media "distort" reality. In representing reality, media makers must select which things to include, which to condense, and which to leave out. There is no way that any medium could compare favorably to the breadth, depth, and complexity of the real world. Media portrayals always lose in that simple comparison.

It is more productive to think about realism as an effect that occurs when our assumptions about what is "realistic" intersect with the techniques that media makers use to portray their world. Our individual experiences give each of us specific knowledges about how the world works, but because we live in the world together and we share media, we have developed dependable conventions that media makers can use to encourage us to accept the worlds they present. So realism is both individual and shared. It is not "natural"; it is something that people do.

We begin to judge the realism of media as soon as we begin consuming it, or even before. We recognize strategies that we have seen in other realistic texts, and this recognition serves as a frame that encourages us to interpret the material inside that frame as being more realistic. Even the simple phrase "based on a true story" can alter the way that we think about the world being presented.

The interpretive frame depends on what we know about the source of the media. We have a journalistic contract with certain news providers whom we have grown to trust, and so we might assume that any images they present have passed journalistic standards, giving them added authority. A fiction filmmaker can have a similar authority based on what we know about his or her life experience. I trust that Spike Lee will get the details right when he portrays the Bedford-Stuyvesant neighborhood of New York where he spent his childhood. Even knowing something about the circumstances in which a video was taken can contribute to its realism. Wrongdoing captured on an onlooker's cell phone can trigger political outrage because we treat those images as evidence. The persuasive force of realistic images depends not only on the images themselves but also on the frame we use for interpreting them.

John Caughie (1980) has noted two broad categories of realistic imagery that he calls the "dramatic look" and the "documentary look." The dramatic look is what we call the "invisible" Hollywood style. The conventions of continuity editing and shot composition encourage us to ignore the actual production circumstances (a highly controlled set with lighting, booms, makeup, multiple takes, and many technicians) and to focus on getting emotionally involved in the characters and their predicament. We accept that a sitcom or fiction film will anticipate which character has the next line of dialogue and will cut to that character just in time. The documentary look does not appear to have this kind of magical knowledge about what will happen. We know that documentary filmmakers cannot always ask the real world to "cut!" and do another take, and so the documentary look is messier than the dramatic look. Because we have seen examples of both the documentary and dramatic looks, we can recognize these two broad "flavors" of realism. We can also recognize the component parts of these two styles, and media makers can recombine these techniques to produce multiple "realisms."

The documentary look in particular relies upon our broad assumption that reality is not pretty. We expect that the world of realism will be unplanned and less manicured, and assume that a more spontaneous, less prepared glimpse of the world will potentially glimpse a bit of the unvarnished "truth." If the media maker's technique appears to respond to the spontaneity of the world, then our experience with the documentary look will encourage us to see this as "realistic." For instance, over the years a handheld camera style has come to be associated with the documentary look. The documentary camera often appears to respond to unplanned events in the world, and the swerving path that it takes conveys how visually unpredictable the world appears to be. Similarly, we might assume that a messy realistic world will sound verbally spontaneous. People in real-life unscripted situations do not talk in witty, well-written lines of dialogue; they search for the right word and interrupt each other. Media makers have thus worked to integrate more realistic forms of acting and delivering lines to create various styles of verbal realism.

The word "apparent" is important throughout this discussion of technique because this takes us one step away from having to judge if representations are absolutely "real" or not. We may not have the inside information to determine if content has been staged, but recording in an apparently spontaneous manner has a realistic effect. Even material that is "fake" can be considered realistic if it encourages us to think it is true to life, and media have developed techniques over the years that ask us to place our faith in the worlds they present.

Creative technique is important to realism, but so are the knowledges that we bring to the media. The impression of realism can be broken when media violate our general understanding of how the world works. When media present automatic weapons that never need reloading, or show us the spacious New York apartment where our struggling young protagonist lives, this can trigger our inner plausibility alarm. Our plausibility alarm can sound when media violate our assumptions about how human nature operates. If a character forgives too easily after a painful breakup or recovers too quickly after the death of a loved one, we might object, saying that "people just don't act that way." Plausibility relies upon our individual and shared knowledge of how the world works and how specific types of people act, and if this monitoring is violated, it interrupts our sense of whether a text is "realistic."

Because plausibility is based on how we think the world works, it tends to reinforce our sense that "that's just the way things are" (the basic message of realism). Watching representation after representation that fits our preconceptions can do powerful ideological work to establish that the status quo is simply natural. On the other hand, journalists have long relied on realistic images to punch through our assumptions about how the world works. Uninterrogated plausibility can be a powerful ideologically conservative force; realistic images can also challenge our comfortable assumptions about what is plausible.

Plausibility is closely related to our expectation that the world (real or fictional) is consistent. We are able to navigate confidently through the real world because people and places tend to stay pretty much the same, and we expect our fictional worlds to behave consistently if we are to accept them. Even futuristic, supernatural, and magical worlds are judged by the standards of consistency. If a character suddenly violates the laws of time travel to extricate himself or herself from a trap, we sense the presence of the media maker intervening in the fictional world to solve the character's dilemma. Although we may have no real-world experience with wizards and aliens, we expect that fantastic fictional worlds will play by the rules they establish for themselves, and if a text activates our sense of implausibility or inconsistency, its sense of realism is (at least temporarily) broken.

Some media makers believe that such consistency is itself a kind of lie. Media making involves mistakes, indecisions, and manipulations by creative personnel, and both the dramatic and documentary looks often want to hide the considerable amount of human effort involved so that we may focus on the subject at hand. However, other media makers prefer a reflexive approach that acknowledges the process of storytelling and/or the audience as part of the story. A reflexive film, for instance, might remind us that we are watching a film, not eavesdropping invisibly on a real world. Characters may "break the fourth wall" to speak directly to the unseen audience, or a documentary may show the director's indecision about how to ethically portray the subject. Such interruptions kick us out of standard dramatic/documentary realism, and so reflexivity at times feels like the antithesis of realism, like an acknowledgment of just how false media making is. But to a reflexive filmmaker, this is a more honest stance than allowing us to comfortably immerse ourselves in the manufactured fiction of a consistent realistic world.

Realism involves what we know about how media are made and about the creative technologies used. An awareness of Photoshop's capabilities can change the way we look at a female model on a magazine cover; assuming that such images are untouched can powerfully shape our norms concerning what bodies should look like. As technologies change, so do our assumptions about what is "realistic." "Realism," therefore, is better thought of as many different "realisms."

55
Reflexivity
Mark Andrejevic

Perhaps the founding gesture of philosophy is reflexivity—that is, the turning around of thought upon itself. Unsurprisingly, media practices and technologies are at the core of this turn, according to foundational accounts of the origins of philosophy, in which writing (as distinct from the oral tradition) fixes understandings of the world so as to highlight their transformation over time. This fixity points to competing modes of understanding that require, in turn, reflection on different (and incompatible) "truths" (see, for example, Havelock 2009). Once a truth is fixed in written form, or so the story goes, it cannot adjust, as oral accounts do, to shifts in shared cultural understandings that develop over time: it stands out as an anachronous understanding that needs to be accounted for—hence the link between history and philosophy.

Reflexivity tends to be associated by sociological popularizers of the term (Beck, Giddens, and Lash 1994) with a distinct form of modernity. The process of reflecting upon traditional constraints and truths is a defining attribute of the Enlightenment—one also associated with media technology, specifically the print revolution that enabled widespread access to texts formerly controlled by political and religious elites. As texts themselves became available to a wider audience, authoritative interpretations could be interrogated and reconfigured, dismantling some of the aura and authority of tradition (Eisenstein 1983).

Reflexivity, in this critical sense, refers to a reflection back upon one's own modes of understanding, thinking, or being in the world—not to the apparently opposite sense of an unreflective, automatic reaction (a "reflexive" reaction). Indeed, Ulrich Beck (Beck, Giddens, and Lash 1994) contrasts the process of reflexivization to that of reflection, understood as deliberate contemplation. The former is the cumulative and unintentional result of a range of processes enabled by the development of industrial society—an unintentional consequence of the forms of rational control that generate their own incalculable by-products associated with advent of what he terms the "risk society." He uses the term to refer to a paradoxical feature of modernity: the fact that greater knowledge leads not necessarily to greater control, but rather to the proliferation of seemingly incalculable risks. Consider the development of increasingly powerful and ubiquitous energy technologies that generate environmental feedback effects whose consequences are, as recent debates indicate, largely unknown. We may know that increased concentration of carbon dioxide in the atmosphere will increase Earth's surface temperature, but the complexity of the ecosphere makes it hard to predict what the concrete consequences of this increase might be, socially, politically, economically, and environmentally. For example, if changing growing seasons and patterns disrupt traditional food chains, these changes might lead to forms of political conflict (generated by food scarcity) that escalate regionally or globally. Similarly, nuclear weapons (and nuclear power) raise the prospect of catastrophic risks.

For Beck, Giddens, and Lash (1994), writing in the incunabulum of the World Wide Web, modernization has taken on a new and distinctly form in which "the social and natural worlds . . . are thoroughly infused with reflexive human knowledge. This infusion does not lead to a situation in which collectively we are the masters of our destiny" (vii). On the contrary, hyperreflexivity corresponds to the advent of new landscapes of risk resulting not from external catastrophes (such as a meteorite strike or a natural disaster), but from the very human activities that are directed toward greater forms of control. This sociological formulation is an important one, insofar as it portrays the reflexive gesture as a failed attempt to gain and assert control.

In the context of an information-saturated society, some of the claims of reflexive modernity look prescient: more people may have more access to more information about the world than ever before in human history, and yet this advance in access corresponds with new forms of fragmentation, increases in inequality and insecurity in informed societies, and a range of new forms of information-related risks, from data breaches to cyberterrorism. If the dream underwriting the technological optimism of the Internet era is that an informed society would be a more democratic and peaceful one, it remains unrealized.

And yet, we find ourselves immersed in logics of mediated reflexivity. The generation that came of age in the cable TV era experienced something distantly analogous to the earliest days of writing transposed into the register of broadcasting: formerly ephemeral media experiences became fixed and repeatable, allowing for the collision of TV epochs, thanks to rerun syndication and an increasingly multichannel environment (and eventually to online streaming and file sharing). Viewers switching between *I Love Lucy*, *M*A*S*H*, and *Cops* could get a sense of the sweep of televisual conventions and the changing ways in which audiences are conceived and configured. Once again, it is easier to see how representations are constructed when they are disembedded from their contexts and juxtaposed with one another. Consider, for example, how contrived advertisements from the 1950s look to contemporary viewers.

One result is that the constructed character of mediated representation migrated to the foreground in this environment, contributing to the rise of reality TV and the related subgenres of "behind the scenes" and "the making of" shows. These formats might be described as reflexive in the sense that they foreground the logic of contrivance, conceding the constructed character of televisual representation. In promising to move beyond or to get behind the constructed façade of representation, they cater to a reflexively savvy audience familiar with the understanding that all representations are constructed. They simultaneously preserve the notion of a deferred, unmediated real, if only by inviting the familiar rejoinder that, despite their promise, media texts are "not *really* real" (because they have not captured what they promised).

This double logic of the debunking and conservation of unmediated reality is a hallmark of the operation of reflexivity in an increasingly media-saturated environment. One symptom of this combination is a familiar form of "savviness" that seeks to insulate itself from the threat of being taken in by contrivance and representation: perhaps the defining goal of such reflexivity is not to be fooled. This form of reflexivity combines a "knowing" attitude with a naïve form of direct faith in immediacy. Consider, for example, the 9/11 conspiracy theorist who "sees through" the machinations of all the "mainstream" and "establishment" media outlets, but accepts without question the anonymous claims made on an obscure website about what "really happened." The point here is not to assert that the mainstream media are always right (or that fringe websites are necessarily wrong), but rather to locate the paradox of generalized savviness: it is impossible to take a stance that debunks *all* representations. Even the savviest subject has to believe in something after having leveled the

criteria for distinguishing between opposing accounts or representations. Thus the way is paved for a return to direct sensory appeals that ostensibly bypass mediation, such as the resurgence of "flat earth" theories in early 2016. Such theories simultaneously "debunk" established science as an elitist ruse and make a direct appeal to how the earth looks to someone standing on it (i.e., pretty flat). This form of generalized reflexivity occupies the paradoxical position of having gone both too far (in dissolving the efficacy of representation altogether) and not far enough (by failing to reflect on its own impasses).

A culture of reflexively savvy skepticism is a result not simply of the failure of traditional forms of instrumental rationality to deliver on their promises of progress and control (a failure associated with the rise of the risk society), but also of the multiplication of narratives and counternarratives associated with an ever expanding information environment. The multiplication of forms of "trutherism" in the United States—referring to conspiracy narratives about everything from the 9/11 attacks to health care data—coincides with a reflexive recognition of the always partial and constructed character of mediated representation.

The danger of reflexivity is that it can be demobilizing—not because it slows down the process of understanding, as in the case of reflection, but because it caters to a debilitating savviness. This attitude is properly conservative insofar as it sacrifices the leap of faith associated with social struggle in order to claim the status of the "non-duped." The predominant ideology of contemporary capitalism "concedes the critical point—that, for example, power is increasingly lodged in the hands of a select few who control not just the economy, but politics and the mass media—without becoming the dupe of such critiques and imagining that things could be otherwise" (Andrejevic 2004, 178).

This ideology interpellates a reflexively savvy subject who derives pleasure precisely from not being fooled by either the political and economic elites or their social critics: such a subject knows just how bad things are and just how futile it is to imagine they could be otherwise. The media sociologist Todd Gitlin invokes the example of reflexive political coverage to demonstrate this attitude, arguing that the trend of "meta-coverage," which knowingly documents politicians' attempts to manipulate public opinion, serves to naturalize the manipulation process rather than to debunk it. This meta-coverage trumpets its own failure as its final satisfaction. It paradoxically devotes ever greater resources to "news" that demonstrates the futility of its own premise: that informing the public serves to empower it. His description of savviness highlights the passivity of reflexivity: "One is already participating, in effect, by watching. 'I like to watch' is the premium attitude" (1990, 21).

By contrast, the risk society theorists anticipate that the process of reflexivization opens up new realms of social practice to politicization: "Those decision making areas which had been protected by the political in industrial capitalism—the private sector, business, science, towns, everyday life and so on—are caught in the storms of political conflicts in reflexive modernity" (Beck, Giddens, and Lash 1994, 44). According to this account, the very failure of traditional political institutions and their strategies for control (as evidenced by declining levels of public trust and confidence) necessarily politicizes new realms of social practice. The media studies version of risk society theory is the fan studies work that locates new (sub)political resources in the intersection of interactive technology and popular culture. The notion here is that fan "activism" will, in an era of convergence, carry over into the political realm, fostering new forms of bottom-up politics. How such a politics might overcome the undermining of the effectivity of representation remains to be seen. The hope is that reflexivity can be disarticulated from the demobilizing savviness fostered by reflexive modernity.

56

Representation

Lisa Henderson

People communicate through symbols, like words or images, that stand for other things. This "standing for" is what communication scholars call representation.

Classical definitions of representation emphasize two facets: political (as in elected representatives) and symbolic. These facets cannot be separated in practice, as each embodies the other. In media studies, political representation leads to studies of campaign messages and outcomes, and the media's role in political socialization, or how we come to think about the political sphere more generally. Symbolic representation, as a broader practice of *standing for* across media and genres, is central to media studies as a whole.

In this broader sense, representation is an achievement of language and other symbolic forms, especially visual images and nonverbal sounds, styles, and gestures. Symbolic forms stand for other things. The word "tree" stands for the tall, erect, natural form with trunks, branches, and leaves. Participants in a native language, especially those considered "neurotypical," fuse the word and the object it conjures to create the mental concept "tree." (This is a process best understood by the field of *semiotics* [see Bignell 2002].) We do this over and over again, learning to use language to represent our reality, from cells to trees to constellations or values.

A foundational insight here is that "reality"— the world as we know it—is unavailable to us except through language and other symbolic systems. If a tree falls in the woods, does it make a sound? Yes, it produces electromagnetic phenomena we call sound waves, which require receptors (not only human ones) to decode those signals into "sounds." But what sense do we make of that falling tree? Is it old? Harvested? Stolen? Endangered? Uprooted by erosion and wind? To ask these questions is to submit the phenomenon of a falling tree to frameworks of explanation, in other words to make meaning. As human beings, we cannot *not* make meaning, though the meanings we make vary by era, group, and culture. We are complex meaning-making organisms and groups who depend on learned symbolic systems, from sounds to alphabets, brushstrokes, or equations, for making sense of reality. Does this mean that nothing *exists* without language or other symbolic systems? No. But without language nothing *meaningful* exists (see Hall 1997a).

Once we understand this point, we begin to see our dependence on language and other symbolic systems and, in turn, why media studies is so devoted to the concept of representation. For us to receive people, events, and even future possibilities as meaningful and real, they need a symbolic presence, something representing or standing for them, and nothing concentrates, distributes, or withholds that presence like our everyday media. There, meaning takes shape in the interaction of media systems, their workers or producers, and media audiences.

Since it matters so much, this process of media representation is argued over and fought for: who and what are in or out? *How* do media represent people? The stakes are especially high for groups whose worlds are largely excluded from media repertoires and whose members are largely excluded from the ranks of producers. In current public debates, for instance, do reporters and pundits call non-US nationals who arrive, without papers, to live and work in the United States "illegal aliens" or "undocumented workers"? The phrase selected—the representation—brings with it a world of moral and political meaning and consequence, for speakers and the people spoken about.

From a variety of perspectives, media studies scholars ask how the media represent the world. Most compare media content to the "real world" (as best as they can separate the two), and interpret the differences they find. Scholars have asked, for example, about the gendered world of television in contrast to gender difference in the world outside. Historically, most prime-time, scripted, broadcast television lead actors (on such networks as CBS, ABC, and NBC, for example) were men, despite there being more women than men in the audience and in the US population at large. The over-representation of men among leads, and the under-representation of women, said something about who deserved a profile, who producers believed prime-time audiences wanted to watch in lead roles, and thus who advertisers would support. It wasn't the proportion of women in the world that determined their numbers on prime-time television, it was men's presumed power and desirability in a commercial medium run largely by men. Here, the political and symbolic meanings of representation converge: only some people are selected to represent others, in this case not people elected to Congress but those hired to their role as decision makers and gatekeepers in the media industry.

We can update the gender representation question by considering technological platform and a broader definition of the gender spectrum. First, we might ask whether changes in platform mean changes in the makeup of the world of television characters compared to their real-world counterparts. Broadcast networks have long relied on high ratings—viewers in the millions or tens of millions—in order to draw advertisers, whereas streaming services rely on new subscribers in much smaller numbers. With the change in platform

and business model, representational changes follow: now, content providers on premium cable and streaming services can afford narrower, more defined audiences seeking more specialized or—by mainstream standards—more unusual stories and characters. One estimate comes from television critic David Bianculli (2015), who, in quoting (but not naming) a Hollywood insider, suggests that two hundred thousand new Netflix subscribers attracted by the addition of a series like *House of Cards* means that series will break even. After two hundred thousand, it's "all profit."

With such a different audience scale and no nervous advertisers, do cable and streaming series reach beyond old formulas of power and desirability to better represent the gender spectrum? While gender is still overwhelmingly represented as women and men, girls and boys, and while a majority of US leads across platforms are men, cable and streaming content has introduced lead and continuing characters who identify elsewhere on the gender spectrum, including butch lesbians (Shane on *The L Word* from premium cable's Showtime network); transitioning and transgender women (Maura in *Transparent* on Amazon and her friends Davina and Shea; at Netflix, Sophia on *Orange Is the New Black* and Nomi on *Sense8*); a transgender boy (Cole on *The Fosters* on cable outlet Freeform, formerly ABC Family); and one transgender man (Dale on *Transparent*). From these observations, we can come to a cautious but significant conclusion about the representation of gender difference: though they remain a tiny proportion of the population of scripted television shows, transgender characters and stories have made important representational inroads on new commercial platforms. Their numbers relative to the US population at large are hard to compare (given the limits of transgender census data and current estimates) but their presence resounds for transgender and non-trans viewers alike. The presence of a gender *spectrum* and of gender change, rather than binary opposition and the persistence of one gender over a lifetime, challenges and potentially shifts the broad audience's ideas about how gender works, and even exposes how gender-typical people "perform" (rather than innately embody) their gendered roles and identities. When such portrayals go beyond listless stereotypes to explore a character's life, responses, and social relationships, they reimagine or *re-present* the world of gender for everyone, transgender and non-trans.

When the media include images of groups historically excluded, it can be exciting to group members. In the early 1990s, critic Patricia A. Turner (1992) recalled her family's excitement, when she was a child in the 1960s, whenever a black actor was going to appear on television. It was an occasion for a long-distance phone call to alert family members far away, a gesture usually reserved for births and deaths. When Ellen DeGeneres's lead character came out as lesbian on ABC's *Ellen* in 1997, I watched the show in a roomful of thirty- and forty-something lesbians who never thought they'd live to see an openly identified lesbian character played by an openly identified lesbian actor. In her 2015 Kennedy Center Honors tribute to pioneering Puerto Rican actor Rita Moreno, *Jane the Virgin* star Gina Rodriguez thanked Moreno for being the *one* Latina actor Rodriguez's mother could point to, to encourage her daughter's aspirations.

Such examples, however, make it easy to slide into the conclusion that any historically underrepresented group is adequately represented by a single dimension, whether that be blackness, lesbianism, or Latina ethnicity. For most viewers, however, inclusion is strongest when differences *within* the group are represented. Tender, complex representations that speak "intersectionally" humanize historically excluded or stereotyped populations, and offer a foothold to other audience members who may share one character experience but not another. On *Transparent*, Maura (formerly Mort) Pfefferman and her family are Jewish; Maura's born of a mother who escaped Nazi Germany as a young woman. The legacy of family trauma, which psychologically affects even the youngest generation in Maura's family, is woven into the family's present-day story of change and their good-faith if complicated acceptance of Maura's gender transition in late middle age. Such a tapestry-like script invites any audience member who has experienced or inherited trauma (for instance, as a Jew, someone of African descent, or an exiled national) or deep hurt and loss to receive Maura and her family in terms that are close, not distant, familiar rather than "other."

The Pfefferman family is also conspicuously well-off, with their gracious home in the Pacific Palisades neighborhood of Los Angeles and Maura's career (as Mort) as a professor of political science. As Maura finds friendship and refuge with Davina and Shea, however, sometimes her privileged history reveals itself despite the transphobic aggression she has suffered. When she tells Davina that Davina's boyfriend Sal, recently released from prison, isn't good enough for her, Davina responds, "My God, who do you think you're talking to? . . . I'm a fifty-three-year-old ex-prostitute HIV-positive woman with a dick. And I know what I want and I know what I need. And if Sal is bothering you this much, you should probably sleep somewhere else." Class difference and its tensions are signified within the trans household, and viewers can carry the recognition of Maura as privileged, amid anti-trans discrimination, to other parts of the story. People who are working class, struggling, underemployed, sex workers, or just class conscious might also appreciate Davina's reality check.

One account of the narrative layers in *Transparent* relates the Pfefferman family story to the Jewish upbringing of the show's primary creator Jill Soloway, whose own "Moppa" (formerly her father) is a transgender woman. But, distinctively, the series also employs transgender writers, directors, designers, and actors. On *Transparent*, being transgender is a credential, not a liability. This is one way in which changes in the representational work of the series rely on and enable changes in the makeup of the production sector. A small handful of transgender performers and producers are *getting work*. It isn't a legal watershed, but it is an institutional shift in which transgender producers pool their talents and insights to *stand for* transgender characters and experiences and, by extension, transgender (and non-trans) audience members.

Resemblance, however, is not the only form of representation in scripted television or other media. Viewers also respond to what Ien Ang (1982) called "emotional realism." In their comparisons of media environments and the world outside, many critics seek empirical resemblance or affirmation: an image is only as good as its replication of actually existing contexts. This is understandable, but misses the point of popular drama and fantasy. *Star Wars: The Force Awakens* wouldn't work if you had to be a Jedi knight to enjoy it. (Or, since there are arguably no Jedi knights, surely no one enjoyed *The Force Awakens*—also an untenable claim.) As the film depicts a battle among villains and heroes and fathers and sons, however, viewers attach at the level of feeling; they are likely drawn by this emotional realism regardless of the empirical distance between their lives and fantasy characters'. In parsing the value of representation, however, the distinction between emotional and empirical realism is not simple. Both qualities are deeply bound up in our experience of "feeling represented."

Since the dawn of Web 2.0, many scholars have envisioned a world where all those who want to see themselves can produce and circulate their own representations. From small formats to "prosumer" communities,

the gates of representation, they argue, have burst open, so much so that the history of "symbolic annihilation" or exclusion is over. I share their sense of possibility, though cautiously. Future media studies of representation will return to the cultural braiding of emotional and empirical realism while responding to dramatic changes in media platforms and social opportunities for media making. *Transparent*, recall, arrived on Amazon only in 2014, and any population or community seeking symbolic and political representation must still contend with the issue of who controls the discourse and with what effect. The classical analysis of images *of*, *by*, and *for* whom is now more layered, with more places to look, but it would be a mistake to imagine that symbolic exclusion is over, or that the terms of inclusion have returned to communities seeking to represent themselves. Not quite. Black queer performers and producers in Chicago, for example, have taken to webisode television (with locally produced, four- to six-minute episode series) to make images and develop careers, relying on pooled resources and collective labor in the absence of easy entry into industrial precincts (Christian 2015). Their creative labor must not be set aside in studies of representation, nor should their career prospects and living wages be treated as secure in the "gig" economy. Visibility, moreover, is an ongoing, historical matter, responding to shifting relations of power, autonomy, and voice in any given place and time, not to a menu of groups who take their turn at representation and then are done.

Just as important, however, the question of representation must capture not only the world as we know it but the world as we feel it and as we would like it to be. Among the queer gamers Adrienne Shaw (2014) spoke with, for example, it isn't obvious that resemblance is what they're after—though it's "nice"—so much as diversity and alterity, other ways of being in the world, of imagining and playing out possibilities. A lock-step standard of correspondence between media lives and people outside the stories is more likely to reproduce divisions among niche markets (selling to "teenage boys" or "Hispanic women") than to reenvision the world. Shaw's gamers want vision, not representation in the conventional sense. Media can do that, too. From webisodes to games to youth-authored memes for political candidates, what world do we want, and how can we use our new platforms to imagine it together? How do we connect those platforms and images to the high stakes of enfranchisement in everyday life? US children's television host Fred Rogers famously said that "if you know someone's story, you will love them." Can we produce and expect stories of inclusive regard and solidarity in our representational future?

57

Resistance

Stephen Duncombe

"Resistance," as a keyword for contemporary media studies, has a curious political lineage. It was first adopted by the right, then crossed the aisle to the left; its history marks the evolution of an idea and a transformation in cultural politics.

The English word "resistance" is a derivation of "resist," stemming from the Latin—via the French—and meaning to stand. Resistance has a technical scientific meaning, "the opposition offered by one body to the pressure or movement of another," as well as a later psychoanalytic one: the unconscious opposition to repressed memories or desires. But it is the *Oxford English Dictionary*'s primary definition, "to stop or hinder (a moving body); to succeed in standing against; to prevent (a weapon, etc.) from piercing or penetrating," that conveys the meaning most often used in media studies: resistance is a stand against an oppositional power.

Writing *Reflections on the Revolution in France* in 1790, Edmund Burke is horrified by the French overthrow of birthright authority, the leveling of classes, and other such "usurpation[s] on the prerogatives of nature" (1993, 49). (He is particularly horrified by the thought of the hairdresser who thinks himself the equal of his betters.) The only response to such usurpations is to resist the Revolution, and return to time-tested tradition. But, as Burke understands, this resistance must go deeper, for revolutionary France also holds the intimate danger of "teaching us a servile, licentious and abandoned insolence" (54). Resistance, as such, is a matter of subjectivity as well as statecraft.

Nearly a century later, Burke's countryman, Matthew Arnold, takes up the call of conservative resistance. Arnold's mid-nineteenth-century England was a world of storm and strife: urbanization, industrialization, and class warfare. The republican ideals of the French Revolution had triumphed over Burke's beloved tradition, and "nature," in the age of Darwin, was harnessed to progress. A new principle of resistance was needed, and for Arnold it was culture. As "the best that has ever been thought and said" (1883, xi), culture offered a means to rise above the politics, commerce, and machinery of the day and supply a universal standard upon which to base "a principle of authority, to counteract the tendency to anarchy which seems to be threatening us" (52).

Halfway around the world Mahatma Gandhi (1919) was developing his own ideas of resistance, embracing Arnold's emphasis on culture, yet insisting it was the idea that English culture constituted the "best that has ever been thought and said" that needed to be resisted. To free India of British soldiers and bureaucrats was one thing, but liberation would come only when the country was free of British ideas, prejudices, and technology. A culture of resistance was necessary, and its source, as it was for Burke, was tradition. Gandhi counseled breaking India's economic dependence on Britain by *khaddar*, a return to the hand looming of cloth, and looked to non-Westernized, rural India for political and spiritual models.

Radical resistance, defined in part as the rejection of foreign cultures and the celebration of indigenous traditions, wound its way through the twentieth century, as European colonies in Africa and Asia were swept away by struggles of national liberation. This strain of resistance makes its way back to the metropole with those finding parallels between their own struggles and anticolonialism. A key point of identification was the fight against internalized oppression, what the Algerian writer and activist Albert Memmi (1965/1991) referred to as "the colonizer within." In 1970, the US-based feminist group Radicalesbians issued a manifesto calling for "The Woman-Identified Woman" based in an understanding that "if we are male-identified in our heads, we cannot realize our autonomy as human beings" (n.p.). This sentiment was further developed by the radical black women of the Combahee River Collective, who in 1977 asserted that "we believe that the most profound and potentially radical politics come directly out of our identity" (1977/1983, 272), making the case for resistance based within and upon the unique experiences of a person's ethnicity, gender, or sexual identity.

As the necessity of resistance was recognized at the intimate level of personal identity, the scope of what was to be resisted expanded dramatically. The political failures of student resistance in 1968 confirmed what French scholar Michel Foucault suspected: that power was not something out there, easy to identify and overthrow; instead it was everywhere, continuous, anonymous, intimate and even pleasurable: "the disciplinary grid of society" (1980, 111). Whereas previous critics of totalitarianism, from the left and the right, elevated the ideal of the individual subject resisting against totalizing society, Foucault countered that the subject itself was problematic. This Enlightenment creature that made new ideals of personal freedom possible also opened up a new site of oppression: the individual's mind, body, and spirit. Because power is impressed upon and internalized into the subject, it raised the vexing problem of who resists and what exactly are they resisting. Can one resist the very subject doing the resisting?

Resistance remained a stated goal for Foucault, but it had to be reconceptualized. The ideal of developing the pure subject in opposition to the corrupting object of society was rejected. "Maybe the target nowadays" he suggests, "is not to discover what we are, but to refuse what we are" (1984, 22). Resistance, then, becomes the only legitimate subject position, and resistance becomes an end in itself.

Resistance, as it is encountered in media studies, is most often cultural resistance. As the euphoria of the anticolonization struggles and student uprisings of the 1950s and 1960s gave way to the rise of corruption and dictatorships, noncolonization and neoliberalism, radical scholars began looking for resistance outside of the political sphere: on the street corner, in the living room, or at the dance hall, that is, in cultural expression. Cultural resistance was, of course, first articulated by Matthew Arnold, but it was a figure on the other side of the political spectrum, the Italian Marxist Antonio Gramsci, who framed the contemporary discussion.

Antonio Gramsci (1971), writing from a fascist jail in the 1920s and early 1930s, reflected on why the communist revolutions he labored for in the West had so far failed. Part of the reason, he concluded, was a serious underestimation of culture and civil society. Power resides not just in institutions, but also in the ways people make sense of their world; hegemony is both a political *and* cultural process. Armed with culture instead of guns, one fights a different type of fight. Whereas traditional battles were "wars of maneuver"—frontal assaults which seized the state—cultural battles were "wars of position"—flanking maneuvers, commando raids and infiltrations, staking out positions from which to attack and then reassemble civil society. Thus, part of the revolutionary project was to create "counterhegemonic culture" behind enemy lines. But if this culture was to have real power, and communist integrity, it could not be imposed from above; it must come out of the experiences and consciousness of people. Thus, the job of the revolutionary is to discover the progressive potentialities that reside within popular consciousness and from this material fashion a culture of resistance.

It was this politico-cultural mission that guided the Centre for Contemporary Cultural Studies at the University of Birmingham in the 1970s. The CCCS is best known for its subcultural studies, and it was within these mainly working-class subcultures that researchers found an inchoate politics of resistance: Mods one-upped their bosses with their snappy dress; Punks performed the decline of Britain with lyrics that warned "We're your future, no future"; Skinheads re-created a cohesive white, masculine working-class world that no longer existed; and Rastafarians turned the world upside down by re-reading Christianity into a condemnation of the white man's Babylon. It was through resistant culture that young people contested and rearranged the ideological constructions—the systems of meaning—handed down to them by the dominant powers of postwar Britain.

But cultural resistance needn't always take place *against* the dominant culture, it can also work *through* it. In her groundbreaking 1984 study *Reading the Romance*, folklorist Janice Radway admits the obvious: romance novels, through their depiction of women as driven by and dependent upon the love of a man, articulate and reinforce patriarchal values. Yet when talking to women who enjoyed reading romances, she found something else: a culture of resistance. Instead of celebrating the dependency of a woman upon a man, fans derived a vicarious power through the agency of a heroine who picks and pursues the man of her desire. Furthermore, just reading itself was recognized as an act of resistance: housewives taking time to indulge in a personal pleasure was a silent strike against a patriarchal society that expected them to be entirely other-directed.

The work of the CCCS and scholars like Janice Radway led to a flowering of cultural studies looking at "resistant readings" of the mass media and celebrating the agency of cultural creation, recreation, and interpretation, yet for the CCCS, as well as Radway, cultural resistance is politically ambiguous. Such resistance opens up spaces were dominant ideology is contested and counterhegemonic culture can be created, but these contestations and symbolic victories often remain locked in culture—and thus don't impact significantly the forces being resisted. As John Clarke et al. write in *Resistance through Rituals*, "They 'solve,' but in an imaginary way, problems which at the concrete material level remain unresolved" (2006, 47–48).

Is cultural resistance, resistance at all? Malcolm Cowley (1934/1976) raised this question nearly a century ago in his memoir of his bohemian days in Greenwich Village of the 1920s. Playful nonconformity, Cowley noted, which may have shocked an older bourgeoisie that honored hard work and sober thrift, no longer served the same function. Within the context of consumer capitalism, the bohemian call to be freed from yesterday's conventions translates all too easily into freedom to buy tomorrow's products. He is the jazz fan that Theodor Adorno infamously dismissed as one who "pictures himself as the individualist who whistles at the world. But what he whistles is its melody" (1938/1990, 298). The cultural rebel, far from resisting the system, is fueling its engine.

One needn't be as pessimistic as Adorno to acknowledge that resistance can be problematic. Not only is what is being resisted dependent upon resistance, but resistance depends upon what it resists. In other words, resistance exits only in relation to the force it sets itself against; without that force resistance has little coherence or purpose. To return to our original *Oxford English Dictionary* definition, without something solid to *stand against*, resistance tumbles over. What, then, is the point of resistance if the very thing being resisted must be maintained in order for there to be resistance? If one accepts resistance as an end in itself, then there is no problem. The point of resistance is an existential act, a tactic of survival, as Michel de Certeau (1984) would have it, within a larger strategy forever controlled by the other. If, however, one pins one's hopes upon resistance as a means by which to contest that dominant force and transform the larger culture, then resistance for itself is not enough—it must pass into something else: revolution or reaction.

Reaction is the easier path. At its core resistance was, and is, a conservative strategy. A conservative resists what is new to conserve the old. If this resistance to—this stand against—the new is successful, change is halted, and the opposing force is vanquished, then the conservative can fall comfortably—and victoriously—back upon the old world he or she fought to retain. For progressives, however, the process is more fraught. If the stand is successful, and the force resisted is removed, then in what direction does one fall? Forward, yes, but forward to where? Resistance, with its eyes always upon its adversary does little to provide a vision of the new world to come.

Yet in acts of resistance new worlds can be glimpsed. Culture—contra Arnold—is not delivered intact from on high, but forged piecemeal from people's interactions with the world around them. Reacting against dominant forces, people form new readings, new perspectives, new combination, and new cultures. This is not an autonomous imagination, but a dialectical one. Through resistance against what we do not like we begin to figure out what we do, and standing against can become a means to move forward.

For "resistance" to remain a relevant concern for media studies, it is not good enough to merely ask, resistance to what? We must always also be posing the question, resistance *for* what? Matthew Arnold once wrote that "freedom . . . is a very good horse to ride, but to ride somewhere" (1883, 344). The same might be said of *resistance*.

58

Sound

Michele Hilmes

Communication occurs for human beings through all five senses—sight, sound, touch, taste, smell—but modern media specialize in the first two only, with rare exceptions. Media studies, too, focuses on the "audiovisual" zone, and yet visuality has dominated media analysis, with sound too often regarded as a mere adjunct to much more important work done by the pictures on the screen. The "blind" medium of radio had just begun to be taken seriously by scholars and critics in the 1940s when television arrived to upstage it. By the time that media studies emerged as a field in the 1980s, radio and recordings scarcely entered into the discussion. Recently, however, audio media have come back into the mix, largely due to sound's digital explosion: podcasts, online audio, streaming services, and a much improved access to sound's past via digital archives, often experienced through increasingly mobile reception technology. In fact, sound media have frequently led digital developments while visual media struggle to catch up.

A new term is needed to encompass these sonic forms in a way that at once links them to familiar contexts such as radio broadcasting, points to areas of emerging critical attention such as television sound and voice recordings, and takes new digital forms into account. I propose the term "soundwork" as one that gathers together the momentum of the recent new wave of sound scholarship (see, e.g., Lacey 2013; Loviglio and Hilmes 2013; Morris 2015; Sterne 2012), aimed at addressing this moment of abundance and innovation in the audio side of audiovisual media. Soundwork refers to creative audio presentations that employ sound as their primary expressive tool, combining elements of voice, music, and actuality sound (sometimes referred to as ambient sound, or noise), no matter what the vehicle of delivery or the technological or institutional framework that produces them (Hilmes 2013). Thus soundwork excludes the "raw material" used to construct sonic texts—oral histories, recorded interviews, talks and speeches, environmental sound, music recordings—though of course these are relevant to the creation of soundwork the same way that raw footage is to a film or video. It designates texts that shape, package, and circulate audio elements in expressive ways, such as music presentation, discussion, performance, documentaries, features, and drama.

The concept of soundwork might allow us to revive the attenuated and almost forgotten critical vocabulary of sound, renewing the project of methodically analyzing sound style, affect, form, and genre. Sound criticism has only a few theorists to show for itself since the time of Rudolf Arnheim (1936), Michel Chion (1994), and a handful of others who have made important contributions to sound studies more generally (Schafer 1993; Sterne 2003). This has recently begun to change, with a few hopeful signs such as journals devoted to soundwork (*Radio Journal, Journal of Radio and Audio Media,* and *RadioDoc Review*) and important reevaluations of historical soundwork (Smith 2008; Smith and Verma 2015). Film sound has received more attention, some of it acknowledging radio's influence (Kozloff 1989), though consideration of television sound remains in its infancy (though see Deaville 2011; Rodman 2009).

One strand of soundwork particularly relevant to some of today's most vibrant sonic innovation consists of what was formerly called the "radio feature" or sometimes "radio ballad" tradition, created and carried forward in radio's early years by producers working in the Features Department of the BBC or in creative spaces like CBS's *Columbia Workshop* in the 1930s and 1940s. Hailed as "pure radio" or "photography in sound," the feature form experimented with presenting factual information creatively, stretching the limits of what sound alone could convey.

Today's producers of soundwork are following in this creative tradition, even though they rarely acknowledge it. John Biewen's collection of essays (2010) finds few of today's most influential radio producers reaching back any further than the early days of National Public Radio for their inspiration and stylistic influence, though echoes of influential sonic techniques are everywhere.

Meanwhile, exciting new forms emerge with little critical evaluation or impact on scholarship, like fully dramatized audiobooks, spellbinding semi-documentary podcasts such as *This American Life*, *Serial*, and *Radiolab*, audio self-education platforms such as the phenomenally successful *TED Talks*, and a revival of audio storytelling as varied as *The Moth Radio Hour* and *Welcome to Night Vale*, to name a few. Such soundwork bridges the historical divide between techniques pioneered decades ago by long-forgotten artists and the innovations of today, and links older broadcast forms with new digital experimentation. By gathering up the long-dispersed threads of sound history, criticism, and practice into a new category, soundwork, we can begin to adequately celebrate the neglected sonic side of media creativity.

59

Space

Helen Morgan Parmett

Space means "denoting time or duration" and "area or extension" (*Oxford English Dictionary*). Media are often credited with the annihilation of space in both of these senses through their collapse of time/duration and compression of distance (Harvey 1989). Yet, media also constitute and produce space, symbolically and materially. Media are fundamentally disorienting and orienting—dislodging us, helping us navigate, and producing space simultaneously.

The possibility to transcend time/space was an early promise of mass media. Newspapers emerged amid the desire to bridge distances to bring news from colonies to ensure the success of the imperial mission (Warner 1990). Television too promised a "window to the world," providing increasingly suburbanized audiences what Raymond Williams (1974) called "mobile privatization," or the ability to both travel and stay put. Today, we are enjoined to view the Internet, mobile phones, and social media as creating a global world of interconnectedness, where our place-based affiliations matter little compared to our capacity to bridge distances and differences through interconnectivity.

This sensibility of media as space collapsing echoes Walter Benjamin's influential *The Work of Art in the Age of Mechanical Reproduction* (1936/2008). Benjamin contends that mass reproduction divorces art from its situatedness in a particular space and time, losing its "aura," or uniqueness and permanence. In contrast to his Frankfurt School counterparts who were more skeptical of mass culture, Benjamin saw the loss of aura as a democratizing possibility. Mechanical reproduction would enable art to travel, change, and be politicized and freed from elitist traditions of ownership tied to spaces of origin.

Benjamin, unfortunately, did not foresee the role that copyright law would play in regulating this travel and how media's space-collapsing mobilities bump up against territorializations that reinscribe place and time to establish ownership. For instance, Aaron Swartz—who used digital media's space-compressing capabilities to share scholarly research beyond the hallowed walls of academia—might have been heralded by Benjamin for unhinging art from its elitist institutions, since access to academic research requires institutional privileges that most individuals cannot afford. Despite the medium's capability for peer-to-peer sharing, Swartz faced up to fifty years in prison and a million-dollar million fine for these actions (Gould 2014).

Swartz's case demonstrates how ownership laws are utilized to reinstate hierarchies of bodies and spaces through governing information access and distribution. Media culture thus does not so much collapse space as it reorganizes it, producing new sensibilities of space by creating new geographies, mobilities, and identities (Appadurai 1990). But the capacity for media to reshape geography and mobility is not the result of inherent technical properties of the medium. Instead, these capacities are the result of culturally and historically specific motivations. Television, for example, emerged within a conjuncture marked by the production of social needs that constructed space compression as socially expedient. Within the contours of liberal capitalism and suburbanization, broadcasting served the interests of new institutions of capital, lending, and consumption centered on the home and the subsequent rise of new forms of social organization (Williams 1974).

Although television served the interests of postwar liberalism and consumer capitalism, its space-compressing possibilities also facilitated collective unrest and resistance. For example, broadcast images of police brutality against black citizens are credited with helping fuel whites' investments in the civil rights movement in the 1960s, as many visually witnessed the plight of the black body in America for the first time. Likewise, today, space compression serves the interests of global capital, as digital media help to connect global transnational corporations and facilitate the flow of capital across borders, as well as new social movements that utilize digital and social media to facilitate collective social unrest and to agitate against oppressive forces, including those of global capital.

But media are also bound up with the production of space in a materialist sense. Suburbanization, the isolation of the urban core through the highway system, and the electrical infrastructures that made broadcasting possible are central to understanding the rise of television. And the production of new material infrastructures, such as railways, arcades, and department stores, give way to new media forms, as Anne Friedberg (1993) argued with regard to how new experiences in city space at the turn of the century gave way to early conceptions of film.

The study of media space, however, has been largely concerned with media's representation of space, or more aptly, place. Place is defined by its relationship to a local articulation, marked by its history and specificity in a moment in time (Massey 1994). Constituting a cultural encounter (Morley and Robins 1995), media create new geographies through the travel of images that bring new sensibilities, identities, and ideas from distant places. But representations are also mediated by our situatedness in the places we consume, use, and produce media images. Spaces of media consumption take on a new texture in an era of digital and social media, convergence, and interactivity in which media consumption appears ubiquitous and mobile, where individuals are invited to produce fluid and cosmopolitan senses of identity not bound to a particular place. Even industries of media production, often theorized within a political economic framework that assumes their centralization in place (e.g., Hollywood), are no longer clearly locatable. From the proliferation of media capitals (Curtin 2003) to the ubiquity of producer/consumer (or produser) spaces and the ever presence of location-based media (media that track or invite you to identify your location), contemporary media production practices reorganize spaces and places of everyday life into potential sites of mediation (Morgan Parmett 2014).

Considering media and space as co-constitutive highlights how media are put to work by a variety of social forces to govern everyday spaces in historically and culturally specific ways that can both reinforce and challenge gendered, raced, classed, and sexualized norms. For example, highlighting the significance of early film in instructing audiences on how to adjust to changing gender norms during industrialization and urbanization, Lauren Rabinovitz (1998) demonstrates how film spaces were as important as film content in defining new sensibilities of public and private space that hinged on the production of new gendered norms and identities. Likewise, feminist television scholars Lynn Spigel (1992) and Anna McCarthy (2001) show that television governs uses of domestic and public space, again not just through content, but also through its use in a particular space and context that constitutes and directs the flow and movement of gendered, raced, and classed bodies. Whereas Spigel considers the spatialization of television in domestic spheres to argue that television was a site for working out struggles and anxieties over postwar gender norms in the suburban home, McCarthy considers television in the public sphere, like the pub or airport, where the television's placement governs social practices in site-specific ways. In these senses, media work as a technology for governing through the production, organizing, and disciplining of space. Cameras and screens, for example, guide the appropriate uses of a particular place, biopolitically producing bodies and behaviors or disciplining and excluding those that contradict "appropriate" uses. Likewise, we are encouraged to use media technologies to reorganize our bodily space in terms of calorie counts or steps per minute to produce our bodies as "healthy" and "fit."

These examples suggest that theorizing media space pushes critical media studies in a non-media-centric direction (Moores 2012), focused on practices rather than objects. Media are more than technologies, systems of production, texts, or audiences, and are instead part of a broader matrix and set of contextual relations. It is in understanding social, political, cultural, and economic life in this broader sense that media space research offers the most promise for critical media studies.

60

Stereotype
Ellen Seiter

Media stereotypes are systematic representations, repeated in a variety of forms from jokes and cartoons to news broadcasts, feature films, and television series. A descriptive or designative (based on physical appearance) aspect combines with an evaluative aspect in which people are judged from a particular perspective or point of view. Stereotypes are especially insidious when they become a way for powerful groups to characterize subordinated groups, whether it is men viewing women, whites viewing blacks, or the middle class viewing the working class. What is usually false about a stereotype is the systematic suggestion that all people of a group are this way, and this way by nature, and that we should feel superior to them, whether we despise, fear, or laugh at the stereotype.

The evaluative dimension of stereotypes justifies social differences. This goes for positive stereotypes (the boy genius, the visionary CEO) as well as negative ones (the crack addict, the welfare mother). Positive stereotypes of majority groups are rarely seen as problematic, but it is important to study stereotypes in relationship to one another. For example, stereotypes usually describe (implicitly or explicitly) women in terms of sexuality—typically a nonfactor in stereotypes of heterosexual white men. Yet sexuality becomes a defining aspect in stereotypes of men of color (the hypersexual black athlete, the asexual Asian "overachiever") (Seiter 1986).

Stereotyping is at the core of everyday thinking about media effects because they function as cautionary images—warning who not to be—as well as models of available social identities. The common usage of the term includes only a part of Walter Lippmann's original intention. Coining the term in his 1922 book *Public Opinion*, Lippmann emphasized the commonsense aspect of stereotypes as well as their capacity to legitimize the status quo. For Lippmann, stereotypes are "pictures in our heads" that we use to apprehend the world around us. They result from a useful "economy of effort," a notion that corresponds to the "cognitive" study of stereotypes retained by many social psychologists.

The question of the truth or falsity of stereotypes is immaterial for Lippmann and cannot account for their origin—something to be found in social divisions: "A pattern of stereotypes is not neutral. . . . It is not merely a short cut. . . . It is the guarantee of our self-respect; it is the projection upon the world of our own sense of our own value, our own position and our own rights" (1922, 28, 96). Described in this way, the significance of stereotypes as an operation of ideology becomes clear. Perhaps the most blatant examples in recent US film and television programs are Arab/Muslim stereotypes. Stereotypes (including those of Arabs and Muslims) change over time and are based in history. While Arab Americans were formerly primarily subject to "symbolic annihilation"—Gaye Tuchman's term for groups who are invisible in the media (1978b)—since 9/11 the image of the Arab terrorist has permeated media news, action films, and political thrillers. Stereotypes not only exist in the media; they are made concrete in the everyday lives of Americans who happen to practice Islam or who happen to "look Arab" (including many Latinos), in the incidence of traffic stops, vandalism, and airport security holds. They persist in ignorance. Iranians and Sikhs are not Arab, for example. The largest Muslim populations in the world are not Arab but South Asian. Most Americans of Egyptian or Lebanese descent are, in fact,

Christian. Yet even on shows that have tried to introduce sympathetic Muslim characters—*24*, *Sleeper Cell*, *Homeland*—the sympathetic portrayals often lead to martyrdom, as though screenwriters had exhausted their imaginations spinning a Muslim character positively and could take the character's arc no further. Their persistence in the media can be explained through the lack of more diverse and knowledgeable personnel working behind the cameras; there are only a handful of Muslim screenwriters in the Writers Guild of America, for instance.

Stereotypes can get you killed—as in the case of the Arab "terrorist," or the young black man assumed to be an armed and dangerous "gang" member, or the "fairy" whose effeminacy renders him a target to violent gay bashing. The long history of the jezebel/loose woman/slut "justifies" sexual battery and even murder. In this last case, as with many LGBT stereotypes, there has been an active attempt to protest the stereotype not by denying it but by reclaiming it, as in the "slut walk" protests against sexual violence. In a long-running comedy series such as *I Love Lucy* the dumb blonde/scatterbrained housewife stereotype part can become something understood in a new subversive way that points to the frustrations and oppressions of women's unpaid work. Overall there has been a significant reduction in the stereotyping of white women when more women enjoy executive positions in the TV industry and female characters populate TV screens to a vastly greater extent than they did in the 1980s. Similarly, showrunner Shonda Rhimes has turned many stereotypes of African American women (and men) on their heads with her series of hits, including *Scandal* and *How to Get Away with Murder*.

Lippmann hoped that individuals would hold these "habits of thought" only lightly and would be ready to change their knowledge of a stereotype when new experiences or contradictory evidence was encountered—an ability that Lippmann suspected was related to education. The starting point in any classroom discussions of media stereotypes is neither to shame individuals for their knowledge of stereotypes or to uphold the belief that any of us escapes their influence.

61

Surveillance

Kelly Gates

Surveillance literally means "watching over" and has a string of related associations—monitoring, tracking, observing, examining, regulating, controlling, gathering data, and invading privacy. The word is derived from the French term *veiller* and the Latin *vigilare*. It probably first appeared in the early nineteenth century in administrative reports, such as an 1807 document "Draft decree containing regulation for the maintenance and surveillance of the banks of the Rhine," and an 1812 document "Draft decree on surveillance, organization, administration, accounting, police and discipline of French Theatre" (both French-language documents located using the Google Books search engine). Google Books Ngram Viewer, an imperfect tool that measures the appearance of words and phrases in books printed since 1500, shows a sharp increase in the use of the word "surveillance" in English-language texts beginning in the 1960s. Writing in the early 1970s, a prominent sociologist of bureaucracy defined surveillance as "any form of systematic attention to whether rules are obeyed, to who obeys and who does not, and to how those who deviate can be located and sanctioned" (Rule 1973, 40). The term implies efforts to govern or control the activities of individuals under observation, and in this sense always signifies a power relationship. It is most often associated with preventing certain behaviors, but it can also connote efforts to encourage, enjoin, or even manipulate people into taking certain actions or conducting themselves in

a particular manner. The term is sometimes used in reference to the monitoring of things like plant life, insects, animals, weather, viruses, and machines, but such uses tend to neutralize its political valence and make it synonymous with "observation." While this usage is correct in a literal sense, it robs the word itself of some of its signifying power.

The figure most closely associated with exploding our thinking about surveillance is the French philosopher Michel Foucault. In *Discipline and Punish* (1979), Foucault detailed the principle of continuous surveillance designed into the panoptic architectural form envisioned by the English utilitarian social reformer Jeremy Bentham. The figure of the panoptic prison and the general principle of panopticism have become commonplace conceptual tools for making sense of the complex forms and effects that "watching over" has taken over the period of modern state formation. While Foucault used the panoptic principle to explain the rise of a historically specific set of disciplinary institutions (prisons, hospitals, schools, insane asylums), the concept has been extended to explain the myriad ways in which all manner of physical spaces and technical systems are designed to induce in individuals a state of continuous visibility and vigilance, from modern urban areas and shopping centers to the Internet and social media.

Today, the term "surveillance" is commonly associated with media artifacts like video cameras and camera-embedded devices, microphones, sensors, biometrics, drones, satellites, smartphones apps, and social media platforms. It is partly for this reason that the concept and its material manifestations have become objects of interest to the field of critical media studies: *surveillance* technologies are *media* technologies, and networked digital media are essentially *surveillant media*. "Surveillance" takes both representational and nonrepresentational forms—it can signify either visual or data-oriented forms of monitoring, or "dataveillance" (Clarke 1994). In fact, this conceptual distinction has become increasingly difficult to sustain along with the digitization of visual media. Surveillance now encompasses technologies, formats, practices, and protocols for reproducing and analyzing images, sounds, texts, and transaction-generated and other forms of data. It is used to refer to a wide range of monitoring and tracking systems that are structural features of information infrastructures, like the Internet, the Global Positioning System (GPS), and other networks that support data transfer across interconnected computers and electronic devices. Implied in the term are operations of widely varying scales, from home surveillance to satellite-supported military command-and-control systems. It is also used as a sweeping definition for present social conditions, as in "the surveillance society" (Lyon 2001), a historical phase seen as emerging contemporaneously with the spread of both computerization and closed-circuit television or video monitoring systems.

The term "surveillance" is typically associated with the main activities of the state and state security agencies, but systems designed for monitoring individuals and groups are also defining features of private security, labor management, and consumer research. Private companies engage in a wide range of activities properly termed surveillance, from visually watching over privatized shopping and work spaces for security purposes to monitoring employee conduct and productivity and gathering and analyzing data on customers. The market research industry employs a vast surveillance apparatus that includes everything from point-of-sale systems to social media platforms, experiments with new forms of emotion measurement using technologies like neuroimaging, automated facial expression recognition, and computational linguistics for "sentiment analysis" of text-based media. Global IT companies like Google and Facebook operate enormous monitoring, tracking, and analytic systems, their server farms housing petabytes of data on the online activities and expressions of hundreds of millions of Internet users across the planet.

The significance of the term "surveillance" clearly extends beyond the denotative meaning of "watching over" to encompass a great deal of complex connotations. Just as there is a blurry distinction between visual surveillance and "dataveillance," it is impossible to draw a clear line between state and private-sector forms of surveillance. Federal government and local law enforcement agencies alike contract with private security companies to deploy and operate their surveillance systems. The US National Security Agency likewise relies centrally on government contractors like Booz Allen Hamilton for its mass data collection activities, as well as telecommunications providers like AT&T and Verizon (as revealed by the whistle-blower Edward Snowden, a name now intimately tied to the term "surveillance," and himself a former employee of both Booz Allen and the Central Intelligence Agency). Personal data compiled and processed for commercial purposes can be and have been repurposed and mined for state security reasons. In fact, what characterizes surveillance in late capitalist societies is the complex network of state and private actors involved in system development, monitoring operations, data collection, and analytics. It is now common to encounter references to a "surveillance-industrial complex," an assemblage so vast and sprawling that no one—not even those who hold leadership positions within its organizational structures—knows the full extent of its reach. Much like the "military-industrial complex," a complex set of social and political-economic forces are seen as driving the development of this expansive "surveillant assemblage" (Haggerty and Ericson 2000), from the post-9/11 obsession with security to the rise of neoliberalism.

The range of meanings associated with the term "surveillance" also reflects the fact that surveillance technologies and practices are fully integrated with our cultural imaginaries and present-day "structures of feeling" (Williams 1977). Surveillance themes and narrative structures pervade literature, cinema, television, and visual art. The entire genre of reality TV has become a defining surveillant media form, featuring real people voluntarily laying their lives bare for the cameras. In this way, it has been argued that reality-based shows like *Big Brother* and *Survivor* subtly urge viewers to enact a form of transparent subjectivity, embracing the kind of willing submission to constant monitoring necessary for the success of online economy (Andrejevic 2002, 2004). Celebratory narratives about surveillance are also found in television's fiction genres. For example, the action-drama *Person of Interest* (2011–16) depicts an artificial intelligence system known as "The Machine," which provides always accurate yet incomplete information to the show's human crime fighters. Conversely, popular culture can be a site of commentary and critique about surveillance, a place where cultural anxieties are negotiated and social implications explored. Novels like George Orwell's science fiction classic *1984*, and its social media remake *The Circle* (2013), by Dave Eggers, offer disturbing cautionary tales of life under conditions of extreme transparency. Science fiction films like *Minority Report* (Steven Spielberg 2002) and *Gattaca* (Andrew Niccol 1997) likewise depict sympathetic protagonists fighting against oppressive surveillance regimes. And the historical-realist drama *The Lives of Others* (Florian Henckel von Donnersmarck 2006) critically reflects on the repressive monitoring operations of the East German Stasi in the 1980s.

As suggested by the prevalence of surveillance in science fiction, the term also encompasses ideas about predicting and controlling the future, ideas inflected with technologically determinist tendencies. The primary purpose of surveillance is to foresee, prepare, and control for the range of possible outcomes that could result from present actions and conditions. In recursive fashion, much of the discourse about surveillance suggests that a hypersurveillant future is itself predictable, a foregone conclusion. If such determinist beliefs shape the spectrum of possibilities for how the future is imagined in the present, it seems incumbent on critical media studies to conceptualize and interrogate surveillance in ways that destabilize the logic of inevitability implied in the term.

62

Taste

Elana Levine and Michael Z. Newman

The very presence of media studies in the academy was not a foregone conclusion; it is an effect of changing conceptions of taste over time. Many kinds of media—especially commercial media consumed by broad audiences—were usually beneath consideration, except perhaps as causes of individual or social problems, until the last decades of the twentieth century. Shifting understandings of taste have led to the existence of media studies, and to particular approaches, including taking cultural distinction itself as an object of study.

Several influential conceptions of taste have shaped the field. In *Critique of Judgement* (1790/2007), Immanuel Kant equated taste with the judgment of beauty, and identified beauty as a universally acknowledged quality found in nature and in fine art. In the nineteenth century, literary critic Matthew Arnold (1869/2006, viii) applied similar qualifications to a definition of culture as "the best that has been thought and said," a line of thought central to the premises of formal education worldwide. Each of these thinkers took as universal the values and tastes that were products of their privileged social positions. Dominant Western conceptions of art and culture fell in line with these assumptions well into the twentieth century.

With the growth and spread of mass media from the late nineteenth century on, intellectuals of various stripes began to recognize that traditional boundaries around art and culture were being tested, and many reacted defensively. Marxist critics like Max Horkheimer and Theodor Adorno (1944/2002, 94–136), deeply concerned with staunching the impact of fascism, argued that the masses, so entranced with the new "culture industry" of Hollywood movies and jazz music, were subjecting themselves to the quasi-fascistic control of capitalists. In this account, the standardized, repetitious products of the film and recording industries inculcate distraction in their viewers or listeners, robbing them of their individuality and making it impossible for members of the mass audience to exert any resistance to capitalism. A taste for mass media would be their downfall. By the mid-twentieth century, American culture critics like Dwight Macdonald (1962), a staff writer for the *New Yorker*, further defended "authentic" high culture not just from commercial mass media ("masscult"), which Macdonald proudly despised. He also distinguished it from a newly identified "middlebrow" culture ("midcult"), appealing to the swelling population of middle-class consumers in the postwar years, and perceived as mixing the profundity of elite art with the more popular pleasures associated with commercial mass media.

In the 1970s, sociologists began considering taste as a factor in social class stratification, disputing long-held assumptions about culture and value. In the United States, Herbert Gans (1974/1999, xi) argued that culture was categorized and defined through a taste structure that functioned hierarchically, positioning the tastes of socioeconomic elites most highly. He insisted that cultural forms embraced by those of low status really were culture, "not just commercial menace," and were worthy of sociological exploration. The French sociologist Pierre Bourdieu's (1984) work of the same period drew more explicitly on Marxist theories of economic stratification and inequality. Critiquing the claims to universality long used to position the cultural preferences of the elite as the only legitimate culture, Bourdieu demonstrated that taste was actually an assertion of economic and cultural capital and thereby a tool whereby those advantaged by their class position reproduced their status and power. In elaborating on Bourdieu's ideas, Mike Featherstone (1987) argued that middle-class consumers assert a taste for media such as movies and rock music as a subversion of elite cultural authority, in response to which elites have accepted the legitimacy of these forms as a way of maintaining dominance of the cultural field. Unfortunately, neither Bourdieu nor Featherstone accounted for such factors as gender, race, region, and nation in these assertions of capital.

Still, their recognition of taste as a site of struggle among social groups opened up new possibilities for studies of popular media. No longer as suspicious of commercial culture's pleasures or as concerned for the vulnerability of the masses, many scholars began to take all kinds of media seriously on their own terms. Taking the perspective of British cultural studies, such phenomena as popular media and fandom were understood as cultural practices to be analyzed for the meanings they encouraged and the challenges to dominant value systems they presented (Jenkins 1992). In the cultural studies of John Fiske (1988), popular taste, the taste of the people subordinated by dominant powers, was a cultural strike against conditions of social inequality. To study popular media was to agitate against the hierarchies so long embedded not only in intellectual discourse but also in lived experience.

Seeing cultural distinction as an instrument of power has led to a body of scholarship making taste its direct object of interest. For example, Lawrence Levine (1988) demonstrates the ways that Shakespeare's plays shifted in nineteenth-century America from being the culture of the working classes to that of the elite. In demonstrating that the status of a given cultural object might change over time, such work challenges the notion of universal value. Particular forms that had been low in

status at one point later became elite culture to suit shifting social needs, as happened with cinema in the post–World War II years with the rise of intellectual interest in film as art and in the director as author (Baumann 2007). Such a process of *cultural legitimation* functions to newly align certain kinds of media with certain kinds of audiences. This is often a class upgrade; middlebrow or high culture is associated with middle-class or rich people, while mass culture or popular culture is associated with audiences imagined as an undifferentiated mass or ordinary folks lacking in sophistication and competence. Gender, race and ethnicity, nationality, and many other kinds of social difference also figure into such distinctions, as in the denigration of the feminized genres of the young adult novel or soap opera, and in the rising legitimacy of black music when appropriated by white artists, as in the history of rock and roll.

Studying taste in media means making connections between media and the audiences they address. The result is the analysis of not only texts and their forms and meanings, but also their appeals to consumers, their cultural circulation, and their function within social structures. Our own *Legitimating Television*, which considers media texts and technologies along with discourses of the television industry and TV criticism, argues that television's increased respectability in the era of digital media convergence is a product of its upscaling in class status and its masculinization (Newman and Levine 2011).

It is possible at once to see the aesthetic appeals of a media text and its audience address and surrounding discourses of marketing, promotion, and criticism as functioning to produce distinction. But this does not necessarily require the study of the ways cultural phenomena sell cachet and prestige. Carl Wilson (2007) focuses on the album *Let's Talk About Love*, by Celine Dion (1997), a hugely popular but also much reviled pop star among those of a certain status. Wilson makes his study into an investigation of bad taste rather than an inquiry into the production of distinction. The payoff of looking at debased culture is not so different from that of scholarship on legitimation. It invites a new appreciation of the function of taste to reinforce social identities and distinctions among them. Wilson makes this argument by connecting particular elements of Dion's music, such as its schmaltz, with the social phenomenon of hating her recordings, prevalent among consumers of a certain hip milieu.

In attending to matters of taste, media studies is connected to an interdisciplinary constellation of ideas about social power and media's role in its workings. That this critical perspective has made the field itself possible is but one reason why taste is a key concept for media studies.

63

Technology

Jennifer Daryl Slack

"Technology" is a widely used term that provokes an almost predictable affective response, closes off the possibility of argument, and promises appropriate solutions for whatever problem is at hand. With the addition of "new," the affect multiplies. "New technology" has become a largely unquestioned goal, measure of progress, and promise of the good life. However, the work performed by the term "technology" depends on its mundane, polysemic, and opportunistic recruitment to variable projects and intentions, always with conceptions of reality and relations of power at stake. Interrogating its uses reveals a lot more about what matters in contemporary society than what it "really" means.

The more or less agreed upon definitions of technology typically fail to make visible the tensions, contradictions, and struggles entailed in its use. Technology has roots in the ancient Greek term *techné*, which was used differently by Plato and Aristotle to distinguish between knowledge (universal form for Plato, *epistémé* for Aristotle) and the transformation of that knowledge (*techné* or craft) into some form of practice or practical application. When first used in English in the seventeenth century, technology suggested, in addition to disclosing, a transforming of the natural, eternal, and divine into a discourse (or treatise) that is lesser or degraded. Casaubon (1875, v) wrote in 1612, "Men, void of Gods spirit, commonly and promiscuously did dispute of spirituall things, and convert Theologie into technology." His characterization of technology as something degraded and in opposition to religion appears at the moment when the arts and sciences were developing apart from the church and threatening the hegemony of the religious knowledge. These uses suggest that from the very earliest Greek and English usages, technology has been caught up in philosophical debates about the nature of and relationships between knowledge and embodiment, in the establishment of hierarchies of knowledge, and in the gradual ascendance of science and technology as secular knowledge practices in competition with religion (see Heidegger 1977). The articulation of technology with a sense of ultimate or degraded knowledge and religious or quasi-religious significance has thus had a long history.

From the seventeenth century on, technology has become more narrowly focused on the transformation of scientific knowledge in the service of craft and later industrial production. As this happened, the term became more closely identified with the products—the embodied forms of knowledge—that result from the transformative process of science-based industrial production. It became commonplace to refer to these "things" as technologies: machines, automobiles, televisions, computers, and so on. This shift has been so thorough that when most people use the term "technology" today, they typically seem to be referring to the "things" produced. Transformation remains extant more as affective residue, a sense that valuable things are produced in technological processes. For example, those who attend a technological university expect a STEM education to provide the knowledge and skills that will allow them to produce or manage technological "things," which are inherently valuable. Links to religious or quasi-religious commitments also continue to function, again largely affectively. As David Noble (1997, 3) explains, "the present enchantment with things technological—the very measure of modern enlightenment—is rooted in religious myths and ancient imaginings." So deeply held are these convictions that even to suggest that the development of new technology might be something other than progress is "to run the risk of being dismissed without hearing as a heretic, a Luddite, a fool" (Noble 1982, xiii). In contemporary culture, the constructions "technological progress" and the "technological sublime" are essentially redundant.

We live this legacy with multiple meanings of technology as (1) the disclosing of order, (2) a transformational process, (3) the embodiment of knowledge, and (4) a certain kind of object. Each of these "meanings" is further articulated to cultural "truths": (1) the development of new technology is synonymous with progress and the good life, and (2) technology is the result of scientific and industrial processes. All of these meanings and valences feature a range of debate, difference, and nuance, such that any particular use will—replete with tension and contradiction—enact a complex relationship among them. A single speaker may use the term in mutually exclusive and even contradictory ways, but rarely is that ever even noticed, so powerful is the affect its use conveys.

In the face of such complexity, it is challenging to pass on knowledge about technology both intentionally and thoughtfully, and the choices made in doing so tend to oversimplify and reinforce dominant conceptions of reality and relations of power. Typically, students are taught a version that emphasizes the superiority of science, the link between technology and progress, and an emphasis on things. For example, a recent third grade version of *Scholastic News* (2015) teaches this definition in its "Words to Know" segment: "technology: the use of science to make life easier or solve a problem." Technology as object is hived off to the next entry: "devices: machines that do a specific job." Yet, if you google technology and look past the first Wikipedia-style explanations that link technology to Greek meanings of *techné* and *logia*, you encounter primarily things: facial recognition technologies, patents on technologies, distance education technologies, surveillance technologies, media, robots, and so on. This "thingness" is pervasive, learned through everyday encounters. For example, almost every media outlet has a "technology" segment that usually features the newest gizmos: drones, hoverboards, and so on. Young people memorize great inventions and their inventors, a construction that privileges the production of things as responsible for making the world a better place and entails ideological, economic, political, and environmental assumptions and effects left largely unexamined.

Nowhere is the potency of this mixture of meaning and mattering more evident than in the "technological fix," the pervasive belief that any problem, whether produced by technology or not, can be solved with a technological solution, which does not require any change in culture generally or individual behavior specifically. For example, the widely held belief that new technology will solve the problem of global warming precludes the possibility that we might have to "sacrifice" any of our ways of life. In a mirror image of the fundamental optimism about technology, resistance to technologies based on beliefs in their ill effects has been exercised throughout history; but resistance is currently far less influential than the particular pro-technology formation that operates materially and ideologically. These positions typically rely on technological determinism—a belief that technology is the fundamental foundation of social life and that technological change is the primary determinant of social change (Winner 1977, 76)—which entails largely unexamined assumptions about the technological character of social and cultural life. It is difficult to conscientiously develop, implement,

resist, or even justify resisting particular technologies without a sophisticated understanding of the complex role of technology in everyday life. After all, there is no human life without technology, however it has been defined.

More helpful approaches to understanding technology recognize that technologies are not mere "things" and are better understood as being developed, implemented, and effective as integral to the complex ideological, political, economic, and environmental arrangements that constitute social and cultural life. For example, instead of studying the effects of clocks, Sarah Sharma (2014) addresses the question of culture and temporality, how time is constructed, and how different forms of keeping and marking time intersect in an organization of multiple temporalities. J. Macgregor Wise and I foreground the technological assemblage: an arrangement of humans, nonhumans, actions, and passions that intermingle and connect "practices, representations, experiences, and affects" with particular kinds of effects (Slack and Wise 2015, 157). Shifts such as these radically reformulate the concern for technology away from a fascination and awe of technological "things" to the more difficult but useful interrogation of technological culture.

64

Temporality

Sarah Sharma

The *Oxford English Dictionary*'s entry on "temporality" is a bit tentative: "the state of existing with or having some relationship to time." This relationship to time is a site of deep hypothetical investigation across almost every academic discipline: what is time and how does one experience it? Lurking behind most theorizations one will find references to clocks, clock towers, watches, telegraphs, train schedules, punch cards, stopwatches, airplanes, computers, networks, and fiber optic cables. These are power machines (Mumford 1963)—objects that impose new orders of time on the social field and recalibrate all of life to the dictates of their intrinsic tempos. It is important to note that these power machines are in fact media. But missing in most accounts of temporality is precisely that which makes temporality critical to media studies—the relationship between media and *lived time*. Appealing to a grand order of time, whether it is clock time or digital time, belies the fact that there are a multitude of interdependent temporalities that live, labor, and love under the auspices of contemporary global capitalism.

One of the most ideological statements made about time today is that we live in a culture of speed dominated by accelerated technologies. This is both a popular notion and an enduring academic conceit (Crary 2013; Hassan 2003; Virilio 1986). The imagined problem is the new 24/7 existence where the boundaries between the separate spheres of work, leisure, and sleep are increasingly blurred. The figures that animate this discourse about time include the fast-living and jet-setting business travelers who live in the time-space of the global network (Castells 1996); the flash boys trading at the speed of light (Lewis 2014); and the working mother juggling three shifts and her buzzing smartphone (Hochschild 2012). Temporality is imagined as if it were an individual subjective experience tied to a new dominant technology, yet temporality is not actually lived in this one-dimensional way. These "speeded up" lives depend upon other temporalities to maintain their pace of life, including their attempts to slow down and take "time off" (Sharma 2014). Neglected in this imaginary of speedup are the manicurists, dog walkers, hotel service staff, and UberEATS drivers (to name a few) whose sense of time is actually shaped by the time of these sped-up subjects.

Temporality is not a generalized sense of time particular to a historical epoch or an all-imposing effect of a specific technology, nor is it tied to a singular identity category. Rather, temporality is an intersectional type of social difference structured in specific political economic and geographical contexts. What is shared across the temporal differential is the expectation that one must recalibrate. Recalibration accounts for the multiple ways in which individuals and social groups synchronize their body clocks, their sense of the future or the present, to an exterior relation—be it another person, pace, technology, traditional chronometer, institution, or ideology. Temporalities are not randomly scattered but intricately tied and inexorably shaped by one another. Temporal regimes and strategic dispositions are cultivated in order simply to survive within the normalizing temporal order of everyday life. Individuals habitually discipline and submit to normative time. One's own regimes of time management can function to command another to recalibrate. Moreover, one's overall sense of time and possibility is formed by a differential economy of temporal worth. Invitations to recalibrate appear as cultural norms and expectation, sometimes by force and/or for lifestyle. The lived experience of time is both differential and entirely collective, and it is this mutual imbrication that defines temporality.

Media alter the temporal and spatial parameters of political and social possibility. A culture's dominant media forms will also determine to some extent what is epistemologically possible, including how it is that one even comes to know time in the first place. This is endemic of a strain of thought termed "medium theory" (Meyrowitz 1985). Following from McLuhan, the message of any medium or technology is the change of scale or *pace* or pattern that it introduces into human affairs (1964). And following from Harold A. Innis, who was McLuhan's predecessor, time is a cultural effect of media technologies manifest materially in the formal properties but also the infrastructure of media technologies and systems of communication to which they are tied. Cultures apprehend time and explain time through their technologies at hand (Heidegger 1977; Innis 1951). Temporality as a power relation, then, must also be understood in terms of its discursive power. For example, it is not the speed of life that creates inequalities. Instead it is the *explanatory* power of speed as if it were a uniform experience in the contemporary moment that elevates the time of some over others and also functions to exclude so much of the population who do not experience time in such a universal way.

Thus media studies must expand the scope of understanding even further, asking how different media alter the rhythm of social relations. This means continuing to broaden the definitional boundaries of what a medium is. Time tends to arrive in media studies in terms of the problem it now poses for everyday life, from politics to lifestyle choices (Sharma 2014). In other words the focus is too often on the right time appropriate to communication, the temporal requirement of democracy, issues of the best pace, the quantity of time necessary for this or that, and concerns over what is faster and what is slower. Or, temporality is taken up in terms of a uniform or novel effect of a particular media form. Temporality, or temporal time to use Innis's terminology, forefronts how particular technologies operate within and extend particular margins and centers of power *in time*. The temporal is about power. Temporality is experienced as a form of social difference (margins) and a type of privilege (centers).

What has been learned of clocks and computers might be learned of a slew of other power machines worth considering and finally naming as machines that exacerbate temporal differences. Thus, in the histories of these grand orders of time, one might continue to excavate and locate the temporal differences hidden in the grand story. There are key works in media studies that don't explicitly attest to revealing the temporal, but reveal it nevertheless. And, in fact feminist theorists and postcolonial theorists of media already have their eyes well beyond the domain of clocks and computers. Much of the work concerned with media and social difference already operates with recognition of the nontraditional media object. These are powerful because they slip from popular view but also because these media objects can work to challenge dominant regimes of power and reveal differential time politics as it cuts across gender, race, class, to name a few. Thus there are baby bottles and breast pumps (Wajcman 2004), wombs, and looms (Gajjala 2013). All of these are media technologies that are intimately and intricately tied to the reproduction of the social order, but they are also media technologies that alter the experience of women to seize control of the means of social reproduction. Along with these, there are also raced circuits of belonging that occur in time over that of space (Hegde 2011). We can see that technologies exacerbate temporal relationships under the guise of having access to the time of another in highly gendered ways, such as the history of the telemothering or domestic technologies in the home that promise free time but increase the time of work (Schwartz-Cowan 1983). There are also portable media that lead to a need for more phone chargers in transit spaces, which then reorient labor to maintain and service power outlets rather than people (see Gregg 2015b). At the risk of repetition, shared across the temporal differential is the expectation that one must recalibrate. Temporality for media studies means tracing this out and complicating the grand order of time that comes with the consumer packaging of our latest high-tech gear. It also allows for the opportunity to retrace our steps and locate how other media forms already theorized and taken account of might in fact have more temporal threads worth pulling out.

65

Text

Jonathan Gray

A text is a unit of meaning for interpretation and understanding. As such, most things are (or could be treated as) texts. Within media studies, a text could be a TV program, film, video game, website, book, song, podcast, newspaper article, tweet, or app. Texts matter because they are bearers of communication and movers of meaning. Texts can inspire and delight, or disgust and disappoint, but more importantly they intervene in the world and into culture, introducing new ideas, or variously attacking or reinforcing old ones. Textual analysis has long been a primary mode of "doing" media studies, as scholars seek to ascertain what a text means, *how* it means (what techniques are used to convey meaning), and what its themes, messages, and explicit and implicit assumptions aim to accomplish.

All of this is simple and reasonably unobjectionable. Where texts and textual analysis become tricky is in their connections to the outside world. While they are *treated as* a discrete unit of meaning, texts are never truly discrete, because meaning is always contextual, relative, and situated in a particular place and time. The challenge of working with media texts lies in tracking how context works, and hence in how they connect, to each other, to the outside world, to their producers, and to their audiences.

During the early days of textual studies, from the Victorian era to the late twentieth century, English literature, art history, and then film studies regularly took the text's existence and discreteness for granted, and instead asked questions about how texts such as novels, poems, paintings, sculptures, and films work. It is from these three fields that media studies draws much of its apparatus for answering similar questions of media texts. At times, little work will be required to ascertain a text's dominant meaning, as it may announce it clearly, even ham-handedly. But many meanings are subtle: what might a director or cinematographer be hoping to suggest by shooting a film with a limited color palette, for instance, or how might any other element of a text—its sounds and music, costumes, editing, duration, etc.—convey a meaning? Even when we are faced with a script, lyrics, or writing, texts are not always so straightforward, as Mikhail Bakhtin (1981) famously observed of what he called the "dialogism" of the novel, wherein characters represent various worldviews and beliefs, which then clash with each other in the narrative, requiring the reader to listen through the dialogue to ascertain a message, meanings, or themes. Indeed, though media studies draws from these other fields' techniques of analysis, it has rarely developed its own rigorous forms of textual analysis, at times adopting a more haphazard nonmethod of analysis. As much as media studies—as I will note—moved beyond simply the questions of *how* a text means, it has sometimes done so at the expense of having an actual *method* for working out textual meaning.

Instead, one of media studies' first key interests in the text lay in what audiences do with it. Stuart Hall's canonical encoding/decoding model (1973/1980) notes that every text has two determinate moments wherein meaning is created, the moment when its creators "encode" meaning into it and the moment when audiences "decode" meaning out of it. Hall saw these as equally important moments, but many readers have focused more on the decoding part of his equation, considering the text as written, and regarding acts of interpretation

as the more fascinating "moment." What was called "textual theory" in literary studies was asking similar questions of reception in the 1970s and 1980s. Most infamously, Stanley Fish (1980) insisted that the text was always empty until filled with meaning by its reader, but many others wrote, often with excited poetic flourish, of an "open text." Roland Barthes (1977, 162–63) offered an image of text and audience collaborating to create meaning as a musician riffs off a piece of sheet music. Wolfgang Iser (1978, 57) wrote of readers approaching texts as stargazers approach the night sky, seeing specific points, but needing to connect them in their minds. Michel de Certeau (1984) likened our journeys through a text to strolls through a city, insisting that specific buildings and structures are in place, but that we can choose our own paths, resulting in differing experiences of the text. Others wrote of intertextuality, as will be discussed later. Meanwhile, Hall (1973/1980) saw each text as having "preferred meanings" as well as the potential for any given audience to perform a preferred, oppositional, or negotiated reading. Moreover, Hall saw the communal audience as key to this process, hypothesizing that different identity markers such as class, gender, and race would lead to different readings of texts. The text, therefore, was seen as unable to complete itself or to contain its own meanings; audiences would finish it, edit it, or reproduce it. It's worth pausing on this conclusion briefly, to underline its iconoclasm in refusing that any text—whether a poem or a legal doctrine, a sitcom or a holy text—could ever have an unequivocal, immutable meaning.

But there are other ways in which texts are messy entities. If decoding introduces an element of chaos, as Hall contends, so too does encoding. When Bakhtin wrote of the dialogic novel, he saw *characters* as disagreeing with each other, but most media also have multiple *authors*, so we should expect a broader, more complex level of dialogism wherein messages and meanings conflict because the people creating the text have not reached perfect consensus on what the text should mean. Most texts have someone entrusted with directing traffic, and with bringing all these artistic visions together amid many other commercial pressures, production rituals and routines, and so forth, but they will have various levels of success or failure in doing so. Encoding will always involve extra "noise" too, as social differences and societal ideologies impact the process of creating meaning, however unintentionally.

More profoundly, texts are messy because we can never truly work out where their borders lie. The linguist Valentin Volosinov (1973) broke with the tendency to consider the singular utterance as the object of analysis, to argue that meaning exists only ever within a given context. The "same" sentence can take on a wide variety of meanings depending upon context as well as listeners' varying histories with that sentence and the words in it. If this is true of sentences, it is even more the case for the texts that we analyze in media studies. Texts may mean one thing at a specific place and time, and another in a different place and time. Good, rigorous textual analysis, therefore, should always be sensitive to the geography and to the temporal setting of the text. Russian filmmaker Lev Kuleshov's famous experiment of placing the same still of an actor's face alongside various other images resulted in viewers claiming to see nuances and subtle shifts in the acting, which led to famed Russian filmmaker Sergei Eisenstein and others' realization of the power of juxtaposition, namely that meaning is constructed in part based on what something is next to. "What something is next to" can be interpreted on many levels, however.

Television networks, for instance, have long regarded scheduling as something of an art, realizing that some shows' meanings and success rely upon their neighbors in the schedule. Raymond Williams (1974) discussed "flow" as a central attribute of television, noting that the ads in a commercial break insert themselves into the flow of meaning, changing our experience of a text (as anyone who has watched a show later on DVD without commercial interruption knows) or perhaps even challenging our notion of what the text is—is it the individual show, or the night's viewing? Juxtaposition and flow matter across all media, whether via the practice of planning double features at cinemas, via a playlist of music, or via online ads designed to appear next to specific content. But by no means is flow always planned. Texts and their constituent elements bump into each other all the time, producing meanings via juxtaposition that sometimes were intended, sometimes not. A given video game may introduce one to a specific image, for example, which then takes on unexpected meaning when it appears in another text. This is "intertextuality," but following Bakhtin and Volosinov's lead, all textuality is in truth intertextuality. We know any unit of meaning—whether a letter, a word, an image, a sound, a character, or a genre—only as something we've encountered in other contexts before. Planned and unplanned juxtapositions produce a cacophony of meanings, all rich with resonances of their past meanings.

Intertextual processes produce other forms of texts as well. Star images and genres are both (inter)textual matrices and may at times matter more to us than a given text. When I see Ian McKellen appear alongside Patrick Stewart, for instance, I am aware contextually of their real-life friendship, but also of their conflicted relationship as Magneto and Professor X respectively in the early *X-Men* films. Intertextually I am also aware of their past roles, most prominently as Gandalf and Captain Jean-Luc Picard respectively, but also of McKellen as an aging Nazi in *Apt Pupil*, or as troubled gay director James Whale in *Gods and Monsters*, and of Stewart as Claudius in *Hamlet*, or as a profane, juvenile version of himself on *Extras*. All of these past images come to a head as I watch them, creating a dance of meaning between the past and the present, ensuring that the text at hand is also heavily laden with other texts and their meanings. Another viewer in turn may have other intertextual histories with these two, thereby seeing and feeling other resonances.

"What something is next to" also entails real space, not just space on a schedule or playlist. When we consider *where* to watch an anticipated film, or when we get excited at the prospect of watching a beloved band play a particular venue, we show an awareness of how place affects the text. Different sociopolitical contexts matter, too: what may appear to be a remarkably mundane, unobjectionable website or television program in one country may be targeted by censors in another country. Texts that once mattered, and that were politically charged, may now appear peculiarly irrelevant, their context lost. As Volosinov and Bakhtin noted, nothing appears out of a vacuum, without history, without meanings already attached to it, existing as "pure" meaning; everything is said at a particular time, for a particular reason, contributing to a particular discussion or debate. As such, the proper study of a text requires a sensitivity to history and geography. Thus, for instance, if we want to understand *South Park*, it helps to know what it is mocking, and where it fits in the life of the sitcom, of animation, of satire using children, and of American television more generally, but we should also consider its varying meanings in different countries and over time.

Texts may also draw other elements into their orbits, requiring us to redraw the boundaries of that text. What are called "paratexts" (see Genette 1997; Gray 2010) are especially important in a mediated era in which promotional budgets regularly eclipse the budgets spent on "the thing itself." By the time we even experience "the thing itself," we have likely seen ads that serve as early portals to framing expectations, and merchandise that similarly structures a sense of what the text is actually about; we may have read reviews that point us toward some readings and away from others; and then after experiencing "the thing itself," podcasts, DVD bonus tracks, other merchandise, and more may further toggle our understanding and appreciation of the text. In such cases, these paratexts have become part of the text, as active at creating meaning as is the supposed thing itself. Given that our world is suffused with more texts than we could ever consume, and since promotional culture is constantly encouraging us to consume new texts, we are always being given "taste tests" of texts through their paratexts. With each taste test comes the construction of meaning, *the construction of a text*, such that even if we decide not to consume "the thing itself," we may already have a sense of what it is, what it's doing, what it means. If paratexts were perfectly synched with their accompanying texts, their presence would be irrelevant to textual analysis, but paratexts will regularly amplify some meanings, bury others, and they may edit or transform textual meaning in the process. They meddle with texts, in short, and in doing so they become vital elements to be considered in the process of textual analysis.

Precisely because paratexts can change meanings, they are a site of contestation, as well as reminders that no text is ever finished. Texts don't exist: they only become. As such, paratexts such as interviews or liner notes can be where musicians tell us what they were trying to communicate with a particular song, or where they tell us of what they wanted to do instead. Paratexts such as fan film, fan art, or fan fiction can be where fans announce readings to other fans, sometimes in direct contradiction to the statements/paratexts of producers.

Paratexts can be used to retrofit a text for a different audience, and/or for a different time and place (as with new book covers, ads, or other promotional materials), and they can thereby respond to context. In short, paratexts are where the battle over meaning regularly occurs.

What is called "close reading," a process whereby paratexts, context, and intertext are ignored, is still, unfortunately, all too common a mode of analysis in media studies. But it is a radically troubling mode for any version of media studies that hopes to situate texts as social, cultural actors. A text is a unit of meaning, but a unit whose borders fluctuate, whose very being is predicated on context, intertext, and paratext, and whose meaning depends on them. A true textual analysis would keep all of these processes in mind.

TEXT   JONATHAN GRAY

Works Cited

Abercrombie, Nicholas and Brian Longhurst. *Audiences: A Sociological Theory of Performance and Imagination*. London: Sage, 1998.

Abu-Lughod, Lila. *Dramas of Nationhood: The Politics of Television in Egypt*. Chicago: University of Chicago Press, 2005.

Acland, Charles R. "Introduction: Residual Media." In *Residual Media*, edited by Charles R. Acland, xiii–xxvii. Minneapolis: University of Minnesota Press, 2007.

Adichie, Chimamanda, N. "The Danger of a Single Story." *TED Talks*, July 2009. www.ted.com.

Adorno, Theodor. "Culture Industry Reconsidered." 1967. Translated by Anson G. Rabinbach. *New German Critique* 6 (Fall 1975): 12–19.

———. "On the Fetish-Character in Music and the Regression of Listening." 1938. In *The Essential Frankfurt School Reader*, edited by Andrew Arato and Eike Gebhardt, 270–99. New York: Continuum, 1990.

Adorno, Theodor and Max Horkheimer. *Dialectic of Enlightenment*. 1944. New York: Herder and Herder, 1972.

Agger, Ben. *Cultural Studies as Critical Theory*. London: Falmer Press, 1992.

Ahmad, Aijaz. "The Politics of Literary Postcoloniality." *Race and Class* 36.3 (1995): 1–20.

Ahmed, Sara. *Cultural Politics of Emotion*. New York: Routledge, 2004.

———. *On Being Included: Racism and Diversity in Institutional Life*. Durham, NC: Duke University Press, 2012.

Allen, Robert. *Speaking of Soap Operas*. Chapel Hill: University of North Carolina Press, 1985.

Althusser, Louis. "Ideology and Ideological State Apparatuses." In *Lenin and Philosophy and Other Essays*, translated by Ben Brewster, 127–88. London: Monthly Review Books, 1971.

———. *On the Reproduction of Capitalism: Ideology and Ideological State Apparatuses*. London: Verso, 2014.

Altman, Rick. "Television, Sound." In *Studies in Entertainment*, edited by Tania Modleski, 39–54. Bloomington: Indiana University Press, 1986.

———. *Film/Genre*. London: British Film Institute, 1999.

Amaya, Hector. *Citizenship Excess: Latino/as, Media, and the Nation*. New York: New York University Press, 2013.

Anderson, Benedict. *Imagined Communities: Reflections on the Origin and Spread of Nationalism*. Rev. ed. New York: Verso, 1991.

Andrejevic, Mark. "The Kinder, Gentler Gaze of Big Brother: Reality TV in the Era of Digital Capitalism." *New Media & Society* 4.2 (2002): 251–70.

———. *Reality TV: The Work of Being Watched*. Lanham, MD: Rowman & Littlefield, 2004.

———. "Watching Television Without Pity." *Television & New Media* 9.1 (2008): 24–46.

———. "The Work That Affective Economics Does." *Cultural Studies* 25.4–5 (2011): 604–20.

———. "Authoring User-Generated Content." In *Media Authorship*, edited by Cynthia Chris and David Gerstner, 123–36. New York: Routledge, 2013a.

———. *Infoglut: How Too Much Information Is Changing the Way We Think and Know*. New York: Routledge, 2013b.

———. "The Big Data Divide." *International Journal of Communication* 8.17 (2014): 1673–89.

Ang, Ien. *Watching Dallas: Soap Opera and the Melodramatic Imagination*. New York: Methuen, 1982.

———. *Desperately Seeking the Audience*. London: Routledge, 1991.

———. "Together-in-Difference: Beyond Diaspora, into Hybridity." *Asian Studies Review* 27.2 (2003): 141–54.

Appadurai, Arjun. *Modernity at Large: Cultural Dimensions of Globalization*. Minneapolis: University of Minnesota Press, 1966.

———. "Disjuncture and Difference in the Global Cultural Economy." *Theory, Culture & Society* 7.2 (1990): 295–310.

———. *Fear of Small Numbers*. Durham, NC: Duke University Press, 2006.

Apter, Andrew. "The Subvention of Tradition: A Genealogy of the Nigerian Durbar." In *State/Culture: State Formation after the Cultural Turn*, edited by George Steinmetz, 213–52. Ithaca, NY: Cornell University Press, 1999.

Arnheim, Rudolf. *Radio: An Art of Sound*. London: Da Capo Press, 1936.

Arnold, Matthew. *Culture and Anarchy*. 1869. New York: Oxford University Press, 2006.

———. *Culture and Anarchy, and Friendship's Garland*. New York: Macmillan, 1883.

Aronczyk, Melissa. *Branding the Nation: The Global Business of National Identity*. New York: Oxford University Press, 2013.

Aronczyk, Melissa and Miranda Brady. "Branding History at the Canadian Museum of Civilization." *Canadian Journal of Communication* 40 (2015): 165–84.

Arvidsson, Adam. *Brands: Value and Meaning in a Media Culture*. New York: Routledge, 2006.

Bachmann, Götz and Timon Beyes. "Media Atmospheres: Remediating Sociality." In *Remediate: At the Borders of Film, Internet and Archives*, edited by Mario Doulis and Peter Ott, 131–54. Stuttgart, Germany: Merz Akademie, 2013.

Baker, Catherine. "Wild Dances and Dying Wolves: Simulation, Essentialization, and National Identity at the Eurovision Song Contest." *Popular Communication* 6.3 (2008): 173–89.

Bakhtin, Mikhail. *The Dialogic Imagination*. Edited by Michael Holquist. Translated by Caryl Emerson and Michael Holquist. Austin: University of Texas Press, 1981.

———. *Speech Genres & Other Late Essays*. Austin: University of Texas Press, 1986.

Bandelj, Nina and Frederick Wherry, eds. *The Cultural Wealth of Nations*. Stanford, CA: Stanford University Press, 2011.

Banet-Weiser, Sarah. *Kids Rule! Nickelodeon and Consumer Citizenship*. Durham, NC: Duke University Press, 2007.

———. *Authentic™: The Politics of Ambivalence in a Brand Culture*. New York: New York University Press, 2012.

———. "'Confidence You Can Carry!' Girls in Crisis and the Market for Girls' Empowerment Organizations." *Continuum: Journal of Media and Cultural Studies* 29.2 (2015): 182–93.

Barker, Martin and Ernest Mathijs, eds. *Watching* The Lord of the Rings*: Tolkien's World Audiences*. New York: Peter Lang, 2008.

Barthes, Roland. "The Death of the Author." Translated by Richard Howard. *Aspen* 5–6 (1967): 4–6.

———. *Mythologies*. Translated by Annette Lavers. London: Granada, 1973.

———. *The Pleasure of the Text*. New York: Farrar, Straus & Giroux, 1975.

———. "From Work to Text." In *Image/Music/Text*, translated by Stephen Heath, 155–64. Glasgow: Fontana-Collins, 1977.

Baudrillard, Jean. *In the Shadow of the Silent Majorities*. New York: Semiotext(e), 1983.

Bauman, Zygmunt. *Liquid Life*. Malden, MA: Polity, 2005.

Baumann, Shyon. *Hollywood Highbrow: From Entertainment to Art*. Princeton: Princeton University Press, 2007.

Beck, Ulrich. *Cosmopolitan Vision*. Cambridge: Polity, 2006.

———. "Cosmopolitanized Nations: Re-imagining Collectivity in World Risk Society." *Theory, Culture & Society* 30.2 (2013): 3–31.

Beck, Ulrich, Anthony Giddens, and Scott Lash. *Reflexive Modernization: Politics, Tradition and Aesthetics in the Modern Social Order*. Stanford: Stanford University Press, 1994.

Beck, Ulrich and Natan Szneider. "Unpacking Cosmopolitanism for the Social Sciences: A Research Agenda." *British Journal of Sociology* 57.1 (2006): 1–23.

Becker, Christine. "Televising Film Stardom in the 1950s." *Framework: The Journal of Cinema & Media* 46.2 (2005): 5–21.

Bedell, Sally. *Up the Tube: Prime-Time TV and the Silverman Years*. New York: Viking, 1981.

Beers, David. "Irony Is Dead! Long Live Irony!" *Salon*, September 25, 2001. www.salon.com.

Belcher, Christina. "White Trash Is the New Black." *FlowTV*, July 2014. http://flowtv.org.

Bellamy, Richard. *Citizenship: A Very Short Introduction*. Oxford: Oxford University Press, 2008.

Benjamin, Walter. *Illuminations: Essays and Reflections*. New York: Schocken Books, 1969.

———. *The Work of Art in the Age of Mechanical Reproduction*. 1936. London: Penguin, 2008.

Bennett, Tony, Lawrence Grossberg, and Meaghan Morris, eds. *New Keywords: A Revised Vocabulary of Culture and Society*. Malden, MA: Wiley-Blackwell, 2005.

Berger, John. *Ways of Seeing*. London: Penguin, 1972.

Berlant, Lauren and Elizabeth Freeman. "Queer Nationality." In *National Identities and Post-Americanist Narratives*, edited by Donald E. Pease, 149–80. Durham, NC: Duke University Press, 1994.

Bettie, Julie. "Class Dismissed? *Roseanne* and the Changing Face of Working-Class Iconography." *Social Text* 45 (Winter 1995): 125–49.

Bhabha, Homi. "DissemiNation: Time, Narrative, and the Margins of the Modern Nation." In *Nation and Narration*, edited by Homi Bhabha, 291–322. London: Routledge, 1990.

Bianculli, David. "Another Great Year for TV." *Fresh Air*, National Public Radio, December 24, 2015. www.npr.org.

Biewen, John, ed. *Reality Radio: Telling True Stories in Sound*. Chapel Hill: University of North Carolina Press, 2010.

Bignell, Jonathan. *Media Semiotics: An Introduction*. 2nd ed. Manchester: Manchester University Press, 2002.

Bird, S. Elizabeth. *For Enquiring Minds: A Cultural Study of Supermarket Tabloids*. Knoxville: University of Tennessee Press, 1992.

Blonsky, Marshall, ed. *On Signs: A Semiotics Reader*. Oxford: Blackwell, 1985.

Bobo, Jacqueline. *Black Women as Cultural Readers*. New York: Columbia University Press, 1995.

Bodnar, John, ed. *Bonds of Affection: Americans Define Their Patriotism*. Princeton: Princeton University Press, 1996.

———. *Blue-Collar Hollywood: Liberalism, Democracy, and Working People in American Film*. Baltimore: Johns Hopkins University Press, 2003.

Bolter, Jay David and Richard Grusin. *Remediation: Understanding New Media*. Cambridge, MA: MIT Press, 1999.

Booth, Paul. *Playing Fans*. Iowa City: University of Iowa Press, 2015.

Born, Georgina. *Uncertain Vision: Birt, Dyke and the Reinvention of the BBC*. London: Random House, 2005.

Bourdieu, Pierre. *Distinction: A Social Critique of the Judgment of Taste*. Translated by Richard Nice. Cambridge, MA: Harvard University Press, 1984.

———. *Language and Symbolic Power*. Cambridge: Polity, 1991.

boyd, danah. "Why Youth (Heart) Social Network Sites: The Role of Networked Publics in Teenage Social Life." In *Youth, Identity, and Digital Media*, edited by David Buckingham, 119–42. Cambridge, MA: MIT Press, 2008.

Boyd-Barrett, Oliver. "Media Imperialism Reformulated." In *Electronic Empires: Global Media and Local Resistance*, edited by Daya Kishan Thussu, 157–76. London: Arnold, 1998.

Boyle, James. *The Public Domain: Enclosing the Commons of the Mind*. New Haven, CT: Yale University Press, 2010.

Braderman, Joan. *Joan Does Dynasty*. New York: Video Data Bank, 1986.

Braman, Sandra. "Where Has Media Policy Gone? Defining the Field in the Twenty-First Century." *Communication Law and Policy* 9.2 (2004): 153–82.

Braun, Josh. "Social Media and Distribution Studies." *Social Media & Society* 1.1 (2015): 1–2.

Braverman, Harry. *Labor and Monopoly Capital: The Degradation of Work in the Twentieth Century*. New York: Monthly Review Press, 1974.

Brennan, Teresa. *The Transmission of Affect*. Ithaca, NY: Cornell University Press, 2004.

Brown, Wendy. "Neoliberalism and the End of Liberal Democracy." In *Edgework: Critical Essays on Knowledge and Politics*, 37–59. Princeton: Princeton University Press, 2005.

Browne, Nick. "The Political Economy of the Television (Super) Text." *Quarterly Review of Film Studies* 9.3 (1984): 174–82.

Brubaker, Rogers and Frederick Cooper. "Beyond 'Identity.'" *Theory & Society* 29 (2000): 1–47.

Brumberg, Joan Jacobs. *The Body Project: An Intimate History of American Girls*. New York: Vintage, 1998.

Bruns, Axel. "Produsage: Towards a Broader Framework for User-Led Content Creation." *Proceedings of the ACM Conference on Creativity and Cognition* 6 (2007): 99.

———. *Blogs, Wikipedia, Second Life and Beyond: From Production to Produsage*. New York: Peter Lang, 2008.

Brunsdon, Charlotte. *Screen Tastes: Soap Operas to Satellite Dishes*. New York: Routledge, 1997.

Buchanan, Ian. "Assemblage Theory and Its Discontents." *Deleuze Studies* 9.3 (2015): 382–92.

Burch, Noël and Geneviève Sellier. *Le Cinéma au Prisme des Rapports de Sexe*. Paris: Vrin, 2009.

Burgess, Jean. "From 'Broadcast Yourself' to 'Follow Your Interests': Making Over Social Media." *International Journal of Cultural Studies* 18.3 (2015): 281–85.

Burke, Edmund. *Reflections on the Revolution in France*. 1790. Oxford: Oxford University Press, 1993.

Busby, Linda. "Sex Role Research on the Mass Media." *Journal of Communication* 25.4 (1975): 107–31.

Butler, Judith. *Gender Trouble: Feminism and the Subversion of Identity*. New York: Routledge, 1990.

———. *Bodies That Matter: On the Discursive Limits of Sex*. New York: Routledge, 1993.

Butler, Matilda and William Paisley. *Women and the Mass Media*. New York: Human Sciences Press, 1980.

Butsch, Richard. *The Making of American Audiences: From Stage to Television, 1750–1990*. Cambridge: Cambridge University Press, 2000.

———. *The Citizen Audience: Crowds, Publics and Individuals*. New York: Routledge, 2007.

———. "Six Decades of Social Class in American Television Sitcoms." In *Gender, Race, and Class in Media: A Critical Reader*, 4th ed., edited by Gail Dines and Jean Humez, 507–16. Thousand Oaks, CA: Sage, 2015.

Caillois, Roger. *Man, Play and Games*. Translated by Meyer Barash. Urbana: University of Illinois Press, 2001.

Caldwell, John Thornton. *Production Culture: Industrial Reflexivity and Critical Practice in Film and Television*. Durham, NC: Duke University Press, 2008.

Calhoun, Craig. *Nationalism*. Minneapolis: University of Minnesota Press, 1997.

———. "The Class Consciousness of Frequent Travellers: Towards a Critique of Actually Existing Cosmopolitanism." *South Atlantic Quarterly* 101.4 (2003): 869–97.

Cammaerts, Bart. "Protest Logics and the Mediation Opportunity Structure." *European Journal of Communication* 27.2 (2012): 117–34.

Campbell, Richard, Christopher R. Martin, and Bettina Fabos. *Media and Culture: An Introduction to Mass Communication*. 8th ed. New York: Bedford/St. Martin's, 2011.

Carey, James W. "A Cultural Approach to Communication." In *Communication as Culture*, 11–28. New York: Routledge, 2009.

Carey, James W. and J. J. Quirk. "The Mythos of the Electronic Revolution." *American Scholar* 39.3 (1970): 395–424.

Carpentier, Nico. "Identity, Contingency and Rigidity: The (Counter-)hegemonic Constructions of the Identity of the Media Professional." *Journalism* 6.2 (2005): 199–219.

Carpentier, Nico and Benjamin De Cleen. "Bringing Discourse Theory into Media Studies." *Journal of Language and Politics* 6.2 (2007): 267–95.

Carpentier, Nico and Erik Spinoy, eds. *Discourse Theory and Cultural Analysis: Media, Arts and Literature*. Cresskill, NJ: Hampton Press, 2008.

Carver, Terrell. "Sex, Gender and Heteronormativity: Seeing 'Some Like It Hot' as a Heterosexual Dystopia." *Contemporary Political Theory* 8.2 (2009): 125–51.

Casaubon, Isaac. *The Answere of Master Isaac Casaubon to the Epistle of the Most Illustrious and Most Reverend Cardinall Peron*. 1612. Baltimore: Charles Harvey, 1875.

Castells, Manuel. *The Rise of Network Society*. Malden, MA: Blackwell, 1996.

———. *Communication Power*. Oxford: Oxford University Press, 2009.

Caughie, John. "Progressive Television and Documentary Drama." *Screen* 21.3 (1980): 9–35.

Chan, Anita. *Networking Peripheries: Technological Futures and the Myth of Digital Universalism*. Cambridge, MA: MIT Press, 2014.

Chávez, Christopher. *Reinventing the Latino Television Viewer: Language Ideology and Practice*. Lanham, MD: Rowman & Littlefield, 2015.

Chion, Michel. *Audio-Vision: Sound on Screen*. New York: Columbia University Press, 1994.

Chouliaraki, Lilie. *The Spectatorship of Suffering*. London: Sage, 2006.

———. *The Ironic Spectator. Solidarity in the Age of Post-humanitarianism*. Cambridge: Polity, 2013.

Christensen, Jerome. *America's Corporate Art: The Studio Authorship of Hollywood Motion Pictures*. Stanford: Stanford University Press, 2012.

Christian, Aymar Jean. "Indie TV: Innovation in Series Development." In *Media Independence: Working with Freedom or Working for Free?*, edited by James Bennett and Niki Strange, 159–81. New York: Routledge, 2015.

Christopherson, Susan and Michael Storper. "The Effects of Flexible Specialization on Industrial Politics and the Labor Market: The Motion Picture Industry." *Industrial and Labor Relations Review* 42 (1989): 331–47.

Chun, Wendy. *Control and Freedom: Power and Paranoia in the Age of Fiber Optics*. Cambridge, MA: MIT Press, 2008.

Clarke, John, Stuart Hall, Tony Jefferson, and Brian Roberts. "Subcultures, Cultures and Class." In *Resistance through Rituals: Youth Subcultures in Post-war Britain*, 2nd ed., edited by Stuart Hall and Tony Jefferson, 3–59. New York: Routledge, 2006.

Clarke, Roger. "The Digital Persona and Its Application to Data Surveillance." *Information Society* 10 (1994): 77–91.

Classen, Steve. *Watching Jim Crow*. Durham, NC: Duke University Press, 2004.

Cohen, Lizbeth. *A Consumer's Republic: The Politics of Mass Consumption in Postwar America*. New York: Vintage, 2003.

Coleman, Beth. *Hello Avatar: Rise of the Networked Generation*. Cambridge, MA: MIT Press, 2011.

Coleman, Gabriella. *Coding Freedom: The Ethics and Aesthetics of Hacking*. Princeton: Princeton University Press, 2012.

Collins, Sue. "Making the Most out of 15 Minutes: Reality TV's Dispensable Celebrity." *Television & New Media* 9.2 (2008): 87–110.

Combahee River Collective. "The Combahee River Collective Statement." 1977. In *Home Girls: A Black Feminist Anthology*, edited by Barbara Smith, 264–74. New York: Kitchen Table/Women of Color Press, 1983.

Consalvo, Mia. *Cheating: Gaining Advantage in Videogames*. Cambridge, MA: MIT Press, 2007.

Cook, Guy. *The Discourse of Advertising*. London: Routledge, 1992.

Cooley, Charles Horton. *Social Organization: A Study of the Larger Mind*. New York: Charles Scribner's Sons, 1909.

Coontz, Stephanie. *The Way We Never Were: American Families and the Nostalgia Trap*. New York: Basic Books, 1992.

Corner, John. *Critical Ideas in Television Studies*. New York: Oxford University Press, 1999.

Couldry, Nick. *The Place of Media Power*. London: Routledge, 2000.

———. *Media Rituals: A Critical Approach*. London: Routledge, 2003.

———. *Media, Society, World: Social Theory and Digital Media Practice*. Cambridge: Polity, 2012.

———. "The Necessary Future of the Audience . . . and How to Research It." In *The Handbook of Media Audiences*, edited by Virginia Nightingale, 213–29. Malden, MA: Wiley-Blackwell, 2014.

Cowley, Malcolm. *Exile's Return*. 1934. London: Penguin, 1976.

Crary, Jonathan. *24/7 Late Capitalism and the Ends of Sleep*. London: Verso, 2013.

Crawford, Susan. *Captive Audience*. New Haven, CT: Yale University Press, 2013.

Crenshaw, Kimberlé. "Demarginalizing the Intersection of Race and Sex: A Black Feminist Critique of Antidiscrimination Doctrine, Feminist Theory and Antiracist Politics." *University of Chicago Legal Forum* 1 (1989): 139–68.

Crisell, Andrew. *Liveness & Recording in the Media*. Basingstoke: Palgrave Macmillan, 2012.

Cross, Gary. *All-Consuming Century: Why Commercialism Won in Modern America*. New York: Columbia University Press, 2002.

Croteau, David and William Hoynes. *Media/Society: Industries, Images and Audiences*. 5th ed. London: Sage, 2014.

Culler, Jonathan. *Barthes*. London: Fontana, 1983.

Cunningham, Stuart. "Popular Media as Sphericules for Diasporic Communities." *International Journal of Cultural Studies* 4.2 (1991): 131–47.

Curran, James. "Rethinking the Media as Public Sphere." In *Communication and Citizenship*, edited by Peter Dahlgren and Colin Sparks, 27–57. London: Routledge, 1997.

Curtin, Michael. "Media Capital: Towards the Study of Spatial Flows." *International Journal of Cultural Studies* 6.2 (2003): 202–28.

Czitrom, Daniel. *Media and the American Mind: From Morse to McLuhan*. Chapel Hill: University of North Carolina Press, 1982.

D'Acci, Julie. *Defining Women: The Case of Cagney and Lacey*. Chapel Hill: University of North Carolina Press, 1994.

———. "Cultural Studies, Television Studies, and the Crisis in the Humanities." In *Television after TV: Essays on a Medium in Transition*, edited by Lynn Spigel and Jan Olsson, 418–46. Durham, NC: Duke University Press, 2004.

Dahlberg, Lincoln and Sean Phelan, eds. *Discourse Theory and Critical Media Politics*. New York: Palgrave Macmillan, 2013.

Darling-Wolf, Fabienne. *Imagining the Global: Transnational Media and Popular Culture Beyond East and West*. Ann Arbor: University of Michigan Press, 2015.

Dean, Jodi. *Blog Theory: Feedback and Capture in the Circuits of Drive*. Cambridge: Polity, 2010.

Dean, Mitchel. *Governmentality: Power and Rule in Modern Society*. 2nd ed. London: Sage, 2010.

Deaville, James, ed. *Music in Television: Channels of Listening*. New York: Routledge, 2011.

de Certeau, Michel. *The Practice of Everyday Life*. Translated by Steven F. Rendall. Berkeley: University of California Press, 1984.

De Cleen, Benjamin. "'Flemish Friends, Let Us Separate!' The Discursive Struggle for Flemish Nationalist Civil Society in the Media." *Javnost—The Public* 22.1 (2015): 37–54.

deCordova, Richard. *Picture Personalities: The Emergence of the Star System in America*. Urbana: University of Illinois Press, 2001.

de Grazia, Victoria and Ellen Furlough. *The Sex of Things: Gender and Consumption in Historical Perspective*. Berkeley: University of California Press, 1996.

de Lauretis, Teresa. *Technologies of Gender*. Basingstoke: Macmillan, 1989.

Deleuze, Gilles and Félix Guattari. *Kafka: Toward a Minor Theory of Literature*. 1975. Translated by Dana Polan. Minneapolis: University of Minnesota Press, 1986.

———. *A Thousand Plateaus: Capitalism and Schizophrenia*. 1980. Translated by Brian Massumi. Minneapolis: University of Minnesota Press, 1987.

Denning, Michael. *Mechanic Accents: Dime Novels and Working Class Culture in America*. New York: Verso, 1998.

de Sola Pool, Ithiel. *Technologies of Freedom: On Free Speech in an Electronic Age*. Cambridge, MA: Harvard University Press, 1983.

Deuze, Mark. *Media Work*. Cambridge: Polity, 2007.

Dittmar, Norbert. *Sociolinguistics: A Critical Survey of Theory and Application*. London: Edward Arnold, 1976.

Dixon, Simon. "Ambiguous Ecologies: Stardom's Domestic Mise-en-Scene." *Cinema Journal* 42.2 (2003): 81–100.

Dominick, Joseph R. and Gail E. Rauch. "The Image of Women in Network TV Commercials." *Journal of Broadcasting* 16:3 (1972): 259–65.

Dorfman, Ariel. *The Empire's Old Clothes: What the Lone Ranger, Babar, and Other Innocent Heroes Do to Our Minds*. Translated by Clark Hansen. New York: Pantheon, 1983.

Doty, Alexander. *Making Things Perfectly Queer: Interpreting Mass Culture*. Minneapolis: University of Minnesota Press, 1993.

Douglas, Susan J. *Where the Girls Are: Growing Up Female with the Mass Media*. New York: Times Books, 1994.

———. *The Rise of Enlightened Sexism: How Pop Culture Took Us from Girl Power to Girls Gone Wild*. New York: St. Martin's Griffin, 2010.

Downes, E. J. and S. J. McMillian. "Defining Interactivity: A Qualitative Identification of Key Dimensions." *New Media & Society* 2.2 (2000): 157–79.

Downing, John and Charles Husband. *Representing "Race": Racisms, Ethnicity and the Media*. London: Sage, 2005.

Du Bois, W. E. B. "The Souls of Black Folk." 1903. In *W. E. B. Du Bois: Writings*, edited by Nathan Huggins, 358–547. New York: Library of America, 1986.

Dubrofsky, Rachel E. and Megan M. Wood. "Gender, Race, and Authenticity: Celebrity Women Tweeting for the Gaze." In *Feminist Surveillance Studies*, edited by Rachel E. Dubrofsky and Shoshana Amielle Magnet, 93–106. Durham, NC: Duke University Press, 2015.

Duffett, Mark. *Understanding Fandom: An Introduction to the Study of Media Fan Culture*. New York: Bloomsbury, 2013.

Duffy, Brooke. *Remake, Remodel: Women's Magazines in the Digital Age*. Urbana: University of Illinois Press, 2013.

du Gay, Paul, Stuart Hall, Linda Janes, and Hugh Mackay. *Doing Cultural Studies: The Story of the Sony Walkman*. London: Sage, 1997.

Duncombe, Stephen, ed. *Cultural Resistance Reader*. New York: Verso, 2002.

Dyer, Gillian. *Advertising as Communication*. London: Methuen, 1982.

Dyer, Richard. *Stars*. London: BFI, 1998.

———. *Only Entertainment*. 2nd ed. London: Routledge, 2002.

———. *Heavenly Bodies: Film Stars and Society*. London: Routledge, 2004.

Easterling, Keller. *Extrastatecraft: The Power of Infrastructure Space*. London: Verso, 2014.

Eckert, Charles. "The Carole Lombard in Macy's Window." In *Stardom: Industry of Desire*, edited by Christine Gledhill, 30–40. London: Routledge, 1991.

Eco, Umberto. *Travels in Hyperreality*. London: Picador, 1986.

Edwards, Lillian. "Pornography, Censorship and the Internet." In *Law and the Internet*, edited by Lillian Edwards and Charlotte Waedle, 623–70. Portland: Hart, 2009.

Eisenstein, Elizabeth L. *The Printing Revolution in Early Modern Europe*. Cambridge: Cambridge University Press, 1983.

Eldridge, John. *Glasgow Media Group Reader*. Vol. 1. London: Routledge, 1995.

Elias, Ana Sofia and Rosalind Gill. "Beauty Surveillance: The Digital Self-Monitoring Cultures of Neoliberalism." *European Journal of Cultural Studies* (forthcoming).

Elias, Ana Sofia, Rosalind Gill, and Christina Scharff, eds. *Aesthetic Labour: Rethinking Beauty Politics in Neoliberalism.* Basingstoke: Palgrave, 2016.

Ellcessor, Elizabeth. "Tweeting @feliciaday: Online Social Media, Convergence, and Subcultural Stardom." *Cinema Journal* 51.2 (2012): 46–68.

———. *Restricted Access: Media, Disability, and the Politics of Participation.* New York: New York University Press, 2016.

Epstein, Rebecca L. "Sharon Stone in a Gap Turtleneck." In *Hollywood Goes Shopping*, edited by David Desser and Garth S. Jowett, 179–204. Minneapolis: University of Minnesota Press, 2000.

Fairclough, Norman and Ruth Wodak. "Critical Discourse Analysis." In *Discourse Studies: A Multidisciplinary Introduction. Vol. 2. Discourse as Social Interaction*, edited by Teun A. van Dijk, 258–84. London: Sage, 1997.

Featherstone, Mike. "Lifestyle and Consumer Culture." *Theory, Culture & Society* 4 (1987): 55–70.

Feist Publications, Inc. v. Rural Telephone Service Company, Inc., 499 US 340 (1991).

Ferguson, Roderick. *The Re-order of Things: The University and Its Pedagogies of Minority Difference.* Minneapolis: University of Minnesota Press, 2012.

Fernandes, Leela. *India's New Middle Class: Democratic Politics in an Era of Economic Reform.* Minneapolis: University of Minnesota Press, 2006.

Feuer, Jane. "The Concept of Live Television: Ontology as Ideology." In *Regarding Television: Critical Approaches—An Anthology*, edited by E. Ann Kaplan, 12–21. Los Angeles: American Film Institute, 1983.

Fish, Stanley. *Is There a Text in This Class? The Authority of Interpretive Communities.* Cambridge, MA: Harvard University Press, 1980.

Fiske, John. *Television Culture.* London: Routledge, 1988.

———. *Reading the Popular.* New York: Routledge, 1989.

———. "The Cultural Economy of Fandom." In *The Adoring Audience: Fan Culture and Popular Media*, edited by Lisa A. Lewis, 30–45. New York: Routledge, 1992.

Fiske, John and John Hartley. *Reading Television.* London: Methuen, 1978.

Fleetwood, Nicole R. *Troubling Vision: Performance, Visuality, and Blackness.* Chicago: University of Chicago Press, 2011.

Flew, Terry and Silvio Waisbord. "The Ongoing Significance of National Media Systems in the Context of Media Globalization." *Media, Culture & Society* 37.4 (2015): 620–36.

Ford, Sam, Abigail De Kosnik, and C. Lee Harrington, eds. *The Survival of Soap Opera: Transformations for a New Media Era.* Jackson: University Press of Mississippi, 2012.

Fortunati, Leopoldina. *The Arcane of Reproduction: Housework, Prostitution, Labor and Capital.* Edited by Jim Fleming. Translated by Hilary Creek. Brooklyn: Autonomedia, 1995.

Foucault, Michel. *The Archaeology of Knowledge.* Translated by Alan Sheridan. New York: Pantheon, 1972.

———. *The History of Sexuality, Vol. 1: An Introduction.* Translated by Robert Hurley. New York: Pantheon, 1978.

———. *Discipline and Punish: The Birth of the Prison.* Translated by Alan Sheridan. New York: Vintage, 1979.

———. *Power/Knowledge.* New York: Pantheon, 1980.

———. "The Order of Discourse." In *Untying the Text: A Poststructuralist Reader*, edited by Robert Young, 48–78. London: Routledge, 1981.

———. "What Is an Author?" 1969. In *The Foucault Reader*, edited by Paul Rabinow, 101–20. New York: Vintage, 1984.

———. *The Foucault Reader.* Edited by Paul Rabinow. New York: Pantheon, 1984.

Fowler, Roger. *Language in the News: Discourse and Ideology in the Press.* London: Routledge, 1991.

Frasca, Gonzalo. "Ludologists Love Stories, Too: Notes from a Debate That Never Took Place." In *Level Up: Digital Games Research Conference Proceedings*, edited by Marinka Copier and Joost Raessens. Utrecht: DiGRA and University of Utrecht, 2003. www.digra.org.

Fraser, Nancy. "Rethinking the Public Sphere: A Contribution to the Critique of Actually Existing Democracy." *Social Text* 25/26 (1990): 56–80.

Freedman, Des. *The Politics of Media Policy.* Cambridge: Policy Press, 2008.

———. *The Contradictions of Media Power.* London: Bloomsbury, 2014.

Frey, Mattias. *The Permanent Crisis of Film Criticism: The Anxiety of Authority.* Amsterdam: Amsterdam University Press, 2015.

Friedan, Betty. *The Feminine Mystique.* New York: Norton, 1963.

Friedberg, Anne. *Window Shopping: Cinema and the Postmodern.* Berkeley: University of California Press, 1993.

Fuss, Diana. "Fashion and the Homospectatorial Look." *Critical Inquiry* 18.4 (1992): 713–37.

Gajjala, Rahdika, ed. *Cyberculture and the Subaltern.* Lanham, MD: Lexington, 2013.

Galloway, Alexander R. *Gaming: Essays on Algorithmic Culture.* Minneapolis: University of Minnesota Press, 2006.

Galloway, Alexander R. and Eugene Thacker. *The Exploit: A Theory of Networks.* Minneapolis: University of Minnesota Press, 2007.

Gamson, Joshua. *Freaks Talk Back: Tabloid Talk Shows and Sexual Nonconformity.* Chicago: University of Chicago Press, 1999.

———. "The Unwatched Life Is Not Worth Living: The Elevation of the Ordinary in Celebrity Culture." *PMLA* 126.4 (2011): 1061–69.

Gandhi, M. K. *Hind Swaraj or Indian Home Rule.* 1910. Madras: Ganseh & Co/Nationalist Press, 1919.

Gans, Herbert. *Deciding What's News: A Study of* CBS Evening News, NBC Nightly News, Newsweek, *and* Time. New York: Pantheon, 1979.

———. *Popular Culture and High Culture: An Analysis and Evaluation of Taste.* 1974. New York: Basic Books, 1999.

García-Canclini, Néstor. *Culturas Híbridas: Estrategias Para Entrar y Salir de la Modernidad.* Mexico City: Grijalbo, 1989.

———. *Hybrid Cultures: Strategies for Entering and Leaving Modernity.* Translated by Silvia López and Christopher Schiappari. Minneapolis: University of Minnesota Press, 1995.

———. *Consumers: Globalization and Multicultural Conflicts.* Minneapolis: University of Minnesota Press, 2001.

Garnham, Nicholas. *Emancipation, the Media and Modernity.* Oxford: Oxford University Press, 2000.

Gaytán, Marie Sarita. *¡Tequila! Distilling the Spirit of Mexico.* Stanford: Stanford University Press, 2014.

Gee, James Paul. *Social Linguistics and Literacies: Ideology in Discourses, Critical Perspectives on Literacy and Education.* Bristol: Falmer Press, 1990.

Geertz, Clifford. *The Predicament of Culture: Twentieth-Century Ethnography, Literature, and Art.* Cambridge, MA: Harvard University Press, 1988.

Genette, Gèrard. *Paratexts: Thresholds of Interpretation.* Translated by Jane E. Lewin. Cambridge: Cambridge University Press, 1997.

Georgiou, Myria. *Diaspora, Identity and the Media.* Cresskill, NJ: Hampton Press, 2006.

———. *Media and the City.* Cambridge: Polity, 2013.

Gerbner, George and Larry Gross. "Living with Television: The Violence Profile." *Journal of Communication* 26.2 (1976): 172–94.

Giardina, Michael and Cameron McCarthy. "The Popular Racial Order of Urban America: Sport, Cinema, and the Politics of Culture." *Cultural Studies/Critical Methodologies* 5.2 (2005): 145–73.

Gibbs, Anna. "Disaffected." *Continuum: Journal of Media and Cultural Studies* 16.3 (2002): 335–41.

Giddens, Anthony. *Modernity and Self-Identity: Self and Society in the Late Modern Age.* Cambridge: Polity, 1991.

Gilder, Ken. *The Subcultures Reader.* London: Routledge, 2005.

Gill, Rosalind. *Gender and the Media.* Cambridge: Polity, 2007a.

———. "Postfeminist Media Culture: Elements of a Sensibility." *European Journal of Cultural Studies* 10.2 (2007b): 147–66.

———. "Empowerment/Sexism: Figuring Female Sexual Agency in Contemporary Advertising." *Feminism & Psychology* 18.1 (2008): 35–60.

———. "Unspeakable Inequalities: Postfeminism, Entrepreneurial Subjectivity and the Repudiation of Sexism among Cultural Workers." *Social Politics* 21 (2014): 509–28.

Gill, Rosalind and Shani Orgad. "The Confidence Cult(ure)." *Australian Feminist Studies* 30 (2015): 324–44.

Gillespie, Marie. *Television, Ethnicity, and Cultural Change.* London: Routledge, 1995.

Gillespie, Tarleton. "The Relevance of Algorithms." In *Media Technologies*, edited by Tarleton Gillespie, Pablo Boczkowski, and Kristen Foot, 167–94. Cambridge, MA: MIT Press, 2014.

Gilroy, Paul. "Diaspora and the Detours of Identity." In *Identity and Difference*, edited by Kathryn Woodward, 301–41. London: Sage, 1997.

Gitlin, Todd. *Inside Prime Time.* New York: Pantheon, 1984.

———. "Blips, Bites and Savvy Talk: Television's Impact on American Politics." *Dissent*, Winter 1990, 18–26. www.dissentmagazine.org.

Glebatis Perks, Lisa. *Media Marathoning: Immersions in Morality.* Lanham, MD: Lexington, 2015.

Glynn, Kevin. *Tabloid Culture: Trash Taste, Popular Power, and the Transformation of American Television*. Durham, NC: Duke University Press, 2000.

Godwin, Mike. *Cyber-Rights: Defending Free Speech in the Digital Age*. New York: Random House, 1998.

Goffman, Erving. *The Presentation of Self in Everyday Life*. Harmondsworth: Penguin, 1969.

Goggin, Gerard and Christopher Newell. *Digital Disability: The Social Construction of Disability in New Media*. Lanham, MD: Rowman & Littlefield, 2003.

Goldberg, David T. *The Threat of Race*. Malden, MA: Blackwell, 2009.

Goldman, Robert. *Reading Ads Socially*. London: Routledge, 1992.

Goriunova, Olga. "New Media Idiocy." *Convergence: The International Journal of Research into New Media Technologies* 19.2 (2013): 223–35.

Gould, Rebecca. "Aaron Swartz's Legacy." *Academe: Magazine of the American Association of University Professors* 100.1 (2014): 19–23.

Govil, Nitin. *Orienting Hollywood: A Century of Film Culture between Los Angeles and Bombay*. New York: New York University Press, 2015.

Gramsci, Antonio. *Selections from the Prison Notebooks of Antonio Gramsci*. Edited and translated by Quintin Hoare and Geoffry Nowell Smith. New York: International, 1971.

———. *The Antonio Gramsci Reader: Selected Writings 1916–1935*. London: Lawrence and Wishart, 1999.

Gray, Jonathan. "New Audiences, New Textualities: Anti-fans and Non-fans." *International Journal of Cultural Studies* 6.1 (2003): 64–81.

———. *Show Sold Separately: Promos, Spoilers, and Other Media Paratexts*. New York: New York University Press, 2010.

———. "When Is the Author?" In *A Companion to Media Authorship*, edited by Jonathan Gray and Derek Johnson, 88–111. Malden, MA: Wiley-Blackwell, 2013.

Gray, Jonathan, Jeffrey P. Jones, and Ethan Thompson, eds. *Satire TV: Politics and Comedy in the Post-network Era*. New York: New York University Press, 2009.

Gray, Jonathan, Cornel Sandvoss, and C. Lee Harrington, eds. *Fandom: Identities and Communities in a Mediated World*. New York: New York University Press, 2007.

Gregg, Melissa. *Work's Intimacy*. Cambridge: Polity, 2011.

———. "Inside the Data Spectacle." *Television & New Media* 16 (January 2015a): 37–51.

———. "Power Out." *HomeCookedTheory*, April 19, 2015b. www.homecookedtheory.com.

Gregg, Melissa and Greg Seigworth, eds. *The Affect Theory Reader*. Durham, NC: Duke University Press, 2010.

Grewal, David Singh. *Network Power: The Social Dynamics of Globalization*. New Haven, CT: Yale University Press, 2008.

Grindstaff, Laura. *The Money Shot: Trash, Class, and the Making of TV Talk Shows*. Chicago: University of Chicago Press, 2002.

Gross, Larry. *Up from Invisibility: Lesbians, Gay Men and the Media in America*. New York: Columbia University Press, 2002.

Grossberg, Lawrence. *We Gotta Get Outta This Place: Popular Conservatism and Postmodern Culture*. New York: Routledge, 1992.

———. *Caught in the Crossfire: Kids, Politics and America's Future*. New York: Routledge, 2008.

Grossberg, Lawrence and Stuart Hall. "On Postmodernism and Articulation: An Interview with Stuart Hall." In *Stuart Hall: Critical Dialogues in Cultural Studies*, edited by David Morley and Kuan-Hsing Chen, 131–50. London: Routledge, 1996.

Gutman, Herbert. "Work, Culture and Society in Industrializing America." *American Historical Review* 78.3 (1973): 531–88.

Habermas, Jürgen. "The Public Sphere." *New German Critique* 3 (1974): 49–55.

———. *The Structural Transformation of the Public Sphere*. Cambridge, MA: MIT Press, 1989.

Haggerty, Kevin and Richard Ericson. "The Surveillant Assemblage." *British Journal of Sociology* 51.4 (2000): 605–22.

Halberstam, Judith. *Female Masculinity*. Durham, NC: Duke University Press, 1998.

Hall, Rachel. *The Transparent Traveler: The Performance and Culture of Airport Security*. Durham, NC: Duke University Press, 2015.

Hall, Stuart. "Encoding, Decoding." 1973. In *Culture, Media, Language: Working Papers in Cultural Studies, 1972–1979*, edited by Stuart Hall, Dorothy Hobson, Andrew Lowe, and Paul Willis, 117–28. London: Unwin Hyman, 1980.

———. "Notes on Deconstructing the 'Popular.'" In *People's History and Socialist Theory*, edited by Raphael Samuel, 227–39. London: Routledge and Kegan Paul, 1981.

———. "The Rediscovery of Ideology: Return of the Repressed in Media Studies." In *Culture, Society and the Media*, edited by Michael Gurevitchet et al., 52–86. London: Methuen, 1982.

———. "Cultural Identity and Diaspora." In *Identity: Community, Culture, and Difference*, edited by Jonathan Rutherford, 222–37. London: Lawrence and Wishart, 1990.

———. "The Problem of Ideology: Marxism without Guarantees." In *Stuart Hall: Critical Dialogues in Cultural Studies*, edited by David Morley and Kuan-Hsing Chen, 25–46. London: Routledge, 1996.

———. *Representation and the Media*. Video recording. Directed by Sut Jhally. Media Education Foundation, 1997a.

———. "The Work of Representation." In *Representation: Cultural Representations and Signifying Practices*, edited by Stuart Hall, 13–64. London: Sage, 1997b.

———. "Encoding/Decoding." In *Media and Cultural Studies: Keyworks*, edited by Meenakshi Gigi Durham and Douglas Kellner, 166–76. Malden, MA: Blackwell, 2001.

Hall, Stuart and Tony Jefferson, eds. *Resistance through Rituals*. London: Unwin Hyman, 1976.

Hall, Stuart, Doreen Massey, and Michael Rustin, eds. *The Kilburn Manifesto*. London: Lawrence and Wishart, 2014.

Hardt, Michael and Antonio Negri. *Empire*. Cambridge, MA: Harvard University Press, 2000.

———. *Multitude: War and Democracy in the Age of Empire*. New York: Penguin, 2005.

Hartley, John. *Understanding News*. London: Methuen, 1982.

———. *Communication, Cultural and Media Studies: The Key Concepts*. New York: Routledge, 2011.

Hartley, John, Jean Burgess, and Axel Bruns. "Introducing Dynamics: A New Approach to 'New Media.'" In *A Companion to New Media Dynamics*, edited by John Hartley, Jean Burgess, and Axel Bruns, 1–11. Malden, MA: Wiley-Blackwell, 2013.

Harvey, David. *The Condition of Postmodernity: An Enquiry into the Origins of Cultural Change*. Cambridge: Blackwell, 1989.

———. *A Short History of Neoliberalism*. Oxford: Oxford University Press, 2007.

Haskell, Molly. *From Reverence to Rape: The Treatment of Women in the Movies*. New York: Penguin, 1974.

Hassan, Robert. *The Chronoscopic Society: Globalization, Time, and Knowledge in the Network Economy*. New York: Peter Lang, 2003.

Havelock, Eric A. *Preface to Plato*. Vol. 1. Cambridge, MA: Harvard University Press, 2009.

Havens, Timothy. *Global Television Marketplace*. London: BFI, 2008.

Havens, Timothy and Amanda D. Lotz. *Understanding Media Industries*. 2nd ed. New York: Oxford University Press, 2016.

Havens, Timothy, Amanda D. Lotz, and Serra Tinic. "Critical Media Industry Studies: A Research Approach." *Communication, Culture and Critique* 2 (2009): 234–53.

Hay, James and Nick Couldry. "Rethinking Convergence/Culture." *Cultural Studies* 25.4/5 (2011): 473–86.

Hayles, N. Katherine with Stephen B. Crofts Wiley. "Media, Materiality, and the Human: A Conversation with N. Katherine Hayles." In *Communication Matters: Materialist Approaches to Media, Mobility, and Networks*, edited by Jeremy Packer and Stephen B. Crofts Wiley, 17–34. New York: Routledge, 2012.

Hearn, Alison. "'Meat, Mask, Burden': Probing the Contours of the Branded 'Self.'" *Journal of Consumer Culture* 8.2 (2008): 197–217.

Hearn, Jonathan. *Theorizing Power*. Basingstoke: Palgrave, 2012.

Hebdige, Dick. *Hiding in the Light: On Images and Things*. London: Routledge, 1988.

Hegde, Radha. *Circuits of Visibility: Gender and Transnational Media Cultures*. New York: New York University Press, 2011.

———. *Mediating Migration*. Cambridge: Polity, 2016.

Heidegger, Martin. *The Question Concerning Technology and Other Essays*. Translated by William Lovitt. New York: Harper & Row, 1977.

Held, David. "Principles of Cosmopolitan Order." In *The Cosmopolitanism Reader*, edited by David Held and Garrett Brown, 229–47. Cambridge: Polity, 2010.

Hellekson, Karen and Kristina Busse, eds. *Fan Fiction and Fan Communities in the Age of the Internet*. Jefferson, NC: McFarland, 2006.

———, eds. *The Fan Fiction Studies Reader*. Iowa City: University of Iowa Press, 2014.

Heller, Dana. *Makeover Television: Realities Remodelled*. London: I. B. Tauris, 2007.

Heritage, John. *Garfinkel and Ethnomethodology*. Englewood Cliffs, NJ: Prentice Hall, 1984.

Herzog, Charlotte Cornelia and Jane Gaines. "Puffed Sleeves before Tea-Time: Joan Crawford, Adrian, and Women Audiences." In *Stardom: Industry of Desire*, edited by Christine Gledhill, 77–95. London: Routledge, 1991.

Hesmondhalgh, David. "Bourdieu, the Media and Cultural Production." *Media, Culture & Society* 28.2 (2006): 211–32.

———. "Media Industry Studies, Media Production Studies." In *Media and Society*, edited by James Curran, 3–21. London: Bloomsbury, 2011.

———. *The Cultural Industries*. 3rd ed. Thousand Oaks, CA: Sage, 2013.

Hesmondhalgh, David and Sarah Baker. *Creative Labour: Media Work in Three Cultural Industries*. London: Routledge, 2011.

Higashi, Sumiko. "Vitagraph Stardom: Constructing Personalities for 'New' Middle Class Consumption." In *Reclaiming the Archive: Feminism and Film History*, edited by Vicki Callahan, 264–88. Detroit: Wayne State University Press, 2010.

Hills, Matt. *Fan Cultures*. London: Routledge, 2002.

———. "'Twilight' Fans Represented in Commercial Paratexts and Inter-fandoms: Resisting and Repurposing Negative Fan Stereotypes." In *Genre, Reception, and Adaptation in the "Twilight" Series*, edited by Anne Morey, 113–129. Farnham: Ashgate, 2012.

Hilmes, Michele. "The New Materiality of Radio: Sound on Screens." In *Radio's New Wave: Global Sound in the Digital Era*, edited by Jason Loviglio and Michele Hilmes, 43–61. New York: Routledge, 2013.

Hobsbawm, Eric. *Age of Extremes: The Short Twentieth Century*. London: Abacus, 1995.

Hobsbawm, Eric and Terence Ranger, eds. *The Invention of Tradition*. Cambridge: Cambridge University Press, 1992.

Hochschild, Arlie. *The Outsourced Self: Intimate Life in Market Times*. New York: Metropolitan Books, 2012.

Holmes, Su and Diane Negra. "Introduction." In *In the Limelight and under the Microscope: Forms and Functions of Female Celebrity*, edited by Su Holmes and Diane Negra, 1–16. New York: Bloomsbury, 2011.

Holt, Jennifer. *Empires of Entertainment: Media Industries and the Politics of Deregulation 1980–1996*. New Brunswick, NJ: Rutgers University Press, 2011.

hooks, bell. *Ain't I a Woman: Black Women and Feminism*. London: South End Press, 1981.

———. *Black Looks: Race and Representation*. Boston: South End Press, 1992.

Horkheimer, Max and Theodor W. Adorno. *Dialectic of Enlightenment: Philosophical Fragments*. 1944. Edited by Gunzelin Schmid Noerr. Translated by Edmund Jephcott. Stanford: Stanford University Press, 2002.

Horwitz, Robert. *The Irony of Regulatory Reform*. New York: Oxford University Press, 1989.

Howarth, David. *Discourse*. Buckingham: Open University Press, 2000.

Howarth, David and Yannis Stavrakakis. "Introducing Discourse Theory and Political Analysis." In *Discourse Theory and Political Analysis*, edited by David Howarth, Aletta J. Norval, and Yannis Stavrakakis, 1–23. Manchester: Manchester University Press, 2000.

Huettig, Mae. "Economic Control of the Motion Picture Industry." In *The American Film Industry*, edited by Tino Balio, 285–310. Madison: University of Wisconsin Press, 1985.

Huizinga, Johan. *Homo Ludens: A Study of the Play Element in Culture*. Boston: Beacon, 1955.

Hutcheon, Linda. *Irony's Edge: The Theory and Politics of Irony*. London: Routledge, 1994.

Hyde, Lewis. *The Gift: Creativity and the Artist in the Modern World*. New York: Vintage, 1983.

Innis, Harold A. *The Bias of Communication*. Toronto: University of Toronto Press, 1951.

Irvine, Judith T. and Susan Gal. "Language Ideology and Linguistic Differentiation." In *Linguistic Anthropology: A Reader*, 2nd ed., edited by Alessandro Duranti, 402–34. Malden, MA: Wiley-Blackwell, 2009.

Iser, Wolfgang. *The Act of Reading: A Theory of Aesthetic Response*. London: Routledge and Kegan Paul, 1978.

Iwabuchi, Koichi. *Recentering Globalization: Popular Culture and Japanese Transnationalism*. Durham, NC: Duke University Press, 2002.

Jameson, Frederic. "Reification and Utopia in Mass Culture." *Social Text* 1.1 (1979): 130–48.

Janrain. "Identity-Driven Marketing: Best Practices for Marketing Continuity." White paper, 2015. www.janrain.com.

Jenkins, Henry. *Textual Poachers: Television Fans and Participatory Culture*. New York: Routledge, 1992.

———. *Convergence Culture: Where Old and New Media Collide*. New York: New York University Press, 2006.

Jenkins, Henry, Sam Ford, and Joshua Green. *Spreadable Media: Creating Meaning and Value in a Networked Culture*. New York: New York University Press, 2013.

Jenkins, Henry, Sangita Shresthova, Liana Gamber-Thompson, Neta Kligler-Vilenchik, and Arley M. Zimmerman. *By Any Media Necessary: The New Youth Activism*. New York: New York University Press, 2016.

Johnson, Derek. *Media Franchising: Creative License and Collaboration in the Culture Industries*. New York: New York University Press, 2013.

Johnson, Richard. "What Is Cultural Studies Anyway?" *Social Text* 16 (1986–87): 38–80.

Jones, Deborah and Judith K. Pringle. "Unmanageable Inequalities: Sexism in the Film Industry." *Sociological Review* 63 (2015): 37–49.

Jones, Jeffrey P. "A Cultural Approach to the Study of Mediated Citizenship." *Social Semiotics* 16.2 (2006): 365–82.

Joyrich, Lynne. *Re-viewing Reception: Television, Gender and Postmodern Culture*. Bloomington: Indiana University Press, 1996.

Ju, Hyejung and Soobum Lee. "The Korean Wave and Asian Americans: The Ethnic Meanings of Transnational Korean Pop Culture in the USA." *Continuum: Journal of Media and Cultural Studies* 29.3 (2015): 323–38.

Kackman, Michael, Marnie Binfield, Matthew Thomas Payne, Allison Perlman, and Bryan Sebok. "Introduction." In *Flow TV: Television in the Age of Media Convergence*, edited by Michael Kackman et al., 1–10. New York: Routledge, 2011.

Kaklamanidou, Betty. *Genre, Gender and the Effects of Neoliberalism: The New Millennium Hollywood Rom Com*. London: Routledge, 2013.

Kant, Immanuel. *Critique of Judgement*. 1790. New York: Oxford University Press, 2007.

Kaplan, E. Ann. *Women and Film: Both Sides of the Camera*. New York: Methuen, 1983.

Kearney, Mary Celeste. *Girls Make Media*. New York: Routledge, 2006.

Keeling, Kara. *The Witch's Flight: The Cinematic, the Black Femme, and the Image of Common Sense*. Durham, NC: Duke University Press, 2007.

———. "Queer OS." *Cinema Journal* 53.2 (2014): 152–56.

Keightley, Emily. *Time, Media, and Modernity*. Basingstoke: Palgrave Macmillan, 2012.

Kelan, Elisabeth K. "Gender Fatigue: The Ideological Dilemma of Gender Neutrality and Discrimination in Organizations." *Canadian Journal of Administrative Sciences/Revue Canadienne des Sciences de l'Administratio* 26.3 (2009): 197–210.

Kendall, Diana. *Framing Class: Media Representations of Wealth and Poverty in America*. 2nd ed. Lanham, MD: Rowman & Littlefield, 2011.

Kennedy, Helen. *Net Work: Ethics and Values in Media Design*. London: Palgrave, 2012.

Kien, Grant. "Actor-Network Theory: Translation as Material Culture." In *Material Culture and Technology in Everyday Life: Ethnographic Approaches*, edited by Phillip Vannini, 27–44. New York: Peter Lang, 2009.

Kintz, Linda. *Between Jesus and the Market: The Emotions That Matter in Right-Wing America*. Durham, NC: Duke University Press, 1995.

Kiousis, S. "Interactivity: A Concept Explication." *New Media & Society* 4.3 (2002): 355–83.

Kittler, Friedrich A. *Gramophone, Film, Typewriter*. Translated by Geoffrey Winthroup-Young and Michael Wutz. Stanford: Stanford University Press, 1999.

Klein, Naomi. *No Logo: No Space, No Choice, No Jobs*. New York: Picador, 2000.

Klinenberg, Eric. *Fighting for Air*. New York: Metropolitan Books, 2007.

Kocurek, Carly. *Coin-Operated Americans: Rebooting Boyhood at the Video Game Arcade*. Minneapolis: University of Minnesota Press, 2015.

Koffman, Ofra, Shani Orgad, and Rosalind Gill. "Girl Power and Selfie Humanitarianism." *Continuum: Journal of Media and Cultural Studies* 29.2 (2015): 157–68.

Kolar-Panov, Dona. *Video, War and the Diasporic Imagination*. London: Routledge, 1997.

Koselleck, Reinhart. *Critique and Crisis: Enlightenment and the Pathogenesis of Modern Society*. Cambridge, MA: MIT Press, 1988.

Kozloff, Sarah. *Invisible Storytellers: Voiceover Narration in American Film*. Berkeley: University of California Press, 1989.

Kraidy, Marwan M. *Hybridity, or the Cultural Logic of Globalization*. Philadelphia: Temple University Press, 2005.

———. *Reality Television and Arab Politics: Contention in Public Life*. New York: Cambridge University Press, 2010.

———. *The Naked Blogger of Cairo: Creative Insurgency in the Arab World*. Cambridge, MA: Harvard University Press, 2016.

Kumar, Shanti. *Gandhi Meets Primetime: Globalization and Nationalism in Indian Television*. Urbana: University of Illinois Press, 2006.

Lacan, Jacques. *The Four Fundamental Concepts of Psycho-Analysis*. Translated by A. Sheridan. New York: Norton, 1981.

Lacey, Kate. *Listening Publics: The Politics and Experience of Listening in the Media Age*. London: Polity, 2013.

Laclau, Ernesto. *Politics and Ideology in Marxist Theory*. London: New Left Books, 1977.

———. "Metaphor and Social Antagonisms." In *Marxism and the Interpretation of Culture*, edited by Cary Nelson and Lawrence Grossberg, 249–57. Urbana: University of Illinois, 1988.

Laclau, Ernesto and Chantal Mouffe. *Hegemony and Socialist Strategy: Towards a Radical Democratic Politics*. London: Verso, 1985.

Landes, Joan. "The Public and the Private Sphere: A Feminist Reconsideration." In *Feminism, the Public and the Private*, edited by Joan B. Landes, 135–63. Oxford: Oxford University Press, 1998.

Larkin, Alile Sharon. "Black Women Film-Makers Defining Ourselves: Feminism in Our Own Voice." In *Female Spectators: Looking at Film and Television*, edited by E. Deirdre Pribam, 157–73. New York: Verso, 1988.

Larrain, Jorge. "Stuart Hall and the Marxist Concept of Ideology." In *Stuart Hall: Critical Dialogues in Cultural Studies*, edited by David Morley and Kuan-Hsing Chen, 46–70. London: Routledge, 1996.

Latonero, Mark. "For Refugees, a Digital Passage to Europe." Thomson Reuters December 27, 2015. http://news.trust.org.

Latour, Bruno. "The Powers of Association." *Sociological Review* 32.S1 (1984): 264–80.

Lauzen, Martha. *Women and the Big Picture: Behind the Scenes Employment on the Top 700 Films of 2014*. San Diego: Centre for the Study of Women in Television, 2015. http://womenintvfilm.sdsu.edu.

Lavers, Annette. *Roland Barthes: Structuralism and After*. London: Methuen, 1982.

Lazar, Michelle M. "Discover the Power of Femininity!" *Feminist Media Studies* 6.4 (2006): 505–17.

Lazzarato, Mauricio. "Immaterial Labor." In *Radical Thought in Italy: A Potential Politics*, edited by Paolo Virno and Michael Hardt, 133–46. Minneapolis: University of Minnesota Press, 1996.

Leaver, Tama. "Joss Whedon, Dr. Horrible, and the Future of Web Media." *Popular Communication* 11.2 (2013): 160–73.

Leaver, Tama and Michele Willson, eds. *Social, Casual and Mobile Games: The Changing Gaming Landscape*. London: Bloomsbury Academic, 2016.

Lee, Paul S. N. "The Absorption and Indigenization of Foreign Media Cultures: A Study of a Cultural Meeting Point of the East and West: Hong Kong." *Asian Journal of Communication* 1.2 (1991): 52–72.

Levina, Marina. "Googling Your Genes: Personal Genomics and the Discourse of Citizen Bioscience in the Network Age." *Journal of Science Communication* 9.1 (2010): 1–8.

———. "From Feminism without Bodies, to Bleeding Bodies in Virtual Spaces." *Communication and Critical/Cultural Studies* 11.3 (2014): 278–81.

Levina, Marina and Grant Kien, eds. *Post-global Network and Everyday Life*. New York: Peter Lang, 2010.

Levine, Lawrence. *Highbrow/Lowbrow: The Emergence of Cultural Hierarchy in America*. Cambridge, MA: Harvard University Press, 1988.

Lévi-Strauss, Claude. *The View from Afar*. Chicago: University of Chicago Press, 1985.

Lewis, Justin. *Beyond Consumer Capitalism: Media and the Limits to Imagination*. London: Polity, 2013.

Lewis, Lisa A., ed. *The Adoring Audience: Fan Culture and Popular Media*. New York: Routledge, 1992.

Lewis, Michael. *Flash Boys: A Wall Street Revolt*. New York: Norton, 2014.

Lewis, Reina and Katrina Rolley. "Ad(dressing) the Dyke: Lesbian Looks and Lesbian Looking." In *Outlooks: Lesbian and Gay Sexualities and Visual Cultures*, edited by Peter Horne and Reina Lewis, 178–90. New York: Routledge, 1996.

Linklater, Andrew. "Distant Suffering and Cosmopolitan Obligations." *International Politics* 44.1 (2007): 19–36.

Lippmann, Walter. *Public Opinion*. New York: Macmillan, 1922.

Lipsitz, George. *Time Passages: Collective Memory and American Popular Culture*. Minneapolis: University of Minnesota Press, 1990.

———. *The Possessive Investment in Whiteness: How White People Profit from Identity Politics*. Philadelphia: Temple University Press, 1998.

Livingstone, Sonia. "On the Relation between Audiences and Publics." In *Audiences and Publics: When Cultural Engagement Matters for the Public Sphere*, edited by Sonia Livingstone, 17–41. Bristol: Intellect, 2005.

Lobato, Ramon and Julian Thomas. *The Informal Media Economy*. Cambridge: Polity, 2015.

Lodziak, Conrad. *The Power of Television*. London: Frances Pinter, 1987.

Losh, Elizabeth. "Hashtag Feminism and Twitter Activism in India." *Social Epistemology Review and Reply Collective* 3.3 (2014): 11–22.

Lotz, Amanda D. and Horace Newcomb. "The Production of Entertainment Media." In *A Handbook of Media and Communication Research*, 2nd ed., edited by Klaus Bruhn Jensen, 71–86. New York: Routledge, 2011.

Loviglio, Jason and Michele Hilmes, eds. *Radio's New Wave: Global Sound in the Digital Era*. New York: Routledge, 2013.

Lowe, Donald. *History of Bourgeois Perception*. Chicago: University of Chicago Press, 1982.

Lukes, Steven. *Power: A Radical Approach*. 2nd ed. Basingstoke: Palgrave, 2005.

Lunenfeld, Peter. "Unfinished Business." In *The Digital Dialectic: New Essays on New Media*, edited by Peter Lunenfeld, 7–22. Cambridge, MA: MIT Press, 1999.

Lunt, Peter and Paul Stenner. "*The Jerry Springer Show* as an Emotional Public Sphere." *Media Culture & Society* 27.1 (2005): 59–81.

Lury, Celia. *Brands: The Logos of the Global Economy*. New York: Routledge, 2004.

Lyon, David. *Surveillance Society: Monitoring Everyday Life*. Buckingham: Open University Press, 2001.

Macdonald, Dwight. *Against the American Grain*. New York: Random House, 1962.

Macdonald, Myra. *Representing Women: Myths of Femininity in the Popular Media*. London: Edward Arnold, 1995.

Machin, David and Joanna Thornborrow. "Branding and Discourse: The Case of Cosmopolitan." *Discourse & Society* 14.4 (2003): 453–71.

Manovich, Lev. *The Language of New Media*. Cambridge, MA: MIT Press, 2001.

Manzerolle, Vincent and Atle Kjosen. "*Dare et Compare*: Virtuous Mesh and a Targeting Diagram." In *The Imaginary App*, edited by Paul D. Miller and Svitlana Matviyenko, 143–62. Cambridge, MA: MIT Press, 2014.

Marks, Laura U. "Video Haptics and Erotics." *Screen* 39.4 (1998): 331–47.

Martín-Barbero, Jesús. *De Los Medios a Las Mediaciones*. Mexico City: Gustavo Gili, 1987.

———. *Communication, Culture and Hegemony: From the Media to Mediations*. Translated by P. Schlesinger. London: Sage, 1993.

Marvin, Carolyn. *When Old Technologies Were New: Thinking about Electric Communication in the Late 19th Century*. New York: Oxford University Press, 1988.

Marwick, Alice E. *Status Update: Celebrity, Publicity and Branding in the Social Media Age*. New Haven, CT: Yale University Press, 2013.

Marwick, Alice and danah boyd. "I Tweet Honestly, I Tweet Passionately: Twitter Users, Context Collapse, and the Imagined Audience." *New Media & Society* 13.1 (2011): 114–33.

———. "Networked Privacy: How Teenagers Negotiate Context in Social Media." *New Media & Society*" 16.7 (2014): 1051–67.

Marx, Karl. *The Poverty of Philosophy*. New York: Cosimo, 2008.

———. *Capital Volume 1: A Critique of Political Economy*. Mineola, NY: Dover, 2011.

Marx, Karl and Frederick Engels. *The German Ideology*. London: Lawrence & Wishart, 1987.

———. *The Communist Manifesto*. New York: Monthly Review, 1998.

Massey, Doreen. *Space, Place, and Gender*. Minneapolis: University of Minnesota Press, 1994.

Massumi, Brian. *Parables for the Virtual: Movement, Affect, Sensation*. Durham, NC: Duke University Press, 2002.

Masterman, Len. *Television Mythologies: Stars, Shows and Signs*. London: Comedia, 1984.

Mattelart, Armand. *Mapping World Communication: War, Progress, Culture*. Minneapolis: University of Minnesota Press, 1994.

Mayer, Vicki. *Below the Line: Producers and Production Studies in the New Television Economy*. Durham, NC: Duke University Press, 2011.

Mayer, Vicki, Miranda J. Banks, and John Caldwell. "Introduction: Production Studies: Roots and Routes." In *Production Studies: Cultural Studies of Media Industries*, eds. Vicki Mayer, Miranda J. Banks, and John Caldwell, 1–12. New York: Routledge, 2009a.

———, eds. *Production Studies: Cultural Studies of Media Industries*. New York: Routledge, 2009b.

Mazzarella, Sharon R. and Norma Odom Pecora, eds. *Growing Up Girls: Popular Culture and the Construction of Identity*. New York: Peter Lang, 1999.

McCarthy, Anna. *Ambient Television: Visual Culture and Public Space*. Durham, NC: Duke University Press, 2001.

———. *The Citizen Machine: Governing by Television in 1950s America*. New York: New Press, 2010.

McChesney, Robert. *Communications Revolution*. New York: New Press, 2007.

McCracken, Ellen. *Decoding Women's Magazines: From Mademoiselle to Ms*. London: Macmillan, 1993.

McGuigan, James. *Cultural Populism*. London: Routledge, 1992.

McLeod, Kembrew and Peter DiCola. *Creative License: The Law and Art of Digital Sampling*. Durham, NC: Duke University Press, 2011.

McLuhan, Marshall. *Understanding Media*. New York: McGraw-Hill, 1964.

McRobbie, Angela. "Jackie: An Ideology of Adolescent Femininity." CCCS Stenciled Occasional Paper. Birmingham: University of Birmingham, 1978. http://epapers.bham.ac.uk.

———. "Settling Accounts with Subcultures." *Screen Education* 3 (1980): 37–49.

———. *In the Culture Society: Art, Fashion and Popular Music*. London: Routledge, 1999.

———. *The Aftermath of Feminism: Gender, Culture and Social Change*. London: Sage, 2009.

Mead, George. *Mind, Self, and Society*. Chicago: University of Chicago Press, 1934.

Meikle, Graham. *Interpreting News*. Basingstoke: Palgrave, 2009.

Mejias, Ulises. *Off the Network*. Minneapolis: Minnesota University Press, 2013.

Memmi, Albert. *Colonizer and the Colonized*. 1965. Boston: Beacon, 1991.

Meyrowitz, Joshua. *No Sense of Place*. Oxford: Oxford University Press, 1985.

Miège, Bernard. "The Logics at Work in the New Cultural Industries." *Media, Culture & Society* 9 (1987): 273–89.

———. *The Capitalization of Cultural Production*. New York: International General, 1989.

Mill, John S. *On Liberty*. Edited by Simon Shaw-Miller. 1859. New Haven, CT: Yale University Press, 2011.

Miller, Toby. *The Well-Tempered Self: Citizenship, Culture and the Postmodern Subject*. Baltimore: Johns Hopkins University Press, 1993.

Miller, Toby, Nitin Govil, John McMurria, Richard Maxwell, and Ting Wang. *Global Hollywood 2*. London: BFI, 2005.

Mittell, Jason. *Genre and Television: From Cop Shows to Cartoons in American Culture*. New York: Routledge, 2004.

———. *Complex TV: The Poetics of Contemporary Television Storytelling*. New York: New York University Press, 2015.

Modleski, Tania. "The Rhythms of Reception: Daytime Television and Women's Work." In *Regarding Television: Critical Approaches—An Anthology*, edited by E. Ann Kaplan, 67–75. Los Angeles: American Film Institute, 1983.

———. *Loving with a Vengeance: Mass Produced Fantasies for Women*. 2nd ed. New York: Routledge, 2007.

Moor, Liz. *The Rise of Brands*. Oxford: Berg, 2007.

Moore, Candace. "The D Word." In *Loving "The L Word,"* edited by Dana Heller, 191–207. London: I. B. Tauris, 2013.

Moores, Shaun. *Media, Place and Mobility*. New York: Palgrave Macmillan, 2012.

Morgan Parmett, Helen. "Media as a Spatial Practice: *Treme* and the Production of the Media Neighbourhood." *Continuum: Journal of Media and Cultural Studies* 28.3 (2014): 286–99.

Morley, David. *The Nationwide Audience*. London: British Film Institute, 1980.

———. *Home Territories: Media, Mobility and Identity*. London: Routledge, 2000.

———. "Audience." In *New Keywords: A Revised Vocabulary of Culture and Society*, edited by Tony Bennett, Lawrence Grossberg, and Meaghan Morris, 8–10. Malden, MA: Blackwell, 2005.

Morley, David and Kevin Robins. *Spaces of Identity: Global*

Media, Electronic Landscapes, and Cultural Boundaries. New York: Routledge, 1995.

Morris, Jeremy. *Selling Digital Music, Formatting Culture*. Berkeley: University of California Press, 2015.

Morris, Jeremy and Evan Elkins. "There's an App for That: Mundane Software as Commodity." *Fibreculture Journal* 25 (2015): n.p.

Mosco, Vincent. *The Political Economy of Communication*. 2nd ed. Thousand Oaks, CA: Sage, 2009.

Mottahedeh, Negar. *#Iranelection: Hashtag Solidarity and the Transformation of Online Life*. Palo Alto, CA: Stanford University Press, 2015.

Mouffe, Chantal. *On the Political*. London: Routledge, 2005.

Mukherjee, Roopali. "Antiracism Limited." *Cultural Studies* 30.1 (2015): 47–77.

Mulvey, Laura. "Visual Pleasure and Narrative Cinema." *Screen* 16.3 (1975): 6–18.

Mumford, Lewis. *Technics and Civilization*: Cambridge, MA: Harvard University Press, 1963.

Muñoz, José Esteban. *Disidentifications: Queers of Color and the Performance of Politics*. Minneapolis: University of Minnesota Press, 1999.

———. *Cruising Utopia: The Then and There of Queer Futurity*. New York: New York University Press, 2009.

Murdock, Graham. "Political Economies as Moral Economies: Commodities, Gifts, and Public Goods." In *The Handbook of Political Economy of Communications*, edited by Janet Wasko, Graham Murdock, and Helena Sousa, 13–40. Malden, MA: Wiley-Blackwell, 2011.

Murdock, Graham and Peter Golding. "For a Political Economy of Mass Communications." *Socialist Register* 10 (1973): 205–34.

Murray, Susan. *Hitch Your Antenna to the Stars: Early Television and Broadcast Stardom*. New York: Routledge, 2005.

Myers, Greg. *Words in Ads*. London: Edward Arnold, 1994.

Naficy, Hamid. *The Making of Exile Cultures: Iranian Television in Los Angeles*. Minneapolis: University of Minnesota Press, 1993.

Napoli, Philip. *The Foundations of Communication Policy*. Cresskill, NJ: Hampton Press, 2001.

Nasaw, David. *Going Out: The Rise and Fall of Public Amusements*. New York: Basic Books, 1993.

Nelmes, Jill. *Introduction to Film Studies*. 5th ed. New York: Routledge, 2011.

Newcomb, Horace and Robert Alley. *The Producer's Medium: Conversations with Creators of American TV*. New York: Oxford University Press, 1983.

Newman, Michael Z. and Elana Levine. *Legitimating Television: Media Convergence and Cultural Status*. New York: Routledge, 2011.

Nightingale, Virginia, ed. *The Handbook of Media Audiences*. Malden, MA: Wiley-Blackwell, 2014.

Nissenbaum, Helen. *Privacy in Context: Technology, Policy, and the Integrity of Social Life*. Stanford: Stanford University Press, 2009.

Noble, David F. "Introduction." In *Architect or Bee? The Human/Technology Relationship*, by Mike Cooley, edited by Shirley Cooley, xi–xxi. Boston: South End Press, 1982.

———. *The Religion of Technology: The Divinity of Man and the Spirit of Invention*. New York: Knopf, 1997.

Ofek, Elie, Sang-Hoon Kim, and Michael Norris. "CJ E&M: Creating a K-Culture in the U.S." Harvard Business School Case 515-015, January 2015.

Olson, Scott. *Hollywood Planet: Global Media and the Competitive Advantage of Narrative Transparency*. Mahwah, NJ: Lawrence Erlbaum, 1999.

Ong, Walter. *Orality and Literature: The Technologizing of the Word*. London: Routledge, 1982.

OpenNet Initiative. "Filtering Data." 2014. https://opennet.net.

Ortiz, Fernando. *Contrapunteo Cubano del Tabaco y el Aazúcar*. 1940. Havana: Editorial de Ciencias Sociales, 1983.

———. *Cuban Counterpoint: Tobacco and Sugar*. Translated by H. de Onís. Durham, NC: Duke University Press, 1995.

Ouellette, Laurie. "TV Viewing as Good Citizenship? Political Rationality, Enlightened Democracy and PBS." *Cultural Studies* 13.1 (1999): 62–90.

———. *Viewers Like You? How Public TV Failed the People*. New York: Columbia University Press, 2002.

———. "Citizen Brand: ABC and the Do Good Turn in US Television." In *Commodity Activism: Cultural Resistance in Neoliberal Times*, edited by Roopali Mukherjee and Sarah Banet-Weiser, 57–75. New York: New York University Press, 2012.

Ouellette, Laurie and James Hay. *Better Living through Reality TV: Television and Post-welfare Citizenship*. Malden, MA: Blackwell, 2008.

Packer, Jeremy and Stephen B. Crofts Wiley, eds. *Communication Matters: Materialist Approaches to Media, Mobility, and Networks*. New York: Routledge, 2012.

Papacharissi, Zizi. *A Private Sphere: Democracy in a Digital Age*. Cambridge: Polity, 2010.

———. *Affective Publics: Sentiment, Technology, and Politics*. Oxford University Press, 2014.

Papacharissi, Zizi and Emily Easton. "In the Habitus of the New: Structure, Agency and the Social Media Habitus." In *A Companion to New Media Dynamics*, edited by John Hartley, Jean Burgess, and Axel Bruns, 171–84. Malden, MA: Wiley-Blackwell, 2013.

Parikka, Jussi. *Insect Media: An Archeology of Animals and Technology*. Minneapolis: University of Minnesota Press, 2010.

Parks, Lisa. "'Stuff You Can Kick': Toward a Theory of Media Infrastructure." In *Between Humanities and the Digital*, edited by Patrik Svennson and David Theo Goldberg, 355–74. Cambridge, MA: MIT Press, 2015.

Parks, Lisa and Nicole Starosielski, eds. *Signal Traffic: Critical Studies of Media Infrastructures*. Urbana: University of Illinois Press, 2015.

Peirce, Charles S. *Selected Writings (Values in a Universe of Chance)*. Edited by P. Wiener. New York: Dover, 1958.

Perren, Alisa. *Indie, Inc.: Miramax and the Transformation of Hollywood in the 1990s*. Austin: University of Texas Press, 2013a.

———. "Rethinking Distribution for the Future of Media Industry Studies." *Cinema Journal* 52.3 (2013b): 165–71.

Perry, Imani. *More Beautiful and More Terrible: The Embrace and Transcendence of Racial Inequality in the United States*. New York: New York University Press, 2011.

Peters, John Durham. *Courting the Abyss: Free Speech and the Liberal Tradition*. Chicago: University of Chicago Press, 2005.

———. *The Marvelous Clouds: Toward a Philosophy of Elemental Media*. Chicago: University of Chicago Press, 2015.

Petersen, Jennifer. *Murder, the Media and the Politics of Public Feelings: Remembering Matthew Shepard and James Byrd Jr*. Bloomington: Indiana University Press, 2011.

———. "Can Moving Pictures Speak? Film, Speech and Social Science in Early Twentieth-Century Law." *Cinema Studies* 53.3 (2014): 76–99.

Philips, Louise and Marianne W. Jørgensen. *Discourse Analysis as Theory and Method*. London: Sage, 2002.

Pinedo, Isabel Cristina. *Recreational Terror: Women and the Pleasures of Horror Film Viewing*. Albany: State University of New York Press, 1997.

Pingree, Suzanne, Robert Parker Hawkins, Matilda Butler, and William Paisley. "A Scale for Sexism." *Journal of Communication* 26.4 (1976): 193–200.

Ponce de Leon, Charles. *Self Exposure: Human Interest Journalism and the Emergence of Celebrity in America, 1890–1940*. Urbana: University of Illinois Press, 2002.

Press, Andrea. *Women Watching Television*. Philadelphia: University of Pennsylvania Press, 1991.

Pries, Ludger and Martin Seeliger. "Translational Social Spaces." In *Beyond Methodological Nationalism: Research Methodologies for Cross-Border Studies*, edited by Anna Amelina, 219–38. London: Routledge, 2012.

Prodnik, Jernej. "A Note on the Ongoing Processes of Commodification: From the Audience Commodity to the Social Factory." *tripleC* 10.2 (2012): 274–301.

Pryke, Michael. "Money's Eyes: The Visual Preparation of Financial Markets." *Economy and Society* 39.4 (2010): 427–59.

Puar, Jasbir. *Terrorist Assemblages: Homonationalism in Queer Times*. Durham, NC: Duke University Press, 2007.

Rabinovitz, Lauren. *For the Love of Pleasure: Women, Movies, and Culture in Turn-of-the-Century Chicago*. New Brunswick, NJ: Rutgers University Press, 1998.

Radicalesbians. "The Woman-Identified Woman." New York: Gay Flames, 1970.

Radway, Janice. *Reading the Romance*. Chapel Hill: University of North Carolina Press, 1984.

Rambukkana, Nathan, ed. *Hashtag Publics: The Power and Politics of Discursive Networks*. New York: Peter Lang, 2015.

Rantanen, Terhi. "In Nationalism We Trust?" In *Aftermath: The Cultures of the Economic Crisis*, edited by Manuel Castells, João Caraça, and Gustavo Cardoso, 132–53. London: Oxford University Press, 2012.

Reagle, Joseph M. *Reading the Comments: Likers, Haters and Manipulators at the Bottom of the Web*. Cambridge, MA: MIT Press, 2015.

Redmond, Sean. "The Whiteness of Stars: Looking at Kate Winslet's Unruly White Body." In *Stardom and Celebrity: A Reader*, edited by Su Holmes and Sean Redmond, 263–75. London: Sage, 2007.

Renan, Ernst. "What Is a Nation?" In *Nation and Narration*, edited by Homi K. Bhabba, 8–22. New York: Routledge, 1990.

Rentschler, Carrie. "Rape Culture and the Feminist Politics of Social Media." *Girlhood Studies* 7.1 (2014): 65–82.

Rhee, Margaret and Amanda Phillips. "Queer & Feminist New Media Spaces—HASTAC." Online forum. 2015. http://hastac.org.

Rich, B. Ruby. *New Queer Cinema: The Director's Cut*. Durham, NC: Duke University Press, 2013.

Ringrose, Jessica, Laura Harvey, Rosalind Gill, and Sonia Livingstone. "Teen Girls, Sexual Double Standards and 'Sexting': Gendered Value in Digital Image Exchange." *Feminist Theory* 14.3 (2013): 305–23.

Ringrose, Jessica and Valerie Walkerdine. "Regulating the Abject: The TV Makeover as Site of Neo-liberal Reinvention towards Bourgeois Femininity." *Feminist Media Studies* 8.3 (2008): 227–46.

Roberts, Dorothy. *Fatal Invention: How Science, Politics, and Big Business Re-create Race in the Twenty-first Century*. New York: New Press, 2011.

Roberts, Kevin. *Love Marks: The Future beyond Brands*. New York: Powerhouse Books, 2005.

Robins, Kevin. "Becoming Anybody: Thinking against the Nation and through the City." *City* 5.1 (2001): 77–90.

Robinson, Cedric J. *Forgery of Memory & Meaning: Blacks and the Regimes of Race in American Theater and Film before World War II*. Chapel Hill: University of North Carolina Press, 2007.

Rodman, Ron. *Tuning In: American Narrative Television Music*. New York: Oxford University Press, 2009.

Rodriguez, Clemencia and Patrick D. Murphy. "The Study of Communication and Culture in Latin America: From Laggards and the Oppressed to Resistance and Hybrid Cultures." *Journal of International Communication* 4.2 (1997): 24–45.

Rogin, Michael. *Blackface/White Noise: Jewish Immigrants in the Hollywood Melting Pot*. Berkeley: University of California Press, 1996.

Roscoe, Jane. "*Big Brother Australia*: Performing the Real Twenty-Four Seven." *International Journal of Cultural Studies* 4.4 (2001): 473–88.

Rose, Nikolas. *Governing the Soul: The Shaping of the Private Self*. London: Free Association Books, 1999.

Rosen, Jay. "The People Formerly Known as the Audience." *PressThink: Ghost of Democracy in the Media Machine*, June 27, 2006. http://journalism.nyu.edu.

Rosen, Marjorie. *Popcorn Venus: Women, Movies & the American Dream*. New York: Coward, McCann & Geohegan, 1973.

Rosenblatt, Roger. "The Age of Irony Comes to an End." *Time*, September 24, 2001.

Ross, Steven. *Working-Class Hollywood: Silent Film and the Shaping of Class in America*. Princeton: Princeton University Press, 1998.

Rule, James. *Private Lives, Public Surveillance*. London: Allen Lane, 1973.

Rushkoff, Douglas. *Present Shock: When Everything Happens Now*. New York: Current Books, 2013.

Ryan, Charlotte. *Prime Time Activism: Media Strategies for Grassroots Activism*. Boston: South End Press, 1991.

Ryan, Michael and Douglas Kellner. *Camera Politica: The Politics and Ideology of Contemporary Hollywood Film*. Bloomington: Indiana University Press, 1988.

Said, Edward. *Orientalism*. London: Pantheon, 1978.

Sandberg, Sheryl. *Lean In: Women, Work, and the Will to Lead*. New York: Knopf, 2013.

Sandvoss, Cornel. *Fans: The Mirror of Consumption*. London: Polity, 2005.

Saussure, Ferdinand de. *Course in General Linguistics*. 1915. Edited by C. Bally, A. Sechehaye, and A. Riedlinger. Translated by W. Baskin. London: Fontana, 1974.

Scannell, Paddy. *Radio, Television, and Modern Life: A Phenomenological Approach*. London: Sage, 1996.

Schafer, R. Murray. *The Soundscape: Our Sonic Environment and the Tuning of the World*. Toronto: Destiny Books, 1993.

Schatz, Thomas. *The Genius of the System: Hollywood Filmmaking in the Studio Era*. New York: Pantheon, 1988.

Schickel, Richard. *Intimate Strangers: The Culture of Celebrity*. Chicago: Ivan R. Dee, 2000.

Schiller, Herbert. *The Mind Managers*. Boston: Beacon, 1973.

———. *Culture Inc.: The Corporate Takeover of Public Expression*. New York: Oxford University Press, 1989.

Schlesinger, Philip. *Putting "Reality" Together: BBC News*. Beverly Hills: Sage, 1978.

Scholz, Trebor. *Digital Labor: The Internet as Playground and Factory*. New York: Routledge, 2013.

Schuchman, J. S. *Hollywood Speaks: Deafness and the Film Entertainment Industry*. Urbana: University of Illinois Press, 1988.

Schwartz-Cowan, Ruth. *More Work for Mother: The Ironies of Household Technology from Open Hearth to the Microwave*. New York: Basic Books, 1983.

Seiter, Ellen. "Stereotypes and the Media: A Reevaluation." *Journal of Communication* 36.2 (1986): 14–26.

———. "Semiotics, Structuralism, and Television." In *Channels of Discourse, Reassembled: Television and Contemporary Criticism*, edited by Robert Allen, 31–66. London: Routledge, 1992.

Sender, Katherine. *Business Not Politics: The Making of the Gay Market*. New York: Columbia University Press, 2005.

Senft, Terri. "The Skin of the Selfie." In *Ego Update: The Future of Digital Identity*, edited by Alain Bieber. Dusseldorf: NRW Forum, forthcoming.

Sharma, Sarah. *In the Meantime: Temporality and Cultural Politics*. Durham, NC: Duke University Press, 2014.

Shaw, Adrienne, *Gaming at the Edge: Sexuality and Gender at the Margins of Gamer Culture*. Minneapolis: University of Minnesota Press, 2014.

Shimpach, Shawn. *Television in Transition*. Malden, MA: Wiley-Blackwell, 2010.

Sigart, Miguel. *Play Matters*. Cambridge, MA: MIT Press, 2014.

Silverstone, Roger. *Why Study the Media?* London: Sage, 1999.

———. *Media and Morality: The Rise of the Mediapolis*. London: Polity, 2007.

Skeggs, Beverley and Helen Wood. *Reacting to Reality Television: Performance, Audience and Value*. New York: Routledge, 2012.

Slack, Jennifer Daryl and J. Macgregor Wise. *Culture and Technology: A Primer*. 2nd ed. New York: Peter Lang, 2015.

Sliwinski, Sharon. *Human Rights in Camera*. Chicago: University of Chicago Press, 2011.

Sloterdijk, Peter. *Bubbles. Spheres Volume I: Microspherology*. Translated by Wieland Hoban. Cambridge, MA: MIT Press, 2011.

Smith, Anne-Marie. *Laclau and Mouffe: The Radical Democratic Imaginary*. London: Routledge, 1999.

Smith, Daniel W. "Deleuze and the Question of Desire: Towards an Immanent Theory of Ethics." In *Deleuze and Ethics*, edited by Nathan Jun and Daniel W. Smith, 123–41. Edinburgh: Edinburgh University Press, 2011.

Smith, Jacob. *Vocal Tracks: Performance and Sound Media*. Berkeley: University of California Press, 2008.

Smith, Jacob and Neil Verma. *Anatomy of Sound: Norman Corwin and Media Authorship*. Berkeley: University of California Press, 2015.

Smythe, Dallas W. "Communications: Blindspot of Western Marxism." *Canadian Journal of Political and Social Theory* 1.3 (1977): 1–27.

Spigel, Lynn. *Make Room for TV: Television and the Family Ideal in Postwar America*. Chicago: University of Chicago Press, 1992.

———. "Entertainment Wars: Television Culture after 9/11." In *Television: The Critical View*, 7th ed., edited by Horace Newcomb, 625–41. Oxford: Oxford University Press, 2007.

Stam, Robert, Richard Burgoyne, and Sandy Flitterman-Lewis. *New Vocabularies in Film Semiotics: Structuralism, Poststructuralism and Beyond*. London: Routledge, 1992.

Sterne, Jonathan. *The Audible Past: Cultural Origins of Sound Reproduction*. Durham, NC: Duke University Press, 2003.

———, ed. *The Sound Studies Reader*. New York: Routledge, 2012.

Storey, John. *Cultural Theory and Popular Culture: An Introduction*. London: Routledge, 2009.

Straayer, Chris. *Deviant Eyes, Deviant Bodies*. New York: Columbia University Press, 1996.

Straubhaar, Joseph. *World Television: From Global to Local*. Thousand Oaks, CA: Sage, 2007.

Streeter, Thomas. *Selling the Air*. Chicago: University of Chicago Press, 1996.

———. "Policy, Politics, and Discourse." *Communication, Culture & Critique* 6.4 (2013): 488–501.

Sturken, Marita. *Tangled Memories: The Vietnam War, the AIDS Epidemic, and the Politics of Remembering*. Berkeley: University of California Press, 1997.

Suits, Bernard. *The Grasshopper: Games, Life and Utopia*. Orchard Park, CA: Broadview Press, 2005.

Sullivan, John L. *Media Audiences: Effects, Users, Institutions, and Power*. London: Sage, 2013.

Superstorm Research Lab. "A Tale of Two Sandys." White paper. 2013. http://superstormresearchlab.org.

Sutton-Smith, Brian. *The Ambiguity of Play*. Cambridge, MA: Harvard University Press, 1997.

Szulc, Lukasz. "Banal Nationalism and Queers Online: Enforcing and Resisting Cultural Meanings of .tr." *New Media & Society* 17.9 (2015): 1530–46.

Tarde, Gabriel. "The Public and the Crowd." 1901. In *Gabriel Tarde on Communication and Social Influence*, edited by Terry Clark, 277–96. Chicago: University of Chicago Press, 1969.

Tartikoff, Brandon. *The Last Great Ride*. New York: Random House, 1992.

Tasker, Yvonne and Diane Negra. *Interrogating Post-feminism: Gender and the Politics of Popular Culture*. Durham, NC: Duke University Press, 2007.

Tawil-Souri, Helga. "Colored Identity: The Politics and Materiality of ID Cards in Palestine/Israel." *Social Text* 29 (2011): 67–97.

Taylor, Diana. *Disappearing Acts: Spectacles of Gender and Nationalism in Argentina's "Dirty War."* Durham, NC: Duke University Press, 1997.

Telotte, J. P. *Disney TV*. Detroit: Wayne State University Press, 2004.

Terranova, Tiziana. "Free Labor: Producing Culture for the Digital Economy." *Social Text* 18.2 (2000): 33–58.

———. *Network Culture: Politics for the Information Age*. London: Pluto Press, 2004.

Thompson, John. *The Media and Modernity*. Cambridge: Polity, 1995.

Tomlinson, John. *Globalization and Culture*. Chicago: University of Chicago Press, 1999.

Tongson, Karen. "Queer Fundamentalism." *Social Text* 32.4 (2014): 117–23.

———. "#Normporn." *Public Books*, August 1, 2015. www.publicbooks.org.

Torfing, Jacob. *New Theories of Discourse: Laclau, Mouffe and Žižek*. Oxford: Blackwell, 1999.

Truffaut, François. "A Certain Tendency of French Cinema." 1954. In *Movies and Methods*, vol. 1, edited by Bill Nichols, 9–18. Berkeley: University of California Press, 1976.

Tuchman, Gaye. *Making News: A Study in the Construction of Reality*. New York: Free Press, 1978a.

———. "The Symbolic Annihilation of Women by the Mass Media." In *Hearth and Home: Images of Women in the Mass Media*, edited by Gaye Tuchman, Arlene Kaplan Daniels, and James Benit, 3–38. Oxford: Oxford University Press, 1978b.

Turner, Graeme. *Ordinary People and the Media*. London: Sage, 2010.

———. *Understanding Celebrity*. 2nd ed. London: Sage, 2014.

Turner, Patricia A. *Color Adjustment*. Video recording. Directed by Marlon Riggs. 1992.

Turner, Victor W. *From Ritual to Theater: The Human Seriousness of Play*. New York: Performance Arts Journal Publication, 1982.

Turow, Joseph. *The Daily You: How the New Advertising Industry Is Defining Your Identity and Your Worth*. New Haven, CT: Yale University Press, 2012.

———. *The Aisles Have Eyes: How Retailers Track Your Shopping, Strip Your Privacy, and Define Your Power*. New Haven, CT: Yale University Press, forthcoming.

United Nations Population Fund. "Migration Overview." 2015. www.unfpa.org.

Vaidhyanathan, Siva. *Copyrights and Copywrongs: The Rise of Intellectual Property and How It Threatens Creativity*. New York: New York University Press, 2001.

Valdivia, Angharad N. *Latina/os and the Media*. Cambridge: Polity, 2010.

Van Brussel, Leen. "A Discourse-Theoretical Approach to Death and Dying." In *The Social Construction of Death: Interdisciplinary Perspectives*, edited by Leen Van Brussel and Nico Carpentier, 13–33. New York: Palgrave Macmillan, 2014.

van Dijk, Teun. *Discourse as Structure and Process*. London: Sage, 1997.

Van Zoonen, Liesbet. *Feminist Media Studies*. London: Sage, 1994.

———. *Entertaining the Citizen: When Politics and Popular Culture Converge*. Lanham, MD: Rowman & Littlefield, 2004.

Villarejo, Amy. *Ethereal Queer: Television, Historicity, Desire*. Durham, NC: Duke University Press, 2014.

Virilio, Paul. *Speed and Politics*. Translated by Mark Polizzotti. New York: Semiotext(e), 1986.

Volosinov, Valentin Nikolaevic. *Marxism and the Philosophy of Language*. Translated by Ladislav Metejka and I. R. Titunik. London: Seminar, 1973.

Wajcman, Judy. *TechnoFeminism*. London: Polity, 2004.

Walker, John and Sarah Chaplin. *Visual Culture: An Introduction*. Manchester: Manchester University Press, 1997.

Walters, Suzanna. *All the Rage: The Story of Gay Visibility in America*. Chicago: University of Chicago Press, 2003.

Wang, Georgette and Emile Yeh. "Globalization and Hybridization in Cultural Products: The Cases of Mulan and Crouching Tiger, Hidden Dragon." *International Journal of Cultural Studies* 8.2 (2005): 175–93.

Wanzo, Rebecca. "African American Acafandom and Other Strangers: New Genealogies of Fan Studies." *Transformative Works and Cultures* 20 (2015). http://journal.transformativeworks.org.

Warner, Michael. *The Letters of the Republic: Publication and the Public Sphere in Eighteenth-Century America*. Cambridge, MA: Harvard University Press, 1990.

———. *Publics and Counterpublics*. New York: Zone Books, 2005.

Warshow, Robert. *The Immediate Experience: Movies, Comics, Theatre and Other Aspects of Popular Culture*. Cambridge, MA: Harvard University Press, 2002.

Weber, Brenda R. *Women and Literary Celebrity in the Nineteenth Century: The Transatlantic Production of Fame and Gender*. London: Ashgate, 2012.

Weems, Robert. *Desegregating the Dollar: African American Consumerism in the Twentieth Century*. New York: New York University Press, 1998.

Weheylie, Alexander. *Habeas Viscus: Racializing Assemblages, Biopolitics and Black Feminist Theories of the Human*. Durham, NC: Duke University Press, 2014.

Westbrook, Robert. "'I Want a Girl Just Like the Girl That Married Harry James': American Women and the Problem of Political Obligation in World War II." *American Quarterly* 42.4 (1990): 587–614.

White, Michele. *The Body and the Screen: Theories of Internet Spectatorship*. Cambridge, MA: MIT Press, 2006.

———. *Producing Women: The Internet, Traditional Femininity, Queerness, and Creativity*. New York: Routledge, 2015.

White, Patricia. *Uninvited: Classical Hollywood Cinema and Lesbian Representability*. Bloomington: Indiana University Press, 1999.

———. *Women's Cinema, World Cinema: Projecting Contemporary Feminisms*. Durham, NC: Duke University Press, 2015.

Williams, Linda. "'Something Else Besides a Mother': *Stella Dallas* and the Maternal Melodrama." *Cinema Journal* 24.1 (1984): 2–27.

———. "Mega-Melodrama! Vertical and Horizontal Suspensions of the 'Classical.'" *Modern Drama* 55.4 (2012): 523–43.

Williams, Raymond. *Television: Technology and Cultural Form*. London: Fontana/Collins, 1974.

———. *Marxism and Literature*. New York: Oxford University Press, 1977.

———. *Keywords: A Vocabulary of Culture and Society*. 1976. London: Fontana, 1983.

———. "Mass and Masses." 1961. In *The Media Studies Reader*, edited by Tim O'Sullivan and Yvonne Jewkes, 18–27. New York: Bloomsbury, 1997.

Williamson, Judith. *Decoding Advertisements: Ideology and Meaning in Advertising*. London: Marion Boyars, 1978.

Willson, Michele and Tama Leaver. "Zynga's Farmville, Social Games and the Ethics of Big Data Mining." *Communication Research and Practice* 1.2 (2015): 147–58.

Wilson, Carl. *Let's Talk about Love: A Journey to the End of Taste*. London: Bloomsbury, 2007.

Winch, Alison. *Girlfriends and Postfeminist Sisterhood*. Basingstoke: Palgrave Macmillan, 2014.

Winner, Langdon. *Autonomous Technology: Technics-Out-of-Control as a Theme in Political Thought*. Cambridge, MA: MIT Press, 1977.

Wise, J. Macgregor. "Assemblage." In *Gilles Deleuze: Key Concepts*, edited by Charles Stivale, 91–102. Durham, UK: Acumen, 2011.

Wodak, Ruth. "The Discourse-Historical Approach." In *Methods of Critical Discourse Analysis*, edited by Ruth Wodak and Michael Meyer, 63–95. London: Sage, 2001.

Wollen, Peter. "The *Auteur* Theory." In *Signs and Meanings in the Cinema*, 3rd ed., 73–115. Bloomington: Indiana University Press, 1972.

Wright, Charles R. *Mass Communication*. New York: Random House, 1959.

Wynter, Sylvia. "Unsettling the Coloniality of Being/Power/Truth/Freedom: Towards the Human, after Man, Its Overrepresentation—An Argument." *CR: The New Centennial Review* 3.3 (2003): 257–337.

Xu, Guiquan. "The Articulation of Audience in Chinese Communication Research." In *Meanings of Audiences: Compara-*

tive Discourses, edited by Richard Butsch and Sonia Livingstone, 151–69. London: Routledge, 2014.

Young, Iris Marion. "Impartiality and the Civic Public." In *Feminism, the Public and the Private*, edited by Joan B. Landes, 421–47. Oxford: Oxford University Press, 1998.

Zelizer, Viviana. *Economic Lives: How Culture Shapes the Economy*. Princeton: Princeton University Press, 2011.

Zucker, Henry L. "Working Parents and Latchkey Children." *Annals of the American Academy of Political and Social Science* 236.1 (1944): 43–50.

Contributors

Mark Andrejevic is Researcher at Monash University and Professor of Media Studies at Pomona College. He writes about surveillance, popular culture, and digital media.

Melissa Aronczyk is Associate Professor in the School of Communication & Information at Rutgers University. She is the author of *Branding the Nation: The Global Business of National Identity* and the co-editor of *Blowing Up the Brand: Critical Perspectives on Promotional Culture*.

Sarah Banet-Weiser is Professor and Director of the School of Communication at the Annenberg School for Communication and Journalism at the University of Southern California. Her books include *Kids Rule! Nickelodeon and Consumer Citizenship*, *Authentic™: The Politics of Ambivalence in a Brand Culture*, *Cable Visions: Television Beyond Broadcasting*, and *Commodity Activism: Cultural Resistance in Neoliberal Times*.

Jonathan Bignell is Professor of Television and Film at the University of Reading. His books include two editions of *Media Semiotics*, three editions of *An Introduction to Television Studies*, and studies of the history of television in Britain, Europe, and the United States.

Jack Z. Bratich is Associate Professor and Chair of the Journalism and Media Studies Department at Rutgers University. His work applies autonomist social theory to social movement media, audience studies, and the cultural politics of secrecy. He edited a special issue of *Communication and Critical/Cultural Studies* on Occupy Wall Street.

Jean Burgess (@jeanburgess) is Professor of Digital Media and Director of the Digital Media Research Centre (DMRC) at Queensland University of Technology. Her research focuses on the uses, cultures, and politics of social and mobile media platforms.

Nico Carpentier is Professor in the Department of Informatics and Media of Uppsala University. In addition, he holds two part-time positions, those of Associate Professor in the Communication Studies Department of the Vrije Universiteit Brussel (VUB—Free University of Brussels) and Docent at Charles University in Prague.

Lilie Chouliaraki is Professor of Media and Communications at the London School of Economics and Political Science. Her most recent book is *The Ironic Spectator: Solidarity in the Age of Post-humanitarianism* (Outstanding Book Award 2015, International Communication Association).

Cynthia Chris is Associate Professor in the Department of Media Culture at the College of Staten Island, City University of New York. She is the author of *Watching Wildlife*, and co-editor of *Cable Visions: Television Beyond Broadcasting* and *Media Authorship*.

John Clarke is Professor Emeritus in the Faculty of Social Sciences at the Open University in the United Kingdom, and is also a Visiting Professor at Central European University in Budapest. He works on transformations of the welfare state, public services, and citizenship.

Nick Couldry is Professor of Media Communications and Social Theory at the London School of Economics and Political Science. He is the author or editor of twelve books including most recently *The Mediated Construction of Reality* (with Andreas Hepp) and *Media Society World*.

Amber Day is Associate Professor in the Literary and Cultural Studies Department at Bryant University. She is the author of *Satire and Dissent: Interventions in Contemporary Political Debate* and editor of the anthology *DIY Utopia*.

Susan J. Douglas is Catherine Neafie Kellogg Professor of Communication Studies at the University of Michigan. She is the author, most recently, of *The Rise of Enlightened Sexism: How Pop Culture Took Us from Girl Power to Girls Gone Wild* and of *Where the Girls Are: Growing Up Female with the Mass Media*.

Stephen Duncombe is Professor of Media and Culture at New York University. He is the author or editor of six books, and writes and speaks regularly on the intersection of culture and politics. He is also a lifelong political activist, and is presently co-founder and co-director of the Center for Artistic Activism.

Elizabeth Ellcessor is Assistant Professor in the Media School at Indiana University Bloomington. She is the author of *Restricted Access: Media, Disability, and the Politics of Participation*.

Terry Flew is Professor of Media and Communications at the Queensland University of Technology, with research interests in digital media, global media, media policy, and media economics. He is the author of eight books, and has headed major public enquiries into Australian media law and policy.

Kelly Gates is Associate Professor of Communication and Science Studies at the University of California, San Diego. She is the author of *Our Biometric Future: Facial Recognition Technology and the Culture of Surveillance*. Her work examines surveillance and visual media through the combined lenses of cultural studies and science and technology studies.

Myria Georgiou is Associate Professor in the Department of Media and Communications, London School of Economics and Political Science. She is the author of *Diaspora, Identity and the Media* and of *Media and the City*.

Rosalind Gill is Professor of Social and Cultural Analysis at City University London. She is the author or editor of several books, including *Gender and the Media*, *New Femininities: Postfeminism, Neoliberalism and Subjectivity*, and *Mediated Intimacy: Sex Advice in Media Culture*. Her latest collection (with Ana Sofia Elias and Christina Scharff) is *Aesthetic Labour: Rethinking Beauty Politics in Neoliberalism*.

Lisa Gitelman is Professor of English and Media Studies at New York University. She is the author most recently of *Paper Knowledge*.

Herman Gray is Professor of Sociology at the University of California, Santa Cruz and has published widely in the areas of black cultural politics and media. His books include *Producing Jazz, Watching Race, Cultural Moves,* and, most recently, *Towards a Sociology of the Trace,* co-edited with Macarena Gómez-Barris. His current research considers diversity, difference, and the cultural politics of media visibility.

Jonathan Gray is Professor of Media and Cultural Studies at the University of Wisconsin–Madison. He is the author of *Television Entertainment, Television Studies* (with Amanda D. Lotz), *Show Sold Separately: Promos, Spoilers, and Other Media Paratexts,* and *Watching with The Simpsons: Television, Parody, and Intertextuality,* and co-editor of numerous other collections.

Melissa Gregg is a researcher at Intel Corporation studying the future of work. She is the author of *Work's Intimacy* and *Cultural Studies' Affective Voices,* and co-editor of *The Affect Theory Reader.*

Laura Grindstaff is Professor of Sociology at the University of California, Davis with affiliations in Cultural Studies, Gender Studies, and Performance Studies. An ethnographer by training, she specializes in the study of American popular culture and has published widely on topics ranging from cheerleading to reality television.

Mary Beth Haralovich is Professor in the School of Theatre, Film, and Television, University of Arizona, Tucson. Her social history of the 1950s suburban family domestic comedy has been reprinted many times. She is a founder of the international conference Console-ing Passions.

Alison Hearn is Associate Professor in the Faculty of Information and Media Studies at the University of Western Ontario. She has published widely in such journals as *Continuum, Journal of Consumer Culture,* and *Journal of Communication Inquiry* and in edited volumes including *The Media and Social Theory* and *Blowing Up the Brand.*

Lisa Henderson is Professor of Communication at the University of Massachusetts at Amherst. Her most recent book is *Love and Money: Queers, Class and Cultural Production,* and her current work is on collaboration between scholars and artists.

Matt Hills is Professor of Media and Journalism at the University of Huddersfield. He is the author of six books, from *Fan Cultures* through to *Doctor Who: The Unfolding Event.*

Michele Hilmes is Professor Emerita at the University of Wisconsin–Madison. Her books include *Radio Voices: American Broadcasting 1922-1952, Only Connect: A Cultural History of Broadcasting in the United States,* and, most recently, *Radio's New Wave: Global Sound in the Digital Era.*

Jennifer Holt is Associate Professor of Film and Media Studies at the University of California, Santa Barbara. She is the author of *Empires of Entertainment* and co-editor of *Distribution Revolution, Connected Viewing,* and *Media Industries: History, Theory, Method.*

Henry Jenkins is Provost's Professor of Communication, Journalism, Cinematic Arts, and Education at the University of Southern California. He is the author of seventeen books, including *Textual Poachers: Television Fans and Participatory Culture* and *By Any Media Necessary: The New Youth Activism.*

Derek Johnson is Associate Professor of Media and Cultural Studies in the Department of Communication Arts at the University of Wisconsin–Madison. He is the author of *Media Franchising: Creative License and Collaboration in the Culture Industries*.

Derek Kompare is Associate Professor of Film and Media Arts in the Meadows School of the Arts at Southern Methodist University. He is the author of *Rerun Nation, CSI*, and several articles on television form and history.

Marwan M. Kraidy is Anthony Shadid Chair in Global Media, Politics and Culture at the University of Pennsylvania. His most recent book is *The Naked Blogger of Cairo: Creative Insurgency in the Arab World*.

Tama Leaver is Senior Lecturer in Internet Studies at Curtin University in Western Australia. His books include *Artificial Culture: Identity, Technology and Bodies* and *Social, Casual and Mobile Games: The Changing Gaming Landscape*.

Suzanne Leonard is Associate Professor of English at Simmons College, and the author of *Fatal Attraction* and co-editor of *Fifty Hollywood Directors*. Her monograph *Wife, Inc.: The Business of Marriage in Twenty-First Century American Culture* is forthcoming.

Marina Levina is Associate Professor of Communication at the University of Memphis. She is the author of *Pandemics and the Media*.

Elana Levine is Associate Professor in the Department of Journalism, Advertising, and Media Studies at the University of Wisconsin–Milwaukee. She is the author of *Wallowing in Sex: The New Sexual Culture of 1970s*

American Television and co-author of *Legitimating Television: Media Convergence and Cultural Status*.

Justin Lewis is Professor of Communication at Cardiff University. His most recent book is *Beyond Consumer Capitalism: Media and the Limits to Imagination*.

George Lipsitz is Professor of Black Studies and Sociology at the University of California, Santa Barbara. His publications include *Time Passages, Dangerous Crossroads*, and *Midnight at the Barrelhouse*. He is senior editor of the ethnic studies journal *Kalfou*.

Jo Littler is Reader in Cultural Industries in the Department of Sociology, City University London. She is the author of *Radical Consumption? Shopping for Change in Contemporary Culture* and is currently finishing a book called *Against Meritocracy: Culture, Power and Myths of Mobility*.

Amanda D. Lotz is Professor of Media Studies at the University of Michigan. She is the author of *The Television Will Be Revolutionized, Cable Guys: Television and Masculinities in the 21st Century*, and *Redesigning Women: Television after the Network Era*.

Lev Manovich is the author or editor of eight books, including *Software Takes Command, Soft Cinema: Navigating the Database*, and *The Language of New Media*, which was described as "the most suggestive and broad ranging media history since Marshall McLuhan."

Vicki Mayer is Professor of Communication at Tulane University, coeditor of the journal *Television & New Media*, and author or editor of several books and journal articles about media production, creative industries, and cultural work.

Kembrew McLeod is Professor of Communication Studies at the University of Iowa. He has published and produced several books and documentaries about music and popular culture. His book *Freedom of Expression*® received an ALA book award, and his most recent documentary *Copyright Criminals* aired on PBS.

Jason Mittell is Professor of Film and Media Culture and American Studies at Middlebury College. His books include *Genre and Television: From Cop Shows to Cartoons in American Culture*, *Television and American Culture*, and *Complex Television: The Poetics of Contemporary Television Storytelling*.

Helen Morgan Parmett is Assistant Professor in Communication Studies at Western Washington University. Her research focuses on media's role in the production of space, addressing issues of identity, branding, cultural policy, and governance.

Dawn Nafus is an anthropologist at Intel Labs. She holds a PhD from the University of Cambridge. Her research interests include experiences of time, beliefs about technology and modernity, and the anthropology of numeracies. She is interested in exploring new ways people might relate to their own data.

Diane Negra is Professor of Film Studies and Screen Culture and Head of Film Studies at University College Dublin. A member of the Royal Irish Academy, she is the author, editor, or co-editor of ten books and the co-editor of *Television & New Media*.

Michael Z. Newman is Associate Professor in the Department of Journalism, Advertising, and Media Studies at the University of Wisconsin–Milwaukee. He is the author of *Indie: An American Film Culture* and *Video Revolutions: On the History of a Medium* and the co-author of *Legitimating Television: Media Convergence and Cultural Status*.

Laurie Ouellette is Associate Professor at the University of Minnesota, where she teaches Media Studies and Cultural Sudies. She is the editor of *The Media Studies Reader*, co-author of *Better Living through Reality TV: Television and Post-Welfare Citizenship*, and author of *Lifestyle TV*.

Lisa Parks is Professor of Film and Media Studies at the University of California, Santa Barbara, and author of *Cultures in Orbit: Satellites and the Televisual* and co-editor of *Signal Traffic: Critical Studies of Media Infrastructures*, *Down to Earth: Satellite Technologies, Industries and Cultures*, and *Life in the Age of Drones*.

Matthew Thomas Payne is Assistant Professor of Film, Television, and Theater at the University of Notre Dame. He is the author of *Playing War: Military Video Games after 9/11* and co-editor of the anthologies *Flow TV* and *Joystick Soldiers*.

Jennifer Petersen is Associate Professor of Media Studies at the University of Virginia. She is the author of *Murder, the Media, and the Politics of Public Feelings* and is currently working on a history of how new communication technologies have shaped the understanding of speech within First Amendment law.

Aswin Punathambekar is Associate Professor of Communication Studies and Founding Director of the Global Media Studies Initiative at the University of Michigan. He is the author of *From Bombay to Bollywood: The Making of a Global Media Industry*.

Carrie A. Rentschler is Associate Professor and William Dawson Scholar of Feminist Media Studies in the Department of Art History and Communication Studies at McGill University. She is the author of *Second Wounds: Victims' Rights and the Media in the US* and co-editor of *Girlhood Studies and the Politics of Place*.

Ellen Seiter holds the Nenno Endowed Chair in Television Studies at the University of Southern California School of Cinematic Arts. Some of her books include *The Internet Playground* and *The Creative Artist's Legal Guide* (with co-author Bill Seiter).

Sarah Sharma is Associate Professor and Director of the McLuhan Program in Culture and Technology at the University of Toronto. She is a faculty member at the Institute of Communication, Culture, Information and Technology (Mississauga) and the Faculty of Information (St. George).

Jennifer Daryl Slack is Professor of Communication and Cultural Studies in the Department of Humanities at Michigan Technological University. Her recent books include the second edition of *Culture and Technology: A Primer*, with J. Macgregor Wise, and *Cultural Studies: 1983* by Stuart Hall, edited with Lawrence Grossberg.

Greg M. Smith is Professor of Moving Image Studies at Georgia State University. His books include *What Media Classes Really Want to Discuss* and *Beautiful TV: The Art and Argument of Ally McBeal*.

Beretta E. Smith-Shomade is Associate Professor at Emory University. Her publications include *Shaded Lives: African-American Women and Television, Pimpin' Ain't Easy: Selling Black Entertainment Television*, and the anthology *Watching while Black: Centering the Television of Black Audiences*.

Karen Tongson is Associate Professor of English and Gender Studies at the University of Southern California, and author of *Relocations: Queer Suburban Imaginaries*. She is series editor for *Postmillennial Pop* at New York University Press, and has two books in progress: *Normal Television: Critical Essays on Queer Spectatorship after the "New Normalcy"* and *Empty Orchestra: Karaoke in Our Time*.

Graeme Turner is Emeritus Professor of Cultural Studies in the Institute for Advanced Studies in the Humanities at the University of Queensland. His most recent publications include *Television Histories in Asia* (with Jinna Tay) and *Re-Inventing the Media*.

Joseph Turow is Robert Lewis Shayon Professor of Communication at the Annenberg School for Communication. His most recent book is *The Aisles Have Eyes: How Retailers Track Your Shopping, Strip Your Privacy, and Define Your Power*.

Angharad N. Valdivia—Research Professor in the Institute of Communications Research at the University of Illinois—was Inaugural Head of Media and Cinema Studies and Interim Director of the Institute of Communications Research, 2009 to 2014. She publishes on Latina/o studies, media studies, girls studies, transnationalism, gender, and popular culture.

Brenda R. Weber is Professor and Chair of the Department of Gender Studies and Professor in Cinema and Media Studies in the Media School at Indiana University Bloomington. Her most recent book is *Reality Gendervision: Sexuality and Gender on Transatlantic Reality TV*.

Michele White is Professor of Internet Studies in Tulane University's Department of Communication. Her monographs consist of *The Body and the Screen: Theories of Internet Spectatorship, Buy It Now: Lessons from eBay,* and *Producing Women: The Internet, Traditional Femininity, Queerness, and Creativity.*

J. Macgregor Wise is Professor of Communication Studies at Arizona State University, where he writes and teaches about cultural studies of technology, globalization, surveillance, and popular culture.

434763